R Programming By Example

Practical, hands-on projects to help you get started with R

Omar Trejo Navarro

BIRMINGHAM - MUMBAI

R Programming By Example

First published: December 2017

Production reference: 1201217

Published by Packt Publishing Ltd.
Livery Place
35 Livery Street
Birmingham
B3 2PB, UK.

ISBN 978-1-78829-254-2

www.packtpub.com

Credits

Author
Omar Trejo Navarro

Copy Editor
Pranjali Chury

Reviewer
Peter C. Figliozzi

Project Coordinator
Vaidehi Sawant

Commissioning Editor
Merint Mathew

Proofreader
Safis Editing

Acquisition Editor
Karan Sadawana

Indexer
Tejal Daruwale Soni

Content Development Editor
Rohit Kumar Singh

Graphics
Jason Monteiro

Technical Editor
Ruvika Rao

Production Coordinator
Shraddha Falebhai

About the Author

Omar Trejo Navarro is a data consultant. He co-founded Datata (`datata.mx`), is actively working on CVEST (cvest.tech), and maintains a personal website (`otrenav.com`). He is an applied mathematics and economics double major from ITAM (`itam.mx`) in Mexico City, where he continues to work as a research assistant. He does software development with a focus on data platforms, data science, and web applications. He has worked with clients from all over the world, and is a keen supporter of open source, open data, and open science in general. He can be reached through his personal website (`otrenav.com`).

This book is the product of combined efforts of many people. First of all, I'd like to thank my loved ones for their continued support and patience for my lack of availability. Next, I'd like to thank Peter C. Figliozzi for his valuable comments and feedback.

Also, I'd like to thank Rohit Kumar Singh and Ruvika Rao for their continued support, collaboration, and help during the production of this book.

Finally, I'd like to thank R's amazing community and the innumerable people who contribute to open knowledge through the internet. And, of course, I'd like to thank you, the reader, for picking up this book! I hope it's valuable to you.

About the Reviewer

Peter C. Figliozzi, PhD, is a professional data scientist and software developer. He works on problems in many areas, including anomaly detection, automated trading, and fraud prevention. Peter uses R through RStudio for ad hoc analysis, modeling, and visualization.

www.PacktPub.com

For support files and downloads related to your book, please visit www.PacktPub.com.

Did you know that Packt offers eBook versions of every book published, with PDF and ePub files available? You can upgrade to the eBook version at www.PacktPub.com and as a print book customer, you are entitled to a discount on the eBook copy. Get in touch with us at service@packtpub.com for more details.

At www.PacktPub.com, you can also read a collection of free technical articles, sign up for a range of free newsletters and receive exclusive discounts and offers on Packt books and eBooks.

https://www.packtpub.com/mapt

Get the most in-demand software skills with Mapt. Mapt gives you full access to all Packt books and video courses, as well as industry-leading tools to help you plan your personal development and advance your career.

Why subscribe?

- Fully searchable across every book published by Packt
- Copy and paste, print, and bookmark content
- On demand and accessible via a web browser

Customer Feedback

Thanks for purchasing this Packt book. At Packt, quality is at the heart of our editorial process. To help us improve, please leave us an honest review on this book's Amazon page at https://www.amazon.com/dp/1788292545.

If you'd like to join our team of regular reviewers, you can email us at customerreviews@packtpub.com. We award our regular reviewers with free eBooks and videos in exchange for their valuable feedback. Help us be relentless in improving our products!

Table of Contents

Preface

In a world where data is becoming increasingly important, data analysts, scientists, and business people need tools to analyze and process large volumes of data efficiently. This book is my attempt to pass on what I've learned so far, so that you can quickly become an effective and efficient R programmer. Reading it will help you understand how to use R to solve complex problems, avoid some of the mistakes I've made, and teach you useful techniques that can be helpful in a variety of contexts. In the process, I hope to show you that, despite its uncommon aspects, R is an elegant and powerful language, and is well suited for data analysis and statistics, as well as complex systems.

After reading this book, you will be familiar with R's fundamentals, as well as some of its advanced features. You will understand data structures, and you will know how to efficiently deal with them. You will also understand how to design complex systems that perform efficiently, and how to make these systems usable by other people through web applications. At a lower level, you will understand how to work with object-oriented programming, functional programming, and reactive programming, and what code may be better written in each of these paradigms. You will learn how to use various cutting edge tools that R provides to develop software, how to identify performance bottlenecks, and how to fix them, possibly using other programming languages such as Fortran and C++. Finally, you will be comfortable reading and understanding the majority of R code, as well as provide feedback for others' code.

What this book covers

Chapter 1, *Introduction to R*, covers the R basics you need to understand the rest of the examples. It is not meant to be a thorough introduction to R. Rather, it's meant to give you the very basic concepts and techniques you need to quickly get started with the three examples contained in the book, and which I introduce next.

This book uses three examples to showcase R's wide range of functionality. The first example shows how to analyze votes with descriptive statistics and linear models, and it is presented in Chapter 2, *Understanding Votes with Descriptive Statistics* and Chapter 3, *Predicting Votes with Linear Models*.

Chapter 2, *Understanding Votes with Descriptive Statistics*, shows how to programatically create hundreds of graphs to identify relations within data visually. It shows how to create histograms, scatter plots, correlation matrices, and how to perform **Principal Component Analysis (PCA)**.

Chapter 3, *Predicting Votes with Linear Models*, shows how to programatically find the best predictive linear model for a set of data, and according to different success metrics. It also shows how to check model assumptions, and how to use cross validation to increase confidence in your results.

The second example shows how to simulate data, visualize it, analyze its text components, and create automatic presentations with it.

Chapter 4, *Simulating Sales Data and Working with Databases*, shows how to design data schema and simulate the various types of data. It also shows how to integrate real text data with simulated data, and how to use a SQL database to access it more efficiently.

Chapter 5, *Communicating Sales with Visualization*, shows how to produce basic to advanced graphs, highly customized graphs. It also shows how to create dynamic 3D graphs and interactive maps.

Chapter 6, *Understanding Reviews with Text Analysis*, shows how to perform text analysis step by step using **Natural Language Processing (NLP)** techniques, as well as sentiment analysis.

Chapter 7, *Developing Automatic Presentations*, shows how to put together the results of previous chapters to create presentations that can be automatically updated with the latest data using tools such as knitr and R Markdown.

Finally, the third example shows how to design and develop complex object-oriented systems that retrieve real-time data from cryptocurrency markets, as well as how to optimize implementations and how to build web applications around such systems.

Chapter 8, *Object-Oriented System to Track Cryptocurrencies*, introduces basic object-oriented techniques that produce complex systems when combined. Furthermore, it shows how to work with three of R's most used object models, which are S3, S4, and R6, as well as how to make them work together.

Chapter 9, *Implementing an Efficient Simple Moving Average*, shows how to iteratively improve an implementation for a **Simple Moving Average (SMA)**, starting with what is considered to be bad code, all the way to advanced optimization techniques using parallelization, and delegation to the Fortran and C++ languages.

Chapter 10, *Adding Interactivity with Dashboards*, shows how to wrap what was built during the previous two chapters to produce a modern web application using reactive programming through the Shiny package.

Appendix, *Required Packages*, shows how to install the internal and external software necessary to replicate the examples in the book. Specifically, it will walk through the installation processes for Linux and macOS, but Windows follows similar principles and should not cause any problems.

What you need for this book

This book was written in a Linux environment (specifically Ubuntu 17.10), and was also tested with a macOS, High Sierra. Even though it was not tested on a Windows computer, all of the R code presented in this book should work fine with one. The only substantial difference is that when I show you how to perform a task using a Terminal, it will be the bash terminal, which is available in Linux and macOS by default. In the case of Windows, you will need to use the cmd.exe terminal, for which you can find a lot of information online. Keep in mind that if you're using a Windows computer, you should be prepared to do a bit more research on your end to replicate the same functionality, but you should not have much trouble at all.

In the appendix, I show you how to install the software you need to replicate the examples shown in this book. I show you how to do so for Linux and macOS, specifically Ubuntu 17.10 and High Sierra. If you're using Windows, the same principles apply but the specifics may be a bit different. However, I'm sure it will not be too hard in any case.

There are two types of requirements you need to be able to execute all the code in this book: external and internal. Software outside of R is what I call external requirements. Software inside of R, meaning R packages, is what I refer to as internal requirements. I walk you through the installation of both of them in the appendix.

Who this book is for

This book is for those who wish to develop software in R. You don't need to be an expert or professional programmer to follow this book, but you do need to be interested in learning how R works. My hope is that this book is useful for people ranging from beginners to advanced by providing hands-on examples that may help you understand R in ways you previously did not.

I assume basic programming, mathematical, and statistical knowledge, because there are various parts in the book where concepts from these disciplines will be used, and they will not be explained in detail. If you have programmed something yourself in any programming language, know basic linear algebra and statistics, and know what linear regression is, you have everything you need to understand this book.

This book was written for people in a variety of contexts and with diverse profiles. For example, if you are an analyst employed by an organization that requires you to do frequent data processing to produce reports on a regular basis, and you need to develop programs to automate such tasks, this book is for you. If you are an academic researcher who wants to use current techniques, combine them, and develop tools to test them automatically, this book is for you. If you're a professional programmer looking for ways to take advantage of advanced R features, this book is for you. Finally, if you're preparing for a future in which data will be of paramount importance (it already is), this book is for you.

Conventions

In this book, you will find a number of text styles that distinguish between different kinds of information. Here are some examples of these styles and an explanation of their meaning. Code words in text, database table names, folder names, filenames, file extensions, pathnames, dummy URLs, user input, and Twitter handles are shown as follows: "We can load the contents of the `data.csv` file into a data frame (the most intuitive structure to use with data in CSV format) by using the `read.csv()` function."

A block of code is set as follows:

```
data <- read.csv("./data_brexit_referendum.csv")
data[data$Leave == -1, "Leave"] <- NA
```

When we wish to draw your attention to a particular part of a code block, the relevant lines or items are set in bold:

```
sum(is.na(data$Leave))
#> [1] 267
```

Any command-line input or output is written as follows:

```
$ sudo service mysql start
```

New terms and **important words** are shown in bold. Words that you see on the screen, for example, in menus or dialog boxes, appear in the text like this: "Now that our code is ready, we should see a table appear in the **Data Overview** tab."

Warnings or important notes appear like this.

 Tips and tricks appear like this.

Reader feedback

Feedback from our readers is always welcome. Let us know what you think about this book-what you liked or disliked. Reader feedback is important for us as it helps us develop titles that you will really get the most out of. To send us general feedback, simply email feedback@packtpub.com, and mention the book's title in the subject of your message. If there is a topic that you have expertise in and you are interested in either writing or contributing to a book, see our author guide at www.packtpub.com/authors.

Customer support

Now that you are the proud owner of a Packt book, we have a number of things to help you to get the most from your purchase.

Downloading the example code

You can download the example code files for this book from your account at http://www.packtpub.com. If you purchased this book elsewhere, you can visit http://www.packtpub.com/support and register to have the files emailed directly to you. You can download the code files by following these steps:

1. Log in or register to our website using your email address and password.
2. Hover the mouse pointer on the **SUPPORT** tab at the top.
3. Click on **Code Downloads & Errata**.
4. Enter the name of the book in the **Search** box.
5. Select the book for which you're looking to download the code files.
6. Choose from the drop-down menu where you purchased this book from.
7. Click on **Code Download**.

Once the file is downloaded, please make sure that you unzip or extract the folder using the latest version of:

- WinRAR / 7-Zip for Windows
- Zipeg / iZip / UnRarX for Mac
- 7-Zip / PeaZip for Linux

The code bundle for the book is also hosted on GitHub at `https://github.com/PacktPublishing/R-Programming-By-Example`. We also have other code bundles from our rich catalog of books and videos available at `https://github.com/PacktPublishing/`. Check them out!

Downloading the color images of this book

We also provide you with a PDF file that has color images of the screenshots/diagrams used in this book. The color images will help you better understand the changes in the output. You can download this file from `https://www.packtpub.com/sites/default/files/downloads/RProgrammingByExample_ColorImages.pdf`.

Errata

Although we have taken every care to ensure the accuracy of our content, mistakes do happen. If you find a mistake in one of our books-maybe a mistake in the text or the code-we would be grateful if you could report this to us. By doing so, you can save other readers from frustration and help us improve subsequent versions of this book. If you find any errata, please report them by visiting `http://www.packtpub.com/submit-errata`, selecting your book, clicking on the **Errata Submission Form** link, and entering the details of your errata. Once your errata are verified, your submission will be accepted and the errata will be uploaded to our website or added to any list of existing errata under the Errata section of that title.

To view the previously submitted errata, go to `https://www.packtpub.com/books/content/support` and enter the name of the book in the search field. The required information will appear under the **Errata** section.

Piracy

Piracy of copyrighted material on the internet is an ongoing problem across all media. At Packt, we take the protection of our copyright and licenses very seriously. If you come across any illegal copies of our works in any form on the internet, please provide us with the location address or website name immediately so that we can pursue a remedy.

Please contact us at `copyright@packtpub.com` with a link to the suspected pirated material. We appreciate your help in protecting our authors and our ability to bring you valuable content.

Questions

If you have a problem with any aspect of this book, you can contact us at `questions@packtpub.com`, and we will do our best to address the problem.

1
Introduction to R

In a world where data is becoming increasingly important, business people and scientists need tools to analyze and process large volumes of data efficiently. R is one of the tools that has become increasingly popular in recent years for data processing, statistical analysis, and data science, and while R has its roots in academia, it is now used by organizations across a wide range of industries and geographical areas.

Some of the important topics covered in this chapter are as follows:

- History of R and why it was designed the way it was
- What the interpreter and the console are and how to use them
- How to work with basic data types and data structures of R
- How to divide work by using functions in different ways
- How to introduce complex logic with control structures

What R is and what it isn't

When it comes to choosing software for statistical computing, it's tough to argue against R. Who could dislike a high quality, cross-platform, open source, statistical software product? It has an interactive console for exploratory work. It can run as a scripting language to replicate processes. It has a lot of statistical models built in, so you don't have to reinvent the wheel, but when the base toolset is not enough, you have access to a rich ecosystem of external packages. And, it's free! No wonder R has become a favorite in the age of data.

The inspiration for R – the S language

R was inspired by the S statistical language developed by John Chambers at AT&T. The name S is an allusion to another one-letter-name programming language also developed at AT&T, the famous C language. R was created by Ross Ihaka and Robert Gentleman in the Department of Statistics at the University of Auckland in 1991.

The general S philosophy sets the stage for the design of the R language itself, which many programmers coming from other programming languages find somewhat odd and confusing. In particular, it's important to realize that S was developed to make data analysis as easy as possible.

> *"We wanted users to be able to begin in an interactive environment, where they did not consciously think of programming. Then as their needs became clearer and their sophistication increased, they should be able to slide gradually into programming, when the language and system aspects would become more important."*

> *– John Chambers*

The key part here is the transition from analyst to developer. They wanted to build a language that could easily service both types of users. They wanted to build language that would be suitable for interactive data analysis through a command line but which could also be used to program complex systems, like traditional programming languages.

It's no coincidence that this book is structured that way. We will start doing data analysis first, and we will gradually move toward developing a full and complex system for information retrieval with a web application on top.

R is a high quality statistical computing system

R is comparable, and often superior, to commercial products when it comes to programming capabilities, complex systems development, graphic production, and community ecosystems. Researchers in statistics and machine learning, as well as many other data-related disciplines, will often publish R packages to accompany their publications. This translates into immediate public access to the very latest statistical techniques and implementations. Whatever model or graphic you're trying to develop, chances are that someone has already tried it, and if not, you can at least learn from their efforts.

R is a flexible programming language

As we have seen, in addition to providing statistical tools, R is a general-purpose programming language. You can use R to extend its own functionality, automate processes that make use of complex systems, and many other things. It incorporates features from other object-oriented programming languages and has strong foundations for functional programming, which is well suited for solving many of the challenges of data analysis. R allows the user to write powerful, concise, and descriptive code.

R is free, as in freedom and as in free beer

In many ways, a language is successful inasmuch as it creates a platform with which many people can create new things, and R has proven to be very successful in this regard. One key limitation of the S language was that it was only available in a commercial package, but R is free software. Free as in freedom, and free as in free beer.

The copyright for the primary source code for R is held by the R Foundation and is published under **General Public License (GPL)**. According to the Free Software Foundation (http://www.fsf.org/), with free software (free as in freedom) you are granted the following four freedoms:

- **Freedom 0**: Run the program for any purpose
- **Freedom 1**: Study how the program works and adapt it to your needs
- **Freedom 2**: Redistribute copies so you can help your neighbor
- **Freedom 3**: Improve the program and release your improvements to the public

These freedoms have allowed R to develop strong prolific communities that include world-class statisticians and programmers as well as many volunteers, who help improve and extend the language. They also allow for R to be developed and maintained for all popular operating systems, and to be easily used by individuals and organizations who wish to do so, possibly sharing their findings in a way that others can replicate their results. Such is the power of free software.

What R is not good for

No programming language or system is perfect. R certainly has a number of drawbacks, the most common being that it can be painfully slow (when not used correctly). Keep in mind that R is essentially based on 40-year-old technology, going back to the original S system developed at Bell Labs. Therefore, several of its imperfections come from the fact that it was not built in anticipation for the data age we live in now. When R was born, disk and RAM were very expensive and the internet was just getting started. Notions of large-scale data analysis and high-performance computing were rare.

Fast-forward to the present, hardware cost is just a fraction of what it used to be, computing power is available online for pennies, and everyone is interested in collecting and analyzing data at large scale. This surge in data analysis has brought to the forefront two of R's fundamental limitations, the fact that it's single-threaded and memory-bound. These two characteristics drastically slow it down. Furthermore, R is an interpreted dynamically typed language, which can make it even slower. And finally, R has object immutability and various ways to implement object-oriented programming, both of which can make it hard for people, specially those coming from other languages, to write high-quality code if they don't know how to deal with them. You should know that all of the characteristics mentioned in this paragraph are addressed in `Chapter 9`, *Implementing an Efficient Simple Moving Average*.

A double-edged sword in R, is that most of its users do not think of themselves as programmers, and are more concerned with results than with process (which is not necessarily a bad thing). This means that much of the R code you can find online is written without regard for elegance, speed, or readability, since most R users do not revise their code to address these shortcomings. This permeates into code that is patchy and not rigorously tested, which in turn produces many edge cases that you must take into account when using low-quality packages. You will do well to keep this in mind.

Comparing R with other software

My intention for this section is not to provide a comprehensive comparison between R and other software, but to simply point out a few of R's most noticeable features. If you can, I encourage you to test other software yourself so that you know first-hand what may be the best tool for the job at hand.

The most noticeable feature of R compared to other statistical software such as SAS, Stata, SPSS, and even Python, is the very large number of packages that it has available. At the time of writing this, there are almost 12,000 packages published in The **Comprehensive R Archive Network (CRAN)** (https://cran.r-project.org/), and this does not include packages published in other places, such as Git repositories. This enables R to have a very large community and a huge number of tools for data analysis in areas such as finance, mathematics, machine learning, high-performance computing, and many others.

With the exception of Python, R has much more programming capabilities than SAS, Stata, SPSS, and even more so than Python in some respects (for example, in R, you may use different object models). However, efficient and effective R usage requires the use of code which implies a steep learning curve for some people, while Stata and SPSS have graphical user interfaces that guide the user through many of the tasks with point-and-click wizards. In my opinion, this hand-holding, although nice for beginners, quickly becomes an important restriction for people looking to become intermediate to advanced users, and that's where the advantage of programming really shines.

R has one of the best graphics systems among all existing software. The most popular package for producing graphs in R, which we will use extensively in this book, is the `ggplot2` package, but there are many other great graphing packages as well. This package allows the modification of virtually every aspect of a graph through its graphics grammar, and is far superior to anything I've seen in SPSS, Stata, SAS, or even Python.

R is a great tool, but it's not the right tool for everything. If you're looking to perform data analysis but don't want to invest the time in learning to program, then software like SAS, Stata, or SPSS may be a better option for you. If you're looking to develop analytical software that is very easily integrated into larger systems and which needs to plug into various interfaces, then Python may be a better tool for the job. However, if you're looking to do a lot of complex data analysis and graphing, and you are going to mostly spend your time focused on these areas, then R is a great choice.

The interpreter and the console

As I mentioned earlier, R is an interpreted language. When you enter an expression into the R console or execute an R script in your operating system's terminal, a program called the interpreter parses and executes the code. Other examples of interpreted languages are Lisp, Python, and JavaScript. Unlike C, C++, and Java, R doesn't require you to explicitly compile your programs before you execute them.

All R programs are composed of a series of expressions. The interpreter begins by parsing each expression, substituting objects for symbols where appropriate, evaluates them, and finally return the resulting objects. We will define each of these concepts in the following sections, but you should understand that this is the basic process through which all R programs go through.

The R console is the most important tool for using R and can be thought of as a wrapper around the interpreter. The console is a tool that allows you to type expressions directly into R and see how it responds. The interpreter will read the expressions and respond with a result or an error message, if there was one. When you execute expressions through the console, the interpreter will pass objects to the print() function automatically, which is why you can see the result printed below your expressions (we'll cover more on functions later).

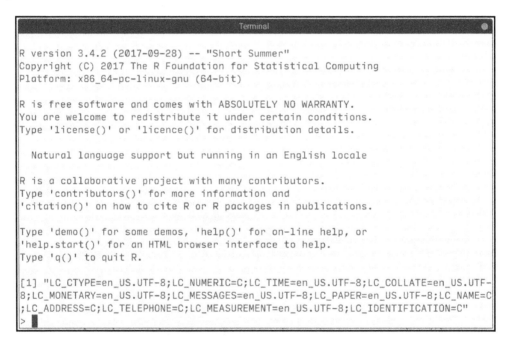

If you've used a command line before (for example, bash in Linux of macOS or cmd.exe in Windows) or a language with an interactive interpreter such as Lisp, Python, or JavaScript, the console should look familiar since it simply is a command-line interface. If not, don't worry. Command-line interfaces are simple to use tools. They are programs that receive code and return objects whose printed representations you see below the code you execute.

When you launch R, you will see a window with the R console. Inside the console you will see a message like the one shown below. This message displays some basic information, including the version of R you're running, license information, reminders about how to get help, and a Command Prompt.

Note that the R version in this case is 3.4.2. The code developed during this book will assume this version. If you have a different version, but in case you end up with some problems, this could be a reason you may want to look into.

You should note that, by default, R will display a greater-than sign (>) at the beginning of the last line of the console, signaling you that it's ready to receive commands. Since R is prompting you to type something, this is called a Command Prompt. When you see the greater-than symbol, R is able to receive more expressions as input. When you don't, it is probably because R is busy processing something you sent, and you should wait for it to finish before sending something else.

For the most part, in this book we will avoid showing such command prompts at all, since you may be typing the code into a source code file or directly into the console, but if we do introduce it, make sure that you don't explicitly type it. For example, if you want to replicate the following snippet, you should only type 1 + 2 in your console, and press the *Enter* key. When you do, you will see a [1] 3 which is the output you received back from R. Go ahead and execute various arithmetic expressions to get a feel for the console:

```
> 1 + 2
[1] 3
```

Note the [1] that accompanies each returned value. It's there because the result is actually a vector (an ordered collection). The [1] means that the index of the first item displayed in that row is 1 (in this case, our resulting vector has a single value within).

Finally, you should know that the console provides tools for looking through previous commands. You will probably find that the up and down arrow keys are the most useful. You can scroll through previous commands by pressing them. The up arrow lets you look at earlier commands, and the down arrow lets you look at later commands. If you would like to repeat a previous command with a minor change, or if you need to correct a mistake, you can easily do so using these keys.

Tools to work efficiently with R

In this section we discuss the tools that will help us when working with R.

Pick an IDE or a powerful editor

For efficient code development, you may want to try a more powerful editor or an **Integrated Development Environment** (**IDE**). The most popular IDE for R is RStudio (`https://www.rstudio.com/`). It offers an impressive feature set that makes interacting with R much easier. If you're new to R, and programming in general, this is probably the way to go. As you can see in the image below it wraps the console (right side) within a larger application which offers a lot of functionality, and in this case, it is displaying the help system (left side). Furthermore, RStudio offers tabs to navigate files, browse installed packages, visualize plots, among other features, as well as a large amount of configuration options under the top menu dropdowns.

Throughout this book, we will not use any functionality provided by RStudio. All I will show you is pure R functionality. I decided to proceed this way to make sure that the book is useful for any R programmer, including those who do not use RStudio. For RStudio users, this means that there may be easier ways to accomplish some of the tasks I will show, and instead of programming a few lines, you could simply click some buttons. If that's something you prefer, I encourage you to take a look through the excellent RStudio Essential webinars,which can be found in RStudio's website at `https://www.rstudio.com/resources/webinars/?wvideo=1xel3j2kos`, as well as Stanford's Introduction to R, RStudio (`https://web.stanford.edu/class/stats101/intro/intro-lab01.html`).

You should be careful to avoid the common mistake of referring to R as RStudio. Since many people are introduced to R through RStudio, they think that RStudio is actually R, which it is not. RStudio is a wrapper around R to extend it's functionality, and is technically known as an IDE.

Experienced programmers may prefer to work with other tools they already know and love and have used for many years. For example, in my case, I prefer to use Emacs (`https://www.gnu.org/software/emacs/`) for any programming I do. Emacs is a very powerful text editor that you can programatically extend to work the way you want it to by using a programming language known as **Elisp**, which is a Lisp extension. In case you use Emacs too, the `ess` package is all you really need.

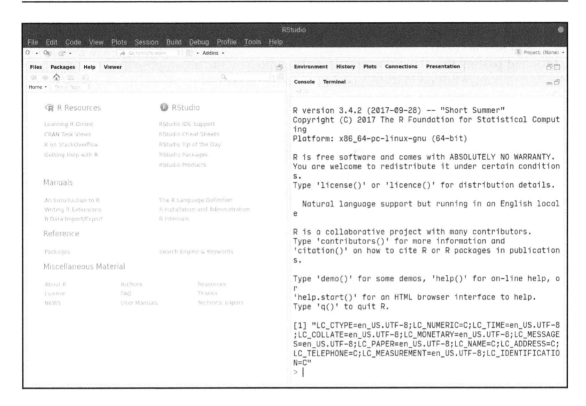

If you're going to use Emacs, I encourage you to take a look through the `ess` package's documentation (`https://ess.r-project.org/Manual/ess.html`) and Johnson's presentation titled *Emacs Has No Learning Curve, University of Kansas, 2015* (`http://pj.freefaculty.org/guides/Rcourse/emacs-ess/emacs-ess.pdf`). If you use Vim, Sublime Text, Atom, or other similar tools, I'm confident you can find useful packages as well.

The send to console functionality

The base R installation provides the console environment we mentioned in the previous section. This console is really all you need to work with R, but it will quickly become cumbersome to type everything directly into it and it may not be your best option. To efficiently work with R, you need to be able to experiment and iterate as fast as you can. Doing so will accelerate your learning curve and productivity.

Whichever tool you use, the key functionality you need is to be able to easily send code snippets into the console without having to type them yourself, or copying them from your editor and pasting them into the console. In RStudio, you can accomplish this by clicking on the Run or Source button in the top-right corner of the code editor panel. In Emacs, you may use the ess-eval-region command.

The efficient write-execute loop

One of the most productive ways to work with R, especially when learning it, is to use the *write-execute* loop, which makes use of the send to console functionality mentioned in the previous section. This will allow you to do two very important things: develop your code through small and quick iterations, which allow you to see step-by-step progress until you converge to the behavior you seek, and save the code you converged to as your final result, which can be easily reproduced using the source code file you used for your iterations. R source code files use the .R extension.

Assuming you have a source code file ready to send expressions to the console, the basic steps through the write-execute loop are as follows:

1. Define what behavior you're looking to implement with code.
2. Write the minimal amount of code necessary to achieve one piece of the behavior you seek in your implementation.
3. Use the send to console functionality to verify that the result in the console is what you expected, and if it's not, to identify possible causes.
4. If it's not what you expected, go back to the second step with the purpose of fixing the code until it has the intended piece of behavior.
5. If it's what you expected, go back to the second step with the purpose of extending the code with another piece of the behavior, until convergence.

This write-execute loop will become second nature to you as you start using it, and when it does, you'll be a more productive R programmer. It will allow you to diagnose issues faster, to quickly experiment with a few ways to accomplishing the same behavior to find which one seems best for your context, and once you have working code, it will also allow you to clean your implementation to keep the same behavior but have better or more readable code.

For experienced programmers, this should be a familiar process, and it's very similar to **Test-Driven Development** (**TDD**), but instead of using unit-tests to automatically test the code, you verify the output in the console in each iteration, and you don't have a set of tests to re-test each iteration. Even though TDD will not be used in this book, you can definitely use it in R.

I encourage you to use this write-execute loop to work through the examples presented in this book. At times, we will show step-by-step progress so that you understand the code better, but it's practically impossible to show all of the write-execute loop iterations I went through to develop it, and much of the knowledge you can acquire comes from iterating this way.

Executing R code in non-interactive sessions

Once your code has the functionality you were looking to implement, executing it through an interactive session using the console may not be the best way to do so. In such cases, another option you have is to tell your computer to directly execute the code for you, in a non-interactive session. This means that you won't be able to type commands into the console, but you'll get the benefit of being able to configure your computer to automatically execute code for you, or to integrate it into larger systems where R is only one of many components. This is known as batch mode.

To execute code in the batch mode, you have two options: the old R CMD BATCH command which we won't look into, and the newer Rscript command, which we will. The **Rscript** is a command that you can execute within your computer's terminal. It receives the name of a source code file and executes its contents.

 In the following example, we will make use of various concepts that we will explain in later sections, so if you don't feel ready to understand it, feel free to skip it now and come back to it later.

Suppose you have the following code in a file named greeting.R. It gets the arguments passed through the command line to Rscript through the args object created with the `commandArgs()` function, assigns the corresponding values to the greeting and name variables, and finally prints a vector that contains those values.

```
args       <- commandArgs(TRUE)
greeting <- args[1]
name       <- args[2]

print(c(greeting, name))
```

Once ready, you may use the Rscript command to execute it from your Terminal (not from within your R console) as is shown ahead. The result shows the vector with the greeting and name variable values you passed it.

 When you see a Command Prompt that begins with the $ symbol instead of of the > symbol, it means that you should execute that line in your computer's Terminal, not in the R console.

```
$ Rscript greeting.R Hi John
[1] "Hi" "John"
```

Note that if you simply execute the file without any arguments, they will be passed as NA values, which allows you to customize your code to deal with such situations:

```
$ Rscript greeting.R
[1] NA NA
```

This was a very simple example, but the same mechanism can be used to execute much more complex systems, like the one we will build in the final chapters of this book to constantly retrieve real-time price data from remote servers.

Finally, if you want to provide a mechanism that is closer to the one in Python, you may want to look into the optparse package to create command-line help pages as well as to parse arguments.

How to use this book

To make the most out of this book, you should recreate on your own the examples shown throughout, and make sure that you understand what each of them is doing in detail. If at some point you feel confused, it's not too difficult to do a couple of searches online to clarify things for yourself. However, I highly recommend that you look into the following books as well, which go into more detail on some of the concepts and ideas presented in this book, and are considered very good references for R programmers:

- *R in a Nutshell, by Adler, O'Reilly, 2010*
- *The Art of R Programming, by Matloff, No Starch Press, 2011*
- *Advanced R, by Wickham, CRC Press, 2015*
- *R Programming for Data Science, by Peng, LeanPub, 2016*

Sometimes all you need to do to clarify something is use R's help system. To get help on a function, you may use the question mark notation, like `?function_name`, but in case you want to search for help on a topic, you may use the `help.search()` function, like `help.search` *(regression)*. This can be helpful if you know what topic you're interested in but can't remember the actual name of the function you want to use. Another way of invoking such functionality is using the double question mark notation, like `??` regression.

Keep in mind that topics in this book are interconnected and not linearly ordered, which means that at times it will seem that we are jumping around. When that happens, it's because a topic can be seen through different points of view. That's why, to make the most out of this book, you should experiment as much as you can in the console and build code progressively using the write-execute loop mentioned earlier. If you simply replicate the code exactly as is shown, you may miss some of the learning that you could have gotten had you built the systems step by step.

Finally, you should know that this book is meant to show how to use R through somewhat real examples, and as such, does not provide too much technical depth or discussion on some of the topics presented. Furthermore, since my objective is to get you quickly working with the real examples, in this first chapter, I explain R fundamentals very briefly, just to introduce the minimum amount of knowledge you need to follow through the real examples presented in the following chapters. Therefore, you should not think that the explanations presented in this chapter are enough for you to understand R's basic constructs. If you're looking for a more in-depth introduction to R fundamentals, you may want to take a look at the references we mentioned previously.

Tracking state with symbols and variables

Like most programming languages, R lets you assign values to variables and refer to these objects by name. The names you use to refer to variables are called symbols in R. This allows you to keep some information available in case it's needed at a later point in time. These variables may contain any type of object available in R, even combinations of them when using lists, as we will see in a later section in this chapter. Furthermore, these objects are immutable, but that's a topic for Chapter 9, *Implementing an Efficient Simple Moving Average*.

In R, the assignment operator is <-, which is a less-than symbol (<) followed by a dash (-). If you have worked with algorithm pseudo code before, you may find it familiar. You may also use the single equals symbol (=) for assignments, similar to many other languages, but I prefer to stick to the <- operator.

An expression like x <- 1 means that the value 1 is assigned to the x symbol, which can be thought of as a variable. You can also assign the other way around, meaning that with an expression like 1 -> x we would have the same effect as we did earlier. However, the assignment from left to right is very rarely used, and is more of a convenience feature in case you forget the assignment operator at the beginning of a line in the console.

Note that the value substitution is done at the time when the value is assigned to z, not at the time when z is evaluated. If you enter the following code into the console, you can see that the second time z is printed, it still has the value that y had when it was used to assign to it, not the y value assigned afterward:

```
x <- 1
y <- 2
z <- c(x, y)
z
#> [1] 1 2

y <- 3
z
#> [1] 1 2
```

It's easy to use variable names like x, y, and z, but using them has a high cost for real programs. When you use names like that, you probably have a very good idea of what values they will contain and how they will be used. In other words, their intention is clear for you. However, when you give your code to someone else or come back to it after a long period of time, those intentions may not be clear, and that's when cryptic names can be harmful. In real programs, your names should be self descriptive and instantly communicate intention.

For a deeper discussion about this and many other topics regarding high-quality code, take a look at Martin's excellent book *Clean Code: A Handbook of Agile Software Craftsmanship,* *Prentice Hall, 2008.*

Standard object names in R should only contain alphanumeric characters (numbers and ASCII letters), underscores (_), and, depending on context, even periods (.). However, R will allow you to use very cryptic strings if you want. For example, in the following code, we show how the variable !A @B #C $D %E ^F name is used to contain a vector with three integers. As you can see, you are even allowed to use spaces. You can use this non-standard name provided that you wrap the string with backticks (` `):

```
`!A @B #C $D %E ^F` <- c(1, 2, 3)
`!A @B #C $D %E ^F`
#> [1] 1 2 3
```

It goes without saying that you should avoid those names, but you should be aware they exist because they may come in handy when using some of R's more advanced features. These types of variable names are not allowed in most languages, but R is flexible in that way. Furthermore, the example goes to show a common theme around R programming: it is so flexible that if you're not careful, you will end up shooting yourself in the foot. It's not too rare for someone to be very confused about some code because they assumed R would behave a certain way (for example, raise an error under certain conditions) but don't explicitly test for such behavior, and later find that it behaves differently.

Working with data types and data structures

This section summarizes the most important data types and data structures in R. In this brief overview, we won't discuss them in depth. We will only show a couple of examples that will allow you to understand the code shown throughout this book. If you want to dig deeper into them, you may look into their documentation or some of the references pointed out in this chapter's introduction.

The basic data types in R are numbers, text, and Boolean values (TRUE or FALSE), which R calls numerics, characters, and logicals, respectively. Strictly speaking, there are also types for integers, complex numbers, and raw data (bytes), but we won't use them explicitly in this book. The six basic data structures in R are vectors, factors, matrices, data frames, and lists, which we will summarize in the following sections.

Numerics

Numbers in R behave pretty much as you would mathematically expect them to. For example, the operation 2 / 3 performs real division, which results in 0.6666667 in R. This natural numeric behavior is very convenient for data analysis, as you don't need to pay too much attention when using numbers of different types, which may require special handling in other languages. Also the mathematical priorities for operators applies, as well the use of parenthesis.

The following example shows how variables can be used within operations, and how operator priorities are handled. As you can see, you may mix the use of variables with values when performing operations:

```
x <- 2
y <- 3
z <- 4
(x * y + z) / 5
#> [1] 2
```

The modulo operation can be performed with the %% symbol, while integer division can be performed with the %/% symbol:

```
7 %% 3
#> [1] 1
7 %/% 3
#> [1] 2
```

Special values

There are a few special values in R. The NA values are used to represent missing values, which stands for not available. If a computation results in a number that is too big, R will return Inf for a positive number and -Inf for a negative number, meaning positive and negative infinity, respectively. These are also returned when a number is divided by 0. Sometimes a computation will produce a result that makes little sense. In these cases, we will get a NaN, which stands for not a number. And, finally, there is a null object, represented by NULL. The symbol NULL always points to the same object (which is a data type on its own) and is often used as a default argument in functions to mean that no value was passed through. You should know that NA, Inf, -Inf, NaN, and NULL are not substitutes for each other.

There are specific NA values for numerics, characters, and logicals, but we will stick to the simple NA, which is internally treated as a logical.

In the following example, you can see how these special values behave when used among themselves in R. Note that 1 / 0 results in Inf, 0 / 0, Inf − Inf, and Inf / Inf results in undefined represented by NaN, but Inf + Inf, 0 / Inf, and Inf / 0, result in Inf, 0, and Inf, respectively. It's no coincidence that these results resemble mathematical definitions. Also note that any operation including NaN or NA will also result in NaN and NA, respectively:

```
1 / 0
#> [1] Inf
-1 / 0
#> [1] -Inf
0 / 0
#> [1] NaN
Inf + Inf
#> [1] Inf
Inf - Inf
#> [1] NaN
Inf / Inf
#> [1] NaN
Inf / 0
#> [1] Inf
0 / Inf
#> [1] 0
Inf / NaN
#> [1] NaN
Inf + NA
#> [1] NA
```

Characters

Text can be used just as easily, you just need to remember to use quotation marks (" ") around it. The following example shows how to save the text Hi, there! and "10" in two variables. Note that since "10.5" is surrounded by quotation marks, it is text and not a numeric value. To find what type of object you're actually dealing with you can use the class(), typeof(), and str() (short for structure) functions to get the metadata for the object in question.

In this case, since the y variable contains text, we can't multiply it by 2, as is seen in the error we get. Also, if you want to know the number of characters in a string, you can use the `nchar()` function, as follows:

```
x <- "Hi, there!"
y <- "10"
class(y)
#> [1] "character"
typeof(y)
#> [1] "character"
str(y)
#> chr "10"
y * 2
#> Error in y * 2: non-numeric argument to binary operator
nchar(x)
#> [1] 10
nchar(y)
#> [1] 2
```

Sometimes, you may have text information, as well as numeric information that you want to combine into a single string. In this case, you should use the `paste()` function. This function receives an arbitrary number of unnamed arguments, which is something we will define more precisely in a later section in this chapter. It then transforms each of these arguments into characters, and returns a single string with all of them combined. The following code shows such an example. Note how the numeric value of 10 in y was automatically transformed into a character type so that it could be pasted inside the rest of the string:

```
x <- "the x variable"
y <- 10
paste("The result for", x, "is", y)
#> [1] "The result for the x variable is 10"
```

Other times, you will want to replace some characters within a piece of text. In that case, you should use the `gsub()` function, which stands for global substitution. This function receives the string to be replaced as its first argument, the string to replace with as its second argument, and it will return the text in the third argument with the corresponding replacements:

```
x <- "The ball is blue"
gsub("blue", "red", x)
#> [1] "The ball is red"
```

Yet other times, you will want to know whether a string contains a substring, in which case you should use the gprel() function. The name for this function comes from terminal command known as grep, which is an acronym for global regular expression print (yes, you can also use regular expressions to look for matches). The l at the end of grepl() comes from the fact that the result is a logical:

```
x <- "The sky is blue"
grepl("blue", x)
#> [1] TRUE
grepl("red", x)
#> [1] FALSE
```

Logicals

Logical vectors contain Boolean values, which can only be TRUE or FALSE. When you want to create logical variables with such values, you must avoid using quotation marks around them and remember that they are all capital letters, as shown here. When programming in R, logical values are commonly used to test a condition, which is in turn used to decide which branch from a complex program we should take. We will look at examples for this type of behavior in a later section in this chapter:

```
x <- TRUE
```

In R, you can easily convert values among different types with the as.*() functions, where * is used as a wildcard which can be replaced with character, numeric, or logical to convert among these types. The functions work by receiving an object of a different type from what the function name specifies and return the object parsed into the specified type if possible, or return an NA if it's not possible. The following example shows how to convert the TRUE string into a logical value, which in this case non-surprisingly turns out to be the logical TRUE:

```
as.logical("TRUE")
#> [1] TRUE
```

Converting from characters and numerics into logicals is one of those things that is not very intuitive in R. The following table shows some of this behavior. Note that even though the `true` string (all lowercase letters) is not a valid logical value when removing quotation marks, it is converted into a `TRUE` value when applying the `as.logical()` to it, for compatibility reasons. Also note that since T is a valid logical value, which is a shortcut for `TRUE`, it's corresponding text is also accepted as meaning such a value. The same logic applies to `false` and F. Any other string will return an `NA` value, meaning that the string could not be parsed as a logical value. Also note that 0 will be parsed as `FALSE`, but any other numeric value, including Inf, will be converted to a `TRUE` value. Finally, note that both `NA` and `NaN` will be parsed, returning NA in both cases.

The `as.character()` and `as.numeric()` functions have less counter-intuitive behavior, and I will leave you to explore them on your own. When you do, try to test as many edge cases as you can. Doing so will help you foresee possible issues as you develop your own programs.

Value	Result	Value	Result
"TRUE"	TRUE	"book"	NA
"true"	TRUE	"1"	NA
"T"	TRUE	"0"	NA
"FALSE"	FALSE	1	TRUE
"false"	FALSE	0	FALSE
"F"	FALSE	-1	TRUE

Before we move on, you should know that these data structures can be organized by their dimensionality and whether they're homogeneous (all contents must be of the same type) or heterogeneous (the contents can be of different types). Vectors, matrices, and arrays are homogeneous data structures, while lists and data frames are heterogeneous. Vectors and lists have a single dimension, matrices and data frames have two dimensions, and arrays can have as many dimensions as we want.

Dimensions	Homogeneous	Heterogeneous
1	Vector	List
2	Matrix	Data frame
n	Array	

When it comes to dimensions, arrays in R are different from arrays in many other languages, where you would have to create an array of arrays to produce a two-dimensional structure, which is not necessary in R.

Vectors

The fundamental data type in R is the vector, which is an ordered collection of values. The first thing you should know is that unlike other languages, single values for numbers, strings, and logicals, are special cases of vectors (vectors of length one), which means that there's no concept of scalars in R. A vector is a one-dimensional data structure and all of its elements are of the same data type.

The simplest way to create a vector is with the `c()` function, which stands for combine, and coerces all of its arguments into a single type. The coercion will happen from simpler types into more complex types. That is, if we create a vector which contains logicals, numerics, and characters, as the following example shows, our resulting vector will only contain characters, which are the more complex of the three types. If we create a vector that contains logicals and numerics, our resulting vector will be numeric, again because it's the more complex type.

Vectors can be named or unnamed. Unnamed vector elements can only be accessed through positional references, while named vectors can be accessed through positional references as well as name references. In the example below, the y vector is a named vector, where each element is named with a letter from A to I. This means that in the case of x, we can only access elements using their position (the first position is considered as 1 instead of the 0 used in other languages), but in the case of y, we may also use the names we assigned.

Also note that the special values we mentioned before, that is NA, NULL, NaN, and Inf, will be coerced into characters if that's the more complex type, except NA, which stays the same. In case coercion is happening toward numerics, they all stay the same since they are valid numeric values. Finally, if we want to know the length of a vector, simply call the `length()` function upon it:

```
x <- c(TRUE, FALSE, -1, 0, 1, "A", "B", NA, NULL, NaN, Inf)
x
#> [1] "TRUE" "FALSE" "-1" "0" "1" "A" "B" NA
#> [9] "NaN" "Inf"
x[1]
#> [1] "TRUE"
x[5]
#> [1] "1"
```

```
y <- c(A=TRUE, B=FALSE, C=-1, D=0, E=1, F=NA, G=NULL, H=NaN, I=Inf)
y
#> A B  C D E F  H   I
#> 1 0 -1 0 1 NA NaN Inf
y[1]
#> A
#> 1
y["A"]
#> A
#> 1
y[5]
#> E
#> 1
y["E"]
#> E
#> 1
length(x)
#> [1] 10
length(y)
#> [1] 8
```

Furthermore, we can select sets or ranges of elements using vectors with index numbers for the values we want to retrieve. For example, using the selector c(1, 2) would retrieve the first two elements of the vector, while using the c(1, 3, 5) would return the first, third, and fifth elements. The : function (yes, it's a function even though we don't normally use the function-like syntax we have seen so far in other examples to call it), is often used as a shortcut to create range selectors. For example, the 1:5 syntax means that we want a vector with elements 1 through 5, which would be equivalent to explicitly using c(1, 2, 3, 4, 5). Furthermore, if we send a vector of logicals, which must have the same length as the vector we want to retrieve values from, each of the logical values will be associated to the corresponding position in the vector we want to retrieve from, and if the corresponding logical is TRUE, the value will be retrieved, but if it's FALSE, it won't be. All of these selection methods are shown in the following example:

```
x[c(1, 2, 3, 4, 5)]
#> [1] "TRUE" "FALSE" "-1" "0" "1"
x[1:5]
#> [1] "TRUE" "FALSE" "-1" "0" "1"
x[c(1, 3, 5)]
#> [1] "TRUE" "-1" "1"
x[c(TRUE, FALSE, TRUE, FALSE, TRUE, FALSE, TRUE,
    FALSE, TRUE, FALSE, TRUE)]
#> [1] "TRUE" "-1" "1" "B" "NaN" NA
```

Next we will talk about operation among vectors. In the case of numeric vectors, we can apply operations element-to-element by simply using operators as we normally would. In this case, R will match the elements of the two vectors pairwise and return a vector. The following example shows how two vectors are added, subtracted, multiplied, and divided in an element-to-element way. Furthermore, since we are working with vectors of the same length, we may want to get their dot-product (if you don't know what a dot-product is, you may take a look at https://en.wikipedia.org/wiki/Dot_product), which we can do using the %*% operator, which performs matrix-like multiplications, in this case vector-to-vector:

```
x <- c(1, 2, 3, 4)
y <- c(5, 6, 7, 8)
x + y
#> [1]  6  8 10 12
x - y
#> [1] -4 -4 -4 -4
x * y
#> [1]  5 12 21 32
x / y
#> [1] 0.2000 0.3333 0.4286 0.5000
x %*% y
#> [,1]
#> [1,] 70
```

If you want to combine multiple vectors into a single one, you can simply use the c() recursively on them, and it will flatten them for you automatically. Let's say we want to combine the x and y into the z such that the y elements appear first. Furthermore, suppose that after we do we want to sort them, so we apply the sort() function on z:

```
z <- c(y, x)
z
#> [1] 5 6 7 8 1 2 3 4
sort(z)
#> [1] 1 2 3 4 5 6 7 8
```

A common source for confusion is how R deals with vectors of different lengths. If we apply an element-to-element operation, as the ones we covered earlier, but using vectors of different lengths, we may expect R to throw an error, as is the case in other languages. However, it does not. Instead, it repeats vector elements in order until they all have the same length. The following example shows three vectors, each of different lengths, and the result of adding them together.

The way R is configured by default, you will actually get a warning message to let you know that the vectors you operated on were not of the same length, but since R can be configured to avoid showing warnings, you should not rely on them:

```
c(1, 2) + c(3, 4, 5) + c(6, 7, 8, 9)
#> Warning in c(1, 2) + c(3, 4, 5):
        longer object length is not a multiple of
#> shorter object length
#> Warning in c(1, 2) + c(3, 4, 5) + c(6, 7, 8, 9):
        longer object length is
#> not a multiple of shorter object length
#> [1] 10 13 14 13
```

The first thing that may come to mind is that the first vector is expanded into `c(1, 2, 1, 2)`, the second vector is expanded into `c(3, 4, 5, 3)`, and the third one is kept as is, since it's the largest one. Then if we add these vectors together, the result would be `c(10, 13, 14, 14)`. However, as you can see in the example, the result actually is `c(10, 13, 14, 13)`. So, what are we missing? The source of confusion is that R does this step by step, meaning that it will first perform the addition `c(1, 2) + c(3, 4, 5)`, which after being expanded is `c(1, 2, 1) + c(3, 4, 5)` and results in `c(4, 6, 6)`, then given this result, the next step that R performs is `c(4, 6, 6) + c(6, 7, 8, 9)`, which after being expanded is `c(4, 6, 6, 4) + c(6, 7, 8, 9)`, and that's where the result we get comes from. It can be confusing at first, but just remember to imagine the operations step by step.

Finally, we will briefly mention a very powerful feature in R, known as vectorization. Vectorization means that you apply an operation to a vector at once, instead of independently doing so to each of its elements. This is a feature you should get to know quite well. Programming without it is considered to be bad R code, and not just for syntactic reasons, but because vectorized code takes advantage of many internal optimizations in R, which results in much faster code. We will show different ways of vectorizing code in Chapter 9, *Implementing An Efficient Simple Moving Average*, and in this chapter, we will see an example, followed by a couple more in following sections.

Even though the phrase vectorized code may seem scary or magical at first, in reality, R makes it quite simple to implement in some cases. For example, we can square each of the elements in the x vector by using the x symbol as if it were a single number. R is intelligent enough to understand that we want to apply the operation to each of the elements in the vector. Many functions in R can be applied using this technique:

```
x^2
#> [1] 1 4 9 16
```

We will see more examples that really showcase how vectorization can shine in the following section about functions, where we will see how to apply vectorized operations even when the operations depend on other parameters.

Factors

When analyzing data, it's quite common to encounter categorical values. R provides a good way to represent categorical values using factors, which are created using the factor() function and are integer vectors with associated labels for each integer. The different values that the factor can take are called levels. The levels() function shows all the levels from a factor, and the levels parameter of the factor() function can be used to explicitly define their order, which is alphabetical in case it's not explicitly defined.

 Note that defining an explicit order can be important in linear modeling because the first level is used as the baseline level for functions like lm() (linear models), which we will use in Chapter 3, *Predicting Votes with Linear Models*.

Furthermore, printing a factor shows slightly different information than printing a character vector. In particular, note that the quotes are not shown and that the levels are explicitly printed in order afterwards:

```
x <- c("Blue", "Red", "Black", "Blue")
y <- factor(c("Blue", "Red", "Black", "Blue"))
z <- factor(c("Blue", "Red", "Black", "Blue"),
            levels=c("Red", "Black", "Blue"))

x
#> [1] "Blue" "Red" "Black" "Blue"
y
#> [1] Blue Red Black Blue
#> Levels: Black Blue Red
z
#> [1] Blue Red Black Blue
#> Levels: Red Black Blue
levels(y)
#> [1] "Black" "Blue" "Red"
levels(z)
#> [1] "Red" "Black" "Blue"
```

Factors can sometimes be tricky to work with because their types are interpreted differently depending on what function is used to operate on them. Remember the `class()` and `typeof()` functions we used before? When used on factors, they may produce unexpected results. As you can see below, the `class()` function will identify x and y as being character and factor, respectively. However, the `typeof()` function will let us know that they are character and integer, respectively. Confusing isn't it? This happens because, as we mentioned, factors are stored internally as integers, and use a mechanism similar to look-up tables to retrieve the actual string associated for each one.

 Technically, the way factors store the strings associated with their integer values is through attributes, which is a topic we will touch on in `Chapter 8`, *Object-Oriented System to Track Cryptocurrencies*.

```
class(x)
#> [1] "character"
class(y)
#> [1] "factor"
typeof(x)
#> [1] "character"
typeof(y)
#> [1] "integer"
```

While factors look and often behave like character vectors, as we mentioned, they are actually integer vectors, so be careful when treating them like strings. Some string methods, like `gsub()` and `grepl()`, will coerce factors to characters, while others, like `nchar()`, will throw an error, and still others, like `c()`, will use the underlying integer values. For this reason, it's usually best to explicitly convert factors to the data type you need:

```
gsub("Black", "White", x)
#> [1] "Blue" "Red" "White" "Blue"
gsub("Black", "White", y)
#> [1] "Blue" "Red" "White" "Blue"
nchar(x)
#> [1] 4 3 5 4
nchar(y)
#> Error in nchar(y): 'nchar()' requires a character vector
c(x)
#> [1] "Blue" "Red" "Black" "Blue"
c(y)
#> [1] 2 3 1 2
```

If you did not notice, the `nchar()` applied itself to each of the elements in the x factor. The "Blue", "Red", and "Black" strings have 4, 3, and 5 characters, respectively. This is another example of the vectorized operations we mentioned in the vectors section earlier.

Matrices

Matrices are commonly used in mathematics and statistics, and much of R's power comes from the various operations you can perform with them. In R, a matrix is a vector with two additional attributes, the number of rows and the number of columns. And, since matrices are vectors, they are constrained to a single data type.

You can use the `matrix()` function to create matrices. You may pass it a vector of values, as well as the number of rows and columns the matrix should have. If you specify the vector of values and one of the dimensions, the other one will be calculated for you automatically to be the lowest number that makes sense for the vector you passed. However, you may specify both of them simultaneously if you prefer, which may produce different behavior depending on the vector you passed, as can be seen in the next example.

By default, matrices are constructed column-wise, meaning that the entries can be thought of as starting in the upper-left corner and running down the columns. However, if you prefer to construct it row-wise, you can send the `byrow` = `TRUE` parameter. Also, note that you may create an empty or non-initialized matrix, by specifying the number of rows and columns without passing any actual data for its construction, and if you don't specify anything at all, an uninitialized 1-by-1 matrix will be returned. Finally, note that the same element-repetition mechanism we saw for vectors is applied when creating matrices, so do be careful when creating them this way:

```
matrix()
#> [,1]
#> [1,] NA

matrix(nrow = 2, ncol = 3)
#> [,1] [,2] [,3]
#> [1,] NA NA NA
#> [2,] NA NA NA

matrix(c(1, 2, 3), nrow = 2)
#> Warning in matrix(c(1, 2, 3), nrow = 2):
#>       data length [3] is not a sub-
#> multiple or multiple of the number of rows [2]
#> [,1] [,2]
#> [1,] 1 3
#> [2,] 2 1
```

```
matrix(c(1, 2, 3), nrow = 2, ncol = 3)
#> [,1] [,2] [,3]
#> [1,] 1 3 2
#> [2,] 2 1 3

matrix(c(1, 2, 3, 4, 5, 6), nrow = 2, byrow = TRUE)
#> [,1] [,2] [,3]
#> [1,] 1 2 3
#> [2,] 4 5 6
```

Matrix subsets can be specified in various ways. Using matrix-like notation, you can specify the row and column selection using the same mechanisms we showed before for vectors, with which you can use vectors with indexes or vectors with logicals, and in case you decide to use vectors with logicals the vector used to subset must be of the same length as the matrix's dimension you are using it for. Since in this case, we have two dimensions to work with, we must separate the selection for rows and columns by using a comma (,) between them (row selection goes first), and R will return their intersection.

For example, x[1, 2] tells R to get the element in the first row and the second column, x[1:2, 1] tells R to get the first through second elements of the third row, which is equivalent to using x[c(1, 2), 3]. You may also use logical vectors for the selection. For example, x[c(TRUE, FALSE), c(TRUE, FALSE, TRUE)] tells R to get the first row while avoiding the second one, and from that row, to get the first and third columns. An equivalent selection is x[1, c(1, 3)]. Note that when you want to specify a single row or column, you can use an integer by itself, but if you want to specify two or more, then you must use vector notation. Finally, if you leave out one of the dimension specifications, R will interpret as getting all possibilities for that dimension:

```
x <- matrix(c(1, 2, 3, 4, 5, 6), nrow = 2, ncol = 3, byrow = TRUE)
x[1, 2]
#> [1] 2
x[1:2, 2]
#> [1] 2 5
x[c(1, 2), 3]
#> [1] 3 6
x[c(TRUE, FALSE), c(TRUE, FALSE, TRUE)]
#> [1] 1 3
x[1, c(1, 3)]
#> [1] 1 3
x[, 1]
#> [1] 1 4
x[1, ]
#> [1] 1 2 3
```

As mentioned earlier, matrices are basic mathematical tools, and R gives you a lot of flexibility when working with them. The most common matrix operation is transposition, which is performed using the t() function, and matrix-vector multiplication, vector-matrix multiplication, and matrix-matrix multiplication, which are performed with the %*% operator we used previously to calculate the dot-product of two vectors.

Note that the same dimensionality restrictions apply as with mathematical notation, meaning that in case you try to perform one of these operations and the dimensions don't make mathematical sense, R will throw an error, as can be seen in the last part of the example:

```
A <- matrix(c(1, 2, 3, 4, 5, 6), nrow = 2, byrow = TRUE)
x <- c(7, 8)
y <- c(9, 10, 11)
A
#> [,1] [,2] [,3]
#> [1,] 1 2 3
#> [2,] 4 5 6
x
#> [1] 7 8
y
#> [1] 9 10 11
t(A)
#> [,1] [,2]
#> [1,] 1 4
#> [2,] 2 5
#> [3,] 3 6
t(x)
#> [,1] [,2]
#> [1,] 7 8
t(y)
#> [,1] [,2] [,3]
#> [1,] 9 10 11
x %*% A
#> [,1] [,2] [,3]
#> [1,] 39 54 69
A %*% t(x)
#> Error in A %*% t(x): non-conformable arguments
A %*% y
#> [,1]
#> [1,] 62
#> [2,] 152
t(y) %*% A
#> Error in t(y) %*% A: non-conformable arguments
A %*% t(A)
#> [,1] [,2]
```

```
#> [1,] 14 32
#> [2,] 32 77
t(A) %*% A
#> [,1] [,2] [,3]
#> [1,] 17 22 27
#> [2,] 22 29 36
#> [3,] 27 36 45
A %*% x
#> Error in A %*% x: non-conformable arguments
```

Lists

A list is an ordered collection of objects, like vectors, but lists can actually combine objects of different types. List elements can contain any type of object that exists in R, including data frames and functions (explained in the following sections). Lists play a central role in R due to their flexibility and they are the basis for data frames, object-oriented programming, and other constructs. Learning to use them properly is a fundamental skill for R programmers, and here, we will barely touch the surface, but you should definitely research them further.

For those familiar with Python, R lists are similar to Python dictionaries.

Lists can be explicitly created using the list() function, which takes an arbitrary number of arguments, and we can refer to each of those elements by both position, and, in case they are specified, also by names. If you want to reference list elements by names, you can use the $ notation.

The following example shows how flexible lists can be. It shows that a list that contains numerics, characters, logicals, matrices, and even other lists (these are known as nested lists), and as you can see, we can extract each of those elements to work independently from them.

This is the first time we show a multi-line expression. As you can see, you can do it to preserve readability and avoid having very long lines in your code. Arranging code this way is considered to be a good practice. If you're typing this directly in the console, plus symbols (+) will appear in each new line, as long as you have an unfinished expression, to guide you along.

```
x <- list(
```

```
    A = 1,
    B = "A",
    C = TRUE,
    D = matrix(c(1, 2, 3, 4), nrow = 2),
    E = list(F = 2, G = "B", H = FALSE)
)

x
#> $A
#> [1] 1
#>
#> $B
#> [1] "A"
#>
#> $C
#> [1] TRUE
#>
#> $D
#> [,1] [,2]
#> [1,] 1 3
#> [2,] 2 4
#>
#> $E
#> $E$F
#> [1] 2
#>
#> $E$G
#> [1] "B"
#>
#> $E$H
#> [1] FALSE

x[1]
#> $A
#> [1] 1

x$A
#> [1] 1

x[2]
#> $B
#> [1] "A"

x$B
#> [1] "A"
```

When working with lists, we can use the `lapply()` function to apply a function to each of the elements in a list. In this case, we want to know the class and type of each of the elements in the list we just created:

```
lapply(x, class)
#> $A
#> [1] "numeric"
#>
#> $B
#> [1] "character"
#>
#> $C
#> [1] "logical"
#>
#> $D
#> [1] "matrix"
#>
#> $E
#> [1] "list"

lapply(x, typeof)
#> $A
#> [1] "double"
#>
#> $B
#> [1] "character"
#>
#> $C
#> [1] "logical"
#>
#> $D
#> [1] "double"
#>
#> $E
#> [1] "list"
```

Data frames

Now we turn to data frames, which are a lot like spreadsheets or database tables. In scientific contexts, experiments consist of individual observations (rows), each of which involves several different variables (columns). Often, these variables contain different data types, which would not be possible to store in matrices since they must contain a single data type. A data frame is a natural way to represent such heterogeneous tabular data. Every element within a column must be of the same type, but different elements within a row may be of different types, that's why we say that a data frame is a heterogeneous data structure.

 Technically, a data frame is a list whose elements are equal-length vectors, and that's why it permits heterogeneity.

Data frames are usually created by reading in a data using the `read.table()`, `read.csv()`, or other similar data-loading functions. However, they can also be created explicitly with the `data.frame()` function or they can be coerced from other types of objects such as lists. To create a data frame using the `data.frame()` function, note that we send a vector (which, as we know, must contain elements of a single type) to each of the column names we want our data frame to have, which are A, B, and C in this case. The data frame we create below has four rows (observations) and three variables, with numeric, character, and logical types, respectively. Finally, extract subsets of data using the matrix techniques we saw earlier, but you can also reference columns using the $ operator and then extract elements from them:

```
x <- data.frame(
    A = c(1, 2, 3, 4),
    B = c("D", "E", "F", "G"),
    C = c(TRUE, FALSE, NA, FALSE)
)
x[1, ]
#> A B C
#> 1 1 D TRUE
x[, 1]
#> [1] 1 2 3 4
x[1:2, 1:2]
#> A B
#> 1 1 D
#> 2 2 E
x$B
#> [1] D E F G
#> Levels: D E F G
x$B[2]
```

```
#> [1] E
#> Levels: D E F G
```

Depending on how the data is organized, the data frame is said to be in either wide or narrow formats (https://en.wikipedia.org/wiki/Wide_and_narrow_data). Finally, if you want to keep only observations for which you have complete cases, meaning only rows that don't contain any NA values for any of the variables, then you should use the complete.cases() function, which returns a logical vector of length equal to the number of rows, and which contains a TRUE value for those rows that don't have any NA values and FALSE for those that have at least one such value.

Note that when we created the x data frame, the C column contains an NA in its third value. If we use the complete.cases() function on x, then we will get a FALSE value for that row and a TRUE value for all others. We can then use this logical vector to subset the data frame just as we have done before with matrices. This can be very useful when analyzing data that may not be clean, and for which you only want to keep those observations for which you have full information:

```
x
#> A B C
#> 1 1 D TRUE
#> 2 2 E FALSE
#> 3 3 F NA
#> 4 4 G FALSE

complete.cases(x)
#> [1] TRUE TRUE FALSE TRUE
x[complete.cases(x), ]
#> A B C
#> 1 1 D TRUE
#> 2 2 E FALSE
#> 4 4 G FALSE
```

Divide and conquer with functions

Functions are a fundamental building block of R. To master many of the more advanced techniques in this book, you need a solid foundation in how they work. We've already used a few functions above since you can't really do anything interesting in R without them. They are just what you remember from your mathematics classes, a way to transform inputs into outputs. Specifically in R, a function is an object that takes other objects as inputs, called arguments, and returns an output object. Most functions are in the following form `f(argument_1, argument_2, ...)`. Where f is the name of the function, and `argument_1`, `argument_2`, and so on are the arguments to the function.

Before we continue, we should briefly mention the role of curly braces ({}) in R. Often they are used to group a set of operations in the body of a function, but they can also be used in other contexts (as we will see in the case of the web application we will build in `Chapter 10`, *Adding Interactivity with Dashboards*). Curly braces are used to evaluate a series of expressions, which are separated by newlines or semicolons, and return only the last expression as a result. For example, the following line only prints the x + y operation to the screen, hiding the output of the x * y operation, which would have been printed had we typed the expressions step by step. In this sense, curly braces are used to encapsulate a set of behavior and only provide the result from the last expression:

```
{ x <- 1; y <- 2; x * y; x + y }
#> [1] 3
```

We can create our own function by using the `function()` constructor and assign it to a symbol. The `function()` constructor takes an arbitrary number of named arguments, which can be used within the body of the function. Unnamed arguments can also be passed using the "..." argument notation, but that's an advanced technique we won't look at in this book. Feel free to read the documentation for functions to learn more about them.

When calling the function, arguments can be passed by position or by name. The positional order must correspond to the order provided in the function's signature (that is, the `function()` specification with the corresponding arguments), but when using named arguments, we can send them in whatever order we prefer. As the following example shows.

In the following example, we create a function that calculates the **Euclidian distance** (`https://en.wikipedia.org/wiki/Euclidean_distance`) between two numeric vectors, and we show how the order of the arguments can be changed if we use named arguments. To realize this effect, we use the `print()` function to make sure we can see in the console what R is receiving as the x and y vectors. When developing your own programs, using the `print()` function in similar ways is very useful to understand what's happening.

Instead of using the function name like `euclidian_distance`, we will use `l2_norm` because it's the generalized name for such an operation when working with spaces of arbitrary number dimensions and because it will make a follow-up example easier to understand. Note that even though outside the function call our vectors are called a and b, since they are passed into the x and y arguments, those are the names we need to use within our function. It's easy for beginners to confuse these objects as being the same if we had used the x and y names in both places:

```
l2_norm <- function(x, y) {
    print("x")
    print(x)
    print("y")
    print(y)
    element_to_element_difference <- x - y
    result <- sum(element_to_element_difference^2)
    return(result)
}

a <- c(1, 2, 3)
b <- c(4, 5, 6)

l2_norm(a, b)
#> [1] "x"
#> [1] 1 2 3
#> [1] "y"
#> [1] 4 5 6
#> [1] 27

l2_norm(b, a)
#> [1] "x"
#> [1] 4 5 6
#> [1] "y"
#> [1] 1 2 3
#> [1] 27

l2_norm(x = a, y = b)
#> [1] "x"
#> [1] 1 2 3
#> [1] "y"
#> [1] 4 5 6
#> [1] 27

l2_norm(y = b, x = a)
#> [1] "x"
#> [1] 1 2 3
#> [1] "y"
```

```
#> [1] 4 5 6
#> [1] 27
```

Functions may use the `return()` function to specify the value returned by the function. However, R will simply return the last evaluated expression as the result of a function, so you may see code that does not make use of the `return()` function explicitly.

Our previous `l2_norm()` function implementation seems to be somewhat cluttered. If the function has a single expression, then we can avoid using the curly braces, which we can achieve by removing the `print()` function calls and avoid creating intermediate objects, and since we know that it's working fine, we can do so without hesitation. Furthermore, we avoid explicitly calling the `return()` function to simplify our code even more. If we do so, our function looks much closer to its mathematical definition and is easier to understand, isn't it?

```
l2_norm <- function(x, y) sum((x - y)^2)
```

Furthermore, in case you did not notice, since we use vectorized operations, we can send vectors of different lengths (dimensions), provided that both vectors share the same length, and the function will work just as we expect it to, without regard for the dimensionality of the space we're working with. As I had mentioned earlier, vectorization can be quite powerful. In the following example, we show such behavior with vectors of dimension 1 (mathematically known as scalars), as well as vectors of dimension 5, created with the ":" shortcut syntax:

```
l2_norm(1, 2)
#> [1] 1
l2_norm(1:5, 6:10)
#> [1] 125
```

Before we move on, I just want to mention that you should always make an effort to follow the Single Responsibility principle, which states that each object (functions in this case) should focus on doing a single thing, and do it very well. Whenever you describe a function you created as doing "*something*" and "*something else,*" you're probably doing it wrong since the "and" should let you know that the function is doing more than one thing, and you should split it into two or more functions that possibly call each other. To read more about good software engineering principles, take a look at Martin's great book title *Agile Software Development, Principles, Patterns, and Practices, Pearson, 2002.*

Optional arguments

When creating functions, you may specify a default value for an argument, and if you do, then the argument is considered optional. If you do not specify a default value for an argument, and you do not specify a value when calling a function, you will get an error if the function attempts to use the argument.

In the following example, we show that if a single numeric vector is passed to our `12_norm()` function as it stands, it will throw an error, but if we redefine it to make the second vector optional, then we will simply return the first vector's norm, not the distance between two different vectors To accomplish this, we will provide a zero-vector of length one, but because R repeats vector elements until all the vectors involved in an operation are of the same length, as we saw before in this chapter, it will automatically expand our zero-vector into the appropriate dimension:

```
12_norm(a)      # Should throw an error because `y` is missing
#> Error in 12_norm(a): argument "y" is missing, with no default

12_norm <- function(x, y = 0) sum((x - y)^2)

12_norm(a)      # Should work fine, since `y` is optional now
#> [1] 14
12_norm(a, b)  # Should work just as before
#> [1] 27
```

As you can see, now our function can optionally receive the y vector, but will also work as expected without it. Also, note that we introduced some comments into our code. Anything that comes after the # symbol in a line, R will ignore, which allows us to explain our code where need be. I prefer to avoid using comments because I tend to think that code should be expressive and communicate its intention without the need for comments, but they are actually useful every now and then.

Functions as arguments

Sometimes when you want to generalize functions, you may want to plug in a certain functionality into a function. You can do that in various ways. For example, you may use conditionals, as we will see in the following section in this chapter, to provide them with different functionality based on context. However, conditional should be avoided when possible because they can introduce unnecessary complexity into our code. A better solution would be to pass a function as a parameter which will be called when appropriate, and if we want to change how a function behaves, we can change the function we're passing through for a specific task.

That may sound complicated, but in reality, it's very simple. Let's start by creating a `l1_norm()` function that calculates the distance between two vectors but uses the sum of absolute differences among corresponding coordinates instead of the sum of squared differences as our `l2_norm()` function does. For more information, take a look at the *Taxicab geometry* article on Wikipedia (`https://en.wikipedia.org/wiki/Taxicab_geometry`).

Note that we use the same *signature* for our two functions, meaning that both receive the same required as well as optional arguments, which are `x` and `y` in this case. This is important because if we want to change the behavior by switching functions, we must make sure they are able to work with the same inputs, otherwise, we may get unexpected results or even errors:

```
l1_norm <- function(x, y = 0) sum(abs(x - y))

l1_norm(a)
#> [1] 6
l1_norm(a, b)
#> [1] 9
```

Now that our `l2_norm()` and `l1_norm()` are built so that they can be switched among themselves to provide different behavior, we will create a third `distance()` function, which will take the two vectors as arguments, but will also receive a norm argument, which will contain the function we want to use to calculate the distance.

Note that we are specifying that we want to use the `l2_norm()` by default in case there's no explicit selection when calling the function, and to do so we simply specify the symbol that contains the function object, without parenthesis. Finally note, that if we want to avoid sending the `y` vector, but we want to specify what norm should be used, then we must pass it through as a named argument, otherwise R would interpret the second argument as the `y` vector, not the norm function:

```
distance <- function(x, y = 0, norm = l2_norm) norm(x, y)

distance(a)
#> [1] 14
distance(a, b)
#> [1] 27
distance(a, b, l2_norm)
#> [1] 27
distance(a, b, l1_norm)
#> [1] 9
distance(a, norm = l1_norm)
#> [1] 6
```

Operators are functions

Now that you have a working understanding of how functions work. You should know that not all function calls look like the ones we have shown so far, where you use the name of the function followed by parentheses that contains the function's arguments. Actually, all statements in R, including setting variables and arithmetic operations, are functions in the background, even if we mostly call them with a different syntax.

Remember that previously in this chapter we mentioned that R objects could be referred to by almost any string, but you should avoid doing so. Well here we show how using cryptic names can be useful under certain contexts. The following example shows how the assignment, selection, and addition operators are usually used with *sugar* syntax (a term used to describe syntax that exists for ease of use), but that in the background they use the functions named [<-, [, and +, respectively.

The [<-() function receives three arguments: the vector we want to modify, the position we want to modify in the vector, and the value we want it to have at that position. The [() function receives two arguments, the vector from which we want to retrieve a value and the position of the value we want to retrieve. Finally, the +() function receives the two values we want to add. The following example shows the syntax sugar, followed by the background function calls R performs for us:

```
x <- c(1, 2, 3, 4, 5)
x
#> [1] 1 2 3 4 5
x[1] <- 10
x
#> [1] 10 2 3 4 5
`[<-`(x, 1, 20)
#> [1] 20 2 3 4 5
x
#> [1] 10 2 3 4 5
x[1]
#> [1] 10
`[`(x, 1)
#> [1] 10
x[1] + x[2]
#> [1] 12
`+`(x[1], x[2])
#> [1] 12
`+`(`[`(x, 1), `[`(x, 1))
#> [1] 20
```

In practice, you would probably never write these statements as explicit function calls. The syntax sugar is much more intuitive and much easier to read. However, to use some of the advanced techniques shown in this book, it is helpful to know that every operation in R is a function.

Coercion

Finally, we will briefly mention what coercion is in R since it's a topic of confusion for newcomers. When you call a function with an argument of a different type than what was expected, R will try to coerce values so that the function will work, and this can introduce bugs if not handled correctly. R will follow a mechanism similar to what was used when creating vectors.

Strongly typed languages (like Java) will raise exceptions when the object passed to a function is of the wrong type, and will try not to convert the object to a compatible type. However, as we mentioned earlier, R was designed to work out of the box with a lot of unforeseen contexts, so coercion was introduced.

In the following example, we show that if we call our `distance()` function and pass logical vectors instead of numeric ones, R will coerce the logical vectors into numeric vectors, using `TRUE` as 1 and `FALSE` as 0, and proceed with the calculations. To avoid this issue in your own programs, you should coerce data types explicitly with the `as.*()` functions we mentioned before:

```
x <- c(1, 2, 3)
y <- c(TRUE, FALSE, TRUE)
distance(x, y)
#> [1] 8
```

Complex logic with control structures

The final topic we should cover is how to introduce complex logic by using control structures. When I write introduce complex logic, I don't mean to imply that it's complex to do so. Complex logic refers to code that has multiple possible paths of execution, but in reality, it's quite simple to implement it.

Nearly every operation in R can be written as a function, and these functions can be passed through to other functions to create very complex behavior. However, it isn't always convenient to implement logic that way and using simple control structures may be a better option sometimes.

The control structures we will look at are if... else conditionals, for loops, and while loops. There are also switch conditionals, which are very much like if... else conditionals, but we won't look at them since we won't use them in the examples contained in this book.

If... else conditionals

As their name states, if...else conditionals will check a condition, and if it is evaluated to be a TRUE value, one path of execution will be taken, but if the condition is evaluated to be a FALSE value, a different path of execution will be taken, and they are mutually exclusive.

To show how if... else conditions work, we will program the same distance() function we used before, but instead of passing it the third argument in the form of a function, we will pass it a string that will be checked to decide which function should be used. This way you can compare different ways of implementing the same functionality. If we pass the l2 string to the norm argument, then the l2_norm() function will be used, but if any other string is passed through, the l1_norm() will be used. Note that we use the double equals operator (==) to check for equality. Don't confuse this with a single equals, which means assignment:

```
distance <- function(x, y = 0, norm = "l2") {
    if (norm == "l2") {
        return(l2_norm(x, y))
    } else {
        return(l1_norm(x, y))
    }
}

a <- c(1, 2, 3)
b <- c(4, 5, 6)

distance(a, b)
#> 27
distance(a, b, "l2")
#> 27
distance(a, b, "l1")
#> 9
distance(a, b, "l1 will also be used in this case")
#> 9
```

As can be seen in the last line of the previous example, using conditionals in a non-rigorous manner can introduce potential bugs, as in this case we used the l1_norm() function, even when the norm argument in the last function call did not make any sense at all. To avoid such situations, we may introduce the more conditionals to exhaust all valid possibilities and throw an error, with the stop() function, if the else branch is executed, which would mean that no valid option was provided:

```
distance <- function(x, y = 0, norm = "l2") {
    if (norm == "l2") {
        return(l2_norm(x, y))
    } else if (norm == "l1") {
        return(l1_norm(x, y))
    } else {
        stop("Invalid norm option")
    }
}

distance(a, b, "l1")
#> [1] 9
distance(a, b, "this will produce an error")
#> Error in distance(a, b, "this will produce an error") :
#>    Invalid norm option
```

Sometimes, there's no need for the else part of the if... else condition. In that case, you can simply avoid putting it in, and R will execute the if branch if the condition is met and will ignore it if it's not.

There are many different ways to generate the logical values that can be used within the if() check. For example, you could specify an optional argument with a NULL default value and check whether it was not sent in the function call by checking whether the corresponding variable still contains the NULL object at the time of the check, using the is.null() function. The actual condition would look something like if(is.null(optional_argument)). Other times you may get a logical vector, and if a single one of its values is TRUE, then you want to execute a piece of code, in that case you can use something like if(any(logical_vector)) as the condition, or in case you require that all of the values in the logical vector are TRUE to execute a piece of code, then you can use something like if(all(logical_vector)). The same logic can be applied to the self-descriptive functions named is.na() and is.nan().

Another way to generate these logical values is using the comparison operators. These include less than (<), less than or equal to (<=), greater than (>), greater than or equal to (>=), exactly equal (which we have seen ,==), and not equal to (!=). All of these can be used to test numerics as well as characters, in which case alphanumerical order is used. Furthermore, logical values can be combined among themselves to provide more complex conditions. For example, the ! operator will negate a logical, meaning that if !TRUE is equal to FALSE, and !FALSE is equal to TRUE. Other examples of these types of operators are the OR operator where in case any of the logical values is TRUE, then the whole expression evaluates to TRUE, and the AND operator where all logical must be TRUE to evaluate to TRUE. Even though we don't show specific examples of the information mentioned in the last two paragraphs, you will see it used in the examples we will develop in the rest of the book.

Finally, note that a vectorized form of the if... else conditional is available under the ifelse() function. In the following code we use the modulo operator in the conditional, which is the first argument to the function, to identify which values are even, in which case we use the TRUE branch which is the second argument to indicate that the integer is *even*, and which are not, in which case we use the FALSE branch which is the third argument to indicate that the integer is *odd*:

```
ifelse(c(1, 2, 3, 4, 5, 6) %% 2 == 0, "even", "odd")
#> [1] "odd" "even" "odd" "even" "odd" "even"
```

For loops

There are two important properties of for loops. First, results are not printed inside a loop unless you explicitly call the print() function. Second, the indexing variable used within a for loop will be changed, in order, after each iteration. Furthermore, to stop iterating you can use the keyword break, and to skip to the next iteration you can use the next command.

For this first example, we create a vector of characters called words, and iterate through each of its elements in order using the for (word in words) syntax. Doing so will take the first element in words, assign it to word, and pass it through the expression defined in the block defined by the curly braces, which in this case print the word to the console, as well as the number of characters in the word. When the iteration is finished, word will be updated with the next word, and the loop will be repeated this way until all words have been used:

```
words <- c("Hello", "there", "dear", "reader")
for (word in words) {
    print(word)
    print(nchar(word))
}
```

```
#> [1] "Hello"
#> [1] 5
#> [1] "there"
#> [1] 5
#> [1] "dear"
#> [1] 4
#> [1] "reader"
#> [1] 6
```

Interesting behavior can be achieved by using *nested for loops* which are `for` loops inside other `for` loops. In this case, the same logic applies, when we encounter a `for` loop we execute it until completion. It's easier to see the result of such behavior than explaining it, so take a look at the behavior of the following code:

```
for (i in 1:5) {
    print(i)
    for (j in 1:3) {
        print(paste("    ", j))
    }
}
#> [1] 1
#> [1] " 1"
#> [1] " 2"
#> [1] " 3"
#> [1] 2
#> [1] " 1"
#> [1] " 2"
#> [1] " 3"
#> [1] 3
#> [1] " 1"
#> [1] " 2"
#> [1] " 3"
#> [1] 4
#> [1] " 1"
#> [1] " 2"
#> [1] " 3"
#> [1] 5
#> [1] " 1"
#> [1] " 2"
#> [1] " 3"
```

Using such nested `for` loops is how people perform matrix-like operations when using languages that do not offer vectorized operations. Luckily, we can use the syntax shown in previous sections to perform those operations without having to use nested for-loops ourselves which can be tricky at times.

Now, we will see how to use the `sapply()` and `lapply()` functions to apply a function to each element of a vector. In this case, we will call use the `nchar()` function on each of the elements in the words vector we created before. The difference between the `sapply()` and the `lapply()` functions is that the first one returns a vector, while the second returns a list. Finally, note that explicitly using any of these functions is unnecessary, since, as we have seen before in this chapter, the `nchar()` function is already vectorized for us:

```
sapply(words, nchar)
#> Hello there dear reader
#> 5      5     4    6
lapply(words, nchar)
#> [[1]]
#> [1] 5
#>
#> [[2]]
#> [1] 5
#>
#> [[3]]
#> [1] 4
#>
#> [[4]]
#> [1] 6
nchar(words)
#> [1] 5 5 4 6
```

When you have a function that has not been vectorized, like our `distance()` function. You can still use it in a vectorized way by making use of the functions we just mentioned. In this case we will apply it to the x list which contains three different numeric vectors. We will use the `lapply()` function by passing it the list, followed by the function we want to apply to each of its elements (`distance()` in this case). Note that in case the function you are using receives other arguments apart from the one that will be taken from x and which will be passed as the first argument to such function, you can pass them through after the function name, like we do here with the `c(1, 1, 1)` and `l1_norm` arguments, which will be received by the `distance()` function as the y and norm arguments, and will remain fixed for all the elements of the x list:

```
x <- list(c(1, 2, 3), c(4, 5, 6), c(7, 8, 9))
lapply(x, distance, c(1, 1, 1), l1_norm)
#> [[1]]
#> [1] 3
#>
#> [[2]]
#> [1] 12
#>
#> [[3]]
```

```
#> [1] 21
```

While loops

Finally, we will take a look at the `while` loops which use a different way of looping than `for` loops. In the case of `for` loops, we know the number of elements in the object we use to iterate, so we know in advance the number of iterations that will be performed. However, there are times where we don't know this number before we start iterating, and instead, we will iterate based on some condition being true after each iteration. That's when `while` loops are useful.

The way `while` loops work is that we specify a condition, just as with `if...else` conditions, and if the condition is met, then we proceed to iterate. When the iteration is finished, we check the condition again, and if it continues to be true, then we iterate again, and so on. Note that in this case if we want to stop at some point, we must modify the elements used in the condition such that it evaluates to `FALSE` at some point. You can also use break and next inside the `while` loops.

The following example shows how to print all integers starting at 1 and until 10. Note that if we start at 1 as we do, but instead of adding 1 after each iteration, we subtracted 1 or didn't change x at all, then we would never stop iterating. That's why you need to be very careful when using `while` loops since the number of iterations can be infinite:

```
x <- 1
while (x <= 10) {
    print(x)
    x <- x + 1
}
#> [1] 1
#> [1] 2
#> [1] 3
#> [1] 4
#> [1] 5
#> [1] 6
#> [1] 7
#> [1] 8
#> [1] 9
#> [1] 10
```

In case you do want to execute an infinite loop, you may use the `while` loop with a `TRUE` value in the place of the conditional. If you do not include a `break` command, the code will effectively provide an infinite loop, and it will repeat itself until stopped with the *CTRL + C* keyboard command or any other stopping mechanism in the IDE you're using. However, in such cases, it's cleaner to use the repeat construct as is shown below. It may seem counter intuitive, but there are times when using infinite loops is useful. We will see one such case in `Chapter 8`, *Object-Oriented System to Track Cryptocurrencies*, but in such cases, you have an external mechanism used to stop the program based on a condition external to R.

Executing the following example will crash your R session:

```
# DO NOTE EXCEUTE THIS, IT's AN INFINITE LOOP

x <- 1
repeat {
    print(x)
    x <- x + 1
}

#> [1] 1
#> [1] 2
#> [1] 3
#> [1] 4
#> [1] 5
#> [1] 5
...
```

The examples in this book

To end this introductory chapter, I want to introduce you to the three examples we will develop throughout the rest of the book. The first one is the Brexit Votes example, in which we are going to use real Brexit votes data, and, with descriptive statistics and linear models, we will attempt to understand the population dynamics at play behind the results. If you're not familiar with Brexit, it is the popular term for the prospective withdrawal of the United Kingdom from the European Union after a referendum which took place on June 23, 2016 (`https://en.wikipedia.org/wiki/Brexit`). This example will be developed through `Chapter 2`, *Understanding Votes with Descriptive Statistics*, and `Chapter 3`, *Predicting Votes with Linear Models*.

The second one is The Food Factory example, in which you will learn how to simulate various kinds of data for a hypothetical company called The Food Factory, as well as integrate real data from other sources (customer reviews in this case) to complement our simulations. The data will be used to develop various kinds of visualizations, text analysis, and presentations that are updated automatically. This example will be developed through; Chapter 4, *Simulating Sales Data and Working with Databases*; Chapter 5, *Communicating Sales with Visualizations*; Chapter 6, *Understanding Reviews with Text Analysis*; and Chapter 7, *Developing Automatic Presentations*.

The third and final one is the *Cryptocurrencies Tracking System* example, in which we will develop an object-oriented system that will be used to retrieve real-time price data from cryptocurrency markets and the amount of cryptocurrencies assets we hold. We will then show how to compute a simple moving average efficiently using performance optimization techniques, and finally we will show how to build interactive web applications using only R. This example will be developed through Chapter 8, *Object-Oriented System to Track Cryptocurrencies*; Chapter 9, *Implementing an Efficient Simple Moving Average*; and Chapter 10, *Adding Interactivity with Dashboards*.

Summary

In this chapter, we introduced the book by mentioning its intended audience, as well as our intentions for it, which are to provide examples that you can use to understand how real-world R applications are built using a high-quality code, and the useful guidelines of what to do and not to do when building your own applications.

We also introduced R's basic constructs and prepared the baseline we need to work through the examples developed in the rest of the book. Specifically, we looked at how to work with the console, how to create and use variables, how to work with R basic data types like numerics, characters, and logicals, as well as how to handle special values, and how to make basic use of data structures like vectors, factors, matrices, data frames, and lists. Finally, we showed how to create our own functions and how to provide multiple paths of execution with control structures.

I hope this book is useful to you and that you enjoy reading it.

2
Understanding Votes with Descriptive Statistics

This chapter shows how to perform a descriptive statistics analysis to get a general idea about the data we're dealing with, which is usually the first step in data analysis projects and is a basic ability for data analysts in general. We will learn how to clean and transform data, summarize data in a useful way, find specific observations, create various kinds of plots that provide intuition for the data, use correlations to understand relations among numerical variables, use principal components to find optimal variable combinations, and put everything together into code that is reusable, understandable, and easily modifiable.

Since this is a book about programming with R and not about doing statistics with R, our focus will be on the programming side of things, not the statistical side. Keep that in mind while reading it.

Some of the important topics covered in this chapter are as follows:

- Cleaning, transforming, and operating on data
- Creating various kinds of graphs programmatically
- Performing qualitative analysis with various tools in R
- Building new variables with Principal Components Analysis
- Developing modular and flexible code that is easy to work with

This chapter's required packages

During this chapter we will make use of the following R packages. If you don't already have them installed, you can look into `Appendix`, *Required Packages* for instructions on how do so.

Package	Used for
ggplot2	High-quality graphs
viridis	Color palette for graphs
corrplot	Correlation plots
ggbiplot	Principal components plots
progress	Show progress for iterations

The Brexit votes example

In June 2016, a referendum was held in the **United Kingdom** (**UK**) to decide whether or not to remain part of the **European Union** (**EU**). 72% of registered voters took part, and of those, 51.2% voted to leave the EU. In February 2017, Martin Rosenbaum, freedom of information specialist at BBC News, published the article, *Local Voting Figures Shed New Light on EU Referendum* (http://www.bbc.co.uk/news/uk-politics-38762034). He obtained data from 1,070 electoral wards (the smallest administrative division for electoral purposes in the UK), with numbers for **Leave** and **Remain** votes in each ward.

Martin Rosenbaum calculated some statistical associations between the proportion of **Leave** votes in a ward and some of its social, economic, and demographic characteristics by making use of the most recent UK census, which was conducted in 2011. He used his data for a university class, and that's the data we will use in this example, with some variables removed. The data is provided in a CSV file (`data_brexit_referendum.csv`) which can be found in the accompanying code repository for this book (https://github.com/PacktPublishing/R-Programming-By-Example). The table shows the variables included in the data:

No.	Variable	Description
1	ID	Ward ID number from 1 to 1,070
2	RegionName	Name of the region within which the ward is situated
3	NVotes	Total number of votes ('Leave' + 'Remain')
4	Leave	Number of 'Leave' votes
5	Residents	Number of permanent residents
6	Household	Number of households
7	MeanAge	Mean age of permanent residents
8	AdultMeanAge	Mean age of adult permanent residents
9	Age_0to4	% of permanent residents aged 0-4
10	Age_5to7	% of permanent residents aged 5-7
11	Age_8to9	% of permanent residents aged 8-9
12	Age_10to14	% of permanent residents aged 10-14
13	Age_15	% of permanent residents aged 15
14	Age_16to17	% of permanent residents aged 16-17
15	Age_18to19	% of permanent residents aged 18-19
16	Age_20to24	% of permanent residents aged 20-24
17	Age_25to29	% of permanent residents aged 25-29
18	Age_30to44	% of permanent residents aged 30-44
19	Age_45to59	% of permanent residents aged 45-59
20	Age_60to64	% of permanent residents aged 60-64
21	Age_65to74	% of permanent residents aged 65-74
22	Age_75to84	% of permanent residents aged 75-84
23	Age_85to89	% of permanent residents aged 85-89
24	Age_90plus	% of permanent residents aged 90 and above
25	White	% of permanent residents self-identifying as white
26	Black	% of permanent residents self-identifying as black
27	Asian	% of permanent residents self-identifying as Asian
28	Indian	% of permanent residents self-identifying as Indian
29	Pakistani	% of permanent residents self-identifying as Pakistani
30	Owned	% of households owning their accommodation
31	OwnedOutright	% of households owning their accommodation without mortgage
32	SocialRent	% of households renting from social landlords
33	PrivateRent	% of households renting from private landlords
34	NoQuals	% of permanent residents with no academic qualifications
35	L4Quals_plus	% of permanent residents with a degree education or above
36	Students	% of permanent residents who are students
37	Unemp	% of permanent residents who are unemployed
38	UnempRate_EA	% of economically active residents who are unemployed
39	HigherOccup	% permanent residents in 'higher-level' occupations
40	Density	Population density (permanent residents per hectare)
41	Deprived	% of households that are 'deprived' in at least one of four dimensions
42	MultiDeprived	% of households that are 'deprived' in at least two of four dimensions

Data variable descriptions

Cleaning and setting up the data

Setting up the data for this example is straightforward. We will load the data, correctly label missing values, and create some new variables for our analysis. Before we start, make sure the `data.csv` file is in the same directory as the code you're working with, and that your *working directory* is properly setup. If you don't know how to do so, setting up your working directory is quite easy, you simply call the `setwd()` function passing the directory you want to use as such. For example, `setwd(/home/user/examples/)` would use the `/home/user/examples` directory to look for files, and save files to.

If you don't know how to do so, setting up your working directory is quite easy, you simply call the `setwd()` function passing the directory you want to use as such. For example, `setwd(/home/user/examples/)` would use the /home/user/examples directory to look for files, and save files to.

We can load the contents of the `data.csv` file into a data frame (the most intuitive structure to use with data in CSV format) by using the `read.csv()` function. Note that the data has some missing values in the `Leave` variable. These values have a value of -1 to identify them. However, the proper way to identify missing values in R is with `NA`, which is what we use to replace the -1 values.

```
data <- read.csv("./data_brexit_referendum.csv")
data[data$Leave == -1, "Leave"] <- NA
```

To count the number of missing values in our data, we can use the `is.na()` function to get a logical (Boolean) vector that contains `TRUE` values to identify missing values and `FALSE` values to identify non-missing values. The length of such a vector will be equal to the length of the vector used as input, which is the `Leave` variable in our case. Then, we can use this logical vector as input for `sum()` while leverage the way R treats such `TRUE`/`FALSE` values to get the number of missing values. `TRUE` is treated as 1, while `FALSE` is treated as 0. We find that the number of missing values in the `Leave` variable is 267.

```
sum(is.na(data$Leave))
#> [1] 267
```

If we want to, we can use a mechanism to fill the missing values. A common and straightforward mechanism is to impute the variable's mean. In our case, in Chapter 3, *Predicting Votes with Linear Models*, we will use linear regression to estimate these missing values. However, we will keep things simple for now and just leave them as missing values.

We now proceed to defining a new variable, `Proportion`, which will contain the percentage of votes in favor of leaving the EU. To do so we divide the `Leave` variable (number of votes in favor of leaving) by the `NVotes` variable (number of votes in total), for each ward. Given the vectorized nature of R, this is straightforward:

```
data$Proportion <- data$Leave / data$NVotes
```

 We are creating a new variable in the data frame by simply assigning to it. There's no difference between creating a new variable and modifying an existing one, which means that we need to be careful when doing so to make sure we're not overwriting an old variable by accident.

Now, create a new variable that contains a classification of whether most of the wards voted in favor of leaving or remaining in the EU. If more than 50 percent of each ward's votes were in favor of leaving, then we will mark the ward as having voted for leaving, and vice versa for remaining. Again, R makes this very simple with the use of the `ifelse()` function. If the mentioned condition (first parameter) holds true, then the value assigned will be `"Leave"` (second parameter); otherwise it will be `"Remain"` (third parameter). This is a vectorized operation, so it will be done for each observation in the data frame:

```
data$Vote <- ifelse(data$Proportion > 0.5, "Leave", "Remain")
```

Sometimes, people like to use a different syntax for these types of operations; they will use a *subset-assign approach,* which is slightly different from what we used. We won't go into the details of the differences among these approaches, but keep in mind that the latter approach may give you an error in our case:

```
data[data$Proportion >  0.5, "Vote"] <- "Leave"
data[data$Proportion <= 0.5, "Vote"] <- "Remain"

#> Error in `[<-.data.frame`(`*tmp*`, data$Proportion 0.5, "Vote", value =
"Leave"):
#>   missing values are not allowed in subscripted assignments of data
frames
```

This happens because the `Proportion` variable contains some missing values that were consequences of the `Leave` variable having some `NA` values in the first place. Since we can't compute a `Proportion` value for observations with `NA` values in `Leave`, when we create it, the corresponding values also get an `NA` value assigned.

If we insist on using the *subset-assign approach,* we can make it work by using the `which()` function. It will ignore (returning as `FALSE`) those values that contain `NA` in the comparison. This way it won't give us an error, and we will get the same result as using the `ifelse()` function. We should use the `ifelse()` function when possible because it's simpler, easier to read, and more efficient (more about this in `Chapter 9`, *Implementing an Efficient Simple Moving Average*).

```
data[which(data$Proportion >  0.5), "Vote"] <- "Leave"
data[which(data$Proportion <= 0.5), "Vote"] <- "Remain"
```

Down the road we will want to create plots that include the `RegionName` information and having long names will most likely make them hard to read. To fix that we can shorten those names while we are in the process of cleaning the data.

```
data$RegionName <- as.character(data$RegionName)
data[data$RegionName == "London", "RegionName"]                     <- "L"
data[data$RegionName == "North West", "RegionName"]                 <- "NW"
data[data$RegionName == "North East", "RegionName"]                 <- "NE"
data[data$RegionName == "South West", "RegionName"]                 <- "SW"
data[data$RegionName == "South East", "RegionName"]                 <- "SE"
data[data$RegionName == "East Midlands", "RegionName"]              <- "EM"
data[data$RegionName == "West Midlands", "RegionName"]              <- "WM"
data[data$RegionName == "East of England", "RegionName"]            <- "EE"
data[data$RegionName == "Yorkshire and The Humber", "RegionName"] <- "Y"
```

Note that the first line in the previous code block is assigning a transformation of the `RegionName` into character type. Before we do this, the type of the variable is factor (which comes from the default way of reading data with `read.csv()`), and it prevents us from assigning a different value from the ones already contained in the variable. In such a case, we will get an error, `Invalid factor level, NA generated`. To avoid this problem, we need to perform the type transformation.

We now have clean data ready for analysis. We have created a new variable of interest for us (`Proportion`), which will be the focus of the rest of this chapter and the next one, since in this example, we're interested in finding out the relations among other variables and how people voted in the referendum.

Summarizing the data into a data frame

To get a summary of the data, we may execute summary(data) and see the relevant summaries for each type of variable. The summary is tailored for each column's data type. As you can see, numerical variables such as ID and NVotes get a quantile summary, while factor (categorical) variables get a count for each different category, such as AreaType and RegionName. If there are many categories, the summary will show the categories that appear the most and group the rest into a (Other) group, as we can see at the bottom of RegionName.

```
summary(data)
#>       ID             RegionName              NVotes              Leave
#> Min.    : 1      Length: 1070        Min.    : 1039     Min.    : 287
#> 1st Qu.: 268     Class : character   1st Qu.: 4252      1st Qu.: 1698
#> Median : 536     Mode  : character   Median : 5746      Median : 2874
#> Mean    : 536                        Mean    : 5703     Mean    : 2971
#> 3rd Qu.: 803                         3rd Qu.: 7020      3rd Qu.: 3936
#> Max.    : 1070                       Max.    : 15148    Max.    : 8316
(Truncated output)
```

From here, we can see that London is the region to which more wards belong, followed by the North West and West Midlands. We can also see that the ward with the least votes in all of the data had only 1,039 votes, the one with the most votes had 15,148, and the mean number of votes per ward was 5,703. We will take a deeper look into these kinds of analyses later in the chapter. For now we'll focus on making this summary data useful for further analysis. As you may have noticed, we can't use the summary() results to make computations. We can try to save the summary into a variable, find out the variable type, and traverse it in an appropriate way. However, if we do that we will find that it's text data, which means that we can't use it for computations as it is:

```
summary <- summary(data)
class(summary)
#> [1] "table"
summary[1]
#> [1] "Min.    : 1  "
class(summary[1])
#> [1] "character"
```

Surely, there must be a way to get the `summary` data into a data frame for further analysis. This is R, so you can bet there is! The first thing we should note is that we can't directly translate the output of the `summary()` function into a data frame because of the non-numerical variables. These non-numerical variables contain a different summary structure which is not composed of the minimum, first quartile, median, mean, third quartile, and maximum values. This means that we first need to subset the data to get only the numerical variables. After all, a data frame is a rectangular structure with well defined rows and columns. If we tried to mix types (by including numerical and non-numerical summaries) into the data frame, we would have a hard time doing so.

To find if a column is numeric or not, we can use the `is.numeric()` function. For example, we can see that the `Proportion` column is numeric and the `RegionName` is not:

```
is.numeric(data$Proportion)
#> [1] TRUE
is.numeric(data$RegionName)
#> [1] FALSE
```

We can then apply `is.numeric()` to each column by using the `sapply()` function. This will give us a logical (Boolean) vector with a `TRUE` or `FALSE` value for each column, indicating whether or not it's numeric. Then we can use this logical vector to subset our data and get only the numerical columns with `data[, numerical_variables]`. As you can see, there are no non-numerical columns in the `data_numerical` object:

```
numerical_variables <- sapply(data, is.numeric)
numerical_variables
#>           ID   RegionName        NVotes        Leave     Residents
#>         TRUE        FALSE          TRUE         TRUE          TRUE
#>   Households      MeanAge  AdultMeanAge    Aget_0to4     Age_5to7
#>         TRUE         TRUE          TRUE         TRUE          TRUE
(Truncated output)

data_numerical <- data[, numerical_variables]
colnames(data_numerical)
#>  [1] "ID"           "Nvotes"       "Leave"          "Residents"
#>  [5] "Households"   "MeanAge"      "AdultMeanAge"   "Age_0to4"
#>  [9] "Age_5to7"     "Age_8to9"     "Age_10to14"     "Age_15"
#> [13] "Age_16to17"   "Age_18to19"   "Age_20to24"     "Age_25to29"
(Truncated output)
```

Since it doesn't make much sense to get the `summary` values for the `ID` variable, we can remove it from the logical vector, effectively treating it as a non-numerical variable. If we do, we must remember to recreate the `data_numeric` object to make sure it doesn't include the `ID` variable also:

```
numerical_variables[["ID"]] <- FALSE
data_numerical <- data[, numerical_variables]
```

To create our numerical variables summary, we first will apply the `summary()` function we used before to each numerical column using the `lapply()` function. The `lapply()` function returns a named list, where each list member has the corresponding column name:

```
lapply(data[, numerical_variables], summary)
#> $NVotes
#>    Min. 1st Qu. Median  Mean 3rd Qu.   Max.
#>    1039    4252   5746  5703    7020  15148
#>
#> $Leave
#>    Min. 1st Qu. Median  Mean 3rd Qu.   Max.
#>     287    1698   2874  2971    3936   8316
#>
#> $Residents
#>    Min. 1st Qu. Median   Mean 3rd Qu.   Max.
#>    1932    8288  11876  11646   14144  34098
#>
(Truncated output)
```

Now we need to put each member of this list together into a data frame. To do so, we will use the `cbind()` and `do.call()` functions. `do.call()` will consecutively apply `cbind()` to each member of the list generated by `lapply()` and return them all together. To get a reminder on how these vectorized operations work, take a look at Chapter 1, *Introduction to R*:

```
numerical_summary <- do.call(cbind, lapply(data_numerical, summary))
#> Warning in (function (..., deparse.level = 1) : number of rows of result
is
#> not a multiple of vector length (arg 1)

numerical_summary
#>         NVotes Leave Residents Households MeanAge AdultMeanAge Age_0to4
#> Min.      1039   287      1932        779   27.80        29.20    2.200
#> 1st Qu.   4252  1698      8288       3466   35.60        44.10    5.400
#> Median    5746  2874     11876       4938   38.70        47.40    6.300
#> Mean      5703  2971     11646       4767   38.45        46.85    6.481
#> 3rd Qu.   7020  3936     14144       5832   41.40        49.90  7.50058
#> Max.     15148  8316     34098      15726   51.60        58.10   12.300
#> NA's      1039   267      1932        779   27.80        29.20    2.200
```

We got our results, but not so fast! We got a warning, and it looks suspicious. What does this `number of rows of result is not a multiple of vector length` message mean? Aha! If we take a more detailed look at the list we previously got from our `lapply()` function, we can see that in the case of `Leave` (and `Proportion`) we get an extra column for `NA`s that we don't get for any other column. That means that when we try to use `cbind()` on these columns, the extra `NA`s column will create an extra space that needs to be filled. This is a problem we looked at in `Chapter 1`, *Introduction to R*.

As we saw, then, R deals with it by repeating the vectors in order until all spaces are filled. In our case this means that the first element, the one corresponding to the minimum value, will be repeated for the `NA`s space for each column that doesn't have an `NA`s space. You can verify this by comparing the numbers of the `Min` and `NA`s columns for variables other than `Leave` or `Proportion` (for these two, the values should actually be different).

To fix it we can just remove the extra `NA` value's row from the resulting data frame, but this would not deal with the warning's source, only the symptom. To deal with the source, we need to have the same number of columns for each variable before we apply `cbind()`. Since we already know that we have 267 missing values for the `Leave` variable, which then affects the `Proportion` variable, we can easily fix this by just ignoring that information. To do so, we simply use the *complete cases*, meaning that we keep observations that don't have any `NA` values in any of their variables; or, put another way, we drop every observation that contains at least one `NA`. Once we do that, we get our results back and we don't get any warnings:

```
data <- data[complete.cases(data), ]
data_numerical <- data[, numerical_variables]
numerical_summary <- do.call(cbind, lapply(data_numerical, summary))
numerical_summary
#>          NVotes Leave Residents Households MeanAge AdultMeanAge Age_0to4
#> Min.       1039   287      1932        779   28.40        30.50    2.200
#> 1st Qu.    4242  1698      8405       3486   35.70        44.10    5.400
#> Median     5739  2874     11911       4935   38.60        47.40    6.300
#> Mean       5725  2971     11739       4793   38.43        46.83    6.479
#> 3rd Qu.    7030  3936     14200       5850   41.40        49.90    7.500
#> Max.      15148  8316     34098      15726   47.30        56.10   12.300
(Truncated output)
```

If we want to get the summary values as columns and the variables as rows, we can use the `rbind()` function instead of `cbind()`. The structure we actually end up using will depend on what we want to do with it. However, we can easily change between them later if we need to:

```
do.call(rbind, lapply(data_numerical, summary))
#>                   Min.   1st Qu.    Median      Mean    3rd Qu.
Max.
#> NVotes       1039.0000  4241.5000  5.739e+03  5.725e+03  7.030e+03
1.515e+04
#> Leave         287.0000  1697.5000  2.874e+03  2.971e+03  3.936e+03
8.316e+03
#> Residents    1932.0000  8405.0000  1.191e+04  1.174e+04  1.420e+04
3.410e+04
#> Households    779.0000  3486.0000  4.935e+03  4.793e+03  5.850e+03
1.573e+04
#> MeanAge        28.4000    35.7000  3.860e+01  3.843e+01  4.140e+01
4.730e+01
```

Now that we have this `numerical_summary` object, we can use it to perform computations, such as finding the range between the wards with the least and most proportions of votes in favor of leaving (0.6681), which may be useful to interpret the big difference among the *types* of wards we may find in the UK. If we want to know which wards are being used to get to this result, we can search for the wards with the least and most proportion of votes:

```
numerical_summary["Max.", "Proportion"] - numerical_summary["Min.",
"Proportion"]
desired_variables <- c(
    "ID",
    "NoQuals",
    "Proportion",
    "AdultMeanAge",
    "L4Quals_plus",
    "RegionName"
)

>data[which.max(data$Proportion), desired_variables]
#>        ID NoQuals Proportion AdultMeanAge L4Quals_plus RegionName
#> 754   754    35.8     0.7897         48.7         13.7          L

data[which.min(data$Proportion), desired_variables]
#>        ID NoQuals Proportion AdultMeanAge L4Quals_plus RegionName
#> 732 732     2.8     0.1216         31.2         44.3         EE
```

As you can see, this analysis already shows some interesting results. The UK ward that voted to leave the EU the most is characterized by older people (MeanAge) with low education levels (NoQuals, L4Quals_plus). On the other hand, the UK ward that voted to remain in the EU the most is characterized by younger people with much higher education levels. Of course, this is not the full picture, but it's a hint about the direction in which we need to look to further understand what's going on. For now, we have found that education and age seem to be relevant variables for the analysis.

Getting intuition with graphs and correlations

Now that we have some clean data to work with, we will create lots of plots to build intuition about the data. In this chapter, we will work with plots that are easy to create and are used for exploratory purposes. In Chapter 4, *Simulating Sales Data and Working with Databases*, we will look into publication ready plots that are a little more verbose to create.

Visualizing variable distributions

Our first plot is a simple one and shows the proportion of votes by each RegionName. As you can see in the plot shown below, the London, North West, and West Midlands regions account for around 55 percent of the observations in the data.

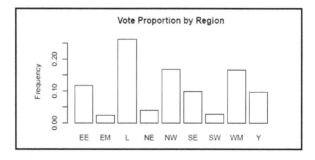

Vote Proportion by Region

To create the plot, we need to create a table for the frequencies of each region in RegionName with the table() function, then we feed that to the prop.table() function, which computes the corresponding proportions, which in turn are used as heights for each bar.

We use the `barplot()` function to produce the plot, and we can specify some options, such as the title (`main`), the *y* axis label (`ylab`), and the color for the bars (`col`). As always, you can find out more about in the function's parameters with ? `barplot`:

```
table(data$RegionName)
#> EE EM   L NE  NW SE SW  WM  Y
#> 94 20 210 32 134 79 23 133 78

prop.table(table(data$RegionName))
#>      EE      EM       L      NE      NW      SE      SW      WM       Y
#> 0.11706 0.02491 0.26152 0.03985 0.16687 0.09838 0.02864 0.16563 0.09714

barplot(
    height = prop.table(table(data$RegionName)),
    main = "Vote Proportion by Region",
    ylab = "Frequency",
    col = "white"
)
```

Our next plot, shown below, is a little more eye-catching. Each point represents a ward observation, and it shows the `Proportion` of `Leave` votes for each ward, arranged in vertical lines corresponding to `RegionName` and colored by the proportion of white population for each ward. As you can see, we have another interesting finding; it seems that the more diversified a ward's population is (seen in the darker points), the more likely it is for the ward to vote in favor of remaining in the EU (a lower `Proportion` value).

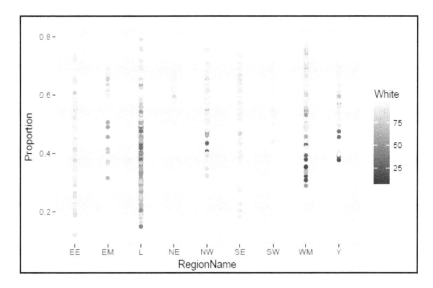

Proportion by RegionName and White Population Percentage

To create the plot, we need to load the `ggplot2` and `viridis` packages; the first one will be used to create the actual plot, while the second one will be used to color the points with a scientifically interesting color palette called **Viridis** (it comes from color perception research done by Nathaniel Smith and Stéfan van der Walt, `http://bids.github.io/colormap/`). The details of the `ggplot2` syntax will be explained in Chapter 4, *Simulating Sales Data and Working with Databases*, but for now, all you need to know is that the function receives as a first parameter the data frame with the data that will be used for the plot, and as a second parameter an aesthetics object (`aes`), created with the `aes()` function, which in turn can receive parameters for the variable that should be used in the *x* axis, *y* axis, and color. After that, we add a *points layer* with the `geom_points()` function, and the Viridis color palette with the `scale_color_viridis()` function. Notice how we are adding plot objects while we work with `ggplot2`. This is a very convenient feature that provides a lot of power and flexibility. Finally, we show the plot with the `print()` function (in R, some functions used for plotting immediately show the plot (for example, `barplot`), while others return a plot object (for example, `ggplot2`) and need to be printed explicitly):

```
library(ggplot2)
library(viridis)

plot <- ggplot(data, aes(x = RegionName, y = Proportion, color = White))
plot <- plot + geom_point() + scale_color_viridis()
print(plot)
```

The next set of plots, shown below, display histograms for the `NoQuals`, `L4Quals_plus`, and `AdultMeanAge` variables. As you can see, the `NoQuals` variable appears to be normally distributed, but the `L4Quals_plus` and `AdultMeanAge` variables seemed to be skewed towards the left and right, correspondingly. These tell us that most people in the sample don't have high education levels and are past 45 years of age.

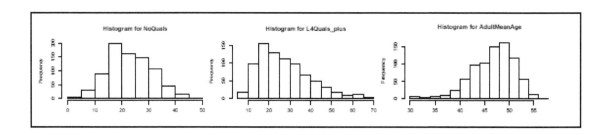

Histogram for NoQuals, L4Quals_plus, and AdultMeanAge

Creating these plots is simple enough; you just need to pass the variable that will be used for the histogram into the `hist()` function, and optionally specify a title and *x* axis label for the plots (which we leave empty, as the information is already in the plot's title).

For the book, we arranged plots in such a way that their spacing and understanding is efficient, but when you create the plots using the code shown, you'll see them one by one. There are ways to group various plots together, but we'll look at them in `Chapter 4`, *Simulating Sales Data and Working with Databases*).

Let's have a look at the following code:

```
hist(data$NoQuals, main = "Histogram for NoQuals", xlab = "")
hist(data$L4Quals_plus, main = "Histogram for L4Quals_plus", xlab = "")
hist(data$AdultMeanAge, main = "Histogram for AdultMeanAge", xlab ="")
```

Now that we understand a bit more about the distribution of the `NoQuals`, `L4Quals_plus`, and `AdultMeanAge` variables, we will see their joint-distribution in the scatter plots shown below. We can see how these scatter plots resemble the histograms by comparing the *x* axis and *y* axis in the scatter plots to the corresponding *x* axis in the histograms, and comparing the frequency (height) in the histograms with the point density in the scatter plots.

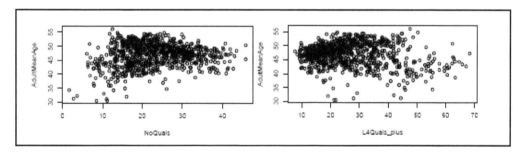

Scatter plots for NoQuals, L4Quals_plus vs AdultMeanAge

We find a slight relation that shows that the older the people, the lower the levels of education they have. This can be interpreted in a number of ways, but we'll leave that as an exercise, to keep focus on the programming, not the statistics. Creating these scatter plots is also very simple. Just send the `x` and `y` variables to the `plot()` function, and optionally specify labels for the axes.

```
plot(x = data$NoQuals, y = data$AdultMeanAge, ylab = "AdultMeanAge", xlab =
"NoQuals")
plot(x = data$L4Quals_plus, y = data$AdultMeanAge, ylab = "AdultMeanAge",
xlab = "L4Quals_plus")
```

Using matrix scatter plots for a quick overview

What happens if we want to visualize a lot of scatter plots in a single graph to quickly get a sense for the data? In that case, we need *matrix scatter plots*. We have various package options to create such matrix scatter plots (such as the `car` package). However, to keep things simple, we will use a built-in function instead of an external package.

By looking at the graph shown below, we can get a big-picture view of the interactions among variables. The purpose of this type of visualization is not to provide details, but to provide a general overview. To read this plot we need to look at any interesting scatter plot in the matrix, and move both horizontally and vertically until we find the name associated with its axis.

For example, if you look at the plot immediately to the right of `NoQuals` and simultaneously immediately on top of `L4Quals_plus`, what you're looking at is at the relation between those two variables (`NoQuals` in the *y* axis, `L4Quals_plus` in the *x* axis), and we find that it's an inverse relation; the higher the percentage of people in a ward with high levels of education, the lower the percentage of people with low levels of education. Another obvious relation is that the higher the education level (`L4Quals_plus`), the higher the occupation (`HigherOccup`).

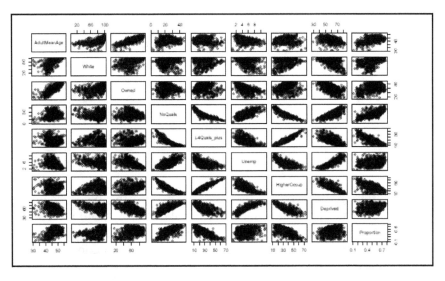

Matrix scatter plot

Due to space restrictions, we were not able to show all variable relations, since the scatter plots would be too small to make sense of. However, we encourage the reader to add more variables to the matrix. There are some non-obvious relations. Finding them is left as an exercise for the reader:

```
desired_variables <- c(
    "AdultMeanAge",
    "White",
    "Owned",
    "NoQuals",
    "L4Quals_plus",
    "Unemp",
    "HigherOccup",
    "Deprived",
    "Proportion"
)
pairs(data[, desired_variables])
```

Getting a better look with detailed scatter plots

Now that we know how to get a big-picture view of the scatter plots to get a general sense of the relations among variables, how can we get a more detailed look into each scatter plot? Well, I'm glad you asked! To achieve this, we'll do it in two steps. First, we are going to work on producing a single, detailed scatter plot that we're happy with. Second, we're going to develop a simple algorithm that will traverse all variable combinations and create the corresponding plot for each of them:

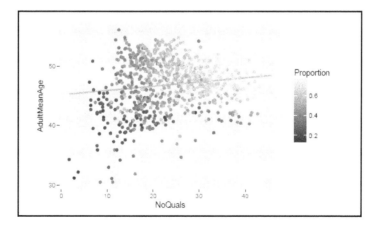

Scatter plot for NoQuals vs AdultMeanAge vs Proportion with Regression Line

The graph shown above shows our prototype scatter plot. It has a combination of variables in the x and y axes, `NoQuals` and `AdultMeanAge` in our case, assigns a color according to the corresponding `Proportion`, and places a line corresponding to a linear regression on top to get a general sense of the relation among the variables in the axes. Compare this plot to the left scatter plot of previous pair of scatter plots. They are the same plot, but this one is more detailed and conveys more information. This plot seems good enough for now.

```
plot <- ggplot(data, aes(x = NoQuals, y = AdultMeanAge, color =
Proportion))
plot <- plot + stat_smooth(method = "lm", col = "darkgrey", se = FALSE)
plot <- plot + scale_color_viridis()
plot <- plot + geom_point()
print(plot)
```

Now we need to develop the algorithm that will take all variable combinations and create the corresponding plots. We present the full algorithm and explain part by part. As you can see, we start defining the `create_graphs_iteratively` function, which receives two parameters: the `data` and the `plot_function`. The algorithm will get the variable names for the data and store them in the `vars` variables. It will then remove `Proportion` from such variables, because they will be used to create the combinations for the axis, and `Proportion` will never be used in the axis; it will be used exclusively for the colors.

Now, if we imagine all the variable combinations in a matrix like the one for the matrix scatter plot shown previously, then we need to traverse the upper triangle or the lower triangle to get all possible combinations (in fact, the upper and lower triangles from matrix of scatter plots are symmetrical because they convey the same information). To traverse these triangles, we can use a *known pattern,* which uses two for-loops, each for one axis, and where the inner loop need only start at the position of the outer loop (this is what forms a triangle). The −1 and +1 are there to make sure we start and finish in appropriate places in each loop without getting an error for array boundaries.

Inside the inner loop is where we will create the name for the plot as a combination of the variable names and concatenate them using the `paste()` function, as well as create the plot with the `plot_function` we will send as a parameter (more on this ahead). The `png()` and `dev.off()` functions are there to save the plots to the computer's hard drive. Think of the `png()` function as the place where R starts looking for a graph, and `dev.off()` as the place where it stops the saving process. Feel free to look into their documentation or read more about *devices* in R.

```
create_plots_iteratively <- function(data, plot_function) {
    vars <- colnames(data)
    vars <- vars(!which(vars == "Proportion"))
    for (i in 1:(length(vars) - 1)) {
```

```
        for (j in (i + 1):length(vars)) {
            save_to <- paste(vars[i], "_", vars[j], ".png", sep = "")
            plot_function(data, vars[i], vars[j], save_to)
        }
    }
}
```

We're almost done; we just need to wrap the code we used to turn our plot prototype into a function and we will be all set. As you can see, we extracted the x, y, and `color` parameters for the `aes()` function as variables that are sent as parameters to the function (this is called **parametrizing arguments**), and we switched the `aes()` function with the `aes_string()` function, which is able to receive variables with strings for the parameters. We also added the option to send the `var_color` as FALSE to avoid using a color-version of the plot. Everything else is kept the same:

```
prototype_scatter_plot <- function(data, var_x, var_y, var_color =
"Proportion", save_to = "") {
    if (is.na(as.logical(var_color))) {
        plot <- ggplot(data, aes_string(x = var_x, y = var_y, color =
var_color))
    } else {
        plot <- ggplot(data, aes_string(x = var_x, y = var_y))
    }
    plot <- plot + stat_smooth(method = "lm", col = "darkgrey", se = FALSE)
    plot <- plot + scale_color_viridis()
    plot <- plot + geom_point()
    if (not_empty(save_to)) png(save_to)
    print(plot)
    if (not_empty(save_to)) dev.off()
}
```

Since we will be checking in various places whether the `save_to` string is empty, we name the check and wrap it in the `not_empty()` function. Now it's a bit easier to read our code.

```
not_empty <- function(file) {
    return(file != "")
}
```

With this `prototype_scatter_plot()` function, we can re-create the right scatter plots shown previously, as well as any other variable combination, quite easily. This seems pretty powerful, doesn't it?

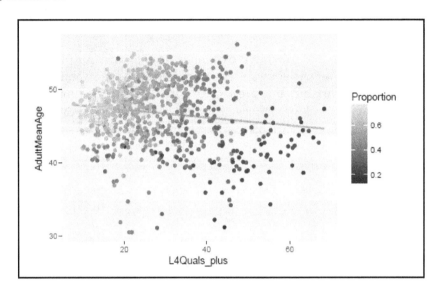

Scatter plot for L4Quals_plus vs AdultMeanAge vs Proportion with Regression Line

Let's have a look at the following code:

```
prototype_scatter_plot(data, "L4Quals_plus", "AdultMeanAge")
```

Now that we have done the hard work, we can create all possible combinations quite easily. We just need to call the `create_plots_iteratively()` function with our data and the `prototype_scatter_plot()` function. Using functions as parameters for other functions is known as the **strategy pattern**. The name comes from the fact that we can easily change our strategy for plotting for any other one we want that receives the same parameters (`data`, `var_x`, and `var_y`) to create plots, without having to change our algorithm to traverse the variable combinations. This kind of flexibility is very powerful:

```
create_plots_iteratively(data, prototype_scatter_plot)
```

This will create all the plots for us and save them to our hard drive. Pretty cool, huh? Now we can look at each of them independently and do whatever we need with them, as we already have them as PNG files.

Understanding interactions with correlations

The correlation is a measure of the linear relation among two variables. Its value ranges from −1, representing a perfect inverse relation, to 1, representing a perfect direct relation. Just as we created a matrix of scatter plots, we will now create a matrix of correlations, and resulting graph is shown below. Large circles mean high absolute correlation. Blue circles mean positive correlation, while red circles mean negative correlation.

To create this plot we will use the `corrplot()` function from the `corrplot` package, and pass it the correlations data computed by the `cor()` function in R, and optionally some parameters for the text labels (`tl`), such as color (`color`) and size (`cex`).

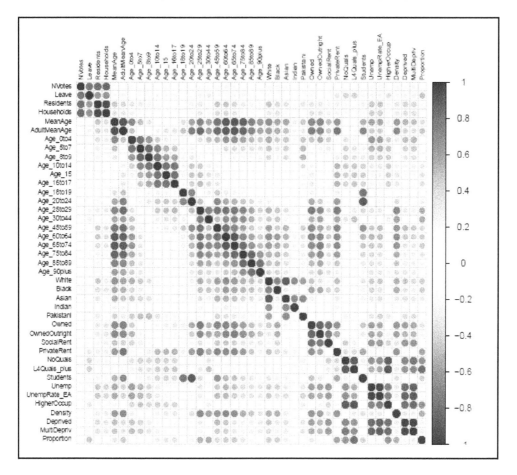

Variable Correlations

Now, let's look at the following code:

```
library(corrplot)
corrplot(corr = cor(data_numerical), tl.col = "black", tl.cex = 0.6)
```

If we look at the relation among the `Proportion` variable and the other variables, variables in large blue circles are positively correlated with it, meaning that the more that variable increases, the more likely it is for the `Proportion` variable to also increase. For examples of this type, look at the relations among `AdultMeanAge` and `NoQuals` with `Proportion`. If we find large red circles among `Proportion` and other variables, it means that the more that variable increases, the more `Proportion` is likely to decrease. For examples of this type, look at the relations among `Age_25to29`, `Age_30to44`, and `L4Quals_plus` with `Proportion`:

Creating a new dataset with what we've learned

What we have learned so far in this chapter is that age, education, and ethnicity are important factors in understanding the way people voted in the Brexit Referendum. Younger people with higher education levels are related with votes in favor of remaining in the EU. Older white people are related with votes in favor of leaving the EU. We can now use this knowledge to make a more succinct data set that incorporates this knowledge. First we add relevant variables, and then we remove non-relevant variables.

Our new relevant variables are two groups of age (adults below and above 45), two groups of ethnicity (whites and non-whites), and two groups of education (high and low education levels):

```
data$Age_18to44 <- (
    data$Age_18to19 +
    data$Age_20to24 +
    data$Age_25to29 +
    data$Age_30to44
)
data$Age_45plus <- (
    data$Age_45to59 +
    data$Age_60to64 +
    data$Age_65to74 +
    data$Age_75to84 +
    data$Age_85to89 +
    data$Age_90plus
)
```

```
data$NonWhite <- (
    data$Black +
    data$Asian +
    data$Indian +
    data$Pakistani
)
data$HighEducationLevel <- data$L4Quals_plus
data$LowEducationLevel  <- data$NoQuals
```

Now we remove the old variables that were used to create our newly added variables. To do so without having to manually specify a full list by leveraging the fact that all of them contain the word "Age", we create the age_variables logical vector, which contains a TRUE value for those variables that contain the word "Age" inside (FALSE otherwise), and make sure we keep our newly created Age_18to44 and Age_45plus variables. We remove the other ethnicity and education levels manually:

```
column_names <- colnames(data)
new_variables <- !logical(length(column_names))
new_variables <- setNames(new_variables, column_names)
age_variables <- sapply(column_names, function(x) grepl("Age", x))
new_variables[age_variables]        <- FALSE
new_variables[["AdultMeanAge"]]   <- TRUE
new_variables[["Age_18to44"]]     <- TRUE
new_variables[["Age_45plus"]]     <- TRUE
new_variables[["Black"]]          <- FALSE
new_variables[["Asian"]]          <- FALSE
new_variables[["Indian"]]         <- FALSE
new_variables[["Pakistani"]]      <- FALSE
new_variables[["NoQuals"]]        <- FALSE
new_variables[["L4Quals_plus"]]   <- FALSE
new_variables[["OwnedOutright"]]  <- FALSE
new_variables[["MultiDeprived"]]  <- FALSE
```

We save our created data_adjusted object by selecting the new columns, create our new numerical variables for the new data structure, and save it as a CSV file:

```
data_adjusted <- data[, new_variables]
numerical_variables_adjusted <- sapply(data_adjusted, is.numeric)
write.csv(data_adjusted, file = "data_brexit_referendum_adjusted.csv")
```

Building new variables with principal components

Principal Component Analysis (PCA) is a dimensionality reduction technique that is widely used in data analysis when there are many numerical variables, some of which may be correlated, and we would like to reduce the number of dimensions required to understand the data.

It can be useful to help us understand the data, since thinking in more than three dimensions can be problematic, and to accelerate algorithms that are computationally intensive, especially with large numbers of variables. With PCA, we can extract most of the information into only one or two variables constructed in a very specific way, such that they capture the most variance while having the added benefit of being uncorrelated among them by construction.

The first principal component is a linear combination of the original variables which captures the maximum variance (information) in the dataset. No other component can have higher variability than the first principal component. Then, second principal component is orthogonal to the first one and is computed in such a way that it captures the maximum variance left in the data. And so on. The fact that all variables are linear combinations that are orthogonal among themselves is the key for them being uncorrelated among each other. Enough statistics talk; let's get on with the programming!

When performing PCA in R, we have a variety of functions which can do the task. To mention some of them, we have `prcomp()` and `princomp()` from the `stats` package (built-in), `PCA()` from the `FactoMineR` package, `dudi.pca()` from the `ade4` package, and `acp()` from the `amap` package. In our case, we'll use the `prcomp()` function that is built into R.

To perform our PCA, we will use the adjusted data from the previous section. First, we remove numerical variables which are correlated with `Proportion`. Then we perform the PCA by sending the numerical data to the `prcomp()` function, as well as some normalization parameters. `center = TRUE` will subtract each variable's mean from itself, and `scale. = TRUE` will make each variable's variance unitary, effectively normalizing the data. Normalizing the data is very important when performing PCA, as it's a method sensitive to scales:

```
numerical_variables_adjusted[["NVotes"]] <- FALSE
numerical_variables_adjusted[["Leave"]]  <- FALSE
data_numerical_adjusted <- data_adjusted[, numerical_variables_adjusted]
pca <- prcomp(data_numerical_adjusted, center = TRUE, scale. = TRUE)
```

```
pca
#> Standard deviations (1, .., p=21):
#> [1] 2.93919 2.42551 1.25860 1.13300 1.00800 0.94112 0.71392 0.57613
#> [9] 0.54047 0.44767 0.37701 0.30166 0.21211 0.17316 0.13759 0.11474
#> [17] 0.10843 0.09797 0.08275 0.07258 0.02717
#>
#> Rotation (n x k) = (21 x 21):
#>                         PC1         PC2       PC3        PC4        PC5
#> ID              0.008492   -0.007276   0.14499   0.174484  -0.82840
#> Residents       0.205721    0.004321   0.54743   0.303663   0.06659
#> Households      0.181071    0.008752   0.49902   0.470793   0.13119
#> AdultMeanAge   -0.275210    0.192311   0.14601  -0.011834   0.12951
#> White          -0.239842    0.112711  -0.25766   0.471189  -0.02500
#> Owned          -0.289544    0.085502   0.26954  -0.179515  -0.11673
(Truncated output)
```

When we print the `pca` object, we can see the standard deviations for each variable, but more importantly, we can see the weights used for each variable to create each principal component. As we can see, when we look at the full output in our computer, among the most important weights (the largest absolute values) we have the age and ethnicity variables, as well as others, such as home ownership.

If you want to get the axis value for each observation in the new coordinate system composed of the principal components, you simply need to multiply each observation in your data (each row) with the corresponding weights from the rotation matrix from the `pca` object (`pca$rotation`). For example, to know where the first observation in the data should be placed in regards to the second principal component, you can use the following:

```
as.matrix(data_numerical_adjusted[1, ]) %*% pca$rotation[, 1]
```

In general, you can apply matrix operations to get coordinates for all the observations in your data in regards to all the principal components in your `pca` object by using the following line, which will perform a matrix multiplication. Note that you don't need to do this yourself since R will do it automatically for you when analyzing the results.

```
as.matrix(data_numerical_adjusted) %*% pca$rotation
```

When we look at the summary of `pca`, we can see the standard deviations for each principal component, as well as its proportion of the variance captured and its accumulation. This information is useful when deciding how many principal components we should keep for the rest of the analysis. In our case, we find that with just the first two principal components, we have captured approximately 70 percent of the information in the data, which for our case may be good enough.

The 70% number can be arrived at by adding the `Proportion of variance` value for the principal components we want to consider (in order and starting at `PC1`). In this case, if we add the `Proportion of variance` for `PC1` and `PC2`, we get $0.411 + 0.280 = 0.691$, which is almost 70 percent. Note that you can simply look at the `Cumulative proportion` to find this number without having to perform the sum yourself, as it accumulates the `Proportion of variance` incrementally, starting at `PC1`.

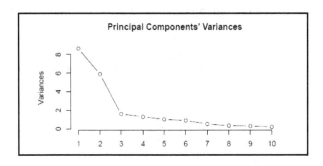

Principal Component's Variances

Take one moment to think about how powerful this technique is: with just two variables, we are able to capture 70 percent of the information contained in the original 40 variables:

```
summary(pca)
#> Importance of components:
#>                          PC1     PC2     PC3     PC4     PC5     PC6     PC7
#> Standard deviation       2.939   2.426   1.2586  1.1330  1.0080  0.9411  0.7139
#> Proportion of Variance   0.411   0.280   0.0754  0.0611  0.0484  0.0422  0.0243
#> Cumulative Proportion    0.411   0.692   0.7670  0.8281  0.8765  0.9186  0.9429
#>                          PC8     PC9     PC10    PC11    PC12    PC13
#> Standard deviation       0.5761  0.5405  0.44767 0.37701 0.30166 0.21211
#> Proportion of Variance   0.0158  0.0139  0.00954 0.00677 0.00433 0.00214
#> Cumulative Proportion    0.9587  0.9726  0.98217 0.98894 0.99327 0.99541
#>                          PC14    PC15    PC16    PC17    PC18    PC19
#> Standard deviation       0.17316 0.1376  0.11474 0.10843 0.09797 0.08275
#> Proportion of Variance   0.00143 0.0009  0.00063 0.00056 0.00046 0.00033
#> Cumulative Proportion    0.99684 0.9977  0.99837 0.99893 0.99939 0.99971
(Truncated output)
```

In the graph shown above, we can see the variances (in the form of squared standard deviations) from the `summary(pca)` results. We can see how each subsequent principal component captures a lower amount of the total variance:

```
plot(pca, type = "l", main = "Principal Components' Variances" )
```

Finally, following graph shows a scatter plot of the ward observations (points) over a plane created by the two principal components from our analysis; it is called a **biplot**. Since these two principal components are formed as linear combinations of the original variables, we need some guidance when interpreting them. To make it easy, the arrows point towards the direction of that variable's association to the principal component axis. The further the arrow is from the center, the stronger the effect on the principal components.

PCA Biplot

With this biplot, we can see that `Proportion` is strongly related to the wards that voted to leave the EU, which is obvious since that's by construction. However, we can also see some other interesting relations. For example, other than the effects we have found so far (age, education, and ethnicity), people owning their own homes is also slightly associated with a higher tendency towards voting to leave the EU. On the other side, a previously unknown relation is the fact that the more dense a ward's population is (think about highly populated cities), the more likely it is that they will vote to remain in the EU:

```
library(ggbiplot)
biplot <- ggbiplot(pca, groups = data$Vote)
biplot <- biplot + scale_color_discrete(name = "")
biplot <- biplot + theme(legend.position = "top", legend.direction =
"horizontal")
print(biplot)
```

Putting it all together into high-quality code

Now that we have the fundamentals about analyzing data with descriptive statistics, we're going to improve our code's structure and flexibility by breaking it up into functions. Even though this is common knowledge among efficient programmers, it's not a common practice among data analysts. Many data analysts would simply paste the code we have developed all together, as-is, into a single file, and run it every time they wanted to perform the analysis. We won't be adding new features to the analysis. All we'll do is reorder code into functions to encapsulate their inner-workings and communicate intention with function names (this substantially reduces the need for comments).

We'll focus on producing *high-quality* code that is easy to read, reuse, modify, and fix (in case of bugs). The way we actually do it is a matter of style, and different ways of arranging code are fit for different contexts. The method we'll work with here is one that has served me well for a variety of situations, but it may not be the best for yours. If it doesn't suit your needs, feel free to change it. Whichever style you prefer, making an investment in creating a habit of constantly producing high-quality code will make you a more efficient programmer in the long run, and a point will come where you will not want to program inefficiently any more.

Planning before programming

Often, people start programming before having a general idea of what they want to accomplish. If you're an experienced programmer, this may be a good way to get a feel for the problem, since you have already developed intuition, and you'll probably end up throwing away the first couple of attempts anyway. However, if you're a novice programmer, I recommend you make your objectives clear and explicit before writing any code (putting them into writing can help). It will help you make better decisions by asking yourself how a certain way of doing things will affect your objectives. So, before we set up anything, we need to understand and make our general objectives explicit:

1. Understand the big picture of the analysis quickly.
2. Reproduce our analysis automatically by executing a single file.
3. Save all the resulting objects, text, and images for the analysis.
4. Measure the amount of time it takes to perform the full analysis.
5. When working on iterative processes, know the completed percentage.
6. Be able to find and change each part of the analysis easily.

To fulfill these general objectives, we need to develop modular code with well-managed dependencies that are flexible (easy to change) and friendly to side-effects (saving objects, texts, and images). Even if your explicit objectives don't require it, you should make a habit of programming this way, even when just doing data analysis.

Understanding the fundamentals of high-quality code

Code that is modular, flexible, and whose dependencies are well-managed, is said to be **highly-cohesive** and **loosely-coupled**. These terms are mostly used in object-oriented environments (more about these in `Chapter 8`, *Object-Oriented System to Track Cryptocurrencies*), but apply generally to any system. **Highly-cohesive** means that things that are supposed to be together, are. **Loosely-coupled** means that things that are not supposed to be together, are not. The following image shows these characteristics, where each of the circles can be a function or an object in general. These are the basics of dependency management. Many books focused on these topics have been, and continue to be, published. For the interested reader, Steve McConnell's *Code Complete* (Microsoft Press, 2004) and Robert Martin's *Clean Code* (Prentice Hall, 2009) are excellent references. In this book, you'll see some of these techniques applied.

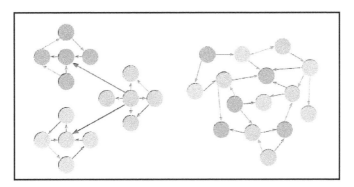

High cohesion and low coupling (left) vs Low cohesion and high coupling (right)

The most important principles for high-quality code are:

1. Make things small and focused on a single responsibility.
2. Make the concrete depend on the abstract (not vice versa).
3. Make things that are highly-cohesive and loosely-coupled.

By *things*, I mean functions, methods, classes, and objects in general. We'll touch more on what these are in Chapter 8, *Object-Oriented System to Track Cryptocurrencies*.

We start by creating two files: functions.R and main.R. The functions.R file contains high-level functions (mainly called from the main.R file) as well as low-level functions (used within other functions). By reading the main.R file, we should have a clear idea of what the analysis does (this is the purpose of the high-level functions), and executing it should re-create our analysis for any data that fits our base assumptions (for this example, these are mainly data structures).

We should always keep related code at the same level of abstraction. This means that we don't want to program things at the big-picture level and implement it with mixed details, and separating our code into the main.R and functions.R is a first step in this direction. Furthermore, none of the code in the main.R file should depend on details of the implementation. This makes it modular in the sense that if we want to change the way something is implemented, we can do so without having to change the high-level code. However, the way we implement things depends on what we want the analysis to ultimately do, which means that concrete implementations should depend on the abstract implementations that in turn depend on our analysis' purpose (stated as code in the main.R file).

When we bring knowledge from one set of code to another, we're generating a dependency, because the code that knows about other code depends on it to function properly. We want to avoid these dependencies as much as possible, and most importantly, we want to manage their direction. As stated before, the abstract should not depend on the concrete, or put another way, the concrete should depend on the abstract. Since the analysis (main.R) is on the abstract side, it should not depend on the implementation details of the concrete functions. But, how can our analysis be performed without knowledge of the functions that implement it? Well, it can't. That's why we need an intermediary, the abstract functions. These functions are there to provide stable knowledge to main.R and guarantee that the analysis its looking for will be performed, and they remove the dependency of main.R on the implementation details by managing that knowledge themselves. This may seem a convoluted way of working and a tricky concept to grasp, but when you do, you'll find out that it's very simple, and you'll be able to create code that is pluggable, which is a big efficiency boost. You may want to take a look at the books referenced previously to get a deeper sense of these concepts.

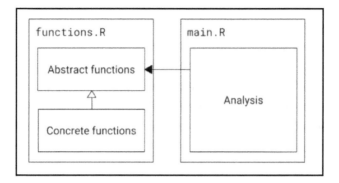

General code structure

The previous graph shows that our analysis depends on the abstract functions (interfaces), as well as the concrete code that implements those interfaces. These abstract functions let us invert the dependency between the concrete functions and the analysis. We'll go deeper into these concepts in Chapter 8, *Object-Oriented System to Track Cryptocurrencies*.

Programming by visualizing the big picture

Now, we will work with a top-down approach, meaning that we'll start with abstract code first and gradually move into the implementation details. Generally I find this approach to be more efficient when you have a clear idea of what you want to do. In our case, we'll start by working with the main.R file.

The first thing to note is that we will use the proc.time() function twice, once at the beginning and once at the end, and we will use the difference among these two values to measure how much time it took for the whole code to execute.

The second thing to note is that the empty_directories() function makes sure each of the specified directories exist, and deletes any files contained in them. We use it to clean up our directories at the beginning of each execution, to make sure we have the latest files, and only the files created in the last run. The actual code is shown below, and it simply iterates through each of the directories passed, removes any files inside recursively with the unlink() function, and makes sure the directory exists with the dir.create() function. It avoids showing any warnings due to the directory already existing, which is not a problem in our case, by using the showWarnings = FALSE parameter.

```
empty_directories <- function(directories) {
    for (directory in directories) {
        unlink(directory, recursive = TRUE)
```

```
            dir.create(directory, showWarnings = FALSE)
        }
    }
```

From Chapter 1, *Introduction to R,* we use of the `print_section()` and `empty_directories()` functions to print headers and delete directory contents (to re-create the results every time we run the function with empty directories), respectively, and we'll use the mechanism shown with `proc.time()` to measure execution time.

Now that the previous two points are out of the way, we proceed to show the full contents of the `main.R` file.

```
start_time <- proc.time()

source("./functions.R")

empty_directories(c(
    "./results/original/",
    "./results/adjusted/",
    "./results/original/scatter_plots/"
))

data <- prepare_data("./data_brexit_referendum.csv", complete_cases = TRUE)

data_adjusted          <- adjust_data(data)
numerical_variables    <- get_numerical_variable_names(data)
numerical_variables_adj <- get_numerical_variable_names(data_adjusted)

print("Working on summaries...")

full_summary(data, save_to = "./results/original/summary_text.txt")
numerical_summary(
    data,
    numerical_variables = numerical_variables,
    save_to = "./results/original/summary_numerical.csv"
)

print("Working on histograms...")

plot_percentage(
    data,
    variable = "RegionName",
    save_to = "./results/original/vote_percentage_by_region.png"
)

print("Working on matrix scatter plots...")
```

```
matrix_scatter_plots(
    data_adjusted,
    numerical_variables = numerical_variables_adj,
    save_to = "./results/adjusted/matrix_scatter_plots.png"
)

print("Working on scatter plots...")

plot_scatter_plot(
    data,
    var_x = "RegionName",
    var_y = "Proportion",
    var_color = "White",
    regression = TRUE,
    save_to = "./results/original/regionname_vs_proportion_vs_white.png"
)
all_scatter_plots(
    data,
    numerical_variables = numerical_variables,
    save_to = "./results/original/scatter_plots/"
)

print("Working on correlations...")

correlations_plot(
    data,
    numerical_variables = numerical_variables,
    save_to = "./results/original/correlations.png"
)

print("Working on principal components...")

principal_components(
    data_adjusted,
    numerical_variables = numerical_variables_adj,
    save_to = "./results/adjusted/principal_components"
)

end_time <- proc.time()
time_taken <- end_time - start_time
print(paste("Time taken:", taken[1]))

print("Done.")
```

As you can see, with just this file, you get the big picture of the analysis, and are able to reproduce your analysis by running a single file, save the results to disk (note the save_to arguments), and measure the amount of time it takes to perform the full analysis. From our general objectives list, objectives one through four are fulfilled by this code. Fulfilling objectives five and six will be accomplished by working on the functions.R file, which contains lots of small functions. Having this main.R file gives us a map of what needs to be programmed, and even though right now it would not work because the functions it uses do not yet exist, by the time we finish programming them, this file will not require any changes and will produce the desired results.

Due to space restrictions, we won't look at the implementation of all the functions in the main.R file, just the representative ones: prepare_data(), plot_scatter_plot(), and all_scatter_plots(). The other functions use similar techniques to encapsulate the corresponding code. You can always go to this book's code repository (https://github. com/PacktPublishing/R-Programming-By-Example) to see the rest of the implementation details. After reading this book, you should be able to figure out exactly what's going on in every file in that repository.

We start with prepare_data(). This function is abstract and uses four different concrete functions to do its job, read.csv(), clean_data(), transform_data(), and, if required, complete.cases(). The first function, namely read.csv(), receives the path to a CSV file to read data from and loads into a data frame object named data in this case. The fourth function you have seen before in Chapter 1, *Introduction to R*, so we won't explain it here. Functions two and three are created by us, and we'll explain them. Note that main.R doesn't know about how data is prepared, it only asks for data to be prepared, and delegates the job to the abstract function prepare_data().

```
prepare_data <- function(path, complete_cases = TRUE) {
    data <- read.csv(path)
    data <- clean_data(data)
    data <- transform_data(data)
    if (complete_cases) {
        data <- data[complete.cases(data), ]
    }
    return(data)
}
```

The `clean_data()` function simply encapsulates the re-coding of -1 for `NA` for now. If our cleaning procedure suddenly got more complex (for example, new data sources requiring more cleaning or realizing we missed something and we need to add it to the cleaning procedure), we would add those changes to this function and we would not have to modify anything else in the rest of our code. These are some of the advantages of encapsulating code into functions that communicate intention and isolate what needs to be done into small steps:

```
clean_data <- function(data) {
    data[data$Leave == -1, "Leave"] <- NA
    return(data)
}
```

To transform our data by adding the extra `Proportion` and `Vote` variables, and re-label the region names, we use the following function:

```
transform_data <- function(data) {
    data$Proportion <- data$Leave / data$NVotes
    data$Vote <- ifelse(data$Proportion > 0.5, "Leave", "Remain")
    data$RegionName <- as.character(data$RegionName)
    data[data$RegionName == "London", "RegionName"]                <-
"L"
    data[data$RegionName == "North West", "RegionName"]            <-
"NW"
    data[data$RegionName == "North East", "RegionName"]            <-
"NE"
    data[data$RegionName == "South West", "RegionName"]            <-
"SW"
    data[data$RegionName == "South East", "RegionName"]            <-
"SE"
    data[data$RegionName == "East Midlands", "RegionName"]         <-
"EM"
    data[data$RegionName == "West Midlands", "RegionName"]         <-
"WM"
    data[data$RegionName == "East of England", "RegionName"]       <-
"EE"
    data[data$RegionName == "Yorkshire and The Humber", "RegionName"] <-
"Y"
    return(data)
}
```

All of these lines of code you have seen before. All we are doing is encapsulating them into functions that communicate intention and allow us to find where certain procedures are taking place so that we can find them and change them easily if we need to do so later on.

Now we look into `plot_scatter_plot()`. This function is between being an abstract and a concrete function. We will use it directly in our `main.R` file, but we will also use it within other functions in the `functions.R` file. We know that most of the time we'll use `Proportion` as the color variable, so we add that as a default value, but we allow for the user to remove the color completely by checking if the argument was sent as `FALSE`, and since we will use this same function to create graphs that resemble all the scatter plots we have created up to this point, we will make the regression line optional.

Note that in the case of the former graphs, the *x* axis is a continuous variable, but in the case of the latter graph, it's a categorical (*factor*) variable. This kind of flexibility is very powerful and is available to us due to `ggplot2`'s capability to adapt to these changes. Formally, this is called **polymorphism**, and it's something we'll explain in `Chapter 8`, *Object-Oriented System to Track Cryptocurrencies*.

Finally, instead of assuming the user will always want to save the resulting graph to disk, we make the `save_to` argument optional by providing an empty string for it. When appropriate, we check to see if this string is empty with `not_empty()`, and if it's not empty, we set up the PNG saving mechanism.

```
plot_scatter_plot <- function(data,
                              var_x,
                              var_y,
                              var_color = "Proportion",
                              regression = FALSE,
                              save_to = "") {
    if (var_color) {
        plot <- ggplot(data, aes_string(x = var_x, y = var_y, color =
var_color))
    } else {
        plot <- ggplot(data, aes_string(x = var_x, y = var_y))
    }
    plot <- plot + scale_color_viridis()
    plot <- plot + geom_point()
    if (regression) {
        plot <- plot + stat_smooth(method = "lm", col = "grey", se = FALSE)
    }
    if (not_empty(save_to)) png(save_to)
    print(plot)
    if (not_empty(save_to)) dev.off()
}
```

Now we look into `all_scatter_plots()`. This function is an abstract function that hides from the user's knowledge the name of the function that will create graphs iteratively, conveniently named `create_graphs_iteratively()`, and the graphing function, the `plot_scatter_plot()` function we saw before. In case we want to improve the iterative mechanism or the graphing function, we can do so without requiring changes from people that use our code, because that knowledge is encapsulated here.

Encapsulate what changes frequently or is expected to change.

The `create_graphs_iteratively()` function is the same we have seen before, except for the progress bar code. The `progress` package provides the `progress_bar$new()` function that creates a progress bar in the terminal while an iterative process is being executed so that we see what percentage of the process has been completed and know how much time is remaining (see `Appendix`, *Required Packages* for more information).

Note the change in the `save_to` argument from the functions `plot_scatter_plot()` and `all_scatter_plots()`. In the former, it's a filename; in the latter, a directory name. The difference is small, but important. The incautious reader might not notice it and it may be a cause for confusion. The `plot_scatter_plot()` function produces a single plot, and thus receives a file name. However, the `all_scatter_plots()` will produce, by making use of `plot_scatter_plot()`, a lot of graphs, so it must know where all of them need to be saved, create the final image names dynamically, and send them one-by-one to `plot_scatter_plot()`. Finally, since we want the regression to be included in these graphs, we just send the `regression = TRUE` parameter:

```
all_scatter_plots <- function(data, numerical_variables, save_to = "") {
    create_graphs_iteratively(data, numerical_variables, plot_scatter_plot,
save_to)
}

create_graphs_iteratively <- function(data,
                                      numerical_variables,
                                      plot_function,
                                      save_to = "") {

    numerical_variables[["Proportion"]] <- FALSE
    variables <- names(numerical_variables[numerical_variables == TRUE])

    n_variables <- (length(variables) - 1)
    progress_bar <- progress_bar$new(
```

```
        format = "Progress [:bar] :percent ETA: :eta",
        total = n_variables
    )
for (i in 1:n_variables) {
    progress_bar$tick()
    for (j in (i + 1):length(variables)) {
        image_name <- paste(
            save_to,
            variables[i], "_",
            variables[j], ".png",
            sep = ""
        )
        plot_function(
            data,
            var_x = variables[i],
            var_y = variables[j],
            save_to = image_name,
            regression = TRUE
        )
    }
}
}
```

The other functions that we have not looked at in detail follow similar techniques as the ones we showed, and the full implementation is available at this book's code repository (`https://github.com/PacktPublishing/R-Programming-By-Example`).

Summary

This chapter showed how to perform a qualitative analysis that is useful as a first step when doing data analysis. We showed some descriptive statistics techniques and how to implement them programmatically. With these skills, we are able to perform simple yet powerful analyses and save the results for later use. Specifically, we showed how to do basic data cleaning, how to create graphs programmatically, how to create matrix scatter plots and matrix correlations, how to perform Principal Component Analysis, and how to combine these tools to understand the data at hand. Finally, we touched on the basics of high-quality code and showed how to transform your initial data analysis code into programs that are modular, flexible, and easy to work with.

In Chapter 3, *Predicting Votes with Linear Models*, we'll show how to extend the current analysis with qualitative tools. Specifically, we'll show how to use linear models to understand the quantitative effects of variables on the proportion of votes in favor of the UK leaving and remaining in the EU, how to make predictions for wards whose vote data we don't have, and how to measure the accuracy of those predictions with the data we do have. These are essential skills for any data analyst and, just as we did in this chapter, we'll see how to implement them programmatically.

3
Predicting Votes with Linear Models

This chapter shows how to work with statistical models using R. It shows how to check data assumptions, specify linear models, make predictions, and measure predictive accuracy. It also shows how to find good models programatically to avoid doing analysis by hand, which can potentially save a lot of time. By the end of this chapter, we will have worked with various quantitative tools that are used in many business and research areas nowadays. The packages used in this chapter are the same ones from the previous chapter.

Just like in the previous chapter, the focus here will be on automating the analysis programatically rather than on deeply understanding the statistical techniques used in the chapter. Furthermore, since we have seen in `Chapter 2`, *Understanding Votes With Descriptive Statistics*, how to work efficiently with functions, we will use that approach directly in this chapter, meaning that when possible we'll work directly with functions that will be used to automate our analysis. We will cover the following:

- Splitting data into training and testing sets
- Creating linear regression models used for prediction
- Checking model assumptions with various techniques
- Measuring predictive accuracy for numerical and categorical data
- Programatically finding the best possible model

Required packages

During this chapter we will make use of the following R packages, which were already used in the previous chapter, so you should be good to go.

Package	Reason
ggplot2	High-quality graphs
corrplot	Correlation plots
progress	Show progress for Iteration

Setting up the data

As it's usual with data analysis, the first step is to understand the data we will be working with. In this case, the data is the same as in Chapter 2, *Understanding Votes with Descriptive Statistics*, and we have already understood some of its main characteristics. Mainly, we've understood that age, education, and race have considerable effects over the propensity to vote in favor of the UK leaving or remaining in the EU.

The focus of this chapter will be on using linear models to predict the Proportion and Vote variables, which contain the percentage of votes in favor of leaving the EU and whether the ward had more votes for "Leave" or "Remain", respectively. Both variables have similar information, the difference being that one is a numerical continuous variable with values between 0 and 1 (Proportion) and the other is a categorical variable with two categories (Vote with Leave and Remain categories).

We'll keep observations that contain *complete cases* in the data object, and observations that have missing values for the Proportion and Vote variables in the data_incomplete object (we'll make predictions over these in the latter part of this chapter). The functions prepare_data(), adjust_data(), and get_numerical_variables() come from Chapter 2, *Understanding Votes with Descriptive Statistics*, so you may want to take a look if you're not clear about what they do. Basically, they load the data with the adjusted version that we created by compressing the data spread among various variables regarding age, education, and race:

```
data <- adjust_data(prepare_data("./data_brexit_referendum.csv"))

data_incomplete       <- data[!complete.cases(data), ]
data                  <- data[ complete.cases(data), ]
numerical_variables   <- get_numerical_variable_names(data)
```

Training and testing datasets

For us to be able to measure the predictive accuracy of our models, we need to use some observations to validate our results. This means that our data will be split into three different groups:

- Training data
- Testing data
- Predicting data

The predicting data is the data that we don't have complete cases for, specifically these are wards for which the `Vote` and `Proportion` variables have `NA` values. Our final objective is to provide predictions for these ward's `Proportion` and `Vote` variables using what we can learn from other wards for which we do have data for these variables, and it's something we'll do toward the end of the chapter.

The data that has complete cases will be split into two parts, training, and testing data. Training data is used to extract knowledge and learn the relationship among variables. Testing is treated as if it had `NA` values for `Proportion` and `Vote`, and we produce predictions for them. These predictions are then compared to the real values in the corresponding observations, and this helps us understand how good our predictions are in a way that is objective since those observations are never seen by the trained models.

We created the predicting data in the previous section, and we called it `data_incomplete`. To create the training and testing data, we use the `sample()` function. It will take as input a list of numbers from which it will pick a certain number of values (`size`). The list of numbers will go from 1 to the total number of observations available in the data with complete cases. We specify the number of observations that will be picked for the training data as around 70% of the total number of observations available, and use the `replace = FALSE` argument to specify that the picked observations may not be duplicated (by avoiding a sample with replacement).

The testing data is composed of the remaining 30% of the observations. Since `sample` is a Boolean vector that contains a `TRUE` or `FALSE` value for each observation to specify whether or not it should be included, respectively, we can negate the vector to pick the other part of the data by prepending a minus sign (–) to the binary vector, effectively making every `TRUE` value a `FALSE` value, and vice versa. To understand this, let's look at the following code:

```
set.seed(12345)

n          <- nrow(data)
sample     <- sample(1:n, size = round(0.7 * n), replace = FALSE)
```

```
data_train <- data[ sample, ]
data_test  <- data[-sample, ]
```

If we did this process various times, we would find that every time we get different samples for the training and testing sets, and this may confuse us about our results. This is because the `sample()` function is stochastic, meaning that it will use *pseudo random number generator* to make the selection for us (computers can not generate real randomness, they simulate numbers that appear to be random even though they are not, that's why it's called **pseudo random**). If we want our process to be reproducible, meaning that, every time we run it the exact same samples are selected, then we must specify an initial seed before applying this process to precondition the pseudo random number generator. To do so, we need to pass an integer to the `set.seed()` function, as we do at the beginning of the code snippet. The seed argument must stay fixed to reproduce the same samples, and with it in place, every time we generate a random sample, we will get the same sample so that our results are reproducible.

Predicting votes with linear models

Before we can make any predictions, we need to specify a model and train it with our training data (`data_train`) so that it learns how to provide us with the predictions we're looking for. This means that we will solve an optimization problem that outputs certain numbers that will be used as parameters for our model's predictions. R makes it very easy for us to accomplish such a task.

The standard way of specifying a linear regression model in R is using the `lm()` function with the model we want to build expressed as a formula and the data that should be used, and save it into an object (in this case `fit`) that we can use to explore the results in detail. For example, the simplest model we can build is one with a single regressor (independent variable) as follows:

```
fit <- lm(Proportion ~ Students, data_train)
```

In this simple model, we would let R know that we want to run a regression where we try to explain the `Proportion` variable using only the `Students` variable in the data. This model is too simple, what happens if we want to include a second variable? Well, we can add it using the plus (+) sign after our other regressors. For example (keep in mind that this would override the previous `fit` object with the new results, so if you want to keep both of them, make sure that you give the resulting objects different names):

```
fit <- lm(Proportion ~ Students + Age_18to44, data_train)
```

This may be a better way of explaining the `Proportion` variable since we are working with more information. However, keep in mind the collinearity problem; it's likely that the higher the students percentage is in a ward (`Students`), the higher the percentage of relatively young people (`Age_18to44`), meaning that we may not be adding independent information into the regression. Of course, in most situations, this is not a binary issue, it's an issue of degree and the analyst must be able to handle such situations. We'll touch more on this when checking the model's assumptions in the next section. For now let's get back to programming, shall we? What if we want to include all the variables in the data? Well, we have two options, include all variables manually or use R's shortcut for doing so:

```
# Manually
fit <- lm(Proportion ~ ID + RegionName + NVotes + Leave + Residents +
Households + White +
          Owned + OwnedOutright + SocialRent + PrivateRent + Students +
Unemp + UnempRate_EA +
          HigherOccup + Density + Deprived + MultiDepriv + Age_18to44 +
Age_45plus + NonWhite +
          HighEducationLevel + LowEducationLevel, data_train)

# R's shortcut
fit <- lm(Proportion ~ ., data_train)
```

These two models are exactly the same. However, there are a couple of subtle points we need to mention. First, when specifying the model manually, we had to leave the `Proportion` variable explicitly out of the regressors (variables after the ~ symbol) so that we don't get an error when running the regressions (it would not make sense for R to allow us to try to explain the `Proportion` variable by using the same `Proportion` variable and other things). Second, if we make any typos while writing the variable names, we will get errors since those names will not be present in the variable names (if by coincidence your typo actually refers to another existing variable in the data it may be a hard mistake to diagnose). Third, in both cases the list of regressors includes variables that should not be there, like `ID`, `RegionName`, `NVotes`, `Leave`, and `Vote`. In the case of `ID` it doesn't make sense for that variable to be included in the analysis as it doesn't have any information regarding the `Proportion`, it's just an identifier. In the case of `RegionName` it's a categorical variable so the regression would stop being a *Standard Multiple Linear Regression* and R would automatically make it work for us, but if we do not understand what we're doing, it may produce confusing results. In this case we want to work only with numerical variables so we can remove it easily from the manual case, but we can't do that in the shortcut case. Finally, in the case of `NVotes`, `Leave`, and `Vote`, those variables are expressing the same information in slightly the same way so they shouldn't be included since we would have a multicollinearity problem.

Let's say the final model we want to work with includes all the valid numerical variables:

```
fit <- lm(Proportion ~ Residents + Households + White + Owned +
OwnedOutright + SocialRent + PrivateRent + Students + Unemp + UnempRate_EA
+ HigherOccup + Density + Deprived + MultiDepriv + Age_18to44 + Age_45plus
+ NonWhite + HighEducationLevel + LowEducationLevel, data_train)
```

> If we want to use the shortcut method, we can make sure that the data does not contain the problematic variables (using the selection techniques we looked at in Chapter 1, *Introduction to R*) and then using the shortcut.

To take a look at the results in detail, we use the summary() function on the fit object:

```
summary(fit)
#>
#> Call:
#> lm(formula = Proportion ~ Residents + Households + White + Owned +
#>     OwnedOutright + SocialRent + PrivateRent + Students + Unemp +
#>     UnempRate_EA + HigherOccup + Density + Deprived + MultiDepriv +
#>     Age_18to44 + Age_45plus + NonWhite + HighEducationLevel +
#>     LowEducationLevel, data = data_train)
#>
#> Residuals:
#>      Min       1Q   Median       3Q      Max
#> -0.21606 -0.03189  0.00155  0.03393  0.26753
#>
#> Coefficients:
#>                   Estimate Std. Error t value Pr(>|t|)
#> (Intercept)       3.30e-02   3.38e-01    0.10  0.92222
#> Residents         7.17e-07   2.81e-06    0.26  0.79842
#> Households       -4.93e-06   6.75e-06   -0.73  0.46570
#> White             4.27e-03   7.23e-04    5.91  6.1e-09 ***
#> Owned            -2.24e-03   3.40e-03   -0.66  0.51071
#> OwnedOutright    -3.24e-03   1.08e-03   -2.99  0.00293 **
#> SocialRent       -4.08e-03   3.60e-03   -1.13  0.25847
#> PrivateRent      -3.17e-03   3.59e-03   -0.89  0.37629
#> Students         -8.34e-04   8.67e-04   -0.96  0.33673
#> Unemp             5.29e-02   1.06e-02    5.01  7.3e-07 ***
#> UnempRate_EA     -3.13e-02   6.74e-03   -4.65  4.1e-06 ***
#> HigherOccup       5.21e-03   1.24e-03    4.21  2.9e-05 ***
#> Density          -4.84e-04   1.18e-04   -4.11  4.6e-05 ***
#> Deprived          5.10e-03   1.52e-03    3.35  0.00087 ***
#> MultiDepriv      -6.26e-03   1.67e-03   -3.75  0.00019 ***
#> Age_18to44        3.46e-03   1.36e-03    2.55  0.01117 *
#> Age_45plus        4.78e-03   1.27e-03    3.75  0.00019 ***
#> NonWhite          2.59e-03   4.47e-04    5.80  1.1e-08 ***
```

```
#> HighEducationLevel -1.14e-02   1.14e-03 -9.93      < 2e-16 ***
#> LowEducationLevel   4.92e-03   1.28e-03  3.85      0.00013 ***
#> ---
#> Signif. codes:  0 '***' 0.001 '**' 0.01 '*' 0.05 '.' 0.1 ' ' 1
#> Residual standard error: 0.0523 on 542 degrees of freedom
#> Multiple R-squared: 0.868, Adjusted R-squared: 0.863
#> F-statistic: 187 on 19 and 542 DF, p-value: <2e-16
```

These results tell us which command was used to create our model, which is useful when you're creating various models and want to quickly know the model associated to the results you're looking at. It also shows some information about the distribution of the residuals. Next, it shows the regression's results for each variable used in the mode. We get the name of the variable ((Intercept) is the Standard Linear Regression intercept used in the model's specification), the coefficient estimate for the variable, the standard error, the *t statistic*, the *p-value*, and a visual representation of the *p-value* using asterisks for significance codes. At the end of the results, we see other results associated with the model, including the *R-squared* and the *F-statistic*. As mentioned earlier, we won't go into details about what each of these mean, and we will continue to focus on the programming techniques. If you're interested, you may look at Casella and Berger's, *Statistical Inference, 2002,* or Rice's, *Mathematical Statistics and Data Analysis, 1995.*

Now that we have a fitted model ready in the fit object, we can use it to make predictions. To do so, we use the predict() function with the fit object and the data we want to produce predictions for, data_test in our case. This returns a vector of predictions that we store in the predictions object. We will get one prediction for each observation in the data_test object:

```
predictions <- predict(fit, data_test)
```

These predictions can be measured for accuracy as we will do in a later section in this chapter. For now, we know how to generate predictions easily with R.

Checking model assumptions

Linear models, as with any kind of models, require that we check their assumptions to justify their application. The accuracy and interpretability of the results comes from adhering to a model's assumptions. Sometimes these will be rigorous assumptions in the sense that if they are not strictly met, then the model is not considered to be valid at all. Other times, we will be working with more flexible assumptions in which a degree of criteria from the analyst will come into play.

For those of you interested, a great article about models' assumptions is David Robinson's, *K-means clustering is not free lunch, 2015* (`http://varianceexplained.org/r/kmeans-free-lunch/`).

For linear models, the following are some of the core assumptions:

- **Linearity**: There is a linear relation among the variables
- **Normality**: Residuals are normally distributed
- **Homoscedasticity**: Residuals have constant variance
- **No collinearity**: Variables are not linear combinations of each other
- **Independence**: Residuals are independent or at least not correlated

We will show how to briefly check four of the them: linearity, normality, homoscedasticity, and no collinearity. We should mention that the independence assumption is probably the most difficult assumption to test, and you can generally handle it with common sense and understanding how the data was collected. We will not get into that here as it's more in the statistics side of things and we want to keep the book focused on programming techniques. For the statistically-interested reader, we recommend looking at Jeffrey M. Wooldridge's, *Introductory Econometrics, 2013* and Joshua D. Angrist and Jorn-Steffen Pischke's, *Mostly Harmless Econometrics, 2008*.

Checking linearity with scatter plots

A basic way of checking the linearity assumption is to make a scatter plot with the dependent variable in the y axis and an independent variable in the x axis. If the relation appears to be linear, the assumption is validated. In any interesting problem it's extremely hard to find a scatter plot that shows a very clear linear relation, and if it does happen we should be a little suspicious and careful with the data. To avoid reinventing the wheel, we will use the `plot_scatterlot()` function we created in Chapter 2, *Understanding Votes with Descriptive Statistics*:

```
plot_scatterplot(
    data = data,
    var_x = "Age_18to44",
    var_y = "Proportion",
    var_color = FALSE,
    regression = TRUE
)
plot_scatterplot(
    data = data,
    var_x = "Students",
```

```
    var_y = "Proportion",
    var_color = FALSE,
    regression = TRUE
)
```

As we can see, the scatter plot on the left shows a clear linear relation, as the percentage of people between 18 and 44 years of age (`Age_18to44`) increases, the proportion of people in favor of leaving the EU (`Proportion`) decreases. On the right hand, we see that the relation among the percentage of students in a ward (`Students`) and `Proportion` is clearly linear in the initial area (where `Students` is between 0 and 20), after that the relation too seems to be linear, but it is polluted by observations with very high percentage of students. However, we can still assume a linear relation between `Students` and `Proportion`.

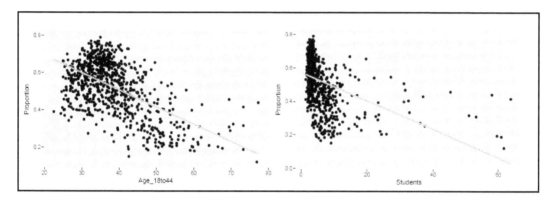

When we're doing a *Multiple Linear Regression* as we're doing here, the assumption should be checked for the rest of the variables, which we omit here to preserve space, but we encourage you to do so. Keep in mind that it's very hard to find a linear relation in all of them, and this assumption is mostly an indicator of the predictive power of the variable in the regression. As long as the relation appears to be slightly linear, we should be all set.

Checking normality with histograms and quantile-quantile plots

We will check normality with two different techniques so that we can exemplify the usage of a technique known as the **strategy pattern**, which is part of a set of patterns from object-oriented programming. We will go deeper into these patterns in `Chapter 8`, *Object-Oriented System to Track Cryptocurrencies*.

For now, you can think of the strategy pattern as a technique that will re-use code that would otherwise be duplicated and simply changes a way of doing things called the **strategy**. In the following code you can see that we create a function called `save_png()` which contains the code that would be duplicated (saving PNG files) and doesn't need to be. We will have two strategies, in the form of functions, to check data normality—histograms and quantile-quantile plots. These will be sent through the argument conveniently named `functions_to_create_images`. As you can see, this code receives some data, a variable that will be used for the graph, the file name for the image, and a function that will be used to create the graphs. This last parameter, the function, should not be unfamiliar to the reader as we have seen in `Chapter 1`, *Introduction to R*, that we can send functions as arguments, and use them as we do in this code, by calling them through their *new name* inside the function, `function_to_create_image()` in this case:

```
save_png <- function(data, variable, save_to, function_to_create_image) {
    if (not_empty(save_to)) png(save_to)
    function_to_create_image(data, variable)
    if (not_empty(save_to)) dev.off()
}
```

Now we show the code that will make use of this `save_png()` function and encapsulate the knowledge of the function that is used for each case. In the case of the histograms, the `histogram()` function shown in the following code simply wraps the `hist()` function used to create the graph with a common interface that will also be used by the other strategies (the `quantile_quantile()` function shown in the following code in this case). This common interface allows us to use these strategies as plugins that can be substituted easily as we do in the corresponding `variable_histogram()` and `variable_qqplot()` functions (they both do the same call, but use a different strategy in each case). As you can see, other details that are not part of the common interface (for example, `main` and `xlab`) are handled within each strategy's code. We could add them as optional arguments if we wanted to, but it's not necessary for this example:

```
variable_histogram <- function(data, variable, save_to = "") {
    save_png(data, variable, save_to, histogram)
}

histogram <- function(data, variable) {
    hist(data[, variable], main = "Histogram", xlab = "Proportion")
}

variable_qqplot <- function(data, variable, save_to = "") {
    save_png(data, variable, save_to, quantile_quantile)
}

quantile_quantile <- function(data, variable) {
```

```
    qqnorm(data[, variable], main = "Normal QQ-Plot for Proportion")
    qqline(data[, variable])
}
```

The following shows the graph for checking proportion normality:

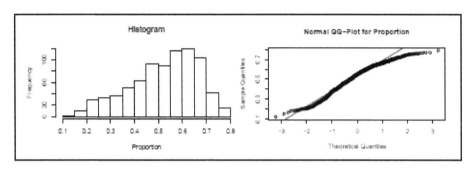

```
quantile_quantile <- function(data, variable) {
    qqnorm(data[, variable], main = "Normal QQ-Plot for Proportion")
    qqline(data[, variable])
}
```

If we wanted to share the code used to create the PNG images with a third (or more) strategies, then we can simply add a strategy wrapper for each new case without worrying about duplicating the code that creates the PNG images. It may seem that this is not a big deal, but imagine that the code used to create the PNG files was complex and suddenly you found a bug. What would you need to fix that bug? Well, you'd have to go to every place where you duplicated the code and fix it there. Doesn't seem very efficient. Now, what happens if you no longer want to save PNG files and want to instead save JPG files? Well, again, you would have to go everywhere you have duplicated your code and change it. Again, not very efficient. As you can see, this way of programming requires a little investment upfront (creating the common interfaces and providing wrappers), but the benefit of doing so will pay for itself through the saved time, you do need to change the code, if only once, as well as more understandable and simpler code. This is a form of **dependency management** and is something you should learn how to do to become a more efficient programmer.

You may have noticed that in the previous code, we could have avoided one function call by having the user call directly the `save_png()` function. However, doing so would require the user to have knowledge of two things, the `save_png()` function to save the image and the `quantile_quantile()` or `histogram()` functions to produce the plots, depending on what she was trying to plot. This extra burden in the user, although seemingly not problematic, could make things very confusing for her since not many users are used to sending functions as arguments, and they would have to know two function signatures, instead of one.

Providing a wrapper whose signature is easily usable as we do with `variable_histogram()` and `variable_qqplot()` makes it easier on the user, and allows us to expand the way we want to show graphs in case we want to change that later without making the user learn a new function signature.

To actually produce the plots we're looking for, we use the following code:

```
variable_histogram(data = data, variable = "Proportion")
variable_qqplot(data = data, variable = "Proportion")
```

As you can see, the histogram shows an approximate normal distribution slightly skewed towards the right, but we can easily accept it as being normal. The corresponding quantile-quantile plot shows the same information in a slightly different way. The line it shows corresponds to the quantiles of the normal distribution, and the dots show the actual distribution in the data. The closer these dots are to the line, the closer the variable's distribution is to being normally distributed. As we can see, for the most part, `Proportion` is normally distributed, and it's at the extremes that we can see a slight deviation, which probably comes from the fact that our `Proportion` variable actually has hard limits at 0 and 1. However, we can also accept it as being normally distributed, and we can proceed to the next assumption safely.

Checking homoscedasticity with residual plots

Homoscedasticity simply means that we need the data to have constant variance in our residuals. To check for it, we can use the `plot(fit)` function call. However, this will show one plot at a time asking you to hit *Enter* on your keyboard to show the next one. This kind of mechanism is not friendly to the automation processes we are creating. So we need a little adjustment. We will use the `par(mfrow = c(2, 2))` call to tell the `plot()` function to graph all four plots at the same time and show it in a single image. We wrap the command around our already familiar mechanism to save PNGs around the `fit_plot()` function, and we're all set:

```
fit_plot <- function(fit, save_to = "") {
    if (not_empty(save_to)) png(save_to)
    par(mfrow = c(2, 2))
    plot(fit)
    if (not_empty(save_to)) dev.off()
}
```

With the `fit_plot()` function in place, we can show the regressions graphical results with the following:

```
fit_plot(fit)
```

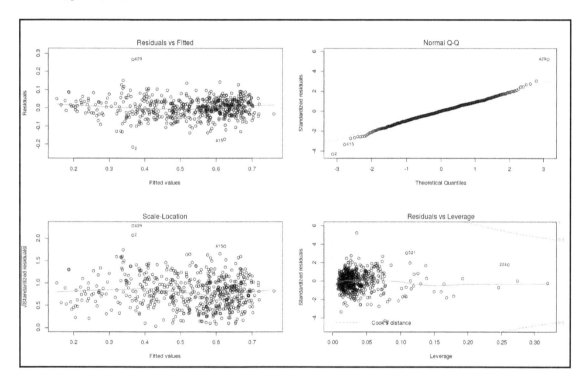

The information we're looking for is in the plots on the left-hand side, where we see fitted values in the x axis and residuals in the y axis. In these plots, we are looking for residuals to be randomly distributed in a tubular pattern, indicated by the dotted lines. We do not want residuals with a pattern that looks similar to a fan or funnel or in any way curvilinear. As we can see, the pattern we see does resemble a tubular pattern, so we can say the assumption of homoscedasticity holds for the data. As an extra, you can also see, in the top-right quantile-quantile plot, that the residuals follow a normal distribution which is also good. The plot on the lower-right shows a statistics concept, which we won't go into, called Cook's distance, which is used to find *influential* observations in a regression. To read more about it, you may look at John Fox's, *Regression Diagnostics, 1991*.

Checking no collinearity with correlations

To check no collinearity, we could use a number of different techniques. For example, for those familiar with linear algebra, the condition number is a measure of how singular a matrix is, where singularity would imply perfect collinearity among the covariates. This number could provide a measure of this collinearity. Another technique is to use the *Variance Inflation Factor*, which is a more formal technique that provides a measure of how much a regression's variance is increased because of collinearity. Another, and a more common, way of checking this is with simple correlations. Are any variables strongly correlated among themselves in the sense that there could be a direct relation among them? If so, then we may have a multicollinearity problem. To get a sense of how correlated our variables are, we will use the correlations matrix techniques shown in `Chapter 2`, *Understanding Votes with Descriptive Statistics*.

The following code shows how correlations work in R:

```
library(corrplot)
corrplot(corr = cor(data[, numerical_variables]), tl.col = "black", tl.cex
= 0.6)
```

As you can see, the strong correlations (either positive or negative) are occurring intra-groups not inter-groups, meaning that variables that measure the same thing in different ways appear to be highly correlated, while variables that measure different things don't appear to be highly correlated.

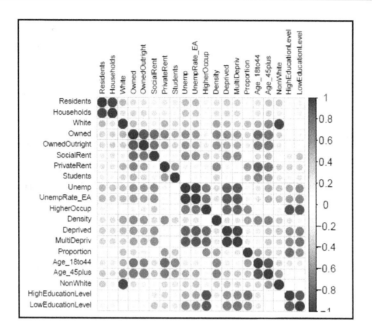

For example, `Age_18to44` and `Age_45plus` are variables that measure age, and we expect them to have a negative relation since the higher the percentage of young people in a ward is, by necessity, the percentage of older people is lower. The same relation can be seen in the housing group (`Owned`, `OwnedOutright`, `SocialRent`, and `PrivateRent`), the employment group (`Unemp`, `UnempRate_EA`, and `HigherOccup`), the deprived group (`Deprived` and `MultiDepriv`), ethnic group (`White` and `NonWhite`), the residency group (`Residents` and `Households`), and the education group (`LowEducationLevel` and `HighEducationLevel`). If you pick variables belonging to different groups, the number of strong correlations is significantly lower, but it's there. For example, `HigherOccup` is strongly correlated to `HighEducationLevel` and `LowEducationLevel`, positively and negatively, respectively. Also, variables in the housing group seem to be correlated with variables in the age group. These kinds of relations are expected and natural since highly educated people will most probably have better jobs, and young people probably can't afford a house yet, so they rent. As analysts, we can assume that these variables are in fact measuring different aspects of society and continue on with our analysis. However, these are still things you may want to keep in mind when interpreting the results, and we may also want to only include one of the variables in each group to avoid inter-group collinearity, but we'll avoid these complexities and continue with our analysis for now.

Linear regression is one of those types of models that require criteria from the analyst to be accepted or rejected. In our specific case, it seems that our model's assumptions are valid enough and we may safely use it to provide credible predictions as we will do in the following sections.

Measuring accuracy with score functions

Now that we have checked our model's assumptions, we turn toward measuring it's predictive power. To measure our predictive accuracy, we will use two methods, one for numerical data (`Proportion`) and the other for categorical data (`Vote`). We know that the `Vote` variable is a transformation from the `Proportion` variable, meaning that we are measuring the same information in two different ways. However, both numerical and categorical data are frequently encountered in data analysis, and thus we wanted to show both approaches here. Both functions, `score_proportions()` (numerical) and `score_votes()` (categorical) receive the data we use for testing and the predictions for each of the observations in the testing data, which come from the model we built in previous sections.

In the numerical case, `score_proportions()` computes a score using the following expression:

$$S = \frac{\sum_{i=1}^{n} \frac{(Y_i - Y_i')^2}{SE_i^2}}{n}$$

Here, `Y_i` is the *real response* variable value for the *i*th observation in the testing data, `Y'_i` is our prediction for that same observation, `SE` is our prediction's standard error, and `n` is the number of observations in the testing data. This equation establishes that the score, which we want to minimize, is the average of *studentized residuals*. Studentized residuals, as you may know, are residuals divided by a measure of the standard errors. This formula gives us an average measure of how close we are to predicting an observation's value correctly relative to the variance observed for that data range. If we have a high degree of variance (resulting in high standard errors), we don't want to be too strict with the prediction, but if we are in a low-variance area, we want to make sure that our predictions are very accurate:

```
score_proportions <- function(data_test, predictions) {
    # se := standard errors
    se <- predictions$se.fit
    real <- data_test$Proportion
```

```
        predicted <- predictions$fit
        return(sum((real - predicted)^2 / se^2) / nrow(data))
}
```

In the categorical case, `score_votes()` computes a score by simply counting the number of times our predictions pointed toward the correct category, which we want to maximize. We do that by first using the same classification mechanism (if the predicted `Proportion` is larger than 0.5, then we classify it as a `"Leave"` vote and vice versa), and compare the categorical values. We know that the sum of Boolean vector will be equal to the number of `TRUE` values, and that's what we're using in the `sum(real == predicted)` expression:

```
score_votes <- function(data_test, predictions) {
    real <- data_test$Vote
    predicted <- ifelse(predictions$fit > 0.5, "Leave", "Remain")
    return(sum(real == predicted))
}
```

To test our model's scores, we do the following:

```
predictions <- predict(fit, data_test, se.fit = TRUE)

score_proportions(data_test, predictions)
#> [1] 10.66
score_votes(data_test, predictions)
#> [1] 216
nrow(data_test)
#> [1] 241
```

In the case of the `score_votes()` function, the measure by itself tells us how well we are doing with our predictions since we can take the number of correct predictions (the output of the function call, which is 216), and divide it by the number of observations (rows) in the `data_test` object (which is 241). This gives us a precision of 89%. This means that if we are given the data from the regressors but we don't know how the ward actually voted, 89% of the time, we would provide a prediction for whether they wanted to leave or remain in the EU, which would be correct. This is pretty good if you ask me.

In the case of the `score_proportions()` function, since we're using a more abstract measure to be able to know how good we're doing, we would like to compare it against other model's scores and get a relative sense of the model's predictive power, and that's exactly what we'll do in the following sections.

Programatically finding the best model

Now that we have seen how to produce scores that represent how good or bad a model's predictive power is, you may go ahead and start specifying lots of models manually by changing the combinations of variables sent to the `lm()` function, compute each model's scores, and then choose the ones with the highest predictive power. This can potentially take a large amount of time, and you may want to delegate it to someone else since it's tedious work. However, fear not. There's a better way! Computers are good at repetitive and tedious tasks, and now we'll see how to tell the computer to find the best model for us with a little bit of programming.

The following sections will increase the programming level, but don't worry we'll explain the code in detail to make sure that everything is understood. If at any point you feel confused, you can always copy-paste small snippets of code into your R terminal and see what each of them are doing individually to gradually get a sense of the whole thing.

Generating model combinations

The first thing we need to do is develop a way of getting the combinations of regressors we want to test. Since this is a combinatorial problem, the number of combinations is exponential with the number of available options. In our case, with the 19 available variables, the number of possible models is the sum of the number of models we can create with one regressor plus the number of models we can create with two regressors, and so on, until we sum the number of models we can create with all 19 regressors. This is what the sum is:

$$\sum_{19}^{i=1} \binom{19}{i} = 524,287$$

Of course, computing so many models, although easy for a computer, may take a while, so we want to limit the minimum and maximum number of regressors allowed in the combinations. To do so, we specify the minimum and maximum percentage of regressors that will be included in the `min_percentage` and `max_percentage` parameters, respectively. In our case, if we specify `min_percentage = 0.9` and `max_percentage = 1.0`, we're asking for all combinations that contain between 17 and 19 of the regressors, which adds up to 191 models. Imagine the time it would take you to generate 191 model specifications manually! Hopefully thinking about that will make you realize the power of this technique.

To start, we create the `generate_combinations_unvectorized()` function that will output the a list with all the possible combinations given the `variables` and the `min_percentage` and `max_percentage` parameters mentioned earlier. The first thing we do is remove the `Proportion` variable by specifying it as `FALSE` in the `variables` vector (the `variables` object here corresponds to the `numerical_variables` object, but we have adjusted its name within this function to make it more readable). The other unwanted variables (`NVotes`, `Leave`, `Vote`, and `RegionName`) were removed in the `get_numerical_variable_names()` function at the beginning of the chapter. Next, we get the actual names of the variables with `TRUE` values so that we can work with string and not Boolean. After that, we compute the total number of variables as `n`, and the actual number of variables we will include in the combinations by taking the percentage parameters, multiplying them by the number of variables, and getting either the *floor* or *ceiling* for that number to make sure that we include the extremes. After that, we initialize the `all_combinations` object that will contain the list of combinations we want. The next part is the progress bar object that we won't explain as we have used it before.

The actual work is done inside the `for` loop. Notice that it goes from the minimum to the maximum number of variables we want inside our combinations. In each iteration, we compute the number of combinations which is returned to us as a matrix where each column represents a different combination and each row contains the index of the variables for that particular combination. This means that we need to add each of those columns to our total list of combinations (`all_combinations`), which is what we do inside the nested `for` loop. Finally, since we have nested lists, we want to use the `unlist()` function to bring them to the *same level*, but we don't want to do it recursively because we would just end with a single long list and we wouldn't be able to differentiate one combination from another.

I encourage you to change the return statement to avoid using the `recursive = FALSE` parameter, as well as avoiding the use of the `unlist()` function at all. Doing so will quickly show you what effect they have on the function's output, and why we need them.

```
library(progress)

generate_combinations_unvectorized <- function(variables, min_percentage,
max_percentage) {
    variables[["Proportion"]] <- FALSE
    variables                 <- names(variables[variables == TRUE])
    n                         <- length(variables)
    n_min                     <- floor(n * min_percentage)
    n_max                     <- ceiling(n * max_percentage)
    all_combinations          <- NULL
```

```
progress_bar <- progress_bar$new(
    format = "Progress [:bar] :percent ETA: :eta",
    total = length(n_min:n_max)
)

for (k in n_min:n_max) {
    progress_bar$tick()
    combinations <- combn(variables, k)
    for (column in 1:ncol(combinations)) {
        new_list <- list(combinations[, column])
        all_combinations <- c(all_combinations, list(new_list))
    }
}
return(unlist(all_combinations, recursive = FALSE))
}
```

A sample output of the object that the `generate_combinations_unvectorized()` function does is shown next. As you can see, it's a list where each element is a vector or type `character`. The first combination created contains only 17 variables, which is the minimum number of variables used when the total number of variables is 19 and the minimum percentage requested is 90%. The last combination (combination number 191), contains all 19 variables and corresponds to the model we built manually earlier in this chapter:

```
combinations <- generate_combinations_unvectorized(
    numerical_variables, 0.9, 1.0
)

combinations
[[1]]
 [1] "Residents"      "Households"     "White"          "Owned"
 [5] "OwnedOutright"  "SocialRent"     "PrivateRent"    "Students"
 [9] "Unemp"          "UnempRate_EA"   "HigherOccup"    "Density"
[13] "Deprived"       "MultiDepriv"    "Age_18to44"     "Age_45plus"
[17] "NonWhite"

...

[[191]]
 [1] "Residents"          "Households"         "White"
 [4] "Owned"              "OwnedOutright"      "SocialRent"
 [7] "PrivateRent"        "Students"           "Unemp"
[10] "UnempRate_EA"       "HigherOccup"        "Density"
[13] "Deprived"           "MultiDepriv"        "Age_18to44"
[16] "Age_45plus"         "NonWhite"           "HighEducationLevel"
[19] "LowEducationLevel"
```

Getting only those combinations that contain between 90% and 100% of the variables may seem a bit restrictive. What if we want to generate all possible combinations? In that case, we would change the first parameter to be 0, but it may not finish in a practical amount of time. The reason is that our `generate_combinations_unvectorized()` function, as the name implies, is not vectorized, and even worse, has nested `for` loops. This is a huge bottleneck in this particular case, and it's something you want to look out for in your own code. One possible solution is to make a *vectorized* version of the function. For those of you interested, we have included a file named `vectorized_vs_unvectorized.R` in this book's code repository (`https://github.com/PacktPublishing/R-Programming-By-Example`), that shows the said implementation. We also include some tests that will show you just how much faster the vectorized implementation is. Just to give you a spoiler, it can be hundreds of times faster! For those cases where vectorizing and other approaches that only depend on R itself are not good enough, you can try delegating the task to a faster (compiled) language. We will see how to do that in `Chapter 9`, *Implementing an Efficient Simple Moving Average.*

Going back to our example, the next thing to do is to create the `find_best_fit()` function, which will go through each of the combinations generated, use the `data_train` data to train a model with the corresponding combination, test it's accuracy with the `measure` selection (either `Proportion` (numerical) or `Vote` (categorical)) and will save the corresponding score in a `scores` vector. Then, it will find the index of the optimal score by either finding the minimum or maximum score, depending on the `measure` selection we're using (`Proportion` requires us to minimize while `Vote` requires us to maximize), and finally it will recreate the optimal model, print it's information, and return the model to the user. The `compute_model_and_fit()`, `compute_score()`, and `print_best_model_info()` functions will be developed next as we're following a top-down approach:

```
find_best_fit <- function(measure, data_train, data_test, combinations) {
    n_cases <- length(combinations)
    progress_bar <- progress_bar$new(
        format = "Progress [:bar] :percent ETA: :eta",
        total = n_cases
    )
    scores <- lapply(1:n_cases, function(i) {
        progress_bar$tick()
        results <- compute_model_and_fit(combinations[[i]], data_train)
        score <- compute_score(measure, results[["fit"]], data_test)
        return(score)
    })
    i <- ifelse(measure == "Proportion", which.min(scores),
which.max(scores))
    best_results <- compute_model_and_fit(combinations[[i]], data_train)
```

```
    best_score <- compute_score(measure, best_results[["fit"]], data_test)
    print_best_model_info(i, best_results[["model"]], best_score, measure)
    return(best_results[["fit"]])
}
```

Next, we create the `compute_model_and_fit()` function, which simply generates the formula for the selected combination and uses it within the `lm()` function. As you can see in the `combinations` object, we returned previously from the `generate_combinations_unvectorized()` function, it's a list with character vectors, it's not a formula we can pass to the `lm()` function; this is why we need the `generate_model()` function, which will take on of these vectors, and concatenate its elements into a single string with the plus (+) sign between them by using the `paste()` function with the `collapse = " + "` argument, and it will prepend the `Proportion ~` string to it. This gives us back a formula object specified by a string like `Proportion ~ Residents + ... + NonWhite`, which contains, instead of the dots, all the variables in the first combination shown in the preceding code. This string is then used inside the `lm()` function to execute our regression, and both `model` and `fit` are returned within a list to be used in the following steps:

```
compute_model_and_fit <- function(combination, data_train) {
    model <- generate_model(combination)
    return(list(model = model, fit = lm(model, data_train)))
}

generate_model <- function(combination) {
    sum <- paste(combination, collapse = " + ")
    return(formula(paste("Proportion", "~", sum)))
}
```

As can be seen by the `score <- compute_score(measure, results[["fit"]], data_test)` line, the `compute_score()` function receives a `measure` object, a `fit` object (which comes from the `results` list), and the data used for testing. It computes the score using the *strategy* pattern mentioned earlier for the plots used to check the normality assumption. Basically, depending on the value of the `measure` string (the chosen strategy), it will choose one of the two functions that share the same signature, and that function will be used to compute the final predictions. We send the `se.fit = TRUE` parameter to the `predict()` function we had seen before because we want the standard errors to also be sent in case we use the numerical score which requires them. The `score_proportions()` and `score_votes()` functions were defined previously in this chapter:

```
compute_score <- function(measure, fit, data_test) {
    if (measure == "Proportion") {
        score <- score_proportions
```

```
    } else {
        score <- score_votes
    }
    predictions <- predict(fit, data_test, se.fit = TRUE)
    return(score(data_test, predictions))
}
```

Finally, we create a little convenience function called print_best_model_info() that will print results about the best model found. It simply takes the index of the best model, the model formula, its score, and the measure type, and prints all of that for the user. As you can see, since the model object is not a simple string but a *formula* object, we need to work a little with it to get the results we want by converting it into a string and splitting it using the plus sign (+) we know is included; otherwise, it would be a very long string:

```
print_best_model_info <- function(i, model, best_score, measure){
    print("*************************************")
    print(paste("Best model number:", i))
    print(paste("Best score:       ", best_score))
    print(paste("Score measure:    ", measure))
    print("Best model:")
    print(strsplit(toString(model), "\\+"))
    print("*************************************")
}
```

We can find the best model, according to the Proportion measure by calling the following:

```
best_lm_fit_by_proportions <- find_best_fit(
    measure = "Proportion",
    data_train = data_train,
    data_test = data_test,
    combinations = combinations
)
#> [1] "*************************************"
#> [1] "Best model number: 3"
#> [1] "Best score:        10.2362983528259"
#> [1] "Score measure:     Proportion"
#> [1] "Best model:"
#> [[1]]
#>  [1] "~, Proportion, Residents " " Households "
#>  [3] " White "                   " Owned "
#>  [5] " OwnedOutright "           " SocialRent "
#>  [7] " PrivateRent "             " Students "
#>  [9] " Unemp "                   " UnempRate_EA "
#> [11] " HigherOccup "             " Density "
#> [13] " Deprived "                " MultiDepriv "
#> [15] " Age_18to44 "              " Age_45plus "
```

```
#> [17] " LowEducationLevel"
#> [1] "***********************************"
```

As we can see, the best model was the third one out of the 191 models, and it had a score of 10.23. We can also see the regressors used in the model. As you can see, `NonWhite` and `HighEducationLevel` were left out by the optimization method, probably due to their counterparts containing all the information necessary for their respective groups. It's no coincidence that those are among the most representative variables in the data.

To find the best model according to the `Vote` measure, we use the following code. Note that given the good techniques we used to create this function, all we have to do is change the value of the `measure` parameter to optimize our search using a different approach:

```
best_lm_fit_by_votes <- find_best_fit(
    measure = "Vote",
    data_train = data_train,
    data_test = data_test,
    combinations = combinations
)
#> [1] "***********************************"
#> [1] "Best model number: 7"
#> [1] "Best score:       220"
#> [1] "Score measure:    Vote"
#> [1] "Best model:"
#> [[1]]
#>  [1] "~, Proportion, Residents " " Households "
#>  [3] " White "                   " Owned "
#>  [5] " OwnedOutright "           " SocialRent "
#>  [7] " PrivateRent "             " Students "
#>  [9] " Unemp "                   " UnempRate_EA "
#> [11] " HigherOccup "             " Density "
#> [13] " Deprived "                " MultiDepriv "
#> [15] " Age_45plus "              " NonWhite "104
#> [17] " HighEducationLevel"
#> [1] "***********************************"
```

In this case, the best model was the seventh one out of the 191 models, with 220 out of 241 correct predictions, which gives us an accuracy of 91%, an improvement given the accuracy we had computed earlier in the chapter. In this case, `LowEducationLevel` and `Age_18to44` were left out. Again, no coincidence that these are part of the most important variables in the data.

Predicting votes from wards with unknown data

Now that we know how to train our models and find the best one possible, we will provide predictions for those wards for which we don't have voting data using the best models we found using the `Vote` measure. To do so, we simply execute the following line:

```
predictions <- predict(best_lm_fit_by_votes, data_incomplete)

predictions
#>    804    805    806    807    808    809    810    811    812    813
#> 0.6845 0.6238 0.5286 0.4092 0.5236 0.6727 0.6322 0.6723 0.6891 0.6004
#>    814    815    816    817    818    819    820    821    822    823
#> 0.6426 0.5854 0.6966 0.6073 0.4869 0.5974 0.5611 0.4784 0.5534 0.6151
(Truncated output)
```

This will take the best model we found earlier using the `Votes` measure and use it to generate predictions for the `Proportion` variable in the `data_incomplete` data, which contains those observations for which we don't have any voting data. These are the best predictions we can provide with what we have done so far and we can expect them to have a 91% accuracy when used to categorize the `Proportion` variable into the `Vote` variable.

Summary

This chapter showed how to use multiple linear regression models, one of the most commonly used family of models, to predict numerical and categorical data. Our focus was on showing programming techniques that allow analysts to be more efficient in the projects while keeping their code quality high. We did so by showing how to create different model combinations programatically, measuring the predictive accuracy, and selecting the best one. The techniques used can easily be used with other, more advanced, types of models, and we encourage you to try to improve on the predictive accuracy by using other families of models. In the code that accompanies this book (`https://github.com/PacktPublishing/R-Programming-By-Example`), you can find an implementation that also uses generalized linear models to produce predictions.

In the following chapter, we will start working with a different and slightly less technical example that uses product data from a hypothetical company to show how to work with manipulative data in a variety of ways and use it with many kinds of visualizations, including 3D, interactive, and geospatial graphs.

4
Simulating Sales Data and Working with Databases

The Food Factory example is about a fictitious company called **The Food Factory**. They sell custom meals for people looking for healthy food. They allow their customers to choose the macronutrients combinations they want, as well as their protein sources. Macronutrients are the base for any diet, and they are composed of carbohydrates, proteins, and fats. Customers can choose the percentage of each macronutrient, as well as their protein source (fish, chicken, beef, or vegetarian); then, The Food Factory will come up with a tasty meal which fulfills their diet specifications. They have found some great combinations this way, and if they continue to do as well as they have, they will add more meal options, as well as fixed recipes, according to what their customers like most.

The Food Factory has done a good job so far and they have a system in place that allows them to collect a good amount of data across their five store locations, as well as keep track of customer messages. Our job in this example will be to analyze the data to diagnose the current state of the business and propose ways to improve it. To do so, we will use lots of visualizations in Chapter 5, *Communicating Sales with Visualizations;* perform text analysis on customer reviews in Chapter 6, *Understanding Reviews with Text Analysis;* and provide automatic diagnosis of the current state of the business in Chapter 7, *Developing Automatic Presentations.* Sounds good, right? However, before we can do all of that, we need to get a hold of the data, and we don't have it yet. We're going to simulate it! This chapter will show you how to design a non-trivial data simulation to produce the data for the example. Furthermore, The Food Factory, as well as many organizations, doesn't always make our lives easier by providing CSV files, and they often have databases we need to work with. This chapter will also show you how to work with such databases.

Some of the important topics covered in this chapter are:

- Designing and implementing non-trivial simulations
- Simulating numbers, categories, strings, and dates
- Function signatures with parameter objects
- Reusing functions in different contexts
- Mixing internal and external data
- Working with relational databases

Required packages

The only package required for this chapter is RMySQL. However, to be able to fully replicate the code shown towards the end of the chapter, you will need a working installation of the MySQL database (https://www.mysql.com/). Specific instructions for Linux and Mac can be found in Appendix, *Required Packages*.

Package	Reason
RMySQL	Interface to MySQL database

Designing our data tables

It's always a good practice to design with paper and a pencil before starting to program. If you do, you'll find that your code is much better because you'll contemplate scenarios that you may not see if you start programming right away, and, instead of hacking your way around what you have already programmed, you'll be able to design solutions beforehand. It's an easy investment that very often pays off, so that's what we will do in this section, we will design our data.

The basic variables

Let's start from the most simple scenario we can imagine and try to find any potential problems we may encounter. For each sale, we would like to have the following variables, the sales DATE, the COST for producing that type of food, the QUANTITY bought, the PRICE for the type food, whether or not we applied a DISCOUNT, the macronutrient percentages for CARBS (carbohydrates), PROTEIN, and FAT, the PROTEIN_SOURCE of the food (either FISH, CHICKEN, BEEF, or VEGETARIAN, if the person does not eat meat), the STORE where it was sold, the DELIVERY method (either send TO LOCATION or deliver IN STORE), the STATUS of the sale, which can be PENDING, DELIVERED, RETURNED, or CANCELLED (a sale can't have two statuses at the same time), whether or not it has been PAID, the client's BIRTH_DATE and GENDER, how many STARS they awarded to the company, the CUSTOMER_SINCE date, and how many messages they sent us related to their order, as well as the DATE, STARS, and actual MESSAGE for each one.

Simplifying assumptions

We can complicate the example as much as we want, but to keep the simulation simple (although not trivial), we are going to assume a couple of things upfront. First, we assume that each sale record contains a single type of food. If a person buys two or more different types of foods, then each of those types will produce a different sale record. However, each sale can contain as many portions of the foods as we want, as long as they are the same type (combination of macronutrients and protein sources). This is the most important simplification, since company sales orders normally have various items per sale, but it will allow us to focus on the programming side of things.

Second, we will not worry about the relation among food types and costs (or prices) being continuous in the mathematical sense. This means that we may find a food type with some combination of macronutrients and protein sources that is very similar to another food's combination, but their production costs, as well as their prices, are very different. Similarly, we assume that each food type has its unique cost and price, and it can vary for different sales (the same food type can have different costs and prices for different sales). This is not a realistic assumption, as most companies have standardized products (including costs and prices), but we can think of The Food Factory as being a craft shop, where each food is unique, and that can generate the differences in costs and prices. If anything, it's adding complexity (fun) to the analysis.

Third, we will not worry about the relation among sales dates and sale statuses, or among sales dates and whether or not a sale has been paid. This means that we may actually find sales that have been delivered and are old, but were not paid. This is something that does happen in some real-life cases, so there's no problem assuming it.

Fourth, the fact that a customer's messages related to a specific sale are rated high or low, does not affect the overall score they gave to The Food Factory. There are two STARS columns, one for overall rating of The Food Factory, and one that will be sent with each message related to an order. This means that a client who in general likes The Food Factory can have a bad experience, and it will not affect how much they continue to like the store. Conversely, a customer who in general does not like The Food Factory, will not start liking it because they had a good experience with it one day. This assumption holds true for people with fixed preferences, but does not hold true in general. If we wanted to, we could include mechanisms in the simulation that take these dynamics into account. As a matter of fact, I encourage you to try to implement some of these mechanisms yourself. It will be good practice.

Fifth, we won't worry about the macronutrients making sense, including the combination with protein sources. A common diet would include approximately 50% protein, 35% carbohydrates, and 15% fat, but we won't worry about our numbers making nutritional sense. That means, please don't think any of these simulated food orders are realistic, or are actually healthy.

Potential pitfalls

Now that we understand the general data structure, we need to find potential pitfalls that should be avoided. We can think about this data structure as a standard table structure (a data frame or a spreadsheet) where each column represents a variable and each row represents an observation (a sales record, in our case).

The too-much-empty-space problem

Let's say we have a sales record; what happens if we get a message related to that order from our customer? Well, we simply add the data to the corresponding columns DATE, STARS, and MESSAGE. What happens if we get another message related to the same order? Well, a possible solution would be to add a new combination of DATE, STARS, and MESSAGE for the new message, but names would collapse.

How would we differentiate among them? Well, we can append a number indicating the actual message number. Then, we would have `DATE_1`, `STARS_1`, and `MESSAGE_1` for the first message, and `DATE_2`, `STARS_2`, and `MESSAGE_2` for the second message. That would fix it, wouldn't it? What happens if we get a third, or more, messages related to the order? Well, we would end up with a lot of variables in our data frame. Specifically, we would have as many combinations as the maximum number of messages that were sent to a single order. What would be the content of the cells for the orders that did not have such a big number of messages? They would be empty. That would be a lot of wasted space! Plus, the general structure for the data would feel awkward. There must be a better way.

If you think about it, it feels like the messages and the sales are two different things and that they should be kept separate, doesn't it? If you think about it that way, you are right. So let's imagine that, let's keep one data frame for the sales orders and another for the messages. There is another problem. Can you see it? How are we going to tell which messages belong to which sales orders? Identifiers to the rescue! We can add `SALE_ID` to the sales data frame, where it should be unique, and we can add the same `SALE_ID` to the messages data frame, where it will not be unique because there can be multiple messages related to the same sales order. This means we have a one-to-many relation. With this in mind, the sales data frame would have all the variables we mentioned earlier, minus the `DATE`, `STARS`, and `MESSAGE` variable for the messages (don't confuse the sales order `DATE` with the `DATE` for each message), and those three variables would conform to the separate messages data frame. Both data frames would have a `SALE_ID` variable. Great; we're past that one.

The too-much-repeated-data problem

What variable do we still have in the sales data frame? Well, to phrase it in such a way as to make the problem very obvious, we still have the sales variables and the customer's variables. So, what might the problem be? Well, each time a customer makes a new purchase, we save her `BIRTH_DATE`, `CLIENT_SINCE`, `GENDER`, and `STARS` information again. What if a frequent customer has 100 different purchases with The Food Factory? Well, her information will be repeated 100 times! We need to fix that. How might we do it? We do the same thing we did before, separate things that are different. That's right. We create a separate data frame for the customer data, and we already know how to link the customers with the sales since we used that same technique in the previous problem, we create identifiers in both data frames. This is a many-to-one relation (from the point of view of the sales data towards the customers' data). I'm sure you can figure out which variables belong to which data frames.

By eliminating the repeated data, we're also eliminating the possibility of accidentally changing some of those repeated values and then being confused about which ones are correct.

To recapitulate, what we have done is break up a huge initial table that contained all the information in a single place into three different tables that are linked through identifiers, in such a way that we represent different things in each table (sales, clients, and client messages), while eliminating a lot of wasted space and repeated values. To get more intuition on how is organized after these adjustments, we can take a look at the following image which shows what data attributes belong to which entities, and how they are related among each other:

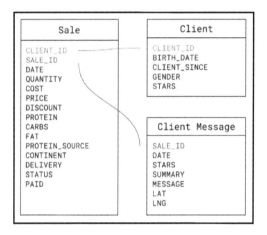

Data entities and attributes for the simulation

These techniques, together with many others, are called **database normalization**, which can be useful in certain scenarios. There are times, however, that we will not want our data to be fully normalized because of performance issues, but those are advanced cases that we won't cover in this book. For the interested reader, I'd recommend looking at Silberschatz, Korth, and Sudarshan's, *Database System Concepts, 2010* for advanced concepts and examples.

Finally, keep in mind that although we are creating our own unique identifiers in this chapter, in real-world applications you will be better off using a well established tool for such a task. The uuid package is specially designed to generate and handle **Universally Unique Identifiers** (**UUIDs**). You can find more information about it in its CRAN page (https://cran.r-project.org/web/packages/uuid/index.html).

Simulating the sales data

Enough concepts; let's start programming. To get a clear idea of where we're heading, we start by initializing the `sales` data frame we will be using, with zero observations for now. We do so by defining the available categories for each factor variable, and defining empty values with the data type we need for each variable. As you can see, it has the identifiers `SALE_ID` and `CLIENT_ID`, which will allow us to link this data with the one from `clients` and `client_messages`. To understand this, let's have a look at the following code:

```
status_levels <- c("PENDING", "DELIVERED", "RETURNED", "CANCELLED")
protein_source_levels <- c("BEEF", "FISH", "CHICKEN", "VEGETARIAN")
continent_levels <- c("AMERICA", "EUROPE", "ASIA")
delivery_levels <- c("IN STORE", "TO LOCATION")
paid_levels <- c("YES", "NO")

sales <- data.frame(
    SALE_ID = character(),
    CLIENT_ID = character(),
    DATE = as.Date(character()),
    QUANTITY = integer(),
    COST = numeric(),
    PRICE = numeric(),
    DISCOUNT = numeric(),
    PROTEIN = numeric(),
    CARBS = numeric(),
    FAT = numeric(),
    PROTEIN_SOURCE = factor(levels = protein_source_levels),
    CONTINENT = factor(levels = continent_levels),
    DELIVERY = factor(levels = delivery_levels),
    STATUS = factor(levels = status_levels),
    PAID = factor(levels = paid_levels)
)
```

This way of initializing an empty data frame, as opposed to many other methods you may find elsewhere, is safer, since you'll have the correct column types from the beginning. If your code relies on some column type checking (as we will do), it will work even with a data frame with zero rows (as is the case here).

Simulating numeric data according to distribution assumptions

We will generate the data for each column separately and then we'll recreate the data frame with it. We want to start with the easy parts first, so we'll take a look at the simulation for QUANTITY, COST, PRICE, and DISCOUNT. The easy way would be to just simulate some random numbers and make sure they are within some range by multiplying or dividing them accordingly. We could also use the round() function to make sure QUANTITY is not fractional. However, if we want to do it the correct way, then we must consider the underlying assumptions in each of those numbers. An image showing the distributions mentioned in the following paragraphs is shown below.

Distributions for COST, PRICE, QUANTITY and DISCOUNT

The COST and PRICE value follow a normal distribution because they are real numbers. On average, COST should be lower than PRICE, so we will set their respective mean parameters accordingly. Note that this allows for the possibility of some foods being sold for less than their production cost, which sometimes happens when companies are trying to minimize losses. DISCOUNT follows an exponential distribution because we want most discounts to be zero, or low (compared to the price). This means that we don't give out discounts often, and when we do, they will be small. QUANTITY follows a *Poisson distribution* because it needs to be an integer. A good resource is Sean Owen's *Common Probability Distributions: The Data Scientist's Crib Sheet, 2015* (https://blog.cloudera.com/blog/2015/12/common-probability-distributions-the-data-scientists-crib-sheet/).

Given these assumptions, we will create three functions. COST and PRICE are simulated with the `random_values()` function, while QUANTITY and DISCOUNT have their own functions. The `random_values()` function uses the `rnorm()` function to simulate n values (where n is the number of rows we want in the data frame) using the normal distribution, with a specific `mean` and standard deviation (`sqrt(variance)`). We then take these values and round them to two decimal places using the `round()` function as shown in the following:

```
random_values <- function(n, mean, variance) {
    return(round(rnorm(n, mean, sqrt(variance)), 2))
}
```

The `random_discounts()` function uses the `rexp()` function to simulate n values using the exponential distribution with the `lambda` parameter, and, as we did before, we use the `round()` function to round the values to two decimal places. When we use this function, we'll use a very high `lambda` parameter (100) to heavily skew the distribution to the right so that we get a lot of zeros in the simulation. However, this will make our values be very small (for example, 0.021). If we use these values directly, our discounts will be of a couple of cents, which is not realistic. Therefore, we multiply these values by 100 to get discounts that are a couple of dollars. Note that if we first round and then multiply by 100, we get full dollar discounts (for example, $2), but if we first multiply by 100 and then round, we get discounts that include cents (for example, $2.1), which is something we prefer to avoid, but it would work just as well. Let's have a look at the following code to understand this:

```
random_discounts <- function(n, lambda) {
    return(round(rexp(n, lambda), 2) * 100)
}
```

The `random_quantities()` function uses the `rpois()` function to simulate n values using the *Poisson distribution* with the `lambda` parameter. In this case, we don't need to round, because the values will already be integers. However, we do add 1 to each value, because we might get zero as a quantity, and having a sales order with zero foods would not make sense. Adding 1 guarantees we have at least one food in each sales order:

```
random_quantities <- function(n, lambda) {
    return(rpois(n, lambda) + 1)
}
```

Simulating categorical values using factors

The `random_levels()` function simulates n categorical values by sampling the `levels` provided with replacement (controlled by the third parameter, which is sent as TRUE). You can think about the `levels` as an array of strings, each of which is a possible value for the simulation. These `levels` will come from the categories defined for factor variables in the data frame (`PROTEIN_SOURCE`, `STORE`, `DELIVERY`, `STATUS`, and `PAID`). A sample with replacement means that every time we pick one of the values from the `levels` object, we return it so that we can pick it again later. Sampling without replacement only makes sense when you want a number of samples that is smaller than the total amount of values available, which is not the case here, since we want to simulate thousands of rows and we won't have that many `levels`.

There's a third parameter that we have not mentioned, the `probabilities` parameter. As you can see, by default it's set to NULL, but we do send an object there; it must be a vector of numbers between 0 and 1, such that they sum to 1 and they represent the probability of picking a specific category. The order of this `probabilities` object must be the same as in the `levels` object. For example, if we have three possible levels and we send the `probabilities` object as `c(0.2, 0.3, 0.5)`, the first level will have a 20% probability of being picked, while the second and third levels will have probabilities of 30% and 50%, respectively. Note that the probabilities add up to one. Let's have a look at the code:

```
random_levels <- function(n, levels, probabilities = NULL) {
    return(sample(levels, n, TRUE, probabilities))
}
```

 Note that we don't check whether the `probabilities` object is being sent as NULL before we pass it along to the `sample()` function. This can be done because the corresponding parameter in the `sample()` function also uses NULL as a default, and interprets it as using equal probabilities for all the values. You can check this in the function's documentation.

To test that the probabilities are being implemented correctly, we can simulate 100 values and then create a table with the results to see the amount of values produced for each of the categories. As you can see, if we simulate 100 values of the categories A, B, and C, with 20%, 30%, and 50% probabilities, we get 18%, 37%, and 45% proportions, respectively. These results are close enough to our specifications, and thus, correct. Note that you will get different values every time you re-execute the code, and they will almost never be the exact values you specified, which is natural in simulations. However, they should almost always be close to the specifications:

```
results <- random_levels(100, c("A", "B", "C"), c(0.2, 0.3, 0.5))
table(results)
#> results
#>  A  B  C
#> 18 37 45
```

Simulating dates within a range

The `random_dates_in_range()` function uses the same `sample()` function we used before, but instead of receiving a list of strings as categories from factor variables, it will receive a list of dates. To generate the full set of valid dates for the simulation, we use the `seq()` function. This function will generate all values from the `start` to the `end` by a specific interval. If we want to generate all odd numbers between 1 and 10, we will use `seq(1, 10, 2)`, which means that it will take 1 and add 2 to it sequentially until 10 is reached. In our case, we want the increment to be a full day, and, conveniently, the `seq()` function provides this capability when sending date objects by sending the increment as the string `"day"`:

```
random_dates_in_range <- function(n, start, end, increasing_prob = FALSE) {
    sequence <- seq(start, end, "day")
    if (increasing_prob) {
        probabilities <- seq(1, length(sequence))^2
        probabilities <- probabilities / sum(probabilities)
        return(sample(sequence, n, TRUE, probabilities))
    } else {
        return(sample(sequence, n, TRUE))
    }
}
```

Note that this will only work when sending *date* objects. If you try to test this function with strings, you will get an error saying that `'from' cannot be NA, NaN, or infinite`. Instead, you should convert those strings to dates with the `as.Date()` function:

```
seq("2017-01-01", "2017-02-01", "day")                       # Error
seq(as.Date("2017-01-01"), as.Date("2017-02-01"), "day")  # Valid
```

Simulating numbers under shared restrictions

As you may remember, The Food Factory creates their foods by receiving a macronutrient specification. Customers can specify whatever combination of percentages they want for each one, as long as they add up to 1. Now we are going to simulate these macronutrient percentages. This will require a little more work than the previous cases.

First, we create a function that will return numeric triples, where each number is between 0 and 1, and together they add up to 1. To accomplish this, we will use two random numbers and make the third one dependent on the first two. We will use the following mathematical fact:

$$abs(a, b) = max(a, b) - min(a, b) \Rightarrow 1 = 1 - max(a, b) + min(a, b) + abs(a, b)$$

This tells us to take one number as *1 - max(a, b)*, another as *min(a, b)*, and the last one as *abs(a, b)*; which is exactly what we do in the `random_triple()` function. Doing so mathematically guarantees that we will get three random numbers between 0 and 1 that together add up to 1. Note that the `random_triple()` is one of the few functions we have created which does not require any arguments at all, which makes sense, since we don't need *external* information to simulate the triple:

```
random_triple <- function() {
    a <- runif(1, 0, 1)
    b <- runif(1, 0, 1)
    PROTEIN <- 1 - max(a, b)
    CARBS <- abs(a - b)
    FAT <- min(a, b)
    return(c(PROTEIN, CARBS, FAT))
}
```

We can test that it's working simply by using `sum()` over the result:

```
triple <- random_triple()
triple
#> [1] 0.05796599 0.76628032 0.17575370

sum(triple)
#> 1
```

Now we want to generate n of these triples. To do so, we use the `replicate()` function to produce n triples. The `TRUE` argument corresponds to the `simplify` argument of the function, which will reduce a list of triples to matrix form, which is easier to work with in this particular case. When we are testing the code and look at the results of `replicate(n, random_triple(), TRUE)`, we will find that the resulting structure is the transpose of what we want, meaning that it has three rows and n columns, where each row represents a macronutrient percentage and each column represents an observation. We want to transpose this structure to get the macronutrient percentages as columns and the observations as rows; to do so, we simply use the `t()` function. After that, we simply create a data frame with the corresponding values for each macronutrient:

```
random_composition <- function(n) {
```

```
    matrix <- t(replicate(n, random_triple(), TRUE))
    return(data.frame(PROTEIN = matrix[, 1],
                      CARBS = matrix[, 2],
                      FAT = matrix[, 3]))
}
```

Simulating strings for complex identifiers

It's time for the most complex part of the simulation, the identifiers. We want to produce n identifiers, and, depending on what identifiers we are simulating, we may want them to be unique. Client identifiers in the client data must be unique, because we don't want two distinct clients with the same identifier, and our clients' data will not have repeated records by design. On the other hand, we don't want unique client identifiers in the sales data, because we want *repeated* clients to appear in there.

We could create two distinct functions that take care of these cases independently, but it's easy enough to combine them into a single function by just using a `reduction` parameter that specifies the percentage of unique identifiers. If the `reduction` parameter is sent as 0 (the default), we assume that full unique identifiers are requested. We will assume that identifiers are composed of a group of letters followed by a group of digits, and each group's length should be specified separately. That's what the `n_letters` and `n_digits` are for. Our implementation will work by creating the letters and digits groups separately and then combining them.

First, we will create the letter combinations by taking a sample from the `LETTERS` group (an internal R object which contains all ASCII letters in the capitalized form) of size n with replacement (we may have repeated letters in each identifier). Then, we are going to replicate this sample for `n_letters`, which is the amount of letters we need in each identifier, and we won't simplify the structure, which is why we send the `FALSE` parameter. This will return a list with `n_letters` elements, where each element is a vector of n letters. Now we want to paste these objects together. To do so, we use the `paste0()` function (which is a shortcut for the `paste()` function that collapses everything together, if you just use `paste()`, you will get spaces between the letters). However, we can't send our construction to `paste0()` because we will get some garbage out. We need to use the `do.call()` function to this properly. To understand what is going on, let's assume that `n_letters` is 5, and see how the code behaves.

```
n_letters <- 5
letters <- do.call(paste0, replicate(
        n_letters, sample(LETTERS, n, TRUE), FALSE))
letters
#> [1] "KXSVT" "HQASE" "DDEOG" "ERIMD" "CQBOY"
```

Now we will focus on the digit combinations. Our objective is to get a number between zero and the number formed of n_digits nines. For example, if n_digits is 5, we want numbers between 0 and 99,999. This will be broken into two steps. First, create the dynamic right-extreme number composed of only nines. Then, make sure that it has exactly n_digit digits, even if the natural way of representing the number does not. This means that if n_digits is 5 and the number we end up sampling is 123, we need to use 00123 as the result, since we need to ensure n_digit digits.

To accomplish the first part, we use replicate() to repeat the string **9** n_digits times. Then we use paste() with collapse = "" to put all the strings together, resulting in a string such as **99999**. Then we convert that string into a number by using the as.numeric() function. We end up with the desired number of nines in the max_number object.

Then we use the sprintf() function to make sure we have n_digits when using the number. To do so, we specify the format with a pre-fill of zeros (using the "%0" syntax), such that we have n_digits (using the n_digits followed by the d letter for digits). We put this inside a paste() function because the format string will be created dynamically. Following the example stated before, it would be "%05d" for 5 digits. For more information on how to use the sprintf() function, take a look at Chapter 1, *Introduction to R*. These lines combined give us:

```
max_number <- as.numeric(paste(replicate(n_digits, 9), collapse = ""))
format <- paste("%0", n_digits, "d", sep = "")
digits <- sprintf(format, sample(max_number, n, TRUE))
digits
#> [1] "84150" "88603" "88640" "24548" "06355"
```

Now we need to paste the letters and digits objects together by using the paste0() function again. Since this is a vectorized operation, we will end up with a single array of n identifiers. Note that even though we have not enforced uniqueness, the probability of the sampling procedures producing repeated identifiers is so extremely low that we won't worry about it here.

Real-world problems have a surprising ability to produce these extremely low probability cases, making careless code fail. If you are developing critical applications, always make sure you check for these cases explicitly.

Finally, if `reduction` is greater than zero, meaning that we want to use only the `reduction` percentage of the identifiers created so far to generate the total of n identifiers, we will use the `sample()` function to get n identifiers from the first `reduction` percentage identifiers, which is computed as an array from 1 to the floor of the percentage (must be an integer) of the `ids`, and we will do it with replacement (hence the `TRUE` parameter). If `reduction` is zero, we simply send the `ids` we have created so far without any modifications:

```
random_strings <- function(n, n_letters, n_digits, reduction = 0) {
    letters <- do.call(paste0, replicate(
                        n_letters, sample(LETTERS, n, TRUE), FALSE))
    max_number <- as.numeric(paste(replicate(n_digits, 9),
                                    collapse = ""))
    format <- paste("%0", n_digits, "d", sep = "")
    digits <- sprintf(format, sample(max_number, n, TRUE))
    ids <- paste0(letters, digits)
    if (reduction > 0) {
        ids <- sample(ids[1:floor(reduction * length(ids))], n, TRUE)
    }
    return(ids)
}
```

Putting everything together

Now that we have done the hard work of creating all our simulation functions, we can just assemble them inside a general function that will use them to easily simulate the data for us. The first thing we note is that there are a lot of parameters that we need to control, and if we create a function signature that contains all of these parameters explicitly, we will be constraining ourselves by having a rigid signature that is hard to work with. We don't want to deal with these parameters by hand because it will make it cumbersome to work with the code. What if we could pass a single parameter that would mutate for us as we require? Well, we can do that! Parameter objects exist for this reason. They are a simple concept to grasp and provide a lot of flexibility. They are lists that are packed before being sent to the function and are unpacked inside the function to be used as needed inside nested functions. This is a form of *encapsulation*. We will look deeper into encapsulation in Chapter 8, *Object-Oriented System to Track Cryptocurrencies*.

Next, we note that since these simulations are stochastic processes, meaning we may get different results every time we execute them, we may lose the reproducibility of our results. To avoid this, we simply set the seed at the beginning of the simulations to make sure we get the same results every time, just as we did in Chapter 3, *Predicting Votes with Linear Models*.

The rest of the code is simply calling the functions we have already created with the appropriate arguments, which come from the parameters object we unpack at the beginning. There are three things worth noting. First, we can't simply use the random_composition() function directly into one of the variables in the data frame we create because the resulting object contains data for three different variables in the data frame. Therefore we need to store an intermediate object with the results, composition, and then use it to extract the information for each macronutrient. Second, we use the stringsAsFactors argument of the data.frame() function as FALSE to make sure that SALE_ID and CLIENT_ID are not treated as factors (since they are strings). When factors start having many categories inside, processing data frames becomes slower, and we can avoid that by treating them as simple strings since we will have lots of unique identifiers. Third, since we are treating all strings as non-factors and we may not get all of the possible categories in our sample when using random_levels() the factor variable may be defined without some of the factors we previously specified. To make sure this doesn't happen we explicitly define the levels inside the factor() function to be the levels in the original sales data frame sent to the function which contains the data from our initial definition:

```
random_sales_data <- function(sales, parameters) {
    n <- parameters[["n"]]
    n_letters <- parameters[["n_letters"]]
    n_digits <- parameters[["n_digits"]]
    reduction <- parameters[["reduction"]]
    date_start <- parameters[["date_start"]]
    date_end <- parameters[["date_end"]]
    quantity_lambda <- parameters[["quantity_lambda"]]
    price_mean <- parameters[["price_mean"]]
    price_variance <- parameters[["price_variance"]]
    cost_mean <- parameters[["cost_mean"]]
    cost_variance <- parameters[["cost_variance"]]
    discount_lambda <- parameters[["discount_lambda"]]
    protein_source_pbs <- parameters[["protein_source_probabilities"]]
    continent_pbs <- parameters[["continent_probabilities"]]
    delivery_pbs <- parameters[["deliver_probabilities"]]
    status_pbs <- parameters[["status_probabilities"]]
    paid_pbs <- parameters[["paid_probabilities"]]
    set.seed(12345)

    composition = random_composition(n)
```

```
    sales <- data.frame(
        SALE_ID = random_strings(n, n_letters, n_digits),
        CLIENT_ID = random_strings(n, n_letters, n_digits, reduction),
        DATE = random_dates_in_range(n, date_start, date_end),
        QUANTITY = random_quantities(n, quantity_lambda),
        COST = random_values(n, cost_mean, cost_variance),
        PRICE = random_values(n, price_mean, price_variance),
        DISCOUNT = random_discounts(n, discount_lambda),
        PROTEIN = composition$PROTEIN,
        CARBS = composition$CARBS,
        FAT = composition$FAT,
        PROTEIN_SOURCE = factor(
            random_levels(n,
                          levels(sales$PROTEIN_SOURCE),
                          protein_source_pbs),
            levels = levels(sales$PROTEIN_SOURCE)
        ),
        CONTINENT = factor(
            random_levels(n, levels(sales$CONTINENT), continent_pbs),
            levels = levels(sales$CONTINENT)
        ),
        DELIVERY = factor(
            random_levels(n, levels(sales$DELIVERY), delivery_pbs),
            levels = levels(sales$DELIVERY)
        ),
        STATUS = factor(
            random_levels(n, levels(sales$STATUS), status_pbs),
            levels = levels(sales$STATUS)
        ),
        PAID = factor(
            random_levels(n, levels(sales$PAID), paid_pbs),
            levels = levels(sales$PAID)
        ),
        stringsAsFactors = FALSE
    )
    sales <- skew_sales_data(sales)
    return(sales)
}
```

Finally, to create our simulation, we create the `parameters` object with the necessary information, and update our `sales` object using the `random_sales_data()` function. In this case we are going to simulate 10,000 sales orders between January 2015 (`date_start`) and today's date (`date_end`, using the `Sys.Date()` function to generate the date for today). We require our identifiers to have five letters (`n_letters`) followed by five digits (`n_digits`), and we want our `CLIENT_ID` to use only the first 25% of the generated identifiers to allow for repeated customers (`reduction`).

We want five foods per sales order on average (quantity_lambda), with production costs with a mean of 30 (cost_mean) and variance of 10 (cost_variance), and prices with a mean of 50 (price_mean) and a variance of 10 (price_variance). We also want discounts around 1 or 2 USD (discount_lambda; remember the transformation we did inside the corresponding function). Finally, we want the probabilities of PENDING, DELIVERED, RETURNED, and CANCELLED as STATUS to be 20%, 60%, 10%, and 10%, respectively. Similarly, we want the probabilities of an order being paid to be 90%:

```
parameters <- list(
    n = 10000,
    n_letters = 5,
    n_digits = 5,
    reduction = 0.25,
    date_start = as.Date("2015-01-01"),
    date_end = Sys.Date(),
    quantity_lambda = 2,
    cost_mean = 12,
    cost_variance = 1,
    price_mean = 15,
    price_variance = 2,
    discount_lambda = 100,
    protein_source_probabilities = c(0.6, 0.2, 0.1, 0.1),
    continent_probabilities = c(0.5, 0.3, 0.2),
    delivery_probabilities = c(0.7, 0.3),
    status_probabilities = c(0.2, 0.6, 0.1, 0.1),
    paid_probabilities = c(0.9, 0.1)
)
sales <- random_sales_data(sales, parameters)
```

You can have fun with these parameters and simulate many different kinds of scenarios. For example, if you want to simulate a company that has been doing very badly with thin margins or even losses, you can bring the means of costs and prices together, and maybe even increase their respective variances to make sure there are a lot of crossovers, meaning losses per sale order.

Congratulations! You now know how to produce non-trivial data simulations. With this knowledge, you can have a lot of fun simulating many kinds of data. We encourage you to expand this example and play around with its analysis using the knowledge from the following chapters.

Simulating the client data

Now that we have gone through the sales data simulation and we have the necessary fundamentals, the rest of the data simulation will be much easier. Furthermore, we will use many of the functions we created before to simulate the client and client messages data, which is great! Reusing functions like this is very efficient, and over time you will get into the habit of doing so. You will build your own collection of reusable code, which will make you increasingly more efficient when programming.

We start by defining the data frame we will use, just as we did before. In this case we will have the CLIENT_ID, BIRTH_DATE, CLIENT_SINCE, GENDER, and STARS variables. The STARS represent a rating between 1 (bad) and 5 (excellent):

```
gender_levels <- c("FEMALE", "MALE")
star_levels <- c("1", "2", "3", "4", "5")

clients <- data.frame(
    CLIENT_ID = character(),
    BIRTH_DATE = as.Date(character()),
    CLIENT_SINCE = as.Date(character()),
    GENDER = factor(levels = gender_levels),
    STARS = factor(levels = star_levels)
)
```

The first thing we note is that the CLIENT_ID information should not be simulated again, because we will get different client identifiers from the ones we already have in the sales data. We want unique client identifiers in the sales data to correspond to a record in the client data, which we accomplish by sending them as the client_ids parameter and assigning them directly into the CLIENT_ID variable in the clients data frame. In this case, n will correspond to the number of unique client identifiers we get, which we get by using the length() function. The other parameters we extract as we normally would with parameter objects. Specifically, we need the range of dates which are valid for our client's birth dates (they must be at least 18 years old), as well as the valid range of dates since they were clients (they couldn't have been a client before the company started operations in January 2015; see the parameters for the sales data simulation). The rest of the code is very similar to what we saw in the sales data simulation, so we won't explain it again. To understand this, let's have a look at the following code:

```
random_clients_data <- function(clients, client_ids, parameters) {
    n <- length(client_ids)
    bd_start <- parameters[["birth_date_start"]]
    bd_end <- parameters[["birth_date_end"]]
    cs_start <- parameters[["client_since_start"]]
    cs_end <- parameters[["client_since_end"]]
```

```
stars_pbs <- parameters[["stars_probabilities"]]
set.seed(12345)

clients <- data.frame(
    CLIENT_ID = client_ids,
    BIRTH_DATE = random_dates_in_range(n, bd_start, bd_end, TRUE),
    CLIENT_SINCE = random_dates_in_range(n, cs_start, cs_end, TRUE),
    GENDER = factor(
        random_levels(n, levels(clients$GENDER)),
        levels = levels(clients$GENDER)
    ),
    STARS = factor(
        random_levels(n, levels(clients$STARS), stars_pbs),
        levels = levels(clients$STARS)
    ),
    stringsAsFactors = FALSE
)
    return(clients)
}
```

To simulate the client data, we simply create the corresponding parameters inside the parameters object and send that to the `random_clients_data()` function to update the `clients` data frame:

```
parameters <- list(
    birth_date_start = as.Date("1950-01-01"),
    birth_date_end = as.Date("1997-01-01"),
    client_since_start = as.Date("2015-01-01"),
    client_since_end = Sys.Date(),
    stars_probabilities = c(0.05, 0.1, 0.15, 0.2, 0.5)
)

clients <- random_clients_data(clients,
                                unique(sales$CLIENT_ID),
                                parameters)
```

Did you notice how easy this was? This is because we created our fundamentals in the previous section, and they drastically simplified following applications of the same concepts. As you increase your programming skills, this will happen more often.

Simulating the client messages data

Simulating text messages that actually make sense is very hard, and we won't attempt it here. Instead, what we'll do is leverage a dataset that was published about food reviews on Amazon. The dataset was published as part of the paper published by McAuley and Leskovec, *From amateurs to connoisseurs: modeling the evolution of user expertise through online reviews, 2013*. You can find the dataset in Kaggle (`https://www.kaggle.com/snap/amazon-fine-food-reviews`). We won't show the code that prepared the data for this example, but basically, what it does is rename the variables we want `STARS`, `SUMMARY`, and `MESSAGE`, delete the rest, and save the data frame into the `reviews.csv` file. For the interested reader, the code that accomplishes this task, as well as the original and processed data, is inside the code repository for this book (`https://github.com/PacktPublishing/R-Programming-By-Example`).

The idea is that since it's hard to simulate this data, we will leverage an already existing dataset with real reviews and sample it to get the messages we want for our example. As before, we start by defining the `client_messages` data frame we will use with the `SALE_ID`, `DATE`, `STARS`, `SUMMARY`, and `MESSAGE` variables as shown in the following code:

```
client_messages <- data.frame(
    SALE_ID = character(),
    DATE = as.Date(character()),
    STARS = factor(levels = star_levels),
    SUMMARY = character(),
    MESSAGE = character(),
    LAT = numeric(),
    LNG = numeric()
)
```

As we have done before, in our `random_client_messages_data()` function, we first unpack the parameter object and set the seed. The next step is to actually retrieve the reviews sample we want with the `random_reviews()` function we will create next. Assuming we have the reviews data ready, we create the `client_messages` data frame by taking a random sample from the `sale_ids` from the sales data so that we can generate a connection among messages and sales orders, and we do so in a way that we can generate various messages for a single sales order, since we use the `replace` argument as `TRUE`. The other parts of the code are similar to what we have seen before. Let's have a look at the following code:

```
random_client_messages_data <- function(client_messages, sales, parameters)
{
    n <- parameters[["n"]]
    date_start <- parameters[["date_start"]]
```

```
        date_end <- parameters[["date_end"]]
        reviews_file <- parameters[["reviews_file"]]
        locations <- parameters[["locations"]]

        set.seed(12345)

        reviews <- random_reviews(n, reviews_file)

        client_messages <- data.frame(
            SALE_ID = sample(unique(sales$SALE_ID), n, TRUE),
            DATE = random_dates_in_range(n, date_start, date_end),
            STARS = factor(reviews$STARS,
                            levels = levels(client_messages$STARS)),
            SUMMARY = reviews$SUMMARY,
            MESSAGE = reviews$MESSAGE,
            LAT = numeric(n),
            LNG = numeric(n),
            stringsAsFactors = FALSE
        )
        client_messages <- add_coordinates(client_messages,
                                            sales,
                                            locations)
        return(client_messages)
    }
```

The `random_reviews()` function takes the CSV file path as an argument in `reviews_file` and uses it to load the data into the `reviews` object. Then it takes a sample of the row indexes without replacement, because we don't want to use the same review twice, and we have enough reviews to make sure that doesn't happen (there are over 5,00,000 reviews in the data). We simply return this subset of the data frame back to be used in the final `client_messages` data frame:

```
    random_reviews <- function(n, reviews_file) {
        reviews <- readRDS(reviews_file)
        return(reviews[sample(1:nrow(reviews), n, FALSE), ])
    }
```

Finally, we create the parameters object with the necessary information, and pass it along to the `random_client_messages_data()` to update the `client_messages` data frame with the simulated data. Make sure you change the `reviews_file` path to the one appropriate for your setup (`./` means that it's in the same directory). Let's have a look at the following code:

```
    parameters <- list(
        n = 1000,
        date_start = as.Date("2015-01-01"),
```

```
        date_end = Sys.Date(),
        reviews_file = "./reviews/data/reviews.rds",
        locations = list(
            "AMERICA" = list(
                list(LAT = 35.982915, LNG = -119.028006),
                list(LAT = 29.023053, LNG = -81.762383),
                list(LAT = 41.726658, LNG = -74.731133),
                list(LAT = 19.256493, LNG = -99.292577),
                list(LAT = -22.472499, LNG = -43.348329)
            ),
            "EUROPE" = list(
                list(LAT = 40.436888, LNG = -3.863850),
                list(LAT = 48.716026, LNG = 2.350955),
                list(LAT = 52.348010, LNG = 13.351161),
                list(LAT = 42.025875, LNG = 12.418940),
                list(LAT = 51.504122, LNG = -0.364277)
            ),
            "ASIA" = list(
                list(LAT = 31.074426, LNG = 121.125328),
                list(LAT = 22.535733, LNG = 113.830406),
                list(LAT = 37.618251, LNG = 127.135865),
                list(LAT = 35.713791, LNG = 139.489820),
                list(LAT = 19.134907, LNG = 73.000993)
            )
        )
    )
)
client_messages <- random_client_messages_data(client_messages, sales,
parameters)
```

We're done! Now we should have a full simulation for sales data, as well as data for clients and their messages for their respective sales orders. Not every sales order will have a message, and some of them may have more than one, and this is by design. Remember that the reviews we used for the example are not necessarily for foods, but the idea was to show how these techniques can be used to simulate new data using already existing datasets.

A look at the three datasets we have simulated should put a smile on our face. Note that we omit the client_messages data because it was too large to be shown here, but you should see it just fine on your computer:

```
head(sales)
#>       SALE_ID   CLIENT_ID       DATE QUANTITY   COST PRICE DISCOUNT
PROTEIN
#> 1 OKRLL75596 EAWPJ80001 2015-01-27        3 27.58 50.79        1
0.12422681
#> 2 ZVTFG64065 WQGVB74605 2015-05-26        7 30.78 51.09        3
0.11387543
#> 3 SPRZD12587 XVRAM64230 2017-01-07        8 33.66 54.46        1
```

```
                 0.54351904
#> 4 YGOLB67346 PDVDC58438 2015-01-12          5 34.85 53.06          1
                 0.49077566
#> 5 CDQRA43926 VJCXI94728 2017-06-21          9 27.35 50.57          0
                 0.01026306
#>
#>       CARBS       FAT PROTEIN_SOURCE    STORE    DELIVERY    STATUS PAID
#> 1 0.1548693 0.72090390        CHICKEN STORE 4    IN STORE DELIVERED  YES
#> 2 0.1251422 0.76098233        CHICKEN STORE 3 TO LOCATION DELIVERED  YES
#> 3 0.2901092 0.16637179     VEGETARIAN STORE 1 TO LOCATION   PENDING  YES
#> 4 0.1841289 0.32509539        CHICKEN STORE 2 TO LOCATION DELIVERED  YES
#> 5 0.2620317 0.72770525     VEGETARIAN STORE 1 TO LOCATION DELIVERED  YES
(Truncated output)

head(clients)
#>    CLIENT_ID BIRTH_DATE CLIENT_SINCE GENDER STARS
#> 1 EAWPJ80001 1974-09-04   2015-05-21   MALE     4
#> 2 WQGVB74605 1987-01-24   2015-12-05 FEMALE     2
#> 3 XVRAM64230 1977-11-18   2017-06-26 FEMALE     2
#> 4 PDVDC58438 1987-11-23   2015-12-20   MALE     2
#> 5 VJCXI94728 1953-07-09   2016-05-03 FEMALE     3
(Truncated output)
```

Working with relational databases

Now that we have the data we need for the rest of the example, we're going to learn how to work with it using databases. In this section, we will learn how to save our data into a relational database, as well as how to read it back. We won't go too deep into advanced operations or workflows. We will only look into the basics, and this section may be skipped if you are not interested in this topic. It's not critical to know this to reproduce the rest of the example in the following chapters.

The first thing we must do is install the RMySQL package. There are various packages for working with databases, and they work almost the same. We chose the RMySQL package because it's designed for the MySQL database, which is very popular and easy to work with in almost all operating systems. To be able to reproduce this code, you will need a MySQL database set up properly in your computer, and we won't go into the details of how to do so here. You can find many good resources online. From this point on, we'll assume you have your database ready:

```
install.packages("RMySQL")
```

The first thing we need to do to work with databases is to connect and disconnect from them. To do so, we use the dbConnect() and dbDisconnect() functions. The dbConnect() function returns an object that contains the connection to the database, and which must be used in all following actions regarding the database. We will call this object db to remind us that it represents the database we're working with:

```
db <- dbConnect(MySQL(), user = <YOUR_USER>, password = <YOUR_PASSWORD>,
host = "localhost")
dbDisconnect(db)
#> [1] TRUE
```

If you're using a database that is not operating on the same computer you're using R from, then you can use the corresponding IP address in the host parameters as you normally would with any SQL remote connection. There's a fifth parameter that we need to use when we know the name of the database we're connecting (a single MySQL server can have multiple databases inside). When you see the TRUE value after trying to disconnect from the database, it means that everything executed correctly.

To send a query into the database server, we use the dbSendQuery() function after having connected to it again. We create the fresh sales database (which will contain our sales, clients, and client_messages tables) in our MySQL server by executing:

```
dbSendQuery(db, "DROP DATABASE IF EXISTS sales;")
dbSendQuery(db, "CREATE DATABSE sales;")
```

Since MySQL syntax requires ";" at the end of each query, depending on your setup, you may get an error if you don't put them in. Now we will disconnect and reconnect to the server, but this time, we will specify which particular database we want to work with (the sales database we just created):

```
dbDisconnect(db)
db <- dbConnect(
    MySQL(),
    user = <YOUR_USER>,
    password = <YOUR_PASSWORD>,
    host = "localhost",
    dbname = "sales"
)
```

Now we're going to write the data we simulated into the MySQL server. To do so, we use the `dbWriteTable()` function. The first argument is the database connection object, the second argument is the name of the table we want to store the data in, the third argument is the data frame that contains the data we want to store, and the fourth argument, as the name suggests, will overwrite (as opposed to append) any data already present in the database.

To read a full table from the MySQL server into R, we use the `dbReadTable()` function. However, note that when we do, any information regarding factors is lost, and the data frame only knows it contains strings, which is the way the data is stored within the MySQL server. To verify this, you can look into the structure of the data being read from the MySQL server with the `str()` function. We won't show the output here to preserve space, but you will find that `sales` does have the factor information, while `sales_from_db` does not:

```
sales_from_db <- dbReadTable(db, "sales")
str(sales)
str(sales_from_db)
```

Not fixing this metadata problem about the factor variables will have implications when we create our visualizations in the next chapter. We can deal with it now or later, but since this chapter is about working with data, we will show how to do so here. First, we will create the `read_table()` function that will wrap the `dbReadTable()` function. This `read_table()` function will check which table is being read and apply the appropriate metadata by calling `add_sales_metadata()`, `add_clients_metadata()`, or `add_client_messages_metadata()`. Note that if the table being read is not one of those three, we will not know what metadata to add for now, so we will just return the table directly:

```
read_table <- function(db, table) {
    data <- dbReadTable(db, table)
    if (table == "sales") {
        return(add_sales_metadata(data))
    } else if (table == "clients") {
        return(add_clients_metadata(data))
    } else if (table == "client_messages") {
        return(add_client_messages_metadata(data))
    } else {
        return(data)
    }
}
```

The way we add metadata to each case is by redefining the factor variables as we did before, as well as transforming the date objects, which are also received as strings. We don't have to change anything else in the data:

```
add_sales_metadata <- function(data) {
    status_levels <- c("PENDING", "DELIVERED", "RETURNED", "CANCELLED")
    protein_source_levels <- c("BEEF", "FISH", "CHICKEN", "VEGETARIAN")
    continent_levels <- c("AMERICA", "EUROPE", "ASIA")
    delivery_levels <- c("IN STORE", "TO LOCATION")
    paid_levels <- c("YES", "NO")
    data$DATE <- as.Date(data$DATE)
    data$PROTEIN_SOURCE <-
    factor(data$PROTEIN_SOURCE, levels = protein_source_levels)

    data$CONTINENT <- factor(data$CONTINENT, levels = continent_levels)
    data$DELIVERY <- factor(data$DELIVERY, levels = delivery_levels)
    data$STATUS <- factor(data$STATUS, levels = status_levels)
    data$PAID <- factor(data$PAID, levels = paid_levels)
    return(data)
}

add_clients_metadata <- function(data) {
    gender_levels <- c("FEMALE", "MALE")
    star_levels <- c("1", "2", "3", "4", "5")
    data$BIRTH_DATE <- as.Date(data$BIRTH_DATE)
    data$CLIENT_SINCE <- as.Date(data$CLIENT_SINCE)
    data$GENDER <- factor(data$GENDER, levels = gender_levels)
    data$STARS <- factor(data$STARS, levels = star_levels)
    return(data)
}

add_client_messages_metadata <- function(data) {
    star_levels <- c("1", "2", "3", "4", "5")
    data$DATE <- as.Date(data$DATE)
    data$STARS <- factor(data$STARS, levels = star_levels)
    return(data)
}
```

Now we can see that both `sales` and `sales_from_db` contain the same metadata. Again, we don't show the output to preserve space, but you'll see that the factor metadata is now preserved when reading from the MySQL server:

```
sales_from_db <- read_table(db, "sales")
str(sales)
str(sales_from_db)
```

Since they have the same data and metadata, it's now safe to completely read the data from the MySQL server whenever we need to work with this data. Just remember to use the `read_table()` function instead of the `dbReadTable()` function.

Reading full tables from the MySQL server with the `dbReadTable()` is only practical when the tables are not too large. If you're working with a database in a real problem, that's probably not the case. If the data you're trying to read is too large, use a combination of the `dbSendQuery()` and `fetch()` functions.

If you want to know what data type will be used in the MySQL server to store the data you're sending, you can use the `dbDataType()` function with the `MySQL()` argument, as well as the data type whose server type you want to find out:

```
dbDataType(MySQL(), "a")
#> [1] "text"
dbDataType(MySQL(), 1.5)
#> [1] "double"
```

Finally, you may use the `dbListTables()` and `dbListFields()` functions to find out the tables available in the database and the fields available for a specific table, respectively. If you followed the example this far, you should see the following:

```
dbListTables(db)
#> [1] "client_messages" "clients" "sales"

dbListFields(db, "sales")
#>    [1] "row_names"     "SALE_ID"      "CLIENT_ID"    "DATE"
#>    [5] "QUANTITY"      "COST"         "PRICE"        "DISCOUNT"
#>    [9] "PROTEIN"       "CARBS"        "FAT"          "PROTEIN_SOURCE"
#>   [13] "STORE"         "DELIVERY"     "STATUS"       "PAID"

dbListFields(db, "clients")
#> [1] "row_names"     "CLIENT_ID"    "BIRTH_DATE"    "CLIENT_SINCE"
"GENDER"
#> [6] "STARS"

dbListFields(db, "client_messages")
#> [1] "row_names" "SALE_ID"    "DATE"      "STARS"     "SUMMARY"
"MESSAGE"
```

Note that you see the `row.names` field because it's necessary for MySQL functionality, but when you actually read the data from the database, you won't get that field. You will get all other fields shown (the ones in capital letters).

These are the basics of working with a MySQL server using R. For the interested reader, a good, concise resource that showcases many other RMySQL features are Squared Academy's *RMySQL Tutorial for Beginners, 2016* slides (`https://www.slideshare.net/RsquaredIn/rmysql-tutorial-for-beginners`).

Summary

In this chapter, we established the fundamentals of the food sales example by presenting the general scenario for The Food Factory: what they do, what they want to accomplish, and, most importantly, how to simulate the data we will need for the rest of the example. We went over various techniques to simulate different kinds of data, like numbers, categories, strings, and dates. The approach we showed is flexible enough to allow you to simulate many different kinds of data in modular and incremental ways. We also showed how to allow flexibility for different assumptions about the simulation to easily take place by using parameter objects. We learned how to create functions that are useful for different scenarios, and how to mix our simulated data with data coming from external sources. Finally, we learned how to work with external MySQL databases.

We are ready to take on the analysis part of the example. In the next chapter, Chapter 5, *Communicating Sales with Visualization*, we will use the data we just simulated to create many visualizations that will allow us to get a good idea of the current status of The Food Factory, as well as its areas for improvement.

5
Communicating Sales with Visualizations

In this chapter, we will explore a very important and useful aspect of data analysis, data visualization. We will show how to create graph functions, which are the functions that encapsulate the process of creating a graph and output a graph object that can be seen or saved to disk. Working with graphs this way increases efficiency, adds flexibility, and provides repeatable processes.

The types of graphs we will create during this chapter include bar graphs, boxplots, scatter plots with marginal distributions, radar graphs, 3D interactive scatter plots, time-series graphs, static and interactive maps, and a cool globe visualization. The chapter will show the fundamentals you need to create a great variety of high-quality graphs.

Some of the important topics covered in this chapter are as follows:

- Working efficiently with graph functions and graph objects
- Working with important graphing packages such as `ggplot2` and `leaflet`
- Data transformations to accommodate different visualizations
- Graph generalization through variable parameterization
- Increasing dimensions shown with colors and shapes
- Extending `ggplot2` with custom graph types
- Numerical data exploration with interactive graphs
- Geographical data exploration with interactive maps

Required packages

During this chapter we will make use of the following R packages. If you don't already have them installed, you can look into `Appendix`, *Required Packages* for instructions on how do so. These packages will fall in one of two categories: packages for creating graphs and packages for working with data. Some of the packages used for interactive graphs (graphs that are not static, meaning you can *move them around* in your screen to see different angles of the data) will require system dependencies to work (for example, `rgl` and `rgdal`), and others will work through your web browser (for example, `threejs`, `leaflet`, and `plotly`). They have been tested using Google Chrome as a web browser. If you encounter any problems with your particular web browser, try using Google Chrome. The *static* graphics will be created using `ggplot2` and some packages that extend it (for example, `viridis` and `ggExtra`).

Package	Reason
ggplot2	High-quality graphs
viridis	Color palette for graphs
ggExtra	Graphs with marginal distributions
threejs	Interactive globe
leaflet	Interactive high-quality maps
plotly	Interactive high-quality graphs
rgl	Interactive 3D graphs
rgdal	Manipulating geographic data
tidyr	Manipulating data

Extending our data with profit metrics

As mentioned earlier, our objective for this chapter is to diagnose the current state of business and find new opportunities. To start with, we will look at three business metrics from different angles. The metrics are number of sales, profits, and profit ratios. They tell us how much The Food Factory is selling in quantity, how much it's earning in money (profit), and where it's growth opportunities are (profit ratio). Keep in mind that this is not a professional financial assessment and, as always, the focus is on the programming techniques not the actual results from the analysis.

The first thing we need to do is add to each sale its corresponding profits and profit ratio. We assume that the only way we can count a profit is if the sale order has been delivered and has been paid. Otherwise, we'll state the profit and profit ratio as zero. If the sale qualifies for a profit, then the profit calculation is *PROFIT = PRICE - COST - DISCOUNT*. Note that this allows for sales that are not profitable (The Food Factory loses money) if the *COST + DISCOUNT > PRICE*. If there's a profit, then the profit ratio is *PROFIT / COST*. What we just described is programmed inside the `add_profits()` function:

```
add_profits <- function(data) {
    unprofitable <- c("RETURNED", "CANCELLED", "PENDING")
    data$PROFIT <- data$PRICE - data$COST - data$DISCOUNT
    data$PROFIT[data$STATUS %in% unprofitable] <- 0
    data$PROFIT[data$PAID == "NO"] <- 0
    data$PROFIT_RATIO <- data$PROFIT / data$COST
    return(data)
}
```

After defining the `add_profit()` function, we simply apply it to our sales data as follows:

```
sales <- add_profits(sales)
```

Building blocks for reusable high-quality graphs

To diagnose the business state and find new opportunities, in this chapter, we will use various types of graphs. When it comes to developing static high-quality graphs, you can't go wrong with the `ggplot2` package. Standard (built-in) graphs in R are fine for exploratory purposes, but are not as flexible or nice-looking as `ggplot2` graphs. Since we want to show how to create high-quality graphs, we will focus on using this package (and others extending it) for static graphs. However, since the vanilla `ggplot2` package only works for static graphs, we will use other packages for high-quality interactive graphs.

A downside of having so much flexibility when using `ggplot2` is that it's very verbose, thus requiring a lot of code to create graphs (specially when compared to standard R built-in graphing functions). We want to avoid having to copy-paste code if we are going to create similar graphs, so we will develop reusable functions that we can use to easily create similar graphs. For example, we could do something like the following instead of repeating more than 10 lines of `ggplot2` code to only make a few small changes:

```
graph_1 <- a_function_that_returns_a_graph_object(
    data_1, other_parameters_1)
```

```
print(graph_1)

graph_2 <- a_function_that_returns_a_graph_object(
    data_2, other_parameters_2)
print(graph_2)
```

Sometimes, people are not comfortable working this way, but these graphing functions are just the same as any other kind of function. The only difference is that, whenever we can, we will return a graph object instead of other data types. These graph objects are a nice feature when working with ggplot2 because they can't be passed to other functions (not all graphing packages are designed this way). For example, while writing this book, we used the following save_png() function, which takes a graph object and saves it to disk. All we needed it to do was to optionally change a graph's dimensions when we saved it to make sure that it's the right size:

```
save_png <- function(graph, save_to, width = 480, height = 480) {
    png(save_to, width = width, height = height)
    print(graph)
    dev.off()
}
```

 If you're working with lots of graphs, if you get an error while creating one of them and you print it, you may be confused to see a previous graph you were working on. To avoid this confusion, you may execute graph <- NULL after every print or save function call to make sure that it's evident where the error occurred.

Now if you want to create a graph and save it into a 1024x768 pixels image, you can use the save_png() function as follows:

```
graph < a_function_that_returns_a_graph_object(data, parameters)
save_png(graph, 1024, 768)
```

The standard way of developing analyzing data is an iterative process closely related to the scientific method. However, we will only focus on the code that generates the graphs during this chapter. We will interpret the results in Chapter 7, *Developing Automatic Presentations*. We think this helps focus on each topic adequately in it's corresponding chapter.

Starting with simple applications for bar graphs

We will start with simple graphs and build our way up towards advanced graphs. The first graph we will create is a bar graph. We will plot a frequency table that shows how many sale orders we have for each QUANTITY number in our sales. To do so, we use the ggplot() function using sales as the data and setting up the aesthetics with the aes() function with QUANTITY in the *x* axis (the first argument).

After we create a graph base with the ggplot() function, we add layers for different objects we want to see in the graph (for example, bars, lines, and points). In this case, we add bars with the geom_bar() function. Note how this layer is added using the + (plus) sign to the graph base. After that, we add another layer for the title with ggtitle(). Finally, we add an *x* axis specification with the scale_x_continuous() function that will allow us to see a number for each bar in the graph. If you don't add this layer, your graph may not show a number for each bar, which may be a little confusing. The way we specify it is by sending a sequence of numbers that should be used as the breaks (where tick data is shown). Since the numbers in the data may vary with different simulations, we make sure that we use the correct numbers by creating a sequence with the seq() function from the minimum number in the QUANTITY variable to the maximum. This will automatically show the correct numbers even if the QUANTITY variable has vastly different ranges.

These may seem like a lot of code to build a simple graph. However, it's precisely the amount of code that allows us to be very specific about what we want to see in the graph as you'll see in the following examples. Also, note that only the ggplot() (with its corresponding aes() function) and geom_bar() functions are required to actually produce the graph. The ggtitle() and scale_x_continuous() functions are only there to improve the graph:

```
graph <- ggplot(sales, aes(QUANTITY)) +
    geom_bar() +
    ggtitle("QUANTITY Frequency") +
    scale_x_continuous(
        breaks = seq(min(sales[, "QUANTITY"]),
        max(sales[, "QUANTITY"]))
    )
```

The following graph shows the **QUANTITY frequency** for the preceding code:

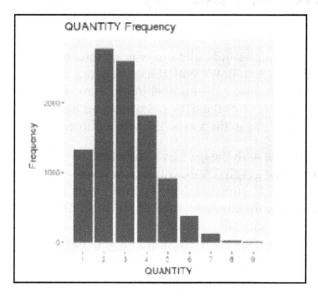

QUANTITY Frequency

Since we will be creating lots of bar graphs, we want to avoid having to copy-paste the code we just wrote, and not only that, but also make it more flexible. To accomplish this, we will generalize our code by parameterizing it and considering different scenarios we should cover.

So, what may we want our custom `graph_bars()` function to allow us to do? To start with, we may want to specify different variables for our *x* axis and *y* axis. To do this, we need to understand how the `geom_bar()` function works internally. If you look back at the code, we never specified the variable for the *y* axis, and `ggplot()` automatically used the number of times a `QUANTITY` number appeared in the data (the frequency).

What if we want to use the PROFIT value for each sale as the variable for the *y* axis? In that case, we need to realize that we have more than 2,000 potentially different values as PROFIT when QUANTITY is two or three, and less so in the other cases. We need to aggregate those PROFIT values somehow before we can use PROFIT in the *y* axis.

Any function that can reduce the PROFIT values into a single value for all the transactions, for each value of QUANTITY, could be used to aggregate the data. However, the most common choices are using the mean or the sum. The mean would show a graph where we see the average PROFIT for each QUANTITY value. The sum would show us the total PROFIT for each QUANTITY value. The same would apply if we want to use PROFIT_RATIO (or any other numerical variable) in the *y* axis. The most intuitive choices are using sum for PROFIT (total profit) and mean for PROFIT_RATIO (average profit ratio), so we will use those.

For the *x* axis, we may have categorical, numerical, or date variables. For this particular case, the default *x* axis options are fine for categorical and date variables, but we still want to see all the numbers in the ticks when working with numerical variables. This means that we need to provide a check for the type of variable in the *x* axis, and if it's numerical, then we need to do the proper adjustment (the same adjustment we saw in the previous code).

What we have explained before is what is programmed in our graph_bars() function. It receives as parameters the data and the *x* axis and *y* axis variables. First, it checks whether or not we specified a particular *y* axis variable. We use the "NULL check" technique mentioned in Chapter 1, *Introduction to R*. If we don't receive a *y* axis variable, then we create a bar graph as we did earlier (using the frequency of the *x* axis variable by default), and we create the corresponding title using the paste() function. If we do get a variable for the *y* axis (meaning that we are in the else block), then we need to find out what type of aggregation we need to do, and we do so using our get_aggregation() function, which returns the sum as the aggregation method if we are asked to graph the PROFIT variable in the *y* axis, and returns the mean in any other case. We then use this function name as the value for the fun.y parameter (which is read as *function for* y), and specify that we are working with a summary function (when you don't need aggregation for a variable you should send the stat = 'identity' parameter to the geom_bar() function and avoid sending it to the fun.y parameter). Then we specify the title of the graph as needed. After the if else block, we check if the variable type for the *x* axis is numeric, and if it is we apply the interval names transformation:

```
graph_bars <- function(data, x, y = NULL) {
    if (is.null(y)) {
        graph <- ggplot(data, aes_string(x)) +
            geom_bar() +
            ggtitle(paste(x, "Frequency")) +
```

```
            ylab("Frequency")
    } else {
        aggregation <- get_aggregation(y)
            graph <- ggplot(data, aes_string(x, y)) +
            geom_bar(fun.y = aggregation, stat = "summary") +
            ggtitle(paste(y, "by", x))
    }
    if (class(data[, x]) == "numeric") {
        graph <- graph +
            scale_x_continuous(
                breaks = seq(min(data[, x]), max(data[, x])))
    }
    return(graph)
}
```

When working with this special-case function, we recommend that you put the special case in the `if` part of the check to make sure that you only catch the special cases we're looking for, and return the generic case otherwise. If you do this the other way around (checking for generic cases first) you'll undoubtedly encounter some tricky bugs:

```
get_aggregation <- function(y) {
    if (y == "PROFIT") {
        return("sum")
    }
    return("mean")
}
```

Now we can create many more bar graphs with our custom `graph_bars()` function:

```
graph_bars(sales, "CONTINENT")
graph_bars(sales, "CONTINENT", "PROFIT")
graph_bars(sales, "CONTINENT", "PROFIT_RATIO")

graph_bars(sales, "PROTEIN_SOURCE")
graph_bars(sales, "PROTEIN_SOURCE", "PROFIT")
graph_bars(sales, "PROTEIN_SOURCE", "PROFIT_RATIO")
```

All of the following graphs are shown together for easier visualization and space preservation, but you would get them one-by-one when executing the code yourself.

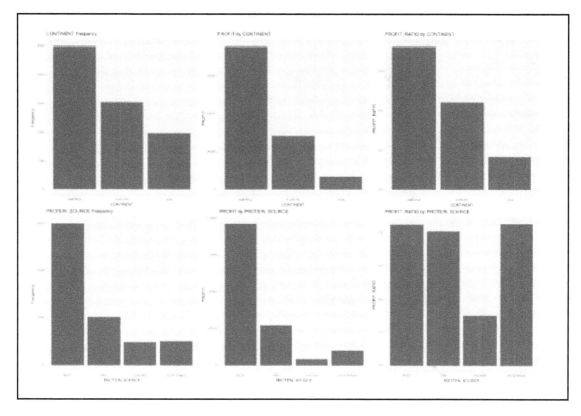

Bar graphs

Adding a third dimension with colors

As often happens, we want to work on some code we had already created to add more features. In this case, we want to add a third dimension to the graphs using colors. We want to be able to specify a `color` variable that will be used to further divide the data in the graph.

To accomplish this, we add a `color` parameter to the function's signature using the "NULL check" pattern and we add the corresponding parameter in each case. Adding the parameter directly in the `aes_string()` function is not problematic in case of `NULL` because `NULL` values indicate to `ggplot()` we don't want to use a fill color for the graph.

However, note that we are not able to use the same technique with y . Instead, we check whether we should send y or not, and only send it to the ggplot () function if we have a non-NULL value. Also, we add the position = "dodge" parameter to the geom_bar () function so that we get unstacked bar graphs. If we don't send this parameter we would get stacked bar graphs, and for these particular graphs, we thought the unstacked version looked better. Feel free to try the stacked version yourself. Let's look at the following code:

```
graph_bars <- function(data, x, y = NULL, color = NULL) {
    if (is.null(y)) {
        graph <- ggplot(data, aes_string(x, fill = color)) +
            geom_bar(position = "dodge") +
            ggtitle(paste(x, "Frequency")) +
            ylab("Frequency")
    } else {
        aggregation <- get_aggregation(y)
        graph <- ggplot(data, aes_string(x, y, fill = color)) +
            geom_bar(
                fun.y = aggregation,
                stat = "summary", position = "dodge") +
                ggtitle(paste(y, "by", x)
            )
    }
    if (class(data[, x]) == "numeric") {
        graph <- graph +
            scale_x_continuous(
                breaks = seq(min(data[, x]),
                max(data[, x]))
            )
    }
    return(graph)
}
```

Note that now we have four different cases we may want to graph, first, when specify only the x value, second, when we specify the x and y values, third, when we specify the x and color values, fourth, when we specify all three of them. Since the ggplot () specification for each of those cases is unique, we can't collapse them into a lower number of cases. You should also note that we only keep inside the conditional blocks the code that is specific for a particular check, and bring out of the conditional block the code that is not specific to the check and should be applied to two cases every time. That's what we do with the ylab () and geom_bar () functions in the outer if block and with the get_aggregation () and geom_bar () functions in the outer else block. Otherwise, we would be repeating code unnecessarily, which is a very bad practice.

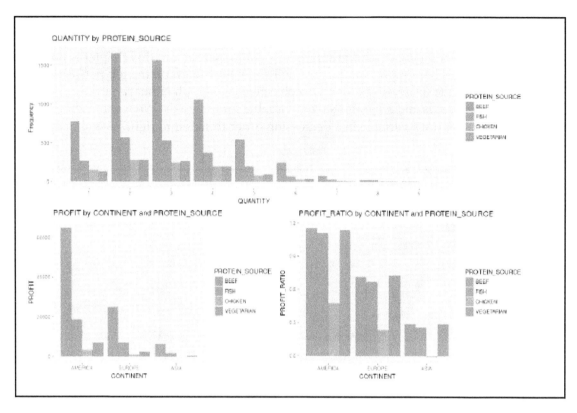

Bar graphs with colors

Now we can produce bar graphs that optionally receive a third parameter `color` (shown above), and if sent, it will be used to divide the data using colors. Note that in the first line of the following code, we need to explicitly send the `color` parameter. This is because we're omitting the `y` parameter from the function call, and if we are not explicit about the `color` parameter, it will be interpreted as being the `x` parameter. You can take a refresher on function calls in Chapter 1, *Introduction to R*:

```
graph_bars(sales, "QUANTITY", color = "PROTEIN_SOURCE")
graph_bars(sales, "CONTINENT", "PROFIT", "PROTEIN_SOURCE")
graph_bars(sales, "CONTINENT", "PROFIT_RATIO", "PROTEIN_SOURCE")
```

Graphing top performers with bar graphs

Bar graphs are one of the most used graphing tools in the world and this chapter is no exception. In our last bar graph example, we will show how to graph the top performers for a given variable in the decreasing order. Our objective is to graph either PROFIT or Frequency in the *y* axis and a parameterized variable for the *x* axis. We want to show the top n performers for the x variable in a decreasing order from left to right, as is shown in the graph below.

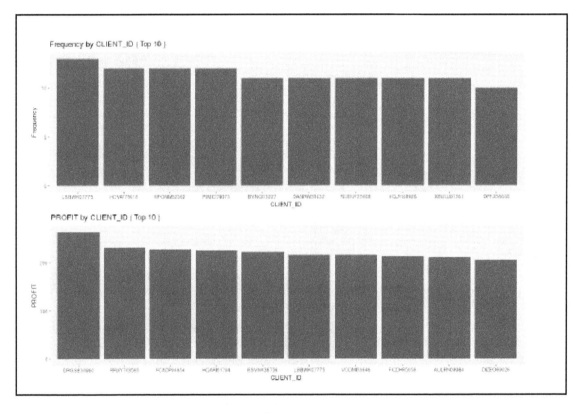

Top n bar graphs

To accomplish this, we receive as parameters the data (sales in this case), the variable that will be used for the *x* axis x, the number of top performers we want to show n, and whether we want to use PROFIT in the *y* axis or not (in which case we will use the Frequency) by using the Boolean by_profit.

The first thing we do is check for the `by_profit` parameter; if it's TRUE, then we aggregate the PROFIT data for each CLIENT_ID with the `aggregate()` function using the sum operator (we want the total profit by client, not the average profit by client). Then we order the results with the `order()` function. The minus sign (−) just before the `profit_by_client$x` value means that we want a decreasing order, and the x that follows `profit_by_client` is because the result of the `aggregate()` function is a data frame with Group.1 and x columns, which store the CLIENT_ID and the PROFIT sum, respectively.

Since we want to avoid unnecessary duplication of the code when we return the graph we want, we need to make sure that both cases in the `if else` block use the same names for the variables we will use in the `ggplot()` function. That's why we explicitly assign the x and `y_bar` names to the `top_df` data frame. If you looked inside the `top_df` object during execution, you would find that it has duplicated data with different column names. We could take care of this by removing the columns with the names we don't want, but it's unnecessary at this point since it's a throwaway object anyway. However, in certain situations this may be a performance issue we need to deal with, but not in this case.

In the case of the `else` block, conceptually we do the same thing. However, technically we implement differently. In this case, we create a table where each entry in the table is a unique CLIENT_ID value and the value for each entry is the number of times the CLIENT_ID appears in the data (Frequency), and we do so with the `table()` function. Then we sort these results in the decreasing order with the `sort()` function and take the top n results. Then we use these results to create the `top_df` data frame with the corresponding columns. Note that we need an auxiliary name `aux_name` for the x variable since we can't create a data frame by specifying a column name with a variable. What we do is then copy the data from the `aux_name` column to the actual name we need (contained in the x variable).

Finally, we create a graph and immediately return it without intermediate storage. The specifics on what each line is doing in that part of the code should be clear to you by this point, so we will avoid explaining that again.

Now you create *top n* graphs easily with the following code. We suggest that you try to create similar graphs for other categorical variables (for example, CONTINENT or PROTEIN_SOURCE). Note that the CLIENT_ID values in each case are different, meaning that the clients that buy the most from The Food Factory are not necessarily the clients that generate the most profit for it:

```
graph_top_n_bars(sales, "CLIENT_ID", 10)
graph_top_n_bars(sales, "CLIENT_ID", 10, TRUE)
```

We wanted to start simple and show the basic concepts of working with graph functions before we complicate things in the following sections.

Graphing disaggregated data with boxplots

Creating bar graphs is useful when presenting results to people who are not familiar with statistics, but the fact that bar graphs aggregate information (just as we did in the bar graphs for top performers) means that, in reality, we lose information due to the reduction. If you're working with people who understand what quartiles are, then boxplots may be a useful visualization. They are an easy way to see individual distributions for different levels of a variable.

Each box represents the first quartile at the bottom, the third quartile at the top, and the median on the line in the middle. The lines that extend vertically reach up to any observation within *1.5 * IQR*, where the **interquartile range (IQR)** is the distance between the first and third quartiles. Any observation beyond *1.5 * IQR* is treated as an outlier and is shown individually.

Our objective is to show the bar graph we created for top performers according to `PROFIT`, but in a disaggregated way. When using bar graphs, the difficulty comes from aggregating the data correctly, but since we don't need to aggregate data for boxplots, their creation is very simple.

Our `graph_top_n_boxplots()` function takes as parameters the `data` value, the variables for the *x* and *y* axis, the number of top performers to show as `n`, and optionally the line and fill colors, as `c` and `f`, respectively. If no colors are specified, a selection of blues is used. The color specification must be done either in a HEX notation (`https://en.wikipedia.org/wiki/Web_colors#Hex_triplet`) or with R color names (`http://sape.inf.usi.ch/quick-reference/ggplot2/colour`). We simply filter the data with our `filter_n_top()` function and use the `boxplot()` layer to produce the boxplots with the adequate colors. We also specify the title as the combination of the parameters received by the function:

```
graph_top_n_boxplots <-
    function(data, x, y, n, f = "#2196F3", c = "#0D47A1") {
    data <- filter_n_top(sales, n, x)
    return(
        ggplot(data, aes_string(x, y)) +
        geom_boxplot(fill = f, color = c) +
        ggtitle(paste(y, "by", x, "( Top", n, ")")))
    )
}
```

The `filter_n_top()` function receives as parameters the `data` value, the number of top performers we want to keep as `n`, and the identifier for the performers as `by`. First, we use the `aggregate()` function to aggregate the `PROFIT` variable by the chosen identifier (which is sent as a list, as is required by the function), and do the aggregation with the `sum` operator to get the total `PROFIT` per client. If we had used the `mean` operator, we would see a graph for the average `PROFIT` per client. Then we order the results, which are contained in the second column of the `aggr` object in decreasing order, and take the top `n` values from the first column, which contain the identifiers (the `CLIENT_ID` values in the example below). Finally, we keep only those observations in the data that correspond to the top identifiers we have in the `top` object.

```
filter_n_top <- function(data, n, by) {
    aggr <- aggregate(data$PROFIT, list(data[, by]), sum)
    top <- aggr[order(-aggr[, 2])[1:n], 1]
    data <- data[data[, by] %in% top, ]
    return(data)
}
```

Now we can easily replicate the bar graph we created in the previous section using boxplots.

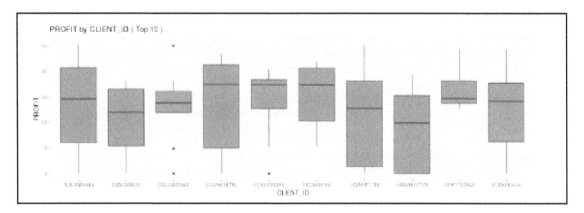

Top m boxplots

As you can see, we have more information shown in the graph, but we loose the ability to easily spot the total `PROFIT` value for each `CLIENT_ID`. Choosing the graph type depends on what information you're trying to communicate:

```
graph_top_n_boxplots(sales, "CLIENT_ID", "PROFIT", 10)
```

Scatter plots with joint and marginal distributions

We have seen how to create scatter plots with `ggplot()` in previous chapters. Therefore, in this section, we will only focus on the parts that we have not seen before. Our objective is to create scatter plots that not only show the scatter plot, but extend it by showing the marginal distributions on both axes. These are called **marginal plots** and are useful for understanding how data is jointly (two variables) as well as marginally (one variable) distributed.

Pricing and profitability by protein source and continent

As usual, we start developing our graph function. We receive as parameters the `data`, and the variables for the *x* axis (`x`) and *y* axis (`y`), and, in this case, we anticipate four cases that correspond to the combinations of including or not the `color` and `shape` variables for the graph. We do the standard checking and create the corresponding graph base. Here comes the different part, we call the `ggMarginal()` function of the `ggExtra` package with the graph object we want (in this case, the base graph plus the points layer), and specify the type of graph to be used for the marginal distributions. You can chose from `density`, `histogram`, and `boxplot`. We choose `histogram`:

```
graph_marginal_distributions <-
function(data, x, y, color = NULL, shape = NULL) {
    if (is.null(color)) {
        if (is.null(shape)) {
            graph <- ggplot(data, aes_string(x, y))
        } else {
            graph <- ggplot(data, aes_string(x, y, shape = shape))
        }
    } else {
        if (is.null(shape)) {
            graph <- ggplot(data, aes_string(x, y, color = color))
        } else {
            graph <- ggplot(data, aes_string(x, y,
                            color = color,
                            shape = shape))
        }
    }
    return(ggMarginal(graph + geom_point(), type = "histogram"))
}
```

Now we are able to easily create scatter plots with marginal distributions on the sides. In the first graph (left), we show the relation among PRICE, COST, PROTEIN_SOURCE, and CONTINENT.

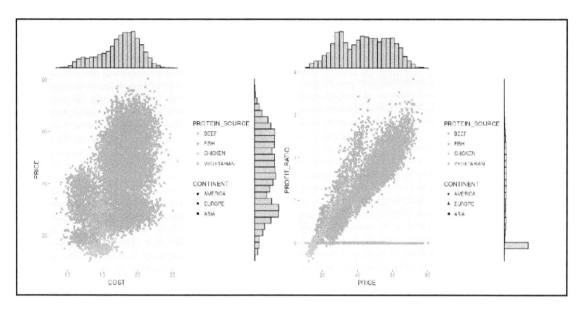

Marginal distributions

Note that there are very distinguishable groups. In the second graph (right), we show the relation among PRICE, PROFIT_RATIO, PROTEIN_SOURCE, and CONTINENT. Note that we find the same relation we did in our 3D interactive scatter plots, the higher the PRICE value, the higher the PROFIT_RATIO value. However, there are two interesting findings here that we will mention in Chapter 7, *Developing Automatic Presentations*. Can you tell what they are?

```
graph_marginal_distributions(sales,
        "COST", "PRICE", "PROTEIN_SOURCE", "CONTINENT")
```

If you use the graph_marginal_distributions() function to graph the combination of COST, PRICE, STATUS, and PAID, you should see no pattern emerge as those distributions were randomly simulated to be normally distributed in Chapter 4, *Simulating Sales Data and Working with Databases*, and no skewing process was applied to them.

Client birth dates, gender, and ratings

A problem you will encounter when programming is that sometimes a function you thought would be general enough needs to be changed in some way. Sometimes the right decision is to change the existing function, but other times, the right decision is to create a new function (maybe based on the original one) that can be modified as needed without breaking old code that used it. This happens when the assumptions for the function are not met, and can't be easily accommodated.

In our case, what happens if we want to use the `clients` data to graph our clients' birth dates using the year in the *x* axis, month in the *y* axis, color by gender, and show the rating adjusting the size of the dots? Well, the *x* axis and the *y* axis data assumptions may be fulfilled with minor data transformations, the color assumption is already met, but the size assumption doesn't seem to fit our previous model.

In our `graph_marginal_distributions()` function, we assumed that we would use the `shape` as the fourth variable to represent categorical variables, but it seems that, even though the `STARS` variable is technically a factor, it would be better represented using size rather than different shapes. The fact that we need to deal with the *x* axis, *y* axis, and size assumptions within special cases for the `clients` data, is reason enough to decide to create its own function based on the original one. If at some point we want to merge these two functions into a single one, we can do so, but there's no need to over complicate things for ourselves at this point.

In our `graph_marginal_distributions_client_birth_dates()` function, we only need to receive the data we will be working on (`clients` in this case). There's no need for other parameters because all the assumptions will be hardcoded inside the function in this case, because we're not looking to generalize the code. To make the code a little more readable, we will use short variable names to contain the string we will use to create the specification for the plot. That's what those `x`, `y`, `x_noise`, and `y_noise` variables are.

As mentioned, we need to slightly transform the data before we are able to produce the plot. First, we need to disaggregate the `BIRTH_DATE` into `BD_YEAR` and `BD_MONTH` (BD is short for birth date). Then we add noise to the dates because if just kept dates as they are, we would get a grid of values, not a distribution, and that's because both the year and the month are integer values, so there would be a lot of dots stacked up on each other and a lot of space empty between them, we can see a mixed version of the data, and that's why we need to add noise to it. See below how both of these functions work internally.

After we have our short names and have transformed our data, we are ready to create a scatter plot just as we have done before. Here's where the distinction between dates with and without noise comes into play. If we used the dates with noise to display the tick values for the axis, we would see year labels like 1953.51, 1973.85, 1993.23, and so on. Clearly, it's not intuitive to display the year axis with such values. Similarly, for the *y* axis, we would see month values like 1.24, 4.09, 8.53, and so on. The same problem. That's why we need two versions of the data, the one with the noise (real values) that is used to place the dots in the graph, and the one without the noise (integer values) that is used to show values in the axis. Finally, we add the axis labels and send the graph through the ggMarginal() function as we had done earlier:

```
graph_marginal_distributions_client_birth_dates <- function(data) {
    x <- "BD_YEAR"
    y <- "BD_MONTH"
    x_noise <- "BD_YEAR_NOISE"
    y_noise <- "BD_MONTH_NOISE"
    data <- disaggregate_dates(data)
    data <- add_dates_noise(data)
    graph <- ggplot(data, aes_string(x_noise,
                                      y_noise,
                                      size = "STARS",
                                      color = "GENDER")) +
        scale_x_continuous(breaks = seq(min(data[, x]),
                                        max(data[, x]), by = 5)) +
        scale_y_continuous(breaks = seq(min(data[, y]),
                                        max(data[, y]))) +
                                        geom_point() +
                                        ylab("MONTH") +
                                        xlab("YEAR")
    return(ggMarginal(graph, type = "histogram"))
}
disaggregate_dates <- function(data) {
    data$BD_YEAR <- as.numeric(format(data$BIRTH_DATE, "%Y"))
    data$BD_MONTH <- as.numeric(format(data$BIRTH_DATE, "%m"))
    return(data)
}
```

Adding noise to the data is straightforward, we simply create new variables (BD_YEAR_NOISE and BD_MONTH_NOISE) that have the original (integer) values and we add a random number from the normal distribution with a mean of 0 and a standard deviation of 0.5. We need a small standard deviation to make sure that our data is not changed too much:

```
add_dates_noise <- function(data) {
    year_noise <- rnorm(nrow(data), sd = 0.5)
```

```
month_noise <- rnorm(nrow(data), sd = 0.5)
data$BD_YEAR_NOISE <- data$BD_YEAR + year_noise
data$BD_MONTH_NOISE <- data$BD_MONTH + month_noise
return(data)
}
```

To disaggregate the dates, we simply create new variables (BD_YEAR and BD_MONTH) that contain the corresponding date value extracted using the date format specification that comes with R (%Y for year and %m for numeric month) converted to numbers (so that we can add noise to them and plot them). For more information on the date format specification, take a look at the *Dates and Times in R* page from Berkeley University (https://www.stat.berkeley.edu/~s133/dates.html).

Let's take a look at the client birth dates with the help of a graph:

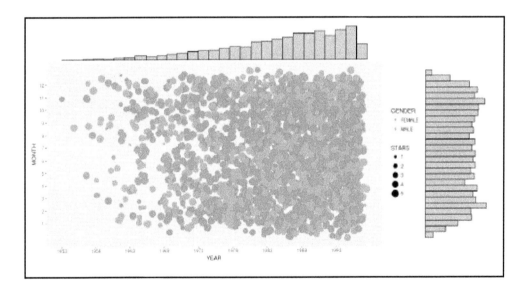

Client birth dates with marginal distribution

Now we can easily create this graph anytime we want without having to worry about the details of how to create it with the following code:

```
graph_marginal_distributions_client_birth_dates(clients)
```

Developing our own graph type – radar graphs

This section will take our graph functions to the next level as we develop our own custom graph type. The ggplot2 package does not have a way to produce radar graphs by default, so we will develop it ourselves during this section. There are packages that extend ggplot2 with radar graph capabilities (for example, ggradar), but we will show how to create it yourself from scratch. After reading this section, you'll be equipped to develop complex graphs on your own.

Radar graphs are plotted on a circular canvas and can show many variables values at the same time. They form a *radar-looking* shape and are useful if you want to compare different variable values among various *entities*. Sometimes they are used to visually get a sense of how similar or different *entities* are. If you're not familiar with this type of graphs, there's one shown in the following image. In our example, instead of measuring speed, durability, comfort, power, and space, as this example does, we will measure the three different macronutrients for The Food Factory's top five clients.

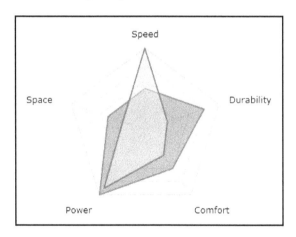

The graph_radar() function receives as parameters the data data frame and the variable by which we want to show radars (CLIENT_ID in our case). First, it transforms the data we need from wide to long format using the gather() function. Then it creates the labels that will be used in top of each radar graph, which show the profit produced by each CLIENT_ID. Finally it returns the graph object, which is created by specifying the macronutrients and percentages, adding a polygon layer groups, colors, and fills by the CLIENT_ID, and adjusting the alpha(transparency) and line size to look good.

The `facet_wrap()` function is used to repeat the same plot for each instance of the `by` variable in the data (`CLIENT_ID` in our case). Since it requires a formula, and we want to generalize its usage, we use a combination of the `as.formula()` and `paste()` functions. To recall how these work, look at `Chapter 3`, *Predicting Votes with Linear Models*. We also pass the `nrow = 1` parameter to make sure that we get a single row of graphs. We remove any legend information with the `guides()` function by sending the `"none"` string to the corresponding legends, apply our `coord_radar()` function (more on this below), and remove the axis labels:

```
graph_radar <- function(data, by) {
    data <- tidyr::gather(
                    data, MACRO, PERCENTAGE,
                    PROTEIN:FAT, factor_key = TRUE)
    data$CLIENT_ID <- paste(
        data$CLIENT_ID, " ($", data$PROFIT, ")", sep = ""
    )
    return(
        ggplot(data, aes(MACRO, PERCENTAGE)) +
        geom_polygon(
            aes_string(group = by, color = by, fill = by),
            alpha = 0.4,
            size = 2
        ) +
        facet_wrap(as.formula(paste("~", by)), nrow = 1) +
        guides(color = "none", fill = "none") +
        coord_radar() +
        xlab("") +
        ylab("")
    )
}
```

The `coord_radar()` function is not a built-in function in the `ggplot2` package, and we need to program it ourselves. The version we will work with here is a slightly modified version of the `coord_radar()` found around the internet first attributed to Hadley Wickham. It leverages the `ggproto()` function to inherit and modify the polar coordinates layer in `ggplot2`, which receives parameters `theta` (angle), `r` (radius), `start` (starting point), `direction` (whether to use positive or negative units), and a hack that returns the function required by the `is_linear` parameter such that its value is always `TRUE`. If we did not send this last hack, we would get circular shapes just as we do with polar coordinates when trying to graph a straight line. The preceding code simply selects the appropriate axis for the angle so that we get the radar shape:

```
coord_radar <- function(theta = "x", start = 0, direction = 1) {
    if (theta == "x") {
        r <- "y"
    } else {
        r <- "x"
    }
    return(ggproto(
        "CordRadar",
        CoordPolar,
        theta = theta,
        r = r,
        start = start,
        direction = sign(direction),
        is_linear = function(coord) { return(TRUE) }
    ))
}
```

The ggproto() function is used as an *internal object system* within the ggplot2 package, and was developed to avoid having to change too much of the code base when implementing layered objects. It's not recommended for you to use it unless absolutely necessary. For more information on object systems, look at Chapter 8, *Object-Oriented System to Track Cryptocurrencies*.

Now that we have our graph function ready, we need to make sure that our data is formatted correctly. To do so, we create the filter_data() function to filter the data and produce the expected structure. The function receives as parameters the data we will use, the number of days to keep backwards from the current date as n_days, the number of top performers we will show as n_top, and the variable we will aggregate by as aggregate_by.

First, we filter the data n days back and then keep the observations only for the n_top performers according to the aggregate_by variable. As we do, we update the data accordingly. Then, we aggregate the data twice, once by PROFIT and the other time by macronutrients (PROTEIN, CARBS, and FAT), and we get back the CLIENT_ID name into the data frame. Doing so produces two data frames, aggr_profit and aggr_macros, where each one aggregates its respective variables for each unique CLIENT_ID. Note that we separate this process into two independent parts because we want to aggregate PROTEIN, CARBS, and FAT with mean to get the average preference for each CLIENT_ID, but at the same time, we want to aggregate PROFIT with sum to get the total profit (not the average profit) for each CLIENT_ID.

Finally, we merge the data with the `merge()` function using our `aggregate_by` variable to be the index by which we join the data, drop residue columns from the data frame, and order it by `PROFIT`:

```
filter_data <- function(data, n_days, n_top, aggregate_by, static = TRUE) {
    data <- filter_n_days_back(data, n_days)
    data <- filter_n_top(data, n_top, aggregate_by)
    if (static) {
        aggr_profit <- aggregate(
            data[, c("PROFIT", "PROFIT_RATIO")],
            list(data[, aggregate_by]),
            sum
        )
        aggr_profit$CLIENT_ID <- aggr_profit$Group.1
        aggr_macros <- aggregate(
            data[, c("PROTEIN", "CARBS", "FAT")],
            list(data[, aggregate_by]),
            mean
        )
        aggr_macros$CLIENT_ID <- aggr_macros$Group.1
        data <- merge(aggr_profit, aggr_macros, by = aggregate_by)
        drop_columns <- c("Group.1.x", "Group.1.y", "PROFIT_RATIO")
        data <- data[, !(names(data) %in% drop_columns)]
        data <- data[order(-data$PROFIT), ]
    }
    return(data)
}
```

If you read the code carefully, you may have noticed a detail we did not mention, the usage of the `PROFIT_RATIO` variable in the aggregation even if we don't use it later in the function. The reason for including `PROFIT_RATIO` in the `aggregate()` computation is because of the side-effect it produces. When specifying two or more variables inside the data for the `aggregate()` function, the result comes back with the actual data frame column names in the resulting data frame `aggr_profit`. If we only specify `PROFIT` by itself, the result will have a column named `x` instead of `PROFIT`, as we have seen and used in the previous code during this chapter. It's an easy way to avoid dealing with variable name changes. In my opinion, the `aggregate()` function should always return the original data frame names, but it does not so we have to work around it. Remember to keep this usability in mind when programming for others.

To see how we actually filter dates, we look inside the `filter_n_days_back()` function. As you can see, we receive as parameter the `data` we want to filter and the number of days we want to keep backwards as `n`. If `n` is `NULL`, meaning that the user did not want to filter the data backward, then we simply return the same `data` we got. If you do receive a number in `n`, then we get the current date and subtract `n` days from it with `Sys.Date()` – `n`. This simple subtraction is automatically done with days as units, thanks to a technique called **operator overloading**. We will look at the details of how it works in `Chapter 8`, *Object-Oriented System to Track Cryptocurrencies*. Finally, we simply keep those dates that is at least the `n_days_back` date (another usage of the *operator overloading* technique which allows us to compare dates). The `filter_n_top()` function is the one we created earlier for the boxplots code:

```
filter_n_days_back <- function(data, n) {
    if (is.null(n)) {
        return(data)
    }
    n_days_back <- Sys.Date() - n
    return(data[data[, "DATE"] >= n_days_back, ])
}
```

Our `filter_data()` function is very useful in itself. For example, we can easily show the average macronutrients for the top 5 clients during the last 30 days by executing:

```
filter_data(sales, 30, 5, "CLIENT_ID")
#>     CLIENT_ID PROFIT   PROTEIN     CARBS       FAT
#> 2 BAWHQ69720 74.298 0.3855850 0.3050690 0.3093460
#> 3 CFWSY56410 73.378 0.4732115 0.3460788 0.1807097
#> 4 CQNQB52245 61.468 0.1544217 0.3274938 0.5180846
#> 1 AHTSR81362 58.252 0.3301151 0.3326516 0.3372332
#> 5 VJAQG30905 53.104 0.2056474 0.5909554 0.2033972
```

Having made the investment in creating the corresponding graph function, we are now able to easily produce our own radar graphs. For example, we can easily produce the corresponding radar graph for the data we just showed earlier with:

```
graph_radar(filter_data(sales, 30, 5, "CLIENT_ID"), "CLIENT_ID")
```

The following image gives a representation of the preceding command:

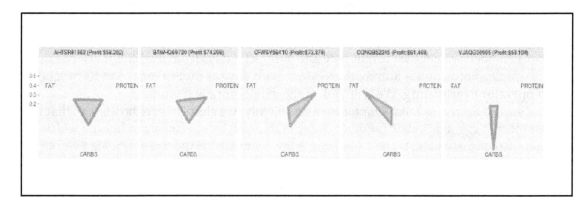

Top clients' macronutrients average radar

Exploring with interactive 3D scatter plots

When exploring data, sometimes it's useful to look at a 3D scatter plot. However, if the scatter plot is fixed (meaning that you cannot move it around), it may not be easy to interpret. Having an interactive plot (one you can move around) to see different angles of the data is very useful in these cases. These graphs don't normally go into static reports because they are hard to interpret correctly when fixed, but are very useful to do data exploration. Luckily, they are also very easy to create with the plot3d() function from the rgl package:

```
library(rgl)
plot3d(sales$PROTEIN, sales$CARBS, sales$FAT)
plot3d(sales$PROFIT_RATIO, sales$PRICE, sales$QUANTITY)
```

Once you create these plots in your computer, remember to move them around with your mouse! The first time you do this, it's pretty amazing. In this case, you can see two phenomenons that occur in the `sales` data. First, macronutrient percentages must add to one, and since there are three of them, what you will see in the graph on the left is a triangle shape in such a way that the sum of the coordinates for each point inside it is equal to one. Second, the graph on the right shows the relation among `PRICE`, `QUANTITY`, and `PROFIT_RATIO`. It shows that there are no fractional quantities in our sales data (just as we designed it), that there are lots of orders with zero `PROFIT_RATIO` because they are not fulfilled or payed for, and that the higher the `PRICE` is, the higher the `PROFIT_RATIO` is.

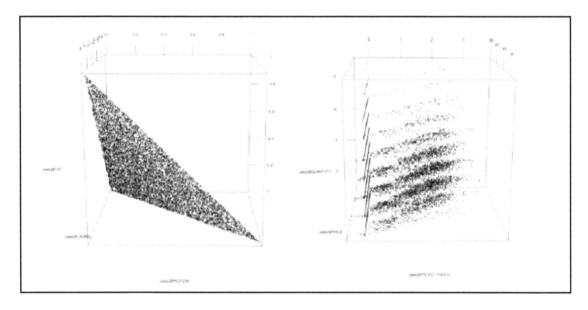

There's not much more to explain about these graphs. They are simple to create, have a simple purpose which sometimes can be very useful, but you will not normally see them in written reports.

Looking at dynamic data with time-series

Now we are going to focus on another very common type of graph: time-series. Our objective is to understand how our data is behaving for the last n days, and, as we have done before, we want to further disaggregate using colors, like the graph below shows:

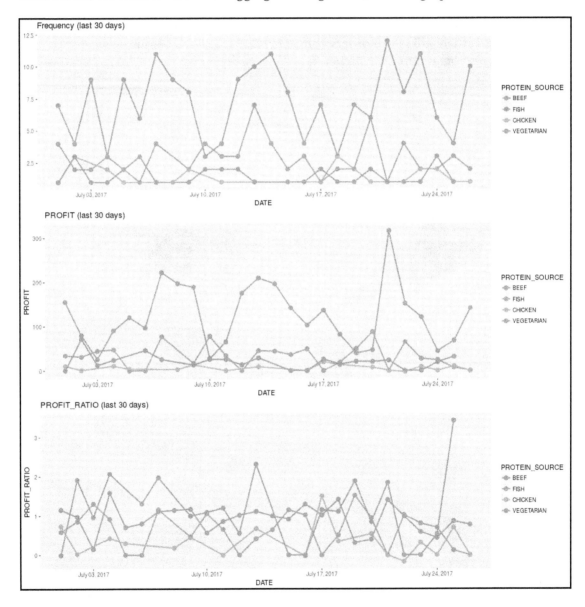

If you have read all the chapter up until this point, you should be able to understand most of what the function is doing. The only new function is `scale_x_date()`. It allows us to specify date formats for the axis ticks other than the default. In this case, we want to use breaks by day (as we had done in some examples before), but we want the format of the labels to be similar to **July 30, 2017**, for example. To do so we make use of the date formats mentioned in a previous section in this chapter and send the desired string structure to the `date_labels` parameter:

```
graph_last_n_days <- function(data, n, y = NULL, color = NULL) {
    subset <- filter_n_days_back(data, n)
    days_range <- paste("(last ", n, " days)", sep = "")
    date_sequence <- seq(min(subset[, "DATE"]),
                         max(subset[, "DATE"]), by = "day")
    if (is.null(y)) {
        graph <-
            ggplot(subset, aes_string(x = "DATE", color = color)) +
            ggtitle(paste("Frequency", days_range)) +
            geom_point(stat = "count", size = 3) +
            geom_line(stat = "count", size = 1)
    } else {
        aggregation <- get_aggregation(y)
        graph <- ggplot(subset, aes_string(
                        x = "DATE",
                        y = y,
                        color = color)) +
            ggtitle(paste(y, days_range)) +
            geom_point(
                fun.y = aggregation,
                stat = "summary", size = 3) +
            geom_line(
                fun.y = aggregation,
                stat = "summary", size = 1)
    }
    graph <- graph +
        ylab(y) +
        scale_x_date(
        breaks = date_sequence,
        date_labels = "%B %d, %Y"
    )
    return(graph)
}
```

If you want to look at simple line graphs that show either the frequency, `PROFIT`, or `PROFIT_RATIO` for the last 30 days, you can use the following code. We don't show these images to preserve space:

```
graph_last_n_days(sales, 30)
graph_last_n_days(sales, 30, "PROFIT")
graph_last_n_days(sales, 30, "PROFIT_RATIO")
```

To look at line graphs for frequency, PROFIT, and PROFIT_RATIO, that distinguish PROTEIN_SOURCE with colors, you can use the following code:

```
graph_last_n_days(sales, 30, color = "PROTEIN_SOURCE")
graph_last_n_days(sales, 30, "PROFIT", "PROTEIN_SOURCE")
graph_last_n_days(sales, 30, "PROFIT_RATIO", "PROTEIN_SOURCE")
```

You can use the graph_last_n_days() function with other data frames. For example, graph the STARS ratings during the last 30 days coming from client_messages, you simply need to transform the categorical variable STARS into a numeric variable with the as.numeric() function so that you don't get errors for type mismatches, and call the function.

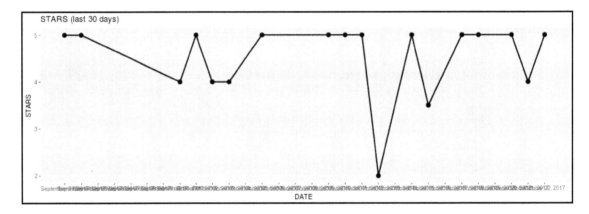

If you don't specify a variable to disaggregate using colors, it will graph with black by default:

```
aux <- client_messages
aux$STARS <- as.numeric(aux$STARS)
graph_last_n_days(aux, 30, "STARS")
```

Looking at geographical data with static maps

Maps can be very useful tools to get an intuition behind geographical data. In this section, we will produce a map with the `ggplot2` package. The objective is to show the location of our client's messages, the `PRICE` associated to their purchases, and the corresponding `PROFIT_RATIO`. This example will show us how to join data from the `sales` and `client_messages` data frames.

Our `graph_client_messages_static()` function receives as parameters the `client_messages` and `sales` data frames, and that's all it needs as we are showing unfiltered (full) datasets. First, we need to merge our two data frames using the identifier they share, which is `SALE_ID`. To do so we use the `merge()` function, and we specify that we want to keep all observation on the x data frame, which is the first one (`client_messages`), and we don't want to keep observations from the y data frame, which is the second one (`sales`), if they don't have a corresponding identifier in the first data frame. This allows us to keep only data that has client messages associated with it. Then we produce the map geographical data with the `map_data()` (it comes in the `ggplot2` package), and we filter it to remove any region marked as `"Antarctica"`.

To actually create the graph we are going to use two main layers. The first one is the geographical data, which is added with the `geom_polygon()` function, using the `world_map` data, specifying the coordinates and groups (groups define countries), and use some dark colors to contrast with our dots. The second layer is the messages data, which is added with the `geom_point()` function, using the merged `data` data frame, with the corresponding coordinates, and adding colors and sizes with `PRICE` and `PROFIT_RATIO`, respectively. Since we are using a numeric variable to specify the color in this example, we will get a gradient of colors instead of discrete colors as in previous examples. Finally, we specify the actual color palette using the `scale_color_viridis()` function, set up the appropriate axis labels, and make the coordinates have equal units with the `coord_fixed()` function. If we don't use this last function, we can get maps which are deformed:

```
graph_client_messages_static <- function(client_messages, sales) {
    data <- merge(
            client_messages, sales,
            "SALE_ID", all.x = TRUE,
            all.y = FALSE
        )
    world_map <- filter(map_data("world"), region != "Antarctica")
    return(
```

```
ggplot() +
geom_polygon(
    data = world_map,
    aes(long, lat, group = group),
    color = "grey60",
    fill = "grey50"
) +
geom_point(
    data = data,
    aes(LNG, LAT, color = PRICE, size = PROFIT_RATIO)
) +
scale_color_viridis(option = "inferno") +
ylab("Latitude") +
xlab("Longitude") +
coord_fixed()
)
}
```

Now we can create our maps with the following function call:

```
graph_client_messages_static(client_messages, sales)
```

Doing so, results in the following graph:

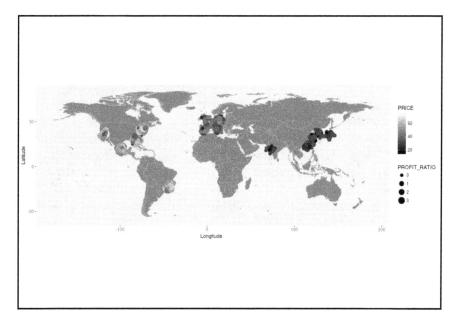

Of course, if you want to generalize this function, you can parameterize some of the variables used for the graph's specification as we have done in previous examples.

Navigating geographical data with interactive maps

We can navigate the geographical data with the help of interactive maps, which are explained in the following sections.

Maps you can navigate and zoom-in to

In this final section, we will create interactive maps that we can navigate. This is a very powerful tool that can be embedded in your R projects, greatly increasing their value and impact on your audience. We will use the `leaflet` package to develop this map. Our objective is to show a map with the locations of the messages we receive from our clients with icons that represent the type of rating we got using the STARS variable of the message and tooltips that show the PROFIT associated to the corresponding purchase of each message.

Our `graph_client_messages_interactive()` function receives the `client_messages` and `sales` data frames. As in the previous map, we will show all data without any filters, so that's all we need as parameters. The first thing we do, as we did earlier, is merge the data so that we keep only observations that have an associated message. Then we add a new variable to the `data` data frame that contains the icon specification that will be used by `leaflet`. To do so, we use the `awesomeIcons()` function (it's part of the `leaflet` package) and specify the functions used to specify the icon, the marker color, and say we want our icons to be white and that they should come from the `ion` icon library (http://ionicons.com/). Other icon libraries available are `glyphicon` (http://glyphicons.com/) and `fa` (fontawesome, http://fontawesome.io/icons/). You may find the icon you're looking for in the referenced websites. Finally, we return the *leaflet graph* by creating markers with the `addAwesomeMarkers()` function, which receives a *leaflet object* created with the `leaflet()` function wrapped around our `data`, the formulas for longitudes and latitudes, the formula for icons, and the formula for the labels. Optionally, we wrap the *leaflet graph* with the `addProviderTiles()` to make sure that we get *tiles* (geographical background images) in our web browser. We need this because at the time of this writing there's a bug that will not show geographic data (only the markers) under specific circumstances and we want to avoid that problem, which we can easily do with the mentioned technique:

```
graph_client_messages_interactive <- function(client_messages, sales) {
    data <- merge(
                client_messages,
```

```
                        sales,
                        "SALE_ID",
                        all.x = TRUE,
                        all.y = FALSE)
    data$ICON <- awesomeIcons(
        markerColor = get_icon_color(data),
        icon = get_icon(data),
        iconColor = 'white',
        library = 'ion'
    )
    return(
        addProviderTiles(addAwesomeMarkers(
            leaflet(data),
            ~LNG, ~LAT,
            icon = ~ICON,
            label = ~paste("Profit:", PROFIT)
        ), providers$OpenStreetMap)
    )
}
```

Now we will explain the functions that specify the icons and marker colors. The get_icon_color() function will receive our data data frame and return a vector with string, which is either "green" or "red", depending on whether or not the associated STARS where higher or equal to 4, or not. We do so using the sapply() function. If you need a refresher on these vectorized functions, take a look at Chapter 1, *Introduction to R*:

```
get_icon_color <- function(data) {
    return(sapply(
        as.numeric(data$STARS),
        function(stars) {
            if (stars >= 4) {
                return("green")
            } else {
                return("red")
            }
        }
    ))
}
```

The get_icon() function is very similar but it will return the name of the icon we want. We got these names from the ion icon library website (referenced earlier):

```
get_icon <- function(data) {
    return(sapply(
        as.numeric(data$STARS),
        function(stars) {
            if (stars >= 4) {
```

```
                    return("ion-android-happy")
                } else {
                    return("ion-android-sad")
                }
            }
        ))
    }
```

Now we can easily produce the interactive maps for our clients' messages using the following code. It will open a web browser and show you a map that you can move around.

```
graph <- graph_client_messages_interactive(client_messages, sales)
print(graph)
```

The initial position for the map will show the full geographical data as is shown in the following image. As you can see, the markers contain either a happy or a sad face, depending on the rating each message had. Also, the color of the marker is either green or red, again depending on the rating.

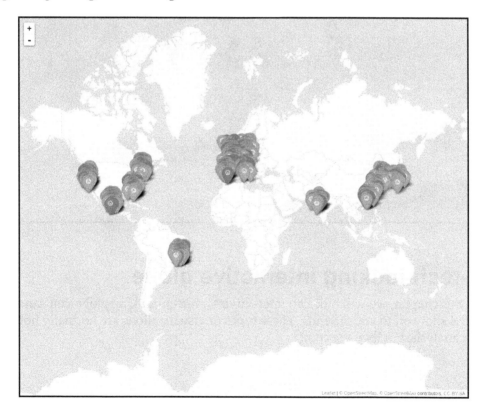

A zoomed-in version of the interactive map can be seen in the following image. Depending on the provider you choose in the `addProviderTiles()` function, you will get different types of geographical images (you can see some of them in action at `htt://leaflet-extras.github.io/leaflet-providers/preview/`).

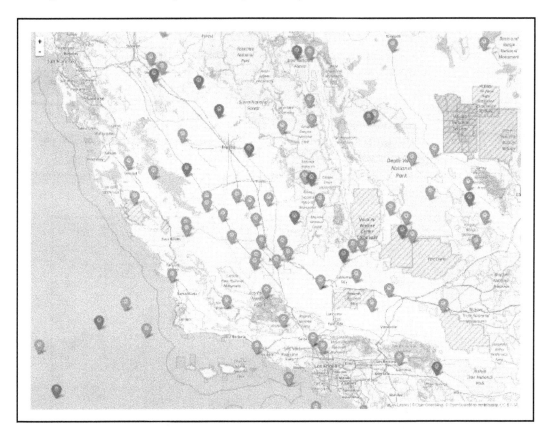

High-tech-looking interactive globe

To finish this chapter, we will build an interactive high-tech-looking globe you can move around and show off to your friends. These types of visualizations are normally not very useful for analysis, but they are cool!

Our objective is to show a globe that will show geographical data coming from clients' messages as well as bars whose height represents the PROFIT associated to each sale and colors for PROTEIN_SOURCE. To accomplish this, we will use the threejs package.

As we did earlier, our graph_client_message_in_globe() function receives the client_messages and sales data and sets it up using the setup_globe_data() function. Then it will get world data using the get_world_map_data() function and append it to the data data frame using the rbind.fill() function from the plyr package. This function resembles R's own rbind() function, but won't complain if columns do not match. Instead, it will fill the empty values with missing data indicators. Finally, we return a globe object with the globejs() function, which receives the coordinates in lat and long, the bar height under the val parameter, which comes from the PROFIT variable, the color which comes from a COLOR variable created during the data setup (see in the following example), and the atmosphere = TRUE parameter to show a glowing effect around the globe:

```
graph_client_messages_in_globe <- function(client_messages, sales) {
    data <- setup_globe_data(client_messages, sales)
    world_map <- get_world_map_data()
    data <- rbind.fill(data, world_map)
    return(globejs(
        lat = data$LAT,
        long = data$LNG,
        val = data$PROFIT^1.2,
        color = data$COLOR,
        pointsize = 1,
        atmosphere = TRUE
    ))
}
```

The setup_globe_data() function does the standard merging we've done with all maps and adds a new variable named COLOR that contains the colors that should be used for each observation. In the case of the ggplot2 package, this color assignment was done automatically for us, but in the threejs package, we need do it ourselves. It will simply be a different color for each value in the PROTEIN_SOURCE variable:

```
setup_globe_data <- function(client_messages, sales) {
    data <- merge(
        client_messages,
        sales,
        "SALE_ID",
        all.x = TRUE,
        all.y = FALSE
    )
```

```
        data$COLOR <- NA
        data[data$PROTEIN_SOURCE == "BEEF", "COLOR"] <- "#aaff00"
        data[data$PROTEIN_SOURCE == "FISH", "COLOR"] <- "#00ffaa"
        data[data$PROTEIN_SOURCE == "CHICKEN", "COLOR"] <- "#00aaff"
        data[data$PROTEIN_SOURCE == "VEGETARIAN", "COLOR"] <- "#0055ff"
        return(data)
    }
```

The `get_world_map_data()` function is somewhat complicated. If you don't understand how it works, don't worry too much, as you probably won't need to do this yourself. We can't just use the data we had used before to create maps that we crated with the `map_data()` function, because the required data structure is different. In this case, we will create a temporary file named `cache` with the `tempfile()` function. Then we will read a binary file coming from a URL with the `url()` and `readBin()` functions. The file is a TIFF file, which we open in a `"raw"` format to keep all the data as is and avoid any data interpretation within R. The n parameter is the maximum number of records to be read from the data, which is 1 million in this case. Then we send this data through the `writeBin()` function so that it gets written to the `cache` file we created before. This mechanism is a way of downloading some temporary data so that we can read it into a function that does not support reading from online resources.

Once we have the temporary file ready, we read it with the `readGDAL()` function from the `rgdal` package, which will read it as geographical data. The specific format for this data includes longitude, latitude, and an altitude metric. The altitude metric is used to identify areas without land (oceans), which contain a value higher than or equal to 255 in this data. We proceed to remove any `NA` values in the data and assign default `PROFIT` and `COLOR` values. Note that we create these `PROFIT` and `COLOR` values to facilitate merging the data later on. We use the `PROFIT` column name for the altitude metric just for convenience since we will want to show the geographic areas with low bars, and we know that we will use `PROFIT` to generate the height for each bar:

```
    get_world_map_data <- function() {
        cache <- tempfile()
        writeBin(readBin(url(
    "http://illposed.net/nycr2015/MOD13A2_E_NDVI_2014-05-25_rgb_360x180.TIFF",
            open = "rb"),
            what = "raw", n = 1e6), con = cache)

        world_map <- readGDAL(cache)
        world_map <- as.data.frame(cbind(
                    coordinates(world_map),
                    world_map@data[,1]))
        names(world_map) <- c("LNG", "LAT", "PROFIT")
```

```
world_map <- world_map[world_map$PROFIT < 255,]
world_map <- na.exclude(world_map)

world_map$PROFIT <- 1
world_map$COLOR <- "#0055ff"
return(world_map)
}
```

Once we invested in creating our graph function, we can create high-tech looking maps that display the location of messages we get from our clients, with bars and colors that indicate related PROFIT and PROTEIN_SOURCE for each message, respectively. Feel free to move the globe around in your web browser:

```
graph_client_messages_in_globe(client_messages, sales)
```

It's a pretty cool effect isn't it?

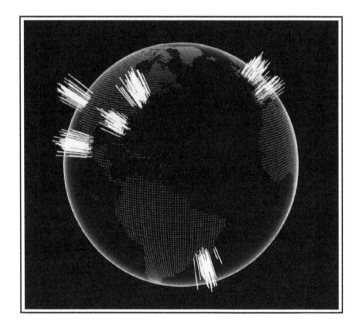

Summary

In this chapter, you learned how to create various types of data visualizations and how to work with graph functions and graph objects efficiently. Apart from the basic graph types, you learned how to create interactive graphs and maps and how to create our own custom types of graphs. The fundamentals shown in this chapter allow you to create high-quality visualizations using important and popular packages such as `ggplot2` and `leaflet`.

In the next chapter, `Chapter 6`, *Understanding Reviews with Text Analysis*, we will analyze the text data we have from client messages as well as data we retrieve from Twitter in real-time. We will show how to generate sentiment analysis given textual data, and we will prepare ourselves to put the graphs in this chapter together with the text analysis in the following chapter into automatic reports in `Chapter 7`, *Developing Automatic Presentations*.

6
Understanding Reviews with Text Analysis

It is well known that a very large percentage of relevant information originates in an unstructured form, an important player being text data. Text analysis, **Natural Language Processing** (**NLP**), **Information Retrieval** (**IR**), and **Statistical Learning** (**SL**) are some areas focused on developing techniques and processes to deal with this data. These techniques and processes discover and present knowledge, facts, business rules, relationships, among others, that is otherwise locked in textual form, impenetrable to automated processing.

Given the explosion of textual data we see nowadays, an important skill for analysts such as statisticians and data scientists is to be able to work efficiently with this data and find the insights they are looking for. In this chapter, we will try to predict whether a customer is going to make repeated purchases given the reviews being sent to The Cake Factory.

Since text analysis is a very broad research area, we need to narrow the techniques we will look at in this chapter to the most important ones. We will take a Pareto approach by focusing on 20% of techniques that will be used 80% of the time when doing text analysis. Some of the important topics covered in this chapter are as follows:

- Document feature matrices as a basic data structure
- Random forests for predictive modeling with text data
- Term frequency-inverse document frequencies for measuring importance
- N-gram modeling to bring back order into the analysis
- Singular vector decomposition for dimensionality reduction
- Cosine similarity to find similar feature vectors
- Sentiment analysis as an added vector feature

This chapter's required packages

Setting up the packages for this chapter may be a bit cumbersome because some of the packages depend on operating system libraries which can vary from computer to computer. Please check `Appendix`, *Required Packages* for specific instructions on how to install them for your operating system.

Package	Reason
lsa	Cosine similarity computation
rilba	Efficient SVD decomposition
caret	Machine learning framework
twitteR	Interface to Twitter's API
quanteda	Text data processing
sentimentr	Text data sentiment analysis
randomForest	Random forest models

We will use the `rilba` package (which depends on C code) to compute a part of the **Singular Value Decomposition** (**SVD**) efficiently using the *Augmented Implicitly Restarted Lanczos Bidiagonalization Methods, by Baglama and Reichel, 2005,* `http://www.math.uri.edu/~jbaglama/papers/paper14.pdf`).

We will use the `parallel` package to perform parallel processing since some text analysis can potentially require a lot of computations. The `parallel` package is the most general parallelization package in R for now, but it has been reported to not work correctly in some systems. Other options are `doParallel`, `doMC` and `doSNOW`. If you run into trouble when using one `parallel`, try switching to one of the other packages. The code to make them work is very similar.

Regarding text data, there are a few packages you can use in R. The most common ones are the `tm` package and the `quanteda` package. Both are excellent, and differ mostly in style. All the functionality we will see in this chapter can be used with either one of them, but we chose to work with the `quanteda` package. It is built with the `stringi` package for processing text, the `data.table` package for large documents, and the `Matrix` package to handle sparse objects. Therefore you can expect it to be very fast and handle Unicode and UTF-8 very well.

If you don't know what Unicode and UTF-8 are, I suggest you read up on them. Very roughly you can think of Unicode as being a standard of IDs for characters, while UTF-8 being a translation of this IDs into bytes computers can understand. During this chapter we won't worry about encodings (all the data is in UTF-8), but it's something that often comes up when working with text data, and is important to handle correctly.

What is text analysis and how does it work?

Text analysis is the process of deriving information from text. Information is typically derived through techniques such as IR, NLP, and SL, and it involves structuring text, deriving patterns with the structured data, and finally evaluating and interpreting the output. The basic models used for text analysis are the bag-of-words models, the vector space model, and the semantic parsing model.

The bag-of-words model is a simplified text representation in which a text (a review in our case) is represented as the set of its terms (words), disregarding grammar and word order but keeping multiplicity (hence the term bag). After transforming the text into a bag-of-words and structuring into a corpus (a structured collection of the text data), we can calculate various measures to characterize the text into a vector space. The bag-of-words model is commonly used in SL methods, and we will use it with random forests in this chapter. In practice, it is used as a tool of feature generation. The following image explains the bag-of-words model:

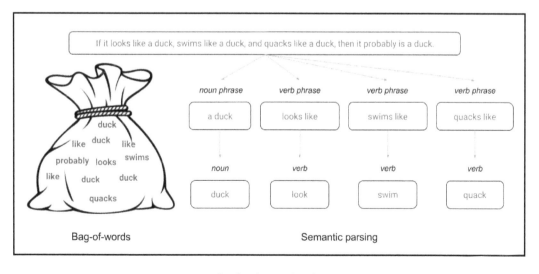

Bag-of-words vs semantic parsing

The vector space model uses the bag-of-words that you extracted from the documents to create a feature vector for each text, where each feature is a term and the feature's value is a term weight. The term weight may be a binary value (1 indicating that the term occurred in the document and 0 indicating that it did not), a **term frequency (TF)** value (indicating how many times the term occurred in the document), or a **term frequency-inverse document frequency (TF-IDF)** value (indicating how important a term is to a text given its corpus). More complex weighting mechanisms exist which are focused on specific problems, but these are the most common ones, and are the ones we will focus on.

Given what we mentioned earlier, a text turns out to be a feature vector, and each feature vector corresponds to a point in a vector space. The model for this vector space is such that there is an axis for every term in the vocabulary, and so the vector space is n-dimensional, where n is the size of the vocabulary in all the data being analyzed (this can be huge). Sometimes, it helps to think about these concepts geometrically. The bag-of-words model and vector space model refer to different aspects of characterizing a body of text, and they complement each other. The following image explains the vector space model:

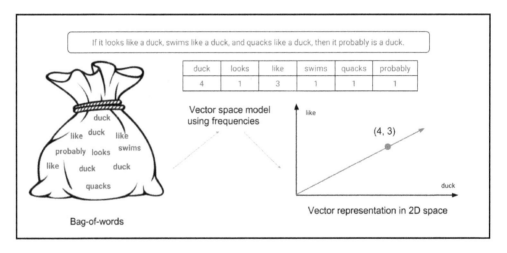

Bag-of-words to vector space

An important weakness of the bag-of-words model is the fact that it ignores the terms' semantic context. More complex models exist that attempt to correct these deficiencies. Semantic parsing is one of them, and it's the process of mapping a natural-language sentence into a formal representation of its meaning. It mainly uses combinations of inductive logic programming and statistical learning. These types of techniques become more useful when dealing with complex texts. Even though we won't touch further on them on this book, they are a powerful tool and are a very interesting area of research.

As an example, if you try to think of the representation of the following quote using the bag-of-words model and the semantic parsing model, you may intuitively think that the first one can give nonsense results while the second one can provide at least some understanding, and you would be correct.

> *"The fish trap exists because of the fish. Once you've gotten the fish you can forget the trap. The rabbit snare exists because of the rabbit. Once you've gotten the rabbit, you can forget the snare. Words exist because of meaning. Once you've gotten the meaning, you can forget the words. Where can I find a man who has forgotten words so I can talk with him?"*

> *– The Writings of Chuang Tzu, 4th century B.C. (Original text in Chinese)*

Preparing, training, and testing data

As always, we will start by setting up our data. In this case, the data is the messages received by our fantasy company, The Cake Factory. These are in the `client_messages.RDS` file that we created in `Chapter 4`, *Simulating Sales Data and Working with Databases*. The data contains 300 observations for 8 variables: `SALE_ID`, `DATE`, `STARS`, `SUMMARY`, `MESSAGE`, `LAT`, `LNG`, and `MULT_PURCHASES`. During this chapter, we will work with the `MESSAGE` and `MULT_PURCHASES` variables.

We will set up our seed to have reproducible results. Keep in mind that this should be before every function call that involves some randomization. We will show it just once here to save space and avoid repeating ourselves, but keep that in mind when you are trying to generate reproducible results:

```
set.seed(12345)
```

Next, we need to make sure that we don't have any missing data in the relevant variables. To do so, we use the `complete.cases()` function together with the negation (`!`) and the `sum()` function to get the total number of `NA` values' in each variable. As you can see, we don't have any missing data:

```
sum(!complete.cases(client_messages$MESSAGE))
#> 0

sum(!complete.cases(client_messages$MULT_PURCHASES))
#> 0
```

If you have missing data, instead of using some imputation mechanism which is normally done in some data analysis scenarios, you want to remove those observations from this data, since it's easier to get this wrong due to the non-continuous characteristics of textual data.

As you will often find when working on interesting real-world problems in predictive analysis, it's not uncommon to work with disproportionate data. In this case, as can be seen with the shown code, we have around 63% of multiple purchases. This is not very disproportionate, but we still have to play on the safe side by keeping the training and testing data with similar proportions:

```
prop.table(table(client_messages$MULT_PURCHASES))
#>      FALSE       TRUE
#> 0.3621262 0.6378738
```

For data with the disproportionality problem, maintaining the same proportions in the testing and training sets is important to get accurate results. Therefore, we need to make sure our sampling method maintains these proportions. To do so, we will use the `createDataPartition()` function from the `caret` package to extract the indexes for each of the training and testing sets. It will create balanced data splits, and, in this case, it will use 70% of the data for training with a single partition:

```
indexes <- createDataPartition(
    client_messages$MULT_PURCHASES,
    list = FALSE,
    times = 1,
    p = 0.7
)
train <- client_messages[ indexes, ]
test <- client_messages[-indexes, ]
```

To make sure that our proportions are being maintained, we can check each of them individually just as we did before with the full data:

```
prop.table(table(train$MULT_PURCHASES))
#>      FALSE       TRUE
#> 0.3632075 0.6367925
```

```
prop.table(table(test$MULT_PURCHASES))
#>      FALSE       TRUE
#> 0.3595506 0.6404494
```

Now that we have our training and testing sets ready, we can start cleaning and setting up our text data as we will do in the next section.

Building the corpus with tokenization and data cleaning

The first thing we need to create when working with text data is to extract the tokens that will be used to create our corpus. Simply, these tokens are all the terms found in every text in our data, put together, and removed the ordering or grammatical context. To create them, we use the `tokens()` function and the related functions from the `quanteda` package. As you can imagine, our data will not only contain words, but also punctuation marks, numbers, symbols, and other characters like hyphens. Depending on the context of the problem you're working with, you may find it quite useful to remove all of them as we do here. However, keep in mind that in some contexts some of these special characters can be meaningful (for example, the hashtag symbol (#) can be relevant when analyzing Twitter data):

```
tokens <- tokens(
    train$MESSAGE,
    remove_punct = TRUE,
    remove_numbers = TRUE,
    remove_symbols = TRUE,
    remove_hyphens = TRUE
)
```

As you can imagine, there will be a huge number of tokens in the data because there must be one for each unique word in our data. These raw tokens will probably be useless (contain a low signal/noise ratio) if we don't apply some filtering. We'll start by ignoring capitalization. In our context, *something* and *something* should be equivalent. Therefore, we use the `tokens_tolower()` function to make all tokens lowercase:

```
tokens <- tokens_tolower(tokens)
```

Also, keep in mind that common words like *the, a,* and *to* are almost always the terms with highest frequency in the text and are not particularly important to derive insights. We should thus remove them, as we do with the `tokens_select()` function:

```
tokens <- tokens_select(tokens, stopwords(), selection = "remove")
```

Word stems allow us to reduce the number of tokens that overall share the same meaning. For example, the words *probability*, *probably*, and *probable* probably have the same meaning and their differences are mostly syntactic. Therefore, we could represent all of them with a single token like *probab* and reduce our feature space considerably. Note that all of these filters have assumptions behind them about the problem we're dealing with, and you should make sure those assumptions are valid. In our case, they are as follows:

```
tokens <- tokens_wordstem(tokens, language = "english")
```

Instead of having to repeat this by hand every time, we want to create tokens; we can wrap all of these filters in a single function and make our lives a little bit easier down the road. The careful reader will note the `token_ngrams()` function and the corresponding `n_grams = 1` default parameter. We dedicate a section to this later, but for now, just know that `n_grams = 1` means that we want single words in our tokens:

```
build_tokens <- function(data, n_grams = 1) {
    tokens <- tokens(
        data,
        remove_punct = TRUE,
        remove_numbers = TRUE,
        remove_symbols = TRUE,
        remove_hyphens = TRUE
    )
    tokens <- tokens_tolower(tokens)
    tokens <- tokens_select(tokens, stopwords(), selection = "remove")
    tokens <- tokens_wordstem(tokens, language = "english")
    tokens <- tokens_ngrams(tokens, n = 1:n_grams)
    return(tokens)
}
```

Now, even though we have shown the code that is used for this chapter's example, we will use a smaller example (one sentence) so that you can get a visual idea of what's going on in each step. You should definitely get in the habit of doing this yourself when exploring a problem to make sure everything is working as you expect it. We put the code for all the steps here and, after reading the preceding paragraphs, you should be able to identify the differences in each step:

```
sentence <- "If it looks like a duck, swims like a duck,
            and quacks like a duck, then it probably is a duck."

tokens <- tokens(sentence)
tokens
#> tokens from 1 document.
#> text1 :
#>  [1] "If"       "it"       "looks"    "like"     "a"        "duck"
```

```
#>   [7] ","           "swims"     "like"       "a"        "duck"      ","
#>  [13] "and"         "quacks"    "like"       "a"        "duck"      ","
#>  [19] "then"        "it"        "probably"  "is"        "a"         "duck"
#>  [25] "."

tokens <- tokens(sentence, remove_punct = TRUE)
tokens
#> tokens from 1 document.
#> text1 :
#>   [1] "If"          "it"        "looks"     "like"      "a"         "duck"
#>   [7] "swims"       "like"      "a"         "duck"      "and"       "quacks"
#>  [13] "like"        "a"         "duck"      "then"      "it"        "probably"
#>  [19] "is"          "a"         "duck"

tokens <- tokens_tolower(tokens)
tokens
#> tokens from 1 document.
#> text1 :
#>   [1] "if"          "it"        "looks"     "like"      "a"         "duck"
#>   [7] "swims"       "like"      "a"         "duck"      "and"       "quacks"
#>  [13] "like"        "a"         "duck"      "then"      "it"        "probably"
#>  [19] "is"          "a"         "duck"

tokens <- tokens_select(tokens, stopwords(), selection = "remove")
tokens
#> tokens from 1 document.
#> text1 :
#>   [1] "looks"       "like"      "duck"      "swims"     "like"      "duck"
#>   [7] "quacks"      "like"      "duck"      "probably"  "duck"

tokens <- tokens_wordstem(tokens, language = "english")
tokens
#> tokens from 1 document.
#> text1 :
#>   [1] "look"      "like"      "duck"      "swim"      "like"      "duck"      "quack"
#>   [8] "like"      "duck"      "probabl"   "duck"
```

Document feature matrices

Once we have our tokens ready, we need to create our corpus. At the most basic level, a **corpus** is a collection of texts that includes document-level variables specific to each text. The most basic *corpus* uses the bag-of-words and vector space models to create a matrix in which each row represents a text in our collection (a client message in our case), and each column represents a term. Each of the values in the matrix would be a 1 or a 0, indicating whether or not a specific term is included in a specific text. This is a very basic representation that we will not use. We will use a **document-feature matrix (DFM)**, which has the same structure but, instead of using an indicator variable (1s and 0s), it will contain the number of times a term occurred within a text, using the multiplicity characteristic from the bag-of-words model. To create it, we use the dfm() function from the quanteda package:

```
train.dfm <- dfm(tokens)
```

To get a visual example, here's the DFM for the example shown in the previous section. We can see a couple of things here. First, it's a special object with some metadata, number of documents (one sentence in our case), number of features (which is the number of tokens), dimensions, and the actual values for each text in our data. This is our corpus. If we had more than one sentence, we would see more than one row in it:

```
dfm(tokens)
#> Document-feature matrix of: 1 document, 6 features (0% sparse).
#> 1 x 6 sparse Matrix of class "dfmSparse"
#>        features
#>   docs   look like duck swim quack probabl
#> text1  1    3    4    1    1      1
```

Now, forget about the one-sentence example, and let's go back to our client messages example. In that case the tokens object will be much larger. Normally, we tokenize and create our DFM in the same way. Therefore, we create the function that makes it a little easier for us:

```
build_dfm <- function(data, n_grams = 1) {
    tokens <- build_tokens(data, n_grams)
    return(dfm(tokens))
}
```

Now we can create our DFM easily with the following:

```
train.dfm <- build_dfm(train$MESSAGE)
```

To get an idea of our DFM's characteristics, you can simply print it. As you can see our training DFM has 212 documents (client messages) and 2,007 features (tokens). Clearly, most documents will not contain most of the features. Therefore we have a sparse structure, meaning that 98.4% of the entries in the DFM are actually zero. The educated reader will identify this as being the curse of dimensionality problem common to machine learning, and specially damaging in text analysis. As we will see later, this can be a computational bottleneck that we need to deal with:

```
train.dfm
#> Document-feature matrix of: 212 documents, 2,007 features (98.4% sparse)
```

Often, tokenization requires some additional pre-processing. As you know by now, the tokens we find in our tokenization process end up being column (feature) names in our DFM. If these names contain symbols inside or start with numbers (for example, *something&odd* or *45pieces*), then some of our analysis algorithms will complain by throwing errors. We want to prevent that when we transform our DFM into a data frame. We can do so with the convenient `make.names()` function. We will also add the `MULT_PURCHASES` value (our dependent variable) to our newly created data frame at this point:

```
dfm.df <- cbind(MULT_PURCHASES = train$MULT_PURCHASES, data.frame(dfm))
names(dfm.df) <- make.names(names(dfm.df))
```

Again, to avoid having to repeat this boilerplate code, we can create our own function that packs this functionality, and easily create our data frame for analysis:

```
build_dfm_df <- function(data, dfm) {
    df <- cbind(MULT_PURCHASES = data$MULT_PURCHASES, data.frame(dfm))
    names(df) <- make.names(names(df))
    return(df)
}
train.dfm.df <- build_dfm_df(train, train.dfm)
```

At this point, our training data is ready for analysis in the form of a data frame that can be used by our predictive models. To finish the section, if you want to know which are the most frequent terms in the data, you can use the `topfeatures()` function. In this case, most of the features can be intuitively guessed in their context. The only one that may require some explanation is the `br` feature. It comes from the fact that our data is coming from HTML pages that contain `<br>` strings that signal for a new line in the text (a break, hence the `br`). We could remove this feature if we wanted to, but we will leave for now:

```
topfeatures(train.dfm)
#>      br    like    tast  flavor     one    just   coffe    good     tri
product
#>     220     107     101      87      82      75      72      71      70
67
```

Training models with cross validation

In this section, we will efficiently train our first predictive model for this example and build the corresponding confusion matrix. Most of the functionality comes from the excellent `caret` package. You can find more information on the vast features within this package that we will not explore in this book in its documentation (`http://topepo.github.io/caret/index.html`).

Training our first predictive model

Following best practices, we will use **Cross Validation** (**CV**) as the basis of our modeling process. Using CV we can create estimates of how well our model will do with unseen data. CV is powerful, but the downside is that it requires more processing and therefore more time. If you can take the computational complexity, you should definitely take advantage of it in your projects.

Going into the mathematics behind CV is outside of the scope of this book. If interested, you can find out more information on Wikipedia (`https://en.wikipedia.org/wiki/Cross-validation_(statistics)`). The basic idea is that the training data will be split into various parts, and each of these parts will be taken out of the rest of the training data one at a time, keeping all remaining parts together. The parts that are kept together will be used to train the model, while the part that was taken out will be used for testing, and this will be repeated by rotating the parts such that every part is taken out once. This allows you to test the training procedure more thoroughly, before doing the final testing with the testing data.

We use the `trainControl()` function to set our repeated CV mechanism with five splits and two repeats. This object will be passed to our predictive models, created with the `caret` package, to automatically apply this control mechanism within them:

```
cv.control <- trainControl(method = "repeatedcv", number = 5, repeats = 2)
```

Our predictive models pick for this example are *Random Forests* (RF). We will very briefly explain what RF are, but the interested reader is encouraged to look into James, Witten, Hastie, and Tibshirani's excellent "*Statistical Learning*" (Springer, 2013). RF are a non-linear model used to generate predictions. A *tree* is a structure that provides a clear path from inputs to specific outputs through a branching model. In predictive modeling they are used to find limited input-space areas that perform well when providing predictions. RF create many such trees and use a mechanism to aggregate the predictions provided by this trees into a single prediction. They are a very powerful and popular Machine Learning model.

Let's have a look at the random forests example:

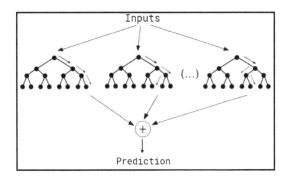

Random forests aggregate trees

To train our model, we use the `train()` function passing a formula that signals R to use `MULT_PURCHASES` as the dependent variable and everything else (~ .) as the independent variables, which are the token frequencies. It also specifies the data, the method (`"rf"` stands for random forests), the control mechanism we just created, and the number of tuning scenarios to use:

```
model.1 <- train(
    MULT_PURCHASES ~ .,
    data = train.dfm.df,
    method = "rf",
    trControl = cv.control,
    tuneLength = 5
)
```

Improving speed with parallelization

If you actually executed the previous code in your computer before reading this, you may have found that it took a long time to finish (8.41 minutes in our case). As we mentioned earlier, text analysis suffers from very high dimensional structures which take a long time to process. Furthermore, using CV runs will take a long time to run. To cut down on the total execution time, use the doParallel package to allow for multi-core computers to do the training in parallel and substantially cut down on time.

We proceed to create the train_model() function, which takes the data and the control mechanism as parameters. It then makes a cluster object with the makeCluster() function with a number of available cores (processors) equal to the number of cores in the computer, detected with the detectCores() function. Note that if you're planning on using your computer to do other tasks while you train your models, you should leave one or two cores free to avoid choking your system (you can then use makeCluster(detectCores() - 2) to accomplish this). After that, we start our time measuring mechanism, train our model, print the total time, stop the cluster, and return the resulting model.

```
train_model <- function(data, cv.control) {
    cluster <- makeCluster(detectCores())
    registerDoParallel(cluster)
    start.time <- Sys.time()
    model <- train(
        MULT_PURCHASES ~ .,
        data = data,
        method = "rf",
        trControl = cv.control,
        tuneLength = 5
    )
    print(Sys.time() - start.time)
    stopCluster(cluster)
    return(model)
}
```

Now we can retrain the same model much faster. The time reduction will depend on your computer's available resources. In the case of an 8-core system with 32 GB of memory available, the total time was 3.34 minutes instead of the previous 8.41 minutes, which implies that with parallelization, it only took 39% of the original time. Not bad right? We will study more the mechanics of parallelization and its advantages and disadvantages more in Chapter 9, *Implementing An Efficient Simple Moving Average*. Let's have look at how the model is trained:

```
model.1 <- train_model(train.dfm.df, cv.control)
```

Computing predictive accuracy and confusion matrices

Now that we have our trained model, we can see its results and ask it to compute some predictive accuracy metrics. We start by simply printing the object we get back from the `train()` function. As can be seen, we have some useful metadata, but what we are concerned with right now is the predictive accuracy, shown in the `Accuracy` column. From the five values we told the function to use as testing scenarios, the best model was reached when we used 356 out of the 2,007 available features (tokens). In that case, our predictive accuracy was 65.36%.

If we take into account the fact that the proportions in our data were around 63% of cases with multiple purchases, we have made an improvement. This can be seen by the fact that if we just guessed the class with the most observations (`MULT_PURCHASES` being true) for all the observations, we would only have a 63% accuracy, but using our model we were able to improve toward 65%. This is a 3% improvement. We will try to increase this improvement as we go through this chapter.

Keep in mind that this is a randomized process, and the results will be different every time you train these models. That's why we want a repeated CV as well as various testing scenarios to make sure that our results are robust:

```
model.1
#> Random Forest
#>
#>  212 samples
#> 2007 predictors
#>    2 classes: 'FALSE', 'TRUE'
#>
#> No pre-processing
#> Resampling: Cross-Validated (5 fold, repeated 2 times)
#> Summary of sample sizes: 170, 169, 170, 169, 170, 169, ...
#> Resampling results across tuning parameters:
#>
#>   mtry  Accuracy   Kappa
#>      2  0.6368771  0.00000000
#>     11  0.6439092  0.03436849
#>     63  0.6462901  0.07827322
#>    356  0.6536545  0.16160573
#>   2006  0.6512735  0.16892126
#>
#> Accuracy was used to select the optimal model using  the largest value.
#> The final value used for the model was mtry = 356.
```

To create a confusion matrix, we can use the `confusionMatrix()` function and send it the model's predictions first and the real values second. This will not only create the confusion matrix for us, but also compute some useful metrics such as sensitivity and specificity. We won't go deep into what these metrics mean or how to interpret them since that's outside the scope of this book, but we highly encourage the reader to study them using the resources cited in this chapter:

```
confusionMatrix(model.1$finalModel$predicted, train$MULT_PURCHASES)
#> Confusion Matrix and Statistics
#>
#>           Reference
#> Prediction FALSE TRUE
#>      FALSE    18   19
#>      TRUE     59  116
#>
#>                Accuracy : 0.6321
#>                  95% CI : (0.5633, 0.6971)
#>     No Information Rate : 0.6368
#>     P-Value [Acc > NIR] : 0.5872
#>
#>                   Kappa : 0.1047
#>  Mcnemar's Test P-Value : 1.006e-05
#>
#>             Sensitivity : 0.23377
#>             Specificity : 0.85926
#>          Pos Pred Value : 0.48649
#>          Neg Pred Value : 0.66286
#>              Prevalence : 0.36321
#>          Detection Rate : 0.08491
#>    Detection Prevalence : 0.17453
#>       Balanced Accuracy : 0.54651
#>
#>        'Positive' Class : FALSE
```

Improving our results with TF-IDF

In general in text analysis, a high raw count for a term inside a text does not necessarily mean that the term is more important for the text. One of the most important ways to normalize the term frequencies is to weigh a term by how often it appears not only in a text, but also in the entire corpus.

The more a word appears inside a given text and doesn't appear too much across the whole corpus, it means that it's probably important for that specific text. However, if the term appears a lot inside a text, but also appears a lot in other texts in the corpus, it's probably not important for the specific text, but for the entire corpus, and this dilutes it's predictive power.

In IR, TF-IDF is one of the most popular term-weighting schemes and it's the mathematical implementation of the idea expressed in the preceding paragraph. The TF-IDF value increases proportionally to the number of times a word appears in a given text, but is diluted by the frequency of the word in the entire corpus (not only the given text), which helps to adjust for the fact that some words appear more frequently in general. It is a powerful technique for enhancing the information contained within a DFM.

The TF normalizes all documents in the corpus to be length independent. The **inverse document frequency** (**IDF**) accounts for the frequency of term appearance in all documents in the corpus. The multiplication of TF by IDF takes both of these concepts into account by multiplying them. The mathematical definitions are as follows:

$$n(DFM) := number\ of\ texts\ in\ DFM$$

$$Freq(term,\ text) := count\ of\ term\ in\ text$$

$$Freq(term,\ DFM) := count\ of\ term\ in\ DFM$$

$$TF(term, text) := \frac{Freq(term, text)}{\sum_i^n Freq(term_i, text)}$$

$$IDF(term, DFM) := log(\frac{n(DFM)}{Freq(term, DFM)})$$

$$TFIDF(term, text, DFM) := TF(term, text) * IDF(term, DFM)$$

Now we are going to show how to program this TF-IDF statistic with R functions. Remember that we're working with a `dfm`, so we can use vectorized operations to make our functions efficient and easy to program. The first three functions `term_frequency()`, `inverse_document_frequency()`, and `tf_idf()`, should be easy to understand.

The `build_tf_idf()` function makes use of these functions to actually build the TF-IDF-weighted DFM. The idea being that we need to apply the functions we created to the rows or columns as necessary using the `apply()` function. We need to transpose the structure we get to get the texts in the rows and the features in the columns which is why we use the `t()` function midway through. Finally, we need to realize that sometimes we get NA's for certain combinations of data (try to figure out these cases yourself to make sure you understand) and we need to substitute them with zeros:

```
build_tf_idf <- function(dfm, idf = NULL) {
    tf <- apply(as.matrix(dfm), 1, term_frequency)
    if (is.null(idf)) {
        idf <- apply(as.matrix(dfm), 2, inverse_document_frequency)
    }
    tfidf <- t(apply(tf, 2, tf_idf, idf = idf))
    incomplete_cases <- which(!complete.cases(tfidf))
    tfidf[incomplete_cases, ] <- rep(0.0, ncol(tfidf))
    return(tfidf)
}
```

Now we can easily build our TF-IDF-weighted DFM using our `build_tf_df()` function and create the corresponding data frame as we have done earlier:

```
train.tfidf <- build_tf_idf(train.dfm)
train.tfidf.df <- build_dfm_df(train, train.tfidf)
```

Now the values inside our TF-IDF-weighted DFM will not only be integer values, which corresponded to frequency counts, but will be floating point values that correspond to the TF-IDF weights instead. We can train our next model using the same `train_model()` we used earlier:

```
model.2 <- train_model(train.tfidf.df, cv.control)
```

This time, our training process took 2.97 minutes. To see the results, simply print the model object. Remember that our previous predictive accuracy was of 65.36%. Now that we have used the TF-IDF-weighted DFM, it increased to 66.48%. This is not a drastic improvement, and it's due to the specific data we are working with. When working with other data or domains, you can expect this increase to be much larger:

```
model.2
#> Random Forest
#>
#>  212 samples
#> 2007 predictors
#>    2 classes: 'FALSE', 'TRUE'
#>
```

```
#> No pre-processing
#> Resampling: Cross-Validated (5 fold, repeated 2 times)
#> Summary of sample sizes: 170, 170, 170, 169, 169, 169, ...
#> Resampling results across tuning parameters:
#>
#>   mtry  Accuracy    Kappa
#>      2  0.6368771   0.00000000
#>     11  0.6368771   0.00000000
#>     63  0.6392580   0.01588785
#>    356  0.6603544   0.13818300
#>   2006  0.6648948   0.18269878
#>
#> Accuracy was used to select the optimal model using  the largest value.
#> The final value used for the model was mtry = 2006.
```

Adding flexibility with N-grams

The bag-of-words model takes into account isolated terms called **unigrams**. This looses the order of the words, which can be important in some cases. A generalization of the technique is called n-grams, where we use single words as well as word pairs or word triplets, in the case of bigrams and trigrams, respectively. The n-gram refers to the general case where you keep up to n words together in the data. Naturally this representation exhibits unfavorable combinatorial complexity characteristics and makes the data grow exponentially. When dealing with a large corpus this can take significant computing power.

With the `sentence` object we created before to exemplify how the tokenization process works (it contains the sentence: `If it looks like a duck, swims like a duck, and quacks like a duck, then it probably is a duck.`) and the `build_dfm()` function we created with the `n_grams` argument, you can compare the resulting DFM with `n_grams = 2` to the one with `n_grams = 1`. After analyzing the features in this DFM, you should have a clear idea on how the tokenization process filters some data out and how the bigrams are created. As you can see, n-grams can potentially bring back some of the lost word ordering, which sometimes can be very useful:

```
build_dfm(sentence, n_grams = 2)
#> Document-feature matrix of: 1 document, 14 features (0% sparse).
#> 1 x 14 sparse Matrix of class "dfmSparse"
#>          features
#>   docs    look like duck swim quack probabl look_like like_duck duck_swim
#> text1     1    3    4    1    1      1        1          3         1
#>          features
#>   docs    swim_like duck_quack quack_like duck_probabl probabl_duck
#> text1     1          1           1           1            1
```

To retrain our full model, we will recreate our TF-IDF-weighted DFM with bigrams this time and its corresponding data frame. Using the function we created earlier, it can easily be done with the following code:

```
train.bigrams.dfm <- build_dfm(train$MESSAGE, n_grams = 2)
train.bigrams.tfidf <- build_tf_idf(train.bigrams.dfm)
train.bigrams.tfidf.df <- build_dfm_df(train, train.bigrams.tfidf)
```

Now we will retrain the model and analyze its results. This can potentially take a lot of time depending on the computer you're using for training it. In our 8-core computer with 32 GB of memory, it took 21.62 minutes when executed in parallel. This is due to the large increase in the number of predictors. As you can see, we now have 9,366 predictors instead of the 2,007 predictors we had before. This huge 4x increase is due to the bigrams.

In this particular case, it seems that the added complexity from the bigrams doesn't increase our predictive accuracy. As a matter of fact, it decreases it. This can be for a couple of reasons, one of which is the increased sparsity, which implies a lower signal/noise ratio. In the next section, we will try to increase this ratio while keeping the bigrams:

```
model.3 <- train_model(train.bigrams.tfidf.df, cv.control)
model.3
#> Random Forest
#>
#>   212 samples
#> 9366 predictors
#>    2 classes: 'FALSE', 'TRUE'
#>
#> No pre-processing
#> Resampling: Cross-Validated (5 fold, repeated 2 times)
#> Summary of sample sizes: 170, 170, 169, 170, 169, 170, ...
#> Resampling results across tuning parameters:
#>
#>   mtry  Accuracy   Kappa
#>      2  0.6368771   0.000000000
#>     16  0.6368771   0.000000000
#>    136  0.6344961  -0.004672897
#>   1132  0.6133998  -0.007950251
#>   9365  0.6109081   0.051144597
#>
#> Accuracy was used to select the optimal model using  the largest value.
#> The final value used for the model was mtry = 2.
```

Reducing dimensionality with SVD

As we have seen in the previous section, the dimensionality course in our data was amplified due to the n-gram technique. We would like to be able to use n-grams to bring back word ordering into our DFM, but we would like to reduce the feature space at the same time. To accomplish this, we can use a number of different dimensionality reduction techniques. In this case, we will show how to use the SVD.

The SVD helps us compress the data by using it's singular vectors instead of the original features. The math behind the technique is out of the scope of the book, but we encourage you to look at Meyer's, *Matrix Analysis & Applied Linear Algebra, 2000*. Basically, you can think of the singular vectors as the important directions in the data, so instead of using our *normal* axis, we can use these singular vectors in a transformed space where we have the largest signal/noise ratio possible. Computing the full SVD can potentially take a very large amount of time and we don't really need all the singular vectors. Therefore, we will use the `irlba` package to make use of the **Implicitly Restarted Lanczos Bidiagonalization Algorithm** (**IRLBA**) for a fast partial SVD, which is much faster.

When using the partial SVD as our DFM, we are actually working in a different vector space, where each feature is no longer a token, but a combination of tokens. These new features are not easy to comprehend and you shouldn't try to. Treat it like a *black-box* model, knowing that you're operating in a higher signal/noise ratio space than you started in while drastically reducing it's dimensions. In our case, we will make the new space 1/4 of the original space. To do so, we will create a wrapper function to measure the time it takes to actually compute the partial SVD. The actual computation will be done with the `irlba()` function, sending the TF-IDF-weighted bigrams DFM and the number of singular vectors we want (1/4 of the possible ones) as the `nv` parameter:

```
build_svd <- function(dfm) {
    dfm <- t(dfm)
    start.time <- Sys.time()
    svd <- irlba(dfm, nv = min(nrow(dfm), ncol(dfm)) / 4)
    print(Sys.time() - start.time)
    return(svd)
}
```

Now we can easily create the partial SVD and the corresponding data frame. We also proceed to retrain our model. Note that even though it is conceptual, the `train.bigrams.svd` is our new DFM, in practice, within R, it's an object that contains our DFM as well as other data. Our DFM is in the v object within the `train.bigrams.svd` object, which is what we send to the `buildf_dfm_df()` function. Another important object within `train.bigrams.svd` is d, which contains the singular values from the decomposition.

As you can see, our feature space was drastically reduced to only 53 features (which is approximately 1/4 of the 212 samples available). However, our predictive accuracy was not higher than our previous results either. This means that probably bigrams are not adding too much information for this particular problem:

```
train.bigrams.svd <- build_svd(train.bigrams.tfidf)
train.bigrams.svd.df <- build_dfm_df(train, train.bigrams.svd$v)
model.4 <- train_model(train.bigrams.svd.df, cv.control)
model.4
#> Random Forest
#>
#> 212 samples
#>  53 predictors
#>   2 classes: 'FALSE', 'TRUE'
#>
#> No pre-processing
#> Resampling: Cross-Validated (5 fold, repeated 2 times)
#> Summary of sample sizes: 169, 170, 170, 170, 169, 170, ...
#> Resampling results across tuning parameters:
#>
#>   mtry  Accuracy   Kappa
#>    2    0.6344408  0.05602509
#>   14    0.6225360  0.06239153
#>   27    0.6272979  0.09265294
#>   40    0.6485604  0.13698858
#>   53    0.6366002  0.12574827
#>
#> Accuracy was used to select the optimal model using  the largest value.
#> The final value used for the model was mtry = 40.
```

Extending our analysis with cosine similarity

Now we proceed to another technique familiar in linear algebra which operates on a vector space. The technique is known as **cosine similarity** (**CS**), and its purpose is to find vectors that are similar (or different) from each other. The idea is to measure the direction similarity (not magnitude) among client messages, and try to use it to predict similar outcomes when it comes to multiple purchases. The cosine similarity will be between 0 and 1 when the vectors are orthogonal and perpendicular, respectively. However, this similarity should not be interpreted as percentage because the movement rate for the cosine function is not linear. This means that a movement from 0.2 to 0.3 does not represent a similar movement magnitude from 0.8 to 0.9.

Given two vectors (rows in our DFM), the cosine similarity among them is computed by taking the dot product between them and dividing it by the product of the Euclidian norms. To review what these concepts mean, take a look at Meyer's, *Matrix Analysis & Applied Linear Algebra, 2000.*

$$cosine\_similarity(V1, V2) = \frac{V1 \cdot V2}{\|V1\|_2 \|V2\|_2}$$

We create the `cosine_similarties()` function that will make use of the `cosine()` function from the lsa package. We send it a data frame and remove the first column, which corresponds to the dependent variable MULT_PURCHASES, and we use the transpose to make sure that we're working with the correct orientation:

```
cosine_similarities <- function(df) {
    return(cosine(t(as.matrix(df[, -c(1)]))))
}
```

Now we create the `mean_cosine_similarities()` function, which will take the cosine similarity among those texts that correspond to clients that have performed multiple purchases and will take the means of these similarities. We need to take the mean because we are computing many similarities among many vectors, and we want to aggregate them for each one of them. We could use other aggregation mechanisms, but the mean is fine for now:

```
mean_cosine_similarities <- function(df) {
    similarities <- cosine_similarities(df)
    indexes <- which(df$MULT_PURCHASES == TRUE)
    df$MULT_PURCHASES_SIMILARITY <- rep(0.0, nrow(df))
    for (i in 1:nrow(df)) {
```

```
        df$MULT_PURCHASES_SIMILARITY[i] <- mean(similarities[i, indexes])
    }
    return(df)
}
```

Now we can use this function to generate a new DFM's data frame that will be used to train a new model, which will take into account the cosine similarity among texts. As we saw earlier, it seems that using bigrams is not helping too much for this particular data. In the next section, we will try a different, very interesting, technique, sentiment analysis. Let's look at the following code:

```
train.bigrams.svd.sim.df <- mean_cosine_similarities(train.bigrams.svd.df)
model.5 <- train_model(train.bigrams.svd.sim.df, cv.control)
model.5
#> Random Forest
#>
#> 212 samples
#>  54 predictors
#>   2 classes: 'FALSE', 'TRUE'
#>
#> No pre-processing
#> Resampling: Cross-Validated (5 fold, repeated 2 times)
#> Summary of sample sizes: 169, 170, 170, 170, 169, 170, ...
#> Resampling results across tuning parameters:
#>
#>   mtry  Accuracy   Kappa
#>    2    0.6460687  0.08590598
#>   15    0.6227021  0.05793928
#>   28    0.6437431  0.12111778
#>   41    0.6296788  0.09535957
#>   54    0.6227021  0.07662715
#>
#> Accuracy was used to select the optimal model using  the largest value.
#> The final value used for the model was mtry = 2.
```

Digging deeper with sentiment analysis

We have now seen that vector space operations did not work too well regarding the predictive accuracy of our model. In this section, we will attempt a technique which is very different and is closer to the semantic parsing model we mentioned at the beginning of this chapter. We will try sentiment analysis.

We will not only take into account the words in a text, but we will also take into account shifters (that is, negators, amplifiers, de-amplifiers, and adversative conjunctions). A negator flips the sign of a polarized word (for example, I do not like it). An amplifier increases the impact of a polarized word (for example, I really like it.). A de-amplifier reduces the impact of a polarized word (for example, I hardly like it). An adversative conjunction overrules the previous clause containing a polarized word (for example, I like it but it's not worth it). This can be very powerful with some types of data.

Our sentiment analysis will produce a number, which will indicate the sentiment measured from the text. These numbers are unbounded and can be either positive or negative, corresponding to positive or negative sentiments. The larger the number, the stronger the inferred sentiment. To implement the technique, we will use the `sentimentr` package, which includes a clever algorithm to compute these sentiments. For the enthusiast, the details of the equation used are in its documentation (https://cran.r-project.org/web/packages/sentimentr/sentimentr.pdf).

To apply this technique, we send messages to the `sentiment_by()` function. This will give us back an object that contains, among other things, the `word_count` value and `ave_sentiment`, which is the average sentiment measured in all the sentences within a given text (`sentinmentr` internally splits each text into its components (sentences) and measures sentiment for each of them). We then add this objects into our DFM and proceed to train our model.

As you can see, this time we get a large increase in the predictive accuracy of the model up to 71.73%. This means that the sentiment feature is highly predictive compared to the other features we engineered in previous sections. Even though we could continue mixing models and exploring to see if we can get even higher predictive accuracy, we will stop at this point since you probably understand how to do these on your own at this point:

```
train.sentiment <- sentiment_by(train$MESSAGE)
train.sentiments.df <- cbind(
    train.tfidf.df,
    WORD_COUNT = train.sentiment$word_count,
    SENTIMENT = train.sentiment$ave_sentiment
)
model.6 <- train_model(train.sentiments.df, cv.control)
model.6
#> Random Forest
#>
#>  212 samples
#> 2009 predictors
#>    2 classes: 'FALSE', 'TRUE'
#>
#> No pre-processing
```

```
#> Resampling: Cross-Validated (5 fold, repeated 2 times)
#> Summary of sample sizes: 170, 170, 169, 170, 169, 170, ...
#> Resampling results across tuning parameters:
#>
#>   mtry  Accuracy   Kappa
#>      2  0.6368771  0.00000000
#>     11  0.6440753  0.04219596
#>     63  0.6863787  0.22495962
#>    356  0.6935770  0.28332726
#>   2008  0.7173198  0.31705425
#>
#> Accuracy was used to select the optimal model using  the largest value.
#> The final value used for the model was mtry = 2008.
```

Sentiment analysis, even though it looks very easy since it did not require a lot of code thanks to the `sentimentr` package, is actually a very hard area with active research behind it. It's very important for companies to understand how their customers feel about them, and do so accurately. It is and will continue to be a very interesting area of research.

Testing our predictive model with unseen data

Now that we have our final model, we need to validate its results by testing it with unseen data. This will give us the confidence that our model is well trained and will probably produce similar results where new data is handed to use.

A careful reader should have noticed that we used the TF-IDF data frame when creating our sentiment analysis data, and not any of the ones we create later with combinations of bigrams, SVDs, and cosine similarities, which operate in a different semantic space due to the fact they are transformations of the original DFM. Therefore, before we can actually use our trained model to make predictions on the test data, we need to transform it into an equivalent space as our training data. Otherwise, we would be comparing apples and oranges, which would give us nonsense results.

To make sure that we're working in the same semantic space, we will apply the TF-IDF weights to our test data. However, if you think about it, there probably are a lot of terms in our test data that were not present in our training data. Therefore, our DFMs will have different dimensions for our training and testing sets. This is a problem, and we need to make sure that they are the same. To accomplish this, we build the DFM for the testing data and apply a filter to it which only keeps the terms that are present in our training DFM:

```
test.dfm <- build_dfm(test)
```

```
test.dfm <- dfm_select(test.dfm, pattern = train.dfm, selection = "keep")
```

Furthermore, if you think about it, the corpus-weighing part of the TF-IDF, that is the IDF, will also be different than these two datasets due to the change in the term space for the corpus. Therefore, we need to make sure that we ignore those terms that are new (that is, were not seen in our training data) and use the IDF from our training procedure to make sure that our tests are valid. To accomplish this, we will first compute only the IDF part of the TF-IDF for our training data and use that when computing the TF-IDF for our testing data:

```
train.idf <- apply(as.matrix(train.dfm), 2, inverse_document_frequency)
test.tfidf <- build_tf_idf(test.dfm, idf = train.idf)
test.tfidf.df <- build_dfm_df(test, test.tfidf)
```

Now that we have the testing data projected into the vector space of the training data, we can compute the sentiment analysis for the new testing DFM and compute our predictions:

```
test.sentiment <- sentiment_by(test$MESSAGE)
test.sentiments.df <- cbind(
    test.tfidf.df,
    WORD_COUNT = test.sentiment$word_count,
    SENTIMENT = test.sentiment$ave_sentiment
)
```

Note that we are not training a new model in this case, we are just using the last model we created and use that to provide predictions for the testing DFM:

```
predictions <- predict(model.6, test.sentiments.df)
```

To know how well we predicted, we can just print a model as we did before because we would just be looking at the results from the training process that does not include predictions for the testing data. What we need to do is create a confusion matrix and compute the predictive accuracy metrics as we did before with the `confusionMatrix()` function.

As you can see, our results seem to be valid since we got a predictive accuracy of 71.91% with previously unseen data, which is very close to the predictive accuracy of the training data, and is 12% more than just guessing actual multiple purchases proportion. For text data and the problem we're dealing with, these results are pretty good.

If you know how to interpret the other metrics, make sure that you compare them to ones we had for our first model to realize how our results evolved during the chapter.

If you're not familiar with them, we suggest you take a look at James, Witten, Hastie, and Tibshirani's, *Statistical Learning, 2013*:

```
confusionMatrix(predictions, test$MULT_PURCHASES)
#> Confusion Matrix and Statistics
#>
#>           Reference
#> Prediction FALSE TRUE
#>      FALSE    11    4
#>      TRUE     21   53
#>
#>                Accuracy : 0.7191
#>                  95% CI : (0.6138, 0.8093)
#>     No Information Rate : 0.6404
#>     P-Value [Acc > NIR] : 0.073666
#>
#>                   Kappa : 0.3096
#>  Mcnemar's Test P-Value : 0.001374
#>
#>             Sensitivity : 0.3438

#>             Specificity : 0.9298
#>          Pos Pred Value : 0.7333
#>          Neg Pred Value : 0.7162
#>              Prevalence : 0.3596
#>          Detection Rate : 0.1236
#>    Detection Prevalence : 0.1685
#>       Balanced Accuracy : 0.6368
#>
#>        'Positive' Class : FALSE
```

If you're going to test with a DFM that was created using an SVD, you need to make the corresponding transformation to make sure you're working in the correct semantic space before producing any predictions. If you used a procedure like the one shown in this chapter, you need to left-multiply the testing DFM (with similar transformations as your training DFM) with the vector of singular values adjusted by sigma, while transposing the structures accordingly. The exact transformation will depend on the data structures you're using and processes you applied to them, but always remember to make sure that both your training and testing data operate in the same semantic space:

```
sigma.inverse <- 1 / train.bigrams.svd$d
u.transpose <- t(train.bigrams.svd$u)
test.bigrams.svd <- t(sigma.inverse * u.transpose %*%
t(test.bigrams.tfidf))
test.bigrams.svd.df <- build_dfm_df(test, test.bigrams.svd)
```

Retrieving text data from Twitter

Before we finish this chapter, we will very briefly touch on a completely different, yet very sought-after topic, that is, getting data from Twitter. In case you want to apply predictive models, you will need to link the Twitter data to a variable you want to predict, which normally comes from other data. However, something you can easily do is measure the sentiment around a topic using the techniques we showed in a previous section.

The `twitteR` package actually makes it very easy for us to retrieve Twitter data. To do so, we will create a **Twitter App** within Twitter, which will give us access to the data feed. To accomplish this, we need to generate four strings within your Twitter account that will be the keys to using the API. These keys are used to validate your permissions and monitor your usage in general. Specifically, you need four strings, the `consumer_key` value, the `consumer_secret`, the `access_token`, and the `access_secret`. To retrieve them, go to the Twitter Apps website (`https://apps.twitter.com/`), click on **Create New App**, and input the information required. The name for your Twitter App must be unique across all of the Twitter Apps. Don't worry about picking a complex name, you'll never use that string again. Also make sure that you read the Twitter Developer Agreement and that you agree with it.

Once inside the dashboard for your app, go to the **Keys and Access Tokens** tab, and generate a key and access token with their corresponding secret keys. Make sure that you copy those strings exactly as they will grant you access to the data feed. Substitute them instead of the ones shown here (which no longer work since they were deleted after writing this book), and execute the `setup_twitter_oauth()` function. If everything went as expected, you should now have connected your R session to the data feed:

```
consumer_key <- "b9SGfRpz4b1rnHFtN2HtiQ9xl"
consumer_secret <- "YMifSUmCJ4dlgB8RVxKRNcTLQw7Y4IBwDwBRkdz2Va1vcQjOP0"
access_token <- "171370802-RT14RBpMDaSFdVf5q9xrSWQKxtae4Wi3y76Ka4Lz"
access_secret <- "dHfbMtmpeA2QdOH5cYPXO5b4hF8Nj6LjxELfOMSwHoUB8"
setup_twitter_oauth(consumer_key, consumer_secret, access_token,
access_secret)
```

To retrieve data, we will create a wrapper function that will save us writing boilerplate again and again every time we want new data. The `get_twitter_data()` function takes a keyword we're searching for within Twitter and the number of messages we want to retrieve. It then goes on to get the data from Twitter using the `searchTwitter()` function (in English), transform the results into a data frame with the `twListToDF()` function, and send that back to the user:

```
get_twitter_data <- function(keyword, n) {
    return(twListToDF(searchTwitter(keyword, n, lang = "en")))
}
```

Now we can easily search for messages that contain the word *"cake"* inside by executing the following code. As you can see, we don't only get the messages, but we also get a lot of metadata, like whether or not the tweet has been favorite; if so, how many times, whether it was a reply, when was it created, and the coordinates of where the tweet was sent if they are available, among other things:

```
cake_data <- get_twitter_data("cake", 250)

names(cake_data)
#>  [1] "text"          "favorited"     "favoriteCount" "replyToSN"
#>  [5] "created"       "truncated"     "replyToSID"    "id"
#>  [9] "replyToUID"    "statusSource"  "screenName"    "retweetCount"
#> [13] "isRetweet"     "retweeted"     "longitude"     "latitude"
```

As an exercise, get data from Twitter with the mechanism shown precedingly and use it to create a world map that shows where the tweets are coming from and colors the pin locations using the sentiment inferred from the tweet. Having a piece of code like that can be fun to play with and joke around with your friends as well as for making real business decisions.

Summary

In this chapter, we showed how to perform predictive analysis using text data. To do so, we showed how to tokenize text to extract relevant words, how to build and work with **document-feature matrices** (**DFMs**), how to apply transformations to DFMs to explore different predictive models using term frequency-inverse document frequency weights, n-grams, partial singular value decompositions, and cosine similarities, and how to use these data structures within random forests to produce predictions. You learned why these techniques may be important for some problems and how to combine them. We also showed how to include sentiment analysis inferred from text to increase the predictive power of our models. Finally, we showed how to retrieve live data from Twitter that can be used to analyze what people are saying in the social network shortly after they have said it.

We encourage you to combine the knowledge from this chapter with that from previous chapters to try to gain deeper insights. For example, what happens if we use trigrams of quadgrams? What happens if we include other features in the data (for example, coordinates or client IDs)? And, what happens if we use other predictive models instead of random forests, such as support vector machines?

In the next chapter, we will look at how to use what we have done during the last three chapters to produce reports that can be automatically generated when we receive new data from The Cake Factory. We will cover how to produce PDFs automatically, how to create presentations that can be automatically updated, as well as other interesting reporting techniques.

7
Developing Automatic Presentations

Have you ever found yourself doing the same mechanical task over and over again? It's surprising how many programmers, statisticians, and scientists, in general, do not invest time to automate many of their activities, especially reporting results. Doing so would allow them to focus deeper on their core competencies. Furthermore, this is not unique to individuals; organizations at large still do not automate many of their processes, especially analytical ones. Remember the graph creation automation we performed in Chapter 2, *Understanding Votes with Descriptive Statistics*, or the regressions automation we performed in Chapter 3, *Predicting Votes with Linear Models*? In this chapter, we will show you how to automate another activity—developing presentations. By this, we don't mean to automate the explanations behind the results, but automate the creation of slides that show tables and graphs of the *current status* of a process. This a very high benefit/cost area that is often overlooked, and a lot of time is wasted producing such presentations for discussion among peers.

This is the last chapter for The Food Factory example, and here, we will automate an activity that people in many organizations find themselves doing over and over again—developing presentations for weekly updates. We will show what a content automation pipeline looks like in R and build a presentation that can be updated automatically with the latest data. To do so, we will use the results we have developed during the previous chapters in this example.

Some of the important topics covered in this chapter are as follows:

- The importance and benefits of automation
- Setting up and running automation pipelines
- Communicating ideas with literate programming
- Writing static content using Markdown
- Developing dynamic content using R Markdown
- Producing presentation and web pages using knitr
- Integrating R resources efficiently

Required packages

There are only two required packages for this chapter and you should be able to install them without a problem in your system. For more information take a look at `Appendix, Required Packages`.

Package	Reason
`ggrepel`	Avoid overlapping labels in graphs
`rmarkdown`	Markdown documents with executable R code

Why invest in automation?

Automation is an investment. It often involves taking different applications and integrating them to make processes happen repeatedly, hopefully seamlessly and effortlessly. Process automation can increase productivity by reducing the time taken to perform repetitive tasks, as well as reduce defects, which also saves time and enhances the value-creation process.

Furthermore, automated systems do not get bored. It's likely that anyone who has to undertake a repetitive task over and over again will get bored. This will slow down their performance and increase the risk of defects. An automated process will not get bored, no matter how often it is run, so performance is not likely to be slowed down.

Scientists can leverage automation to reduce cycle time through scientific methods, which in turn increases learning rates, often exponentially. In my opinion, this is one of the most powerful consequences of automation: accelerating learning processes by removing us (humans) from activities to which we do not add value, and allowing us to focus on activities that (so far) cannot be automated, such as being creative or developing innovative solutions to valuable problems.

Lastly, people often complain about not having enough time. One effective way to get time back is to automate processes, and that's the ultimate benefit of automation—making more of your time.

Literate programming as a content creation methodology

Automation requires us to put different pieces together in such a way that the process is clear for both humans and machines. The process must be reproducible and capable of evolving as new ideas come to us or requirements change. Automating content creation can be achieved with literate programming, which comes from Donald Knuth's *Literate Programming, 1992* (`http://www-cs-faculty.stanford.edu/~knuth/lp.html`). The basic idea is that a document is viewed as a combination of text and code. Code is divided into chunks with text surrounding the code chunks explaining what is going on. Text adapts as necessary to keep the ideas behind the code updated, clear, and accurate.

In this chapter, we use the words *presentation* and *document* interchangeably as you can create both of them with the tools we will show.

Literate programming is not a requisite for automating content creation, but it certainly is a great tool for it. Literate programming has the advantages of being easily readable, just as a manual or instruction set. Also, it allows for where code and natural language need to be combined. Results can be automatically shown as we go through the document. The document itself is simple text, which makes it flexible and easy to change. In general, literate programs are *weaved* to produce human-readable documents and *tangled* to produce machine-readable documents. To make this work, we only need a documentation language and a programming language, which are English and R in our case.

Literate programming seems to have the potential to make many tools obsolete that are currently being used to produce content. However, there are still better tools available if you need to produce documents with very accurate formatting or that require highly technical optimizations. This is not due to any inherent weaknesses in the concept of literate programming, but due to the fact that available tools are not as performant as specialized tools in those aspects.

When it comes to literate programming, R strikes a nice balance between technical complexity and simple presentations, allowing for a wide range of content automation to be developed, and this can produce documents that can serve very well for research and data analysis in general. If at some point you find that you need to make a change, you can easily do so, recompile, and you'll be looking at the latest version in a matter of seconds. That's why it's very handy to develop automated presentations the way we will show you in this chapter.

Reproducibility as a benefit of literate programming

In science, reproducibility is the most important element of verifying and validating analysis findings. The analyses, models, and algorithms we run are much more complicated than they used to be. Having a basic understanding of these algorithms is difficult, even for a sophisticated person, and it's almost impossible to describe with words alone. Understanding what someone did nowadays requires looking at data and code directly, not only at results.

Scientists write a lot of reports describing the results of data analyses. Making those reports reproducible is essential to have your work reviewed by your peers, and it is a very good way to accomplish this with literate programming. With it, the final report depends on code that is executed at the moment of its creation, and thus, reproducibility is embedded in the process. There's a clear and automatic path from data and code to the final report.

Literate programming for data analysis has become quite popular due to the development and communication efficiency it provides. In the following sections, we will show, how to do it using R, R Markdown, and knitr.

The basic tools for an automation pipeline

A pipeline is a process that starts with text, code, and raw data, and ends with the final document or presentation we want to show or distribute. Luckily, much of the hard work is automated for you within R, so there's not much you need to do other than install these tools and set up a compilation file.

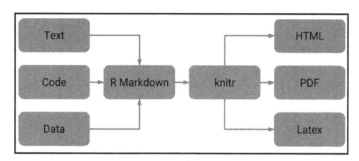

Our pipeline should be general enough to accommodate various use cases without having to be modified substantially. If it is, we can master one set of tools and reuse them for different projects rather than learning a new tool set each time. On the input side, using text, code, and data, is general enough. On the output side, being able to generate HTML, PDF, LaTeX, and even Word documents seems to be general enough so we are good to go.

Markdown is a low-overhead mark-up language (http://spec.commonmark.org/0.28/). Its main benefit for writers is that it allows us to focus on writing as opposed to formatting. It has simple and minimal yet intuitive formatting elements, and there are many programs that can translate Markdown into HTML and PDF files, among many others. R Markdown is an extension of Markdown to incorporate R code (http://rmarkdown.rstudio.com/). Documents written in R Markdown have R code nested inside, which allows us to create dynamic presentations. They can not be evaluated using standard Markdown tools. Instead, R code is evaluated as part of the processing of the R Markdown before the traditional Markdown tools are called.

One of the first literate programming systems in R is **Sweave**, which is used for creating dynamic reports and reproducible research using **LaTeX** (https://www.latex-project.org/). Sweave enables the embedding of R code within LaTeX documents to generate a PDF file that includes text, analysis, graphics, code, and the computation results. knitr (with first letter lowercase) is an R package that adds many new capabilities to Sweave (https://yihui.name/knitr/).

R Markdown can be converted to standard markdown using the knitr package in R, which inserts R results into a Markdown document. Markdown can subsequently be converted to HTML using Pandoc (a very powerful document translator, `https://pandoc.org/`). The use of R Markdown to create reproducible reports has quickly become a core tool for many scientists.

We won't go into details of how Sweave, LaTeX, or Pandoc transform files among different formats, since you won't have to operate them directly. We will focus on using R Markdown and knitr. However, we still need to make sure that we have all these tools installed in our system before we continue. Sweave is shipped within any R distribution. R Markdown and knitr can be installed within R. Pandoc and LaTeX should be installed directly into your computer. Specific instructions for Windows, macOS, and Linux can be found in `Appendix`, *Required Packages*.

Finally, you should note that these are not the only tools available to produce automated content. As literate programming for R has become a topic of high interest, naturally, many tools have been, and continue to be, developed for it. Even though this chapter focuses on R Markdown and knitr, there are other tools such as **R Studio's Presenter** (**RPres**) and **Slidify**. We have not shown this tools in this book because they are either more restricted in their application or more complex in their usage. We believe that the R Markdown-knitr combination strikes a very good balance between power and ease of use, and it's our combination of choice. However, we encourage the reader to research other tools and find the best fit.

A gentle introduction to Markdown

Markdown has various syntax versions that are supported by different systems and platforms. The one we show here is a general one that is useful throughout many systems, including R Markdown.

What we show in the following examples are the basic elements to structure content using Markdown. The actual aesthetics depend on what styles are being applied to your files. The examples shown as follows don't have any aesthetics applied to them. We will show you how to adjust them for our presentation later in the chapter.

Text

If you want simple text, you can simply write as you normally would. If you want to format the text, you can use pairs of asterisks (*) or underscores (_). The following table shows how to use pairs of asterisks. Underscores work the same way.

If we use the following input:

```
Text with *italic* text inside.
Text with **bold** text inside.
Text with **bold and *italic* text**.
```

We get the following output:

Text with *italic* text inside.

Text with **bold** text inside.

Text with ***bold and italic text***.

Headers

If you want, you can have the equivalent to sections (first-level headers), subsections (second-level headers), sub-subsections (third-level headers), and so on. The organizational structures are marked using a number sign, repeated as many times as the depth you want to produce in the document. A string like # Header would produce a first-level header, while ### Header would create a third-level header.

If we use the following input:

```
# Header Level 1

## Header Level 2

### Header Level 3

#### Header Level 4
```

We get the following output:

Header Level 1

Header Level 2

Header Level 3

Header Level 4

Lists

Lists can be ordered, unordered, and can be marked as tasks. These cover most cases you'll need, and they are very simple to use. For ordered lists, you can use hyphens (-) or asterisks (*), and you can nest them to create nested lists. For ordered lists, you can use numbers and letters. Finally, to create task lists, you simply need to put a pair of brackets at the beginning of an item ([]). If the brackets contain an X, then it means that the task has been completed. If the brackets have a space in between them, then the item is still pending.

If we use the following input:

```
1. This is an ordered item
   - This is an unordered item
   - This is another unordered item
2. This is another ordered item
   - [ ] This is a pending task
   - [X] This is a completed task
- [ ] This is another incomplete task
   1. Which contains one ordered item
   - And one unordered item
```

1. This is an ordered item
   - This is an unordered item
   - This is another unordered item
2. This is another ordered item
   - [ ] This is a pending task
   - [X] This is a completed task

- [ ] This is another incomplete task

1. Which contains one ordered item
   - And one unordered item

Tables

Tables are one of the most cumbersome structures to create when using Markdown. Having said that, it's still not hard to create them. If you align them, everything looks normal. However, most of the time, people don't align them, and they seem a bit odd if you're not used to the syntax. By non-aligned tables, we mean that there are no padding spaces after items so that vertical lines align. The table shown as follows is an aligned table.

If we use the following input:

```
| First column | Second column | Third column |
|--------------|---------------|--------------|
| Item one     | Item two      | Item three   |
| Item four    | Item five     | Item six     |
| Item seven   | Item eight    | Item nine    |
```

We get the following output:

First column	Second column	Third column
Item one	Item two	Item three
Item four	Item five	Item six
Item seven	Item eight	Item nine

Links

To provide links, you can simply write the link directly. If you want to name links so that only the name shows but not the URL, like the ones you see in web pages, you can use brackets containing the name followed immediately by parenthesis containing the actual link , in the format "[Name](URL)".

If we use the following input:

```
[The R Project for Statistical Computing](https://www.r-project.org/)
[Packt Publishing](https://www.packtpub.com/)
```

We get the following output:

```
The R Project for Statistical Computing

Packt Publishing
```

Images

Images have a similar structure to links, but they are preceded by an exclamation mark (!). The name for the image (what is contained inside the brackets) is only shown if the actual image was not (for example, the file was not found in the specified route). The URL is replaced by the path to the image you want to show. By default, an image's size will be as large as possible. Under the assumption that the images are within a directory named images in the same directory as the Markdown file is, the following example works.

If we use the following input:

```
[The R Project for Statistical Computing](./images/r.png)

[Packt Publishing](./images/packt-publishing.png)
```

We get the following output:

Quotes

Quotes are very useful when trying to emphasize points to the readers. They are also very easy to create. All you have to do is prepend a greater-than sign (>) followed by a space at the beginning of a line.

If we use the following input:

```
> Look deep into nature, and then you will understand everything better.
>
> —Albert Einstein
```

We get the following output:

> *Look deep into nature, and then you will understand everything better.*
>
> *- Albert Einstein*

Code

Code can be embedded within text using single backticks (`) surrounding it, or can be used in independent blocks by using triple backticks (```). Optionally, you may specify the programming language in the code block to activate syntax highlighting for that code.

If we use the following input:

```r
add_two_numbers <- function(x, y) {
    return(x + y)
}
```

We get the following output:

```
add_two_numbers <- function(x, y) {
    return(x + y)
}
```

Mathematics

Embedding mathematics in Markdown is similar to embedding code. However, instead of using backticks ("'), you use dollar signs ($). If you want to use mathematics blocks, you may use two (instead of three) dollar signs. Keep in mind that this is not a standard Markdown feature, and, even though R Markdown does support it, it may not be supported in other systems. If you're trying to create a web page using Markdown, to be able to use LaTeX-like code, you need to make sure that the system loads the `MathJax` library to the browser.

If we use the following input:

```
$$\Theta = \begin{pmatrix} \alpha & \beta \\ \gamma & \delta
\end{pmatrix}$$
```

We get the following output:

$$\Theta = \begin{pmatrix} \alpha & \beta \\ \gamma & \delta \end{pmatrix}$$

Extending Markdown with R Markdown

As mentioned earlier, R Markdown extends Markdown. It offers many features to enhance it. There are various examples in R Markdown's documentation (`http://rmarkdown.rstudio.com/gallery.html`) where you may get a sense of what's possible. In this section, we will focus on code chunks, tables, graphs, local and global chunk options, and caching.

Code chunks

Code chunks are simply standard Markdown code blocks, which have a special syntax that uses curly braces (`{}`) along the top line of the block to send metadata to knitr, about how the block should be treated. The metadata sent is in the form of parameters with the `key = value` format. We'll cover more on this in the *Chunk options* section.

When you use a block header like (```{r chunk-label}), knitr knows that it's an R code block which will be identified with the `chunk-label` label. The chunk label is not a requirement, and if you do not specify one, one will be automatically created for you, but they are useful when trying to remember the purpose of a code block and to reference images (more on this later).

Finally, you should note that whatever code you write inside a standard Markdown code block is not executed in any way, so it can be full of errors and nothing will happen. However, when using R Markdown code chunks, the code within an R block is actually evaluated when compiling the document, and if it contains errors, the document or presentation will not compile successfully until you fix them.

If we use the following input:

```
```{r optional-label}
1 + 2
```
```

We get the following output:

```
1 + 2
[1] 3
```

Tables

In informal reports, you may just print out a matrix or data frame rather than creating a formal table. If you need to, there are multiple ways to make tables with R Markdown that may look a bit nicer. We show how to use `kable` from the `knitr` package, as it's the simplest one. If you need more control, you may look at the `xtable` package, which gives you complete control. You need to be sure to use `results = "asis"` in the code chunk.

If we use the following input:

```
```{r r-markdown-label, results = "asis"}
library(knitr)
x <- rnorm(100)
y <- 2 * x + rnorm(100)
coeficients <- summary(lm(y ~ x))$coef
kable(coeficients, digits = 2)
```
```

We get the following output:

	Estimate	Std. error	t value	Pr(>|t|)
(Intercept)	0.02	0.10	0.21	0.83
x	2.09	0.09	22.98	0.00

Graphs

Creating graphs with R Markdown is as easy as creating the within R. Actually, you don't need to do anything extra; knitr is smart enough to do it automatically. If you need to, specify the width and height for your image using the corresponding chunk options shown in the next section.

If we use the following input:

```{r basic-r-graph}
attach(mtcars)
plot(wt, mpg)
abline(lm(mpg ~ wt))
title("Regression of MPG on Weight")
```

We get the following output:

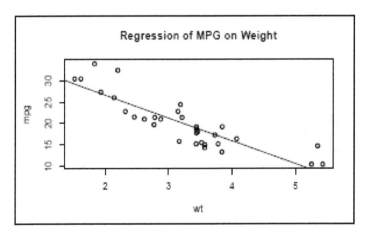

Chunk options

When working with chunks we have a lot of flexibility, and this flexibility can be seen by the many options we may adjust. Here, we will only mention the most common ones. To avoid including the code as output, use `echo = FALSE`. To avoid showing the results, use `include = FALSE`. To avoid evaluating the code block, use `eval = FALSE`. To avoid showing warnings, use `warning = FALSE`. To set the figure width and height, use `fig.height = 10` and `fig.width = 10` with the actual numbers you want (units are inches by default). All of these can be used in the code chunk header shown as follows:

```
```{r some-label, include = TRUE, eval = FALSE}
1 + 2
```
```

Global chunk options

You may use global chunk options rather than repeated local chunk options. Whenever you need to, you can override a global chunk option by specifying a different local chunk option. Using the following code would make every code chunk have the `echo = TRUE` and `eval = FALSE` options enabled, unless otherwise specified at specific blocks:

```
```{r global-options}
knitr::opts_chunk$set(echo = TRUE, eval = FALSE)
```
```

Caching

As we mentioned earlier, knitr is not so useful if you are writing a very long document or one involving complex computations. However, you may avoid some of these problems by using caches. The basic issue is that if you have a long document or one involving lengthy computations, then every time you want to *refresh* your document, you need to recompile it, meaning that you need to rerun all the computations. This may not be a problem if your document is efficient or small. However, it can be inefficient to sit there and wait for every computation to run every single time. Chunk caching is one way to avoid those lengthy computations. By setting the `cache = TRUE` chunk option, knitr runs the chunk once and stores the output in your working directory. When you *reknit* the document, instead of running the code in that particular chunk, knitr will reload the stored output. If the code in the chunk changes at all, knitr will detect it and will rerun the code, storing the updated results.

There are some caveats to caching. In particular, by default, dependencies between chunks are not checked. If the results of a cached chunk depend on a previous chunk that has been modified, those changes will not necessarily propagate down to later cached chunks. Also, chunks with significant side effects, such as those writing output to files or interacting with the external environment in any way, may not be cacheable. As long as you are careful with these, you should not have any issues.

Producing the final output with knitr

Once you have a finished document or are ready to see its next iteration, you may compile within R Studio if you're using it or by executing the code that triggers the compilation. We will show the latter since it's more general and can be used by people who are not necessarily using R Studio. You simply need to execute the following lines, changing the filename "document.Rmd" with your own, and choosing the appropriate output:

```
library(rmarkdown)
outputs <- c("html_document", "pdf_document")
render("document.Rmd", outputs)
```

We suggest that you create a compile.R file that contains those line, and execute it every time you want to recompile your document. The following outputs are available:.

String	Output
html_document	HTML document
pdf_document	PDF document
word_document	Word document
10slides_presentation	HTML presentation, type 1
slidy_presentation	HTML presentation, type 2
beamer_presentation	Beamer (LaTex) PDF presentation

At this point, you should be able to create your own presentations. In the following sections, we will start building the presentation we want to actually develop for The Food Factory example.

Developing graphs and analysis as we normally would

As you saw in previous sections, you can work directly with our R Markdown file for the presentation (`presentation.Rmd`, in our case). However, you can be more productive if you first develop the content for the presentation as you would normally work with R, taking advantage of any configurations and tooling you may be accustomed to. When the code has been finalized, you translate only the necessary parts into the R Markdown file. Even though it seems counter intuitive because it would be more work, it's actually faster to work this way just because you're used to working with R more than with R Markdown, and you'll think about producing modular code that can be plugged into your presentation. This allows your to produce higher quality and reusable code. That's exactly what we will do here. We will start working with our usual `main.R` and `functions.R` files to develop what we need. Then, in a later section, we will migrate the code into our `presentation.Rmd` file.

Since we want to present the analysis we have developed during the last couple of chapters and we shouldn't rewrite code, we will bring some of it back from Chapter 4, *Simulating Sales Data and Working with Databases*, as well as the data that we simulated for **The Food Factory**:

```
source("../../chapter-05/functions.R")
all_time <- readRDS("../../chapter-04/results/sales.rds")
```

Note that using the `source()` function, as we did, loads into memory all of the functions we have in the functions file from Chapter 5, *Communicating Sales with Visualization*. This may or may not be what you actually need, and if you're not careful, you may end up overwriting a function definition when doing so. In this particular case, it's not a problem, so we'll leave it as is. If it were a problem, we could always move the desired function into its own file and just `source` that file. The function we are interested in is the following:

```
filter_n_days_back <- function(data, n) {
    if (is.null(n)) {
        return(data)
    }
    n_days_back <- Sys.Date() - n
    return(data[data[, "DATE"] >= n_days_back, ])
}
```

Let's suppose that a long time has passed since you first simulated the data. If you execute a function call like `filter_n_days_back(data, 7)`, you are not guaranteed to have the data for the previous week, and you'll most likely get an empty result due to `n_days_back <- Sys.Date() - n` containing data of 7 days back from `today`, not the last date recorded in the data. That's a problem.

How to deal with situations like these can take you down a long debate with your peers. In general, we have two options: rewrite an independent function, or fix the code we already have. The right answer will depend on your specific circumstances and context, and both of them have their advantages and disadvantages. In general, when you write a new function, you'll be certain that your code works and that you didn't accidentally break someone else's code, which depended on the previous version. The disadvantage is that you'll have to maintain more code without gaining much functionality, and over time, this can be a huge pain. Remember the DRY principle we mentioned before? **Don't Repeat Yourself (DRY)**. If you decide to fix the current version of the code, you will possibly end up with a more robust code base that you can reuse for even more cases that you initially anticipated without increasing too much (sometimes decreasing) the code you need to maintain. However, there's also the possibility that you break code that depended on the previous functionality, which can be very tricky to fix down the road when you realize that you did.

There are two basic fundamentals that will save you from strong headaches when dealing with these types of situations. We have been using one of them throughout this book: developing small and modular code. By small, we mean code that follows the *Single Responsibility* principle, mentioned in `Chapter 1`, *Introduction to R*. When you do, something magical happens; you start plugging in code to other code and you can easily modify those plugins and create new ones as you need them without too much trouble. The other fundamental is having unit tests for your code. Simply put, unit tests are pieces of code designed to test that other code is performing as it should. Unit testing is out of the scope for this book, but it's something you should definitely study if you don't already know.

Going back to the code for this specific example, we choose to fix the code we already have. For us to make sure that we don't accidentally break other code that depends on this function, we follow the *Open-Closed* principle, which states that objects should be open for extensions and closed for modification (`https://www.cs.duke.edu/courses/fall07/cps108/papers/ocp.pdf`).

Basically, we will extend the interface without modifying it in such a way that the output is the same when using the same previous inputs, but the extended version will allow us to get the new outputs we want. It sounds more cumbersome than it really is. As you can see, we simply add a new optional parameter with a default value of NULL. Then, instead of computing n_days_back with the current date, we check to see if any value was sent; if it was, then we use that as the starting point; if not, we go back to the old behavior:

```
filter_n_days_back <- function(data, n, from_date = NULL) {
    if (is.null(n)) {
        return(data)
    }
    if (is.null(from_date)) {
        from_date <- Sys.Date()
    } else if (is.character(from_date)) {
        from_date <- as.Date(from_date)
    }
    n_days_back <- from_date - n
    return(data[data[, "DATE"] >= n_days_back, ])
}
```

Now that we have this new version of the function, we can actually use it to take the last week in the data by computing the maximum date we have recorded in it, and using that as our from_date parameter. Also, note how easy it is to take not only the data for this week, but also from last week. However, for this to work, we need to make sure that the max_date object is a Date object in R, so that we can subtract 7 from it, and it actually means 7 days. If it's a string instead of a date, we would get an error.

As a side note, note that if were using data that is constantly being recorded, *this week* and *last week* would make perfect sense, but since we're using data we simulated possibly a long time ago, *this week* and *last week* will vary depending on the dates in the actual data we're using. That's not a problem because we're using the *maximum* date in the data, which will be adjusted accordingly for each situation:

```
max_date <- max(all_time$DATE)
this_week <- filter_n_days_back(all_time, 7, max_date)
last_week <- filter_n_days_back(all_time, 7, max_date - 7)
```

Now that we have the three datasets we need (`all_time`, `last_week`, and `this_week`), we can start developing the code that will use them to create the graphs we're looking for. First, we need to get proportion tables for each variable of interest and for each dataset. As always, we want to wrap code that is not very explicit about its functionality into its own function so that we can assign a name to it and quickly know what it's supposed to do. In this case, we create the `proportion_table()` function, which should be self-explanatory, and we apply it as mentioned. Note that we're multiplying by `100`, because we want to show `20%` instead of `0.2` in our graphs:

```
proportions_table <- function(data, variable) {
    return(prop.table(table(data[, variable])))
}

quantity_all <- proportions_table(all_time, "QUANTITY")
continent_all <- proportions_table(all_time, "CONTINENT")
protein_all <- proportions_table(all_time, "PROTEIN_SOURCE")

quantity_last <- proportions_table(last_week, "QUANTITY")
continent_last <- proportions_table(last_week, "CONTINENT")
protein_last <- proportions_table(last_week, "PROTEIN_SOURCE")

quantity_this <- proportions_table(this_week, "QUANTITY")
continent_this <- proportions_table(this_week, "CONTINENT")
protein_this <- proportions_table(this_week, "PROTEIN_SOURCE")
```

At this point, each of these objects should contain a table with the percentage of each category within the variable of interest. Those ending with _all contain the percentages for all the data recorded. Similarly, those ending with _last and _this contain the percentages for last week and this week, respectively. The number of decimal points will depend on the actual data and your configuration. In all cases, the numbers should add up to 100:

```
quantity_all
#>     1      2      3      4      5      6      7      8      9
#> 13.22  27.78  26.09  18.29  9.19  3.77  1.29  0.30  0.07

quantity_last
#>       1       2       3       4       5       6       7       8
#> 12.1387 33.5260 28.3234 12.7160 5.7803 5.7803 1.1560 0.5780

quantity_this
#>  1  2  3  4  5  6  7  8
#> 12 36 25 14  7  4  1  1
```

The careful reader should have noticed that `quantity_all` contains one more category than `quantity_last` and `quantity_this`. That's because in the last two weeks in the data, there were no sales for nine items. This means that when we try to compare the count change in each of these categories, we will have a problem due to the extra category in `quantity_all`. We will deal with it by keeping only categories that are shared among any table pair we're using. The `equal_length_data()` function receives two of these tables as `data_1` and `data_2`, then, it computes the minimum length (`ml`) among them and uses it to get elements up to that point in both `data_1` and `data_2`. Since both of them are tables at this point, we want the numeric array of its values, not the table object, that's why we apply the `as.numeric()`. If we don't do so, `ggplot2` will complain about not knowing how to deal with objects of type `table`. We don't lose the category names by applying the `as.numeric()` function to the tables because we're taking those separately in the `names` element of the returned list. Finally, we want to know if any categories were deleted, and we can know that by checking if the length of any of the data tables contains less categories than the `ml` number indicates. If that's the case, `deleted` will be TRUE and will be sent, and it will be FALSE otherwise:

```
equal_length_data <- function(data_1, data_2) {
    ml <- min(length(data_1), length(data_2))
    return(list(
        names = names(data_1[1:ml]),
        data_1 = as.numeric(data_1[1:ml]),
        data_2 = as.numeric(data_2[1:ml]),
        deleted = ml != length(data_1) || ml != length(data_2))
    )
}
```

We now have access to data with equal length, with the corresponding category names, and with a Boolean value indicating whether any categories were deleted. We can use this object as follows:

```
parts <- equal_length_data(quantity_all, quantity_this)

parts$names
#> [1] "1" "2" "3" "4" "5" "6" "7" "8"

parts$data_1
#> [1] 0.1322 0.2778 0.2609 0.1829 0.0919 0.0377 0.0129 0.0030

parts$data_2
#> [1] 0.12 0.36 0.25 0.14 0.07 0.04 0.01 0.01

parts$deleted
#> [1] TRUE
```

Now, we will focus on preparing the data for our graphs. As we will be using the `ggplot2` package, we know we need to create a dataframe. This dataframe should contain category names in `Category`, the absolute and percent differences among matching categories from the two tables in the `Difference` and `Percent`, respectively, the `Sign` and `Color` depending on whether the absolute difference is positive or negative, and the *before* and *after* data in `Before` and `After`, respectively. Note that the order in which the `parts` were computed is important for the absolute and percent differences, which in turn impact the color and sign. We must be careful of sending the latest data as `data_2` so that we get an interpretation like *compared to last week, this week we had X more*. Otherwise, the interpretation would be inverted:

```
prepare_data <- function(parts) {
    data <- data.frame("Category" = parts$names)
    data$Difference <- parts$data_2 - parts$data_1
    data$Percent <- (parts$data_2 - parts$data_1) / parts$data_1 * 100
    data$Sign <- ifelse(data$Difference >= 0, "Positive", "Negative")
    data$Color <- ifelse(data$Difference &gt;= 0, GREEN, RED)
    data$Before <- parts$data_1
    data$After <- parts$data_2
    return(data)
}
```

We will define two colors using hexadecimal notation so that we can call them by name instead of copying the hexadecimal string every time. Later, if we want to change the colors, we can change them in a single place instead of replacing them everywhere we used them:

```
RED <- "#F44336"
GREEN <- "#4CAF50"
```

If you read Chapter 5, *Communicating Sales with Visualizations*, the `difference_bars()` function should be clear. As you can see, we are computing the `parts` and `data` objects using the functions shown earlier, and then we use the `ggplot2` package to develop the graph. Note that we only add a subtitle containing the indication that some categories have been deleted if the `deleted` Boolean from `parts` is TRUE:

```
difference_bars <- function(data_1, data_2, before, after) {
    parts <- equal_length_data(data_1, data_2)
    data <- prepare_data(parts)
    p <- ggplot(data, aes(Category, Difference, fill = Sign))
    p <- p + geom_bar(stat = "identity", width = 0.5)
    p <- p + scale_fill_manual(values =
    c("Positive" = GREEN, "Negative" = RED))
    p <- p + theme(legend.position = "none",
    text = element_text(size = 14))
    p <- p + scale_y_continuous(labels = scales::percent)
```

```
p <- p + labs(title = paste(before, "vs", after))
p <- p + labs(x = "", y = "")
if (parts$deleted) {
    p <- p + labs(subtitle =
        "(Extra categories have been deleted)")
}
return(p)
}
```

Now we can create some useful graphs, as follows. Keep in mind that the values in the y axis do not indicate a percentage growth, but a change in percentage points. This can be immediately understood by looking at the code, but it is not clear when looking at the graph. In reality, we would have to include some explanation for this in a real presentation:

```
difference_bars(quantity_all, quantity_this, "This week", "All-time")
difference_bars(continent_all, continent_this, "This week", "All-time")
difference_bars(protein_all, protein_this, "This week", "All-time")
```

The resulting graphs are shown as follows:

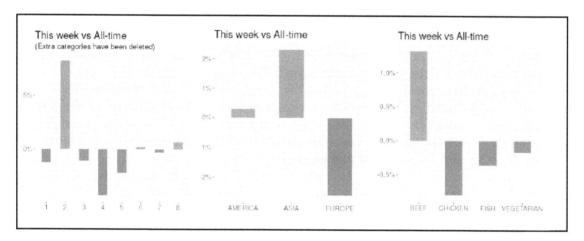

The second type of graph we want to develop is a bit more complex. We will create vertical lines at 1 and 2 along the x axis, place text labels indicating where the percentage for each category is in the `before` and `after` data sets, and the change percentage in the middle. First, we create the `data` object as we did before. Next, we create the labels we will use for each category. The ones one the left are the `before_labels`, the ones in the center are the `percent_labels`, and the ones in the right are the `after_labels`.

The `percent_y` contains the values for the y axis where the `percent_labels` will be placed. The *x* axis value is fixed at 1.5 so that it's between the two vertical lines. To compute the `percent_y` value, we want to get the minimum between the before and after values for each category and add half the difference between them. This will make sure that the value is at the middle of the line that will join both values.

We are now ready to start using the `ggplot2` package. First, we define the data as we normally would and add a segment joining the *before* and *after* values for each category by starting at the $(1, \text{ Before})$ tuple and ending at the $(2, \text{ After})$ tuple, where each tuple has the form (x, y). We will use the `Sign` variable as the *fill* color for the bars, and avoid showing a legend since we will show some labels ourselves. We will use the *scale_color_manual()* function to specify the colors that should be used for each line depending on whether the absolute difference was positive or negative.

Next come the vertical lines, which are created with the `geom_vline()` function. As mentioned before, they will be placed at values 1 and 2 along the *x* axis. We will make the line dashed to improve aesthetics and use a smaller size than the segment lines we created before.

Next, we will place the labels using the `geom_text()` function. We start creating the label for each of the vertical lines, which are created at 0.7 and 2.3 *x* axis values, and a slightly increased maximum of the *before* and *after* values. Then, we place the labels for the categories in the left, center, and right using the `geom_text_repel()` function. This function is not included in the `ggplot2` package, and it's actually an extension for it. It is designed to *repel* (hence the name) labels that overlap each other. To do so, the function moves labels away from the point's position and draws a line that indicates which label belongs to each point. You can find nice examples on its website (`https://cran.r-project.org/web/packages/ggrepel/vignettes/ggrepel.html`). In our case, we remove said line with the *segment.color = NA* parameter and indicate that the direction for adjustment is only along the *y* axis.

In reality, it's very hard for someone to come up with all of this code on their first attempt, and our case was no different. We started with some small plots and continuously added the elements we were looking for through iterated experimentation. In particular, we realized that some labels were overlapping each other, which doesn't look great, and so we decided to use the `geom_text_repl()` package, which we did not previously know, but easily found online since many people have the same problem and luckily someone had developed a solution for it.

The x_adjustment parameter is a result of similar experimentation. We realized that different graph's labels were overlapping the vertical lines depending on the number of characters in the category names. To fix that, we decided to introduce a new parameter that adjusts the position along the x axis that can be experimented with until we find a good parameter for it. All this is to say that you should take advantage of R's rapid experimentation cycles to iteratively produce what you're looking for.

Finally, we remove any text from the x and y axes and limit their range of values because they are unnecessary to read the graph and provide a cleaner visualization. It may take a bit of experimentation for you to understand exactly what each part of the code is doing, which is totally fine, and you should definitely do so:

```
change_lines <- function(data_1, data_2, before, after, x_adjustment) {
    parts <- equal_length_data(data_1, data_2)
    data <- prepare_data(parts)
    percent_labels <- paste(round(data$Percent, 2), "%", sep = "")
    before_labels <- paste(
        data$Category, " (", round(data$Before, 2), "%)", sep = "")
    after_labels <- paste(
        data$Category, " (", round(data$After, 2), "%)", sep = "")
    percent_y <- (
        apply(data[, c("Before", "After")], 1, min) +
        abs(data$Before - data$After) / 2
    )

    p <- ggplot(data)
    p <- p + geom_segment(
        aes(x = 1, xend = 2, y = Before, yend = After, col = Sign),
        show.legend = FALSE,
        size = 1.5)

    p <- p + scale_color_manual(
        values = c("Positive" = GREEN, "Negative" = RED))

    p <- p + geom_vline(xintercept = 1, linetype = "dashed", size = 0.8)
    p <- p + geom_vline(xintercept = 2, linetype = "dashed", size = 0.8)
    p <- p + geom_text(
        label = before,
        x = 0.7,
        y = 1.1 * max(data$Before, data$After),
        size = 7)

    p <- p + geom_text(
        label = after,
        x = 2.3,
        y = 1.1 * max(data$Before, data$After),
```

```
    size = 7)

p <- p + geom_text_repel(
    label = before_labels,
    x = rep(1 - x_adjustment, nrow(data)),
    y = data$Before, size = 5, direction = "y",
    segment.color = NA)

p <- p + geom_text_repel( label = after_labels,
    x = rep(2 + x_adjustment, nrow(data)),
    y = data$After, size = 5,
    direction = "y",
    segment.color = NA)

p <- p + geom_text_repel(label = percent_labels,
    x = rep(1.5, nrow(data)),
    y = percent_y, col = data$Color, size = 5,
    direction = "y",
    segment.color = NA)

p <- p + theme(
    axis.ticks = element_blank(),
    axis.text.x = element_blank(),
    axis.text.y = element_blank()
)

p <- p + ylim(0, (1.1 * max(data$Before, data$After)))
p <- p + labs(x = "", y = "")
p <- p + xlim(0.5, 2.5)
return(p)
}
```

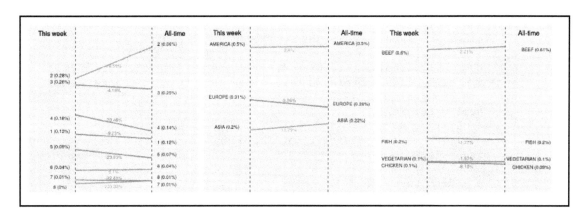

Now, we can present some very useful and nice-looking graphs with the following code:

```
change_lines(quantity_last, quantity_this, "This week", "Last week", 0.2)
change_lines(continent_last, continent_this, "This week", "Last week", 0.3)
change_lines(protein_last, protein_this, "This week", "Last week", 0.5)
```

These graphs can be easily interpreted and don't seem to be as vulnerable to the *x* axis percentage units problem we mentioned for the previous graphs. You can easily see if a category increased or decreased its percentage among periods, and by how much percentage. Keep in mind that the plots for *all-time* also contain *this week* when interpreting them. In reality, this may or may not be correct for your specific use case.

Building our presentation with R Markdown

In this section, we will develop our presentation's R Markdown file. We create an empty file named `presentation.R` and put the following headers in. The quotation marks are not required unless you want to include a colon in the title. As shown in a previous section, using backticks (" '), we can execute R code. In this case, we put the current date automatically in the front page. Finally, we chose `ioslides_presentation` as an output format. Feel free to experiment with the other outputs shown previously:

```
---
title:    "The Food Factory"
author:   "Weekly Update"
date:     "`r Sys.Date()`"
output:   ioslides_presentation
---
```

The following code sets up the default configuration for the *code chunks* in our presentation. We avoid showing code in the presentation with `echo = FALSE` and make each picture full width unless stated otherwise with `out.width = '100%'`:

```
```{r setup, include=FALSE}
knitr::opts_chunk$set(echo = FALSE, out.width = '100%')
```
```

Now, we need to bring all the resources we need for our presentation to work. Specifically, we need to load the functions we have developed along the last three chapters. Load the data `sales` and `client_messages` data and apply the same transformation we have seen in previous chapters to set up the data. Note that in this chapter, we referenced the sales data as `all_time` instead of `sales`, and to avoid changing our code so that we can still easily reference our development files, we simply copy the `sales` object into the `all_time` object. Be careful when doing this if you have tight memory restrictions in your system:

```r
```{r load-functions-and-data, include=FALSE}
source("../functions.R")
source("../../chapter-05/functions.R")
source ("../../chapter-06/functions.R")

sales            <- readRDS("../../chapter-04/results/sales.rds")
client_messages <- readRDS("../../chapter-04/results/client_messages.rds")
sales            <- add_profits(sales)

all_time  <- sales
max_date  <- max(all_time$DATE)
this_week <- filter_n_days_back(all_time, 7, max_date)
last_week <- filter_n_days_back(all_time, 7, max_date - 7)

quantity_all  <- proportions_table(all_time, "QUANTITY")
continent_all <- proportions_table(all_time, "CONTINENT")
protein_all   <- proportions_table(all_time, "PROTEIN_SOURCE")

quantity_last  <- proportions_table(last_week, "QUANTITY")
continent_last <- proportions_table(last_week, "CONTINENT")
protein_last   <- proportions_table(last_week, "PROTEIN_SOURCE")

quantity_this  <- proportions_table(this_week, "QUANTITY")
continent_this <- proportions_table(this_week, "CONTINENT")
protein_this   <- proportions_table(this_week, "PROTEIN_SOURCE")
```
```

Now that our resources have been set up, we can work on the code that will actually show our analysis in the presentation. We start with the slides that use the functions we developed previously in this chapter to show changes using bars and lines. Note that we are specifying different heights in each case for bar and line graphs. Also note that we're using a 50% width for line graphs. That's because we want them to appear vertically in the slide. A 50% width with a height of 10 achieves that distribution.

In reality, you may want to choose better titles for each slide, but we will keep them obvious for this example. Note that working this way, we avoid placing any logic code in our slides, and by simply reading the function titles, we know exactly what will be shown. This lets you easily move things around without breaking things up due to dependencies among pieces of code since we have abstracted that into separate files. If you fill your presentation files with R logic, you'll quickly find it very confusing when you need to change them. It's better to have that logic in an actual `.R` file, as we do with our `functions.R` file. Not to mention that it's also much more reusable that way:

```
## Changes in quantity (1/2)

```{r quantity-bars, fig.height = 2.5}
difference_bars_absolute(quantity_last, quantity_this, "This week", "Last
week")
difference_bars_absolute(quantity_all, quantity_this, "This week", "All-
time")
```

Changes in quantity (2/2)

```{r quantity-lines, out.width = '50%', fig.height = 10}
change_lines(quantity_last, quantity_this, "This week", "Last week", 0.2)
change_lines(quantity_all, quantity_this, "This week", "All-time", 0.2)
```

Changes in continent (1/2)

```{r continent-bars, fig.height = 2.5}
difference_bars_absolute(continent_last, continent_this, "This week", "Last
week")
difference_bars_absolute(continent_all, continent_this, "This week", "All-
time")
```

Changes in continent (2/2)

```{r continent-lines, out.width = '50%', fig.height = 10}
change_lines(continent_last, continent_this, "This week", "Last week", 0.3)
change_lines(continent_all, continent_this, "This week", "All-time", 0.3)
```

Changes in protein source (1/2)

```{r protein-source-bars, fig.height = 2.5}
difference_bars_absolute(protein_last, protein_this, "This week", "Last
week")
```
```

```
difference_bars_absolute(protein_all, protein_this, "This week", "All-
time")
```

```
## Changes in protein source (2/2)
```

```
```{r protein-source-lines, out.width = '50%', fig.height = 10}
change_lines(protein_last, protein_this, "This week", "Last week", 0.5)
change_lines(protein_all, protein_this, "This week", "All-time", 0.5)
```
```

Now, we will add function calls to code we developed in previous chapters. As you can see, the process is exactly the same since we have already loaded those resources at this point in the `load-functions-and-data` code chunk shown earlier. All we have to do is actually call the functions that produce the graphs for us. If you can't remember what these functions do, we suggest to go back to their corresponding chapters to go over the details on how they were created.

As you can see, the last slide from this *code chunk* calls the `graph_client_messages_interactive()` function that produces the interactive map you could move around in Chapter 5, *Communicating Sales with Visualizations*. A great thing about creating presentations this way is that you can actually play around with the map within the presentation! Of course, this will only work if you're using an output format that uses the web browser for visualization (it will not work with PDFs or Word documents, for example), but it can be a fantastic way to add powerful content to your presentations if you're using a web browser to visualize them:

```
## Profit ratio vs continent
```

```
```{r sales-proft-ratio-by-continent-and-protein-source }
graph_bars(sales, "CONTINENT", "PROFIT_RATIO", "PROTEIN_SOURCE")
```
```

```
## Cost vs price
```

```
```{r price-vs-cost}
graph_marginal_distributions(sales, "COST", "PRICE", "PROTEIN_SOURCE",
"CONTINENT")
```
```

```
## Price vs profit
```

```
```{r price-vs-profit-ratio}
graph_marginal_distributions(sales, "PRICE", "PROFIT_RATIO",
"PROTEIN_SOURCE", "CONTINENT")
```
```

```
## Historic pricing

```{r date-vs-frequency-profit-and-profit-ratio, fig.height = 1.8}
graph_last_n_days(sales, 30, color = "PROTEIN_SOURCE")
graph_last_n_days(sales, 30, "PROFIT", "PROTEIN_SOURCE")
graph_last_n_days(sales, 30, "PROFIT_RATIO", "PROTEIN_SOURCE")
```


Top 5 customers' preferences

```{r top-customers-preferences}
subset <- filter_data(sales, 30, 5, "CLIENT_ID")
graph_radar(subset, "CLIENT_ID")
```


Customer messages geolocations

```{r customers-dynamic-map}
graph_client_messages_interactive(client_messages, sales)
```
```

Finally, we want to show the latest tweets using actual live Twitter data. Since The Food Factory company that we have alluded to during this example is fictitious, we can't really get data for it, but we will still search Twitter for *The Food Factory* phrase and show the top 5 results we get back. In reality, you can retrieve tweets that mention a specific account you're interested in, and be more creative with the querying process. We will keep it simple for this example.

The first thing we must do, as shown in Chapter 6, *Understanding Reviews with Text Analysis*, is to identify ourselves with Twitter's API so that we can retrieve data. If you don't remember how to do so, take a look at said chapter. Since we want to execute this piece of code but we don't want to show it or its output, we simply apply the option include = FALSE. Note that we keep the slide title on top of the authentication code as a sign to ourselves that this code belongs to this slide's logic:

```
## Latest messages from Twitter

```{r twitter-setup, include = FALSE}
consumer_key    <- "b9SGfRpz4b1rnHFtN2HtiQ9xl"
consumer_secret <- "YMifSUmCJ4dlgB8RVxKRNcTLQw7Y4IBwDwBRkdz2Va1vcQjOP0"
access_token    <- "171370802-RT14RBpMDaSFdVf5q9xrSWQKxtae4Wi3y76Ka4Lz"
access_secret   <- "dHfbMtmpeA2QdOH5cYPXO5b4hF8Nj6LjxELfOMSwHoUB8"
setup_twitter_oauth(consumer_key, consumer_secret, access_token,
access_secret)
```
```

Next, we put in another *code chunk* that actually produces the output we want to show in the slide. We are getting data from Twitter using the `get_twitter_data()` we created in the previous chapter, and we pass it through the `format_tweets()` function we will show next:

```
```{r twitter-live-data, size = "footnotesize", comment = ""}
format_tweets(get_twitter_data("The Food Factory", 5))
```
```

This `format_tweets()` function was necessary to print the data we are interested in showing in the slide. If you remember, the data we get from the `get_twitter_data()` function contains quite a bit of metadata around each tweet, which is very useful when doing analysis, but for this slide, we would rather show only the screen name for the person who tweeted, the tweet's timestamp, and the actual tweet. We also need to truncate the tweet's length to make sure that it looks fine in the presentation. Even though it's a small function, the code can be a bit complex if you haven't seen those functions before, so we will take it step by step.

The `format_tweets()` function receives a single argument, which is the data we got back from the `get_twitter_data()` function, and we know that data structure contains the `created`, `text`, and `screenName` variables we're interested in. Since this is vectorized code, we don't have to use a for loop to print each tweet independently. We can simply use the arrays of values directly. If you don't remember what vectorized code refers to, you can review it in Chapter 1, *Introduction to R*:

```
format_tweets <- function(data) {
    write(paste(
        data$screenName, " (", data$created, "): \n",
        iconv(enc2utf8(substr(data$text, 1, 65)), sub = ""),
        "(...) \n", sep = ""
    ), stdout())
}
```

The first thing you may notice is that we're not using the `print()` function. We are using the `write()` function passing in the `stdout()` function call. This means that we will *write* an object into the standard output. You can think of this as a *dumb* `print()` function call, where R will not do any processing for us, and will simply show exactly what we tell it to. What this does is avoid printing the numbered lines we normally get when using the print function. Remember those [1], [2], ... at the beginning of the output in the previous code? This `write(..., stdout())` technique avoids them. You normally don't want that, but it's useful for aesthetics purposes in this particular case.

Next, we use the `paste()` function as we have been doing to put together everything we want to print. In this case, we start with screen names, followed by parenthesis enclosing the timestamp (contained in `data$created`), and followed by a combination that indicates a *new line*. The `\n` combination, when used inside the `write()` function, tells R to actually introduce a new line at that point, just as if you had pressed the *return* key (*Enter* key on your keyboard). Next, we pass the actual tweet (`data$text`) to the `substr()` function so that we can get characters 1 through 65. This is done, again, for aesthetic purposes since we don't want very long tweets to take more than one line. That output is sent to the `enc2utf8()` function, which sets the string's encoding to UTF-8, and this output is passed through the `iconv()` function with a `sub = ""` parameter, which will delete any non-convertible characters. Finally, we put a `"(...) \n"` string to show that the tweet was probably truncated, and another *new line* symbol.

When using the `iconv()` function, what happens is that it will try to convert characters one by one, and whenever it can't convert a character, it will replace it with the `sub` string we send. We need to do this because we may get characters from languages like Chinese or Arabic whose output, would contain a Unicode representation which would not make sense to people who are not familiar with these types of encoding issues. We're trying to produce a user-friendly presentation.

> *If you recompile this presentation, the messages you retrieve from Twitter will be different from the ones shown here because they will be retrieved at that moment.*

Now, you can compile your presentation with any of the methods mentioned earlier, and if everything goes fine, you should see a `presentation.html` file in your directory. If you open that file in your web browser, you should see slides similar to the ones shown as follows. You may also open directly the live presentation in the repository for this book. Remember to play around with the interactive map!

```
Session info --------------------------------------------------
setting value
version R version 3.4.2 (2017-09-28)
system x86_64, linux-gnu
ui X11
language (EN)
collate en_US.UTF-8
tz America/Mexico_City
date 2017-10-30

Packages ------------------------------------------------------
package * version date source
assertthat 0.2.0 2017-04-11 CRAN (R 3.3.2)
base * 3.4.2 2017-10-28 local
```

```
base64enc 0.1-3 2015-07-28 CRAN (R 3.3.2)
bindr 0.1 2016-11-13 CRAN (R 3.3.2)
[... truncated ...]
```

Summary

In this chapter, we discussed the benefits of automating tasks as well as content creation. We showed how to integrate automation pipelines for content creation, how to write R Markdown documents, which provide dynamic content, and how to use these documents to produce documents and presentations that look nice and are efficient. We showed how to integrate various R resources to create content that can be updated automatically.

In case you want to develop documents that are more technical or lengthy, the bookdown package may be a good option for you. Its purpose is to make the creation of lengthy documents, such as books, easier using R Markdown. As a matter of fact, this book was written using bookdown, and the process was a really nice one.

In the next chapter, we will start a new example focused on evaluating cryptocurrency trades. We will start by building an object-oriented system that simulates a trading platform and evaluates traders' performances automatically. After that, we will show you how to make our algorithms run faster by using parallelization and delegation, and finally, in the last chapter, we will show you how to create web pages that contain interactive dashboards, all from within R.

8
Object-Oriented System to Track Cryptocurrencies

In this chapter, we will introduce a new way of programming that we have not explicitly used before in the book. It's called object-oriented programming, and it will be used throughout our third and final example in the book. Object-oriented programming is very popular among programmers, and it's mainly used to allow for complex abstraction relations to be modeled and implemented in such a way that the evolution of the system is not jeopardized.

When developing object-oriented systems, and in general when we program, we should strive for simplicity, but it doesn't come naturally. When dealing with a complex domain, it's easier to create complex rather than simple code. Programmers must make an active effort to produce simple code, since simplicity depends mostly on the programmer, not the language. In this chapter, we will show you how to efficiently work with object-oriented code by introducing the ideas and concepts that support it, and we will later illustrate how to implement it using three of R's most used object models.

R has various object models, or object-oriented systems, so it can be a bit intimidating at first. The goal of this chapter is not to make you an expert in object-oriented programming or in each of R's object models, but to help you understand how to implement the basic building blocks of object-oriented programs with R's different object models.

Some of the important topics covered in this chapter are:

- Fundamental object-oriented programming concepts
- Design and architecture of object-oriented systems
- R's parametric polymorphism through generic functions
- The different object models available for R
- Mixing functionality from R's different object models

This chapter's required packages

This chapter will make use of the `methods` and `R6` packages to load the S4 and R6 object models functionality. You should know that interactive R sessions load the `methods` by default, but non-interactive sessions don't, so you need to explicitly load it in such cases. The `jsonlite` and `lubridate` packages are brought to simplify some common tasks like getting data from JSON APIs and transforming dates. For more information, take a look at `Appendix`, *Required Packages*.

Package	Reason
R6	R6 object model
methods	S4 object model
lubridate	Easily transform dates
jsonlite	Retrieve data from JSON APIs

The cryptocurrencies example

A **cryptocurrency** is a digital currency designed to work as a medium of exchange. Cryptocurrencies use cryptography to secure and verify transactions, as well as to control the creation of new units. Simply put, cryptocurrencies are entries in a public and distributed database that can only be changed by algorithmic consensus, and they remove the need for trusted third-parties for transaction handling and currency emission. The concept closely resembles peer-to-peer networks for file sharing, with an algorithmic monetary policy on top. If you want to learn more about cryptocurrencies, you should definitely look at videos starring Andreas Antonopoulos. He can make very complex concepts very easy to understand. You may also want to read his recollection of conferences in his book, *The Internet of Money, by Merkle Bloom LLC, 2016.*

Cryptocurrencies are being heavily developed nowadays to offer many innovative features that will have disruptive effects during upcoming years, but for now, they are mostly used for buying goods and investing. Every transaction consists of the amount of coins transferred, as well as the sender's and recipient's public keys, also known as wallet addresses. We will use these public keys in the example for this chapter to keep track of how many coins we own, and we will also use CoinMarketCap API (`https://coinmarketcap.com/`) to keep track of cryptocurrency prices.

Since this will be a complex system, we will use object-oriented programming to modularize it and build it part by part. At the end of the example, we will have a system that can be turned on to start tracking our cryptocurrency assets as well as their prices, and to save the real-time data to disk for later analysis. Later, in `Chapter 9`, *Implementing an Efficient Simple Moving Average*, we will use this data, in simulated form, to develop various **Simple Moving Average** (**SMA**) implementations to showcase how R code can be improved to become faster, as well as more readable. Finally, in `Chapter 10`, *Adding Interactivity with Dashboards*, we will see how to create a modern web application to show the SMAs developed, as well as the data collected.

A brief introduction to object-oriented programming

As statisticians and data scientists, we strive to build systems that produce valuable insights. To accomplish this, we normally use two tools—mathematics and computers. This book was developed for people who are comfortable with the mathematics side but feel that their R programming skills need improvement.

Normally, when people with mathematical backgrounds are introduced to programming, they are introduced through a *functional approach*, which means that they think in terms of algorithms with inputs and outputs, which are implemented as functions. This way of working is intuitive if you come from a mathematical background and are not dealing with high level abstractions, and it is the way we have been working throughout the book up to this point.

This chapter will show a different way of programming called **object-oriented programming**. Object-oriented programming and the object model are powerful and unifying ideas in many fields and can be found in most popular programming languages, R being no exception. In my experience, people who have not had conscious experience with object-oriented programming normally find it confusing at first and don't understand its potential. They see it as more of a hassle than an enabler, and think that it gets in their way when trying to write some code. In this chapter, we will try to distill the object-oriented paradigm in a way that is understandable to people who feel comfortable with a functional approach (not necessarily with functional programming), and we will show you how to implement a small object-oriented system that continuously retrieves live data from cryptocurrency markets and wallets.

Before we start implementing such a system, we need to introduce the concepts that will be used throughout the rest of the example, including the upcoming two chapters. In the following paragraphs, you will find very general descriptions of the concepts behind the object model, which is implemented with object-oriented programming, as well as explanations that will hopefully convince you that this way of programming can be very powerful for certain problems. For a more exhaustive and formal introduction, you should read the excellent book by Booch, Maksimchuck, Engle, Young, Conallen, and Houston, titled, *Object-Oriented Analysis and Design With Applications, by Addison-Wesley, 2007*.

The purpose of object-oriented programming

The main purpose of object-oriented programming is to efficiently manage complexity. It's a way of organizing code and data such that you can develop well-delimited abstractions with controlled dependencies to evolve a complex system in a controlled manner. These abstractions are called **objects** and they offer behavior in response to messages. The behavior they offer to other objects is cataloged in an interface which is implemented in this object's public methods. Objects request behavior from other objects, and when they do, they are said to depend on them. The messages sent between all these objects and the associated behavior are what make an object-oriented system useful.

Before we go any further, let's explain more about these concepts. An object is an entity in abstract form. For example, integers, cars, dogs, buildings, credit cards, and cryptocurrencies, could all be objects in an object-oriented system. An object is a well-defined idea of something, and we know that different kinds of objects have different kinds of behaviors associated with them, and some of those behaviors require some data, which is normally stored within the object.

For example, the idea of an integer is not associated with any specific number, just as the idea of a car is not associated with any specific model or brand. For those familiar with statistics, think of a random variable as an object, and a realization of that random variable as an instance.

Object-oriented programming is a way of thinking of programs as interactions among objects instead of steps through an algorithm. You can still understand an object-oriented system as a big algorithm with lots of functions calling each other, but for large enough systems this will not be a fruitful or enjoyable process. When dealing with object-oriented systems, you're better off just trying to understand a part of the system by itself and clearly defining how it should communicate with other parts. Trying to fully understand a complex object-oriented system can prove to be quite challenging.

Important concepts behind object-oriented languages

There are many ways to implement the object model in object-oriented languages, and the specific ways it is implemented imply different sets of properties for the language. Some of these properties are encapsulation, polymorphism, generics (parametric polymorphism), hierarchies (inheritance and composition), subtyping, and several others. They are powerful, high-level ideas with precise definitions that impose restrictions on how a language should behave. Don't worry too much about them for now; we will explain the necessary ones as we move forward.

An interesting exercise is to find languages that are considered to be object-oriented, yet don't use one or more of these properties. For example, the class concept is unnecessary, as seen with prototype-based languages like JavaScript. Subtyping is also unnecessary, since it doesn't make sense in dynamically typed languages like R or Python. We could go on and on, but you get the idea—a single language that has all of these properties does not exist. Furthermore, the only property that is found in all object-oriented languages is polymorphism. That's why people commonly say that polymorphism is the essence of object-oriented programming.

Any professional object-oriented programmer should understand these properties and have formal experience with languages that implement them. However, in the following paragraphs, we will give a high-level explanation of the most common ones in R's different object models—encapsulation, polymorphism (with and without generics), and hierarchies.

Encapsulation

Encapsulation is about hiding an object's internals from other objects. As the designer of the C++ language, Bjarne Stroustrup, put it, *Encapsulation hides information not to faciliate fraud, but to prevent mistakes.* By giving other objects a minimal catalog of messages (public methods) that they can send to an object, we are helping them commit less mistakes and avoid getting their hands in tasks that do not pertain them. This, in turn, helps with decoupling objects from themselves and providing cohesiveness within objects.

A common way to think about encapsulation is like when you go to a restaurant—you message the waiter with what you want, and the waiter then delegates the cooking of what you requested to the restaurant's chef. You have no business in going into the restaurant's kitchen and telling the chef how to cook your meal, and if the chef wants to change the way he cooks a certain dish, she can do so without you having to know about it. It's the same with objects; they should not get inside another object and tell it how to do its job. This sounds simple enough, but in practice, it's very easy to violate this principle. We will talk more about this when we reach the *Law of Demeter* section later in this chapter. Technically, the process of separating the interface from the implementation is called **encapsulation**.

Polymorphism

Polymorphism is perhaps the most powerful feature of object-oriented programming languages, next to their support for abstraction, and it is what distinguishes object-oriented programming from more traditional programming with abstract data types. **Polymorphism** literally means many forms, and that's exactly what it is used for in object-oriented programming. The same name will denote different meanings, depending on the context in which it is used, just as with our natural languages. This allows for much cleaner and understandable abstractions, as well as code.

Loosely speaking, polymorphism can be implemented in two different ways: from inside or from outside objects. When it's implemented from inside objects, each object must provide a definition of how it will deal with a given message. This is the most common method, and you can find it in Java or Python. R is very special in this manner and implements the outside approach, formally know as **generics**, or **parametric polymorphism**. This way of programming can be frustrating for people who have only used the inside approach, but it can be very flexible. The outside approach lets you define a generic method or function for types of objects that you have not yet defined, and may never do. Java and Python can also implement this type of polymorphism, but it's not their nature, just as R can also implement the inside, but it's not its nature, either.

Hierarchies

Hierarchies can be formed in two ways—inheritance and composition. The idea of **inheritance** is to form new classes as specialized versions of old ones. The specialized classes are subclasses and the more general ones are superclasses. This type of relationship is often referred to as an **is-a** type of relationship, since *a subclass is a type of the superclass*. For example, a lion is a type of animal, so animal would be the superclass and lion the subclass. Another type of relationship is known as the **has-a** relation. This means that one class has instances of another class. For example, a car has wheels. We wouldn't say that wheels are a type of car, so there's no inheritance there, but we would say that they are part of a car, which implies **composition**.

There are cases where it's not so clear whether a relation should be modeled with inheritance or with composition, and in those cases, you should decide to move along with composition. In general, people agree that composition is a much more flexible way of designing a system, and that you should only use inheritance where you must model the specialization of a class. Note that when you design your systems with composition instead of inheritance, your objects take on different roles and they become more tool-like. That's a good thing, because you can easily plug them into each other and replace them as necessary, and you also usually end up with larger numbers of smaller classes.

Now that you understand some fundamental ideas behind object-oriented programming, you may realize the power that combining these ideas gives you. If you have a system that encapsulates behavior and only publicly offers what is needed by others to operate correctly, which can dynamically respond to abstract ideas with correct and concrete actions and allows for concept hierarchies to interact with other concept hierarchies, then you can rest assured that you can manage quite a bit of complexity.

In the following paragraphs, we will explain some more down-to-earth concepts which are basic building blocks in most object-oriented systems and that you need to understand to be able to follow the code we will develop for the example.

Classes and constructors

Objects must be defined in some way so that we can generate specific instances from them. The most common way to provide those definitions is through classes. A **class** is a piece of code that provides the definition for an object, including the behavior it offers in response to messages from other objects, as well as the internal data it needs to provide that behavior. The behavior for a class is implemented in its methods. More on this in the next section.

Classes must be created at some point, and that's where constructors come into play. The vast majority of the time, when you create an instance of a class, you will want it to contain some data about itself. That data is assigned to the class when it's created through its constructor. Specifically, a **constructor** is a function whose job is to create an instance of a class with a specific set of data. As you know, that data should be kept inside the object, and other objects should not interact with this data directly. Instead, the object should offer public methods that other objects may use to get the data or behavior they need.

Public and private methods

Methods are functions contained within classes, and in general, they will be either public or private. In general, methods have access to classes' data (which should be encapsulated away from other objects), as well as their public and private methods.

Public methods are visible to other objects and should be as stable as possible since other objects may come to depend on them. If you change them, you may unexpectedly break another object's functionality. **Private methods** are visible only to the instance itself, which means that other objects cannot (or should not, as is the case with R) call these methods directly. Private methods are allowed to change as often as necessary.

Public methods make use of other methods, public or private, to further delegate behavior. This delegation breaks up a problem into very small pieces which are easily understandable, and the programmer reserves the right to modify private methods as she sees fit. Other objects should not depend on them.

Note that technically, only public methods exist in R. Under one of R's object models you can hide methods and under another you can put them in a different environment, but that does not make them inaccessible, as the case would be with private methods in other languages. Derived from that, we also don't touch on the concept of protected methods, which are methods that are visible to a class and its subclasses.

 Even if there are technically no private methods in R, we will program as if there were. Not having some type of compiler or error-checking mechanism to tell you that you're accessing private methods when you shouldn't is not an excuse for doing so. You should always be producing high quality code, even if not explicitly enforced by language mechanisms.

What we said previously implies that you should make your objects as private as possible to keep them cohesive and decoupled, which are fancy terms for self-contained and independent. In other words, try to reduce the number of methods in your objects as much as possible. Of course, cohesiveness and decoupleness are far more general ideas than just reducing the number of private methods, but it's a good start.

Interfaces, factories, and patterns in general

An **interface** is the part of a class that is made public for other objects to use. Specifically, it's a set of definitions for the public methods of a class. Of course, the more public methods an object has, the more responsibilities and the less flexibility it has towards the outside world. Note that the interface does not provide any details about implementation; it's just a contract which defines what inputs and what outputs are expected when a method is called.

Sometimes, you want to give yourself the flexibility of changing the object for a given task according to context. You know that as long as the interfaces for the objects you want to interchange are the same, everything should be fine (of course, this assumes that the programmers implement said interfaces correctly). If you don't plan for it in advance, switching these objects can be a difficult task. That's where factories come into play. A factory is a way to choose, at runtime and according to context, which object to use from a set of predefined options.

Factories basically work as `if` statements that choose which class to use for a task based on some condition. They are a way of investing a little more effort today so that you save yourself quite a bit of effort later, when you decide to use a different object for the same interface. They should be used where you anticipate you will be using different kinds of objects in the future.

Factories are one of many know **patterns** for object-oriented programming. These patterns are developed by people with a lot of experience on design decisions, and, as such, they know what solutions can be generally good for certain types of problems. Documenting these patterns is very useful and allows many people to save a lot of time and effort by not having to reinvent the wheel in their own context. A great source for some fundamental object-oriented patterns can be found in Gamma, Vlissides, Johnson, and Helmfamous's famous, *Design Patterns: Elements of Reusable Object-Oriented Software*, by Addison-Wesley, 1994. We encourage the reader to study these patterns, as they will surely prove useful at some point.

Introducing three object models in R – S3, S4, and R6

Now that you have a basic understanding of general object-oriented concepts, we will dig into R's own object models. There are two main sources of confusion when doing object-oriented programming in R. Before we start developing code, we will explain what these sources of confusion are. After we do, we will develop a small example to illustrate inheritance, composition, polymorphism, and encapsulation in R's S3, S4, and R6 object models. The same example will be used for all three models so that the reader can pinpoint precise differences. Specifically, we will model a `Square` inheriting from a `Rectangle`, which is in turn composed with a `Color`.

The first source of confusion – various object models

The way you work with object-oriented programming in R is different from what you may see in other languages, such as Python, Java, C++, and many others. For the most part, these languages have a single object model that all people use. In the case of R, note that we have been writing object models, in plural. That's because R is a very special language and it has various ways of implementing object-oriented systems. Specifically, R has the following object models as of this book's writing—S3, S4, Reference Classes, R6, and Base Types. In the upcoming sections, we will dig deeper into the S3, S4, and R6 models. Now, we will briefly touch on Reference Classes and Base Types.

Reference Classes (**RC**) is the object-model in R that does not require external libraries and is most similar to the well-known object model found in Python, Java, or C++. It implements message-passing as those languages do, meaning that methods belong to classes, not to functions, and objects are mutable, meaning that an instance's data may change in place instead of producing copies with the modified data. We will not dig deeper into this object model, since R6 seems to be a cleaner implementation of such a model. However, R6 does require an external package, as we will see later, which is not a problem, and it is therefore preferred.

Base types are not exactly an object model, per se. They are C implementations that work in R's background and are used to develop the other object models on top of them. Only R's core development team may add new classes to this model, and they very rarely do so (many years can pass before they do). Their usage is very advanced, and we will not dig deeper into them, either.

The decision of what object model to use is an important one, and we will touch more on this after we have shown how to work with them. In general, it will come down to a trade-off between flexibility, formality, and code cleanness.

The second source of confusion – generic functions

Another big difference with popular object-oriented languages like the ones mentioned before is that R implements parametric polymorphism, also known as generic functions, which implies that methods belong to functions, not classes. **Generic functions** allow the same name to be used for many different functions, with many different sets of arguments, from many different classes. This means that the syntax to call a class's method is different from the normally chained syntax you find in other languages (normally implemented with a "." (dot) between a class and the method we want to call), which is called **message-passing**.

R's method calls look just like function calls, and R must know which names require simple function calls and which names require method calls. If you read the previous sections, you should understand why this is important. R must have a mechanism to distinguish what it's supposed to do. That mechanism is called **generic functions**. By using generic functions, we register certain names to be treated as methods in R, and they act as dispatchers. When we call registered generic functions, R will look into a chain of attributes in the object that is being passed in the call, and will look for functions that match the method call for that object's type; if it finds one, it will call it.

You may have noted that the `plot()` and `summary()` functions may return different results, depending on the objects that are being passed to them (for example, a data frame or a linear model instance). That's because those are generic functions that implement polymorphism. This way of working provides simple interfaces for users, which can make their tasks much simpler. For instance, if you are exploring a new package and you get some kind of result at some point derived from the package, try calling `plot(result)`, and you may be surprised to get some kind of plot that makes sense. This is not common in other languages.

When doing object-oriented programming with R's S3 and S4 models, keep in mind that you should not call methods directly, but should declare corresponding generic functions and call those instead. This may be a bit confusing at first, but it's just one of R's unique characteristics that you get used to with time.

The S3 object model

As you may recall, the R language is derived from the S language. S's object model evolved over time, and its third version introduced **class attributes**, which allowed for the S3 object model we find in R today. It is still the object model in R, and most of R's own built-in classes are of the S3 type. It's a valid and very flexible object model, but it's very different from what people who come from other object-oriented languages are used to.

S3 is the least formal object model, so it's lacking in some key respects. For example, S3 does not offer formal class definitions, which implies that there's no formal concept of inheritance or encapsulation, and polymorphism is achieved through generics. It's clear that its functionality is limited in some key respects, but the programmer has quite a bit of flexibility. However, as Hadley Wickham put it in *Advanced R, by Chapman and Hall, 2014*:

> "*S3 has a certain elegance in its minimalism: you can't take away any part of it and still have a useful object-oriented system.*"

Classes, constructors, and composition

The idea of an object is really just to bundle data and corresponding methods together. Lists in R are well-suited to implement this, since they can contain different data types, even functions, which are first class objects that can be assigned or returned like any other. In fact, we can literally create objects of a new class in R by taking a list and simply setting the class attribute of the list to a new value, which is how we create classes in S3.

Instead of providing definitions for S3 classes, we provide constructors. These constructors have the responsibility of creating objects (a string which has the parameter passed in the case of `S3Color` and a list in the case of `S3Rectangle`) and assigning a string to their class attributes. These objects are then returned, and they represent the classes we will be using. In the case of the rectangle, our constructor receives the length, orthogonal sides, and the name of its color. The color constructor only receives the name of the color:

```
color_constructor <- function(color) {
    class(color) <- "S3Color"
    return(color)
}

rectangle_constructor <- function(a, b, color) {
    rectangle <- list(a = a, b = b, color = color_constructor(color))
    class(rectangle) <- "S3Rectangle"
    return(rectangle)
}
```

As you can see, instead of assigning the color string which is passed as a parameter to the rectangle_constructor() function directly in the color element of the rectangle list, we use the color_constructor() function to provide a Color class, not only a string. You should do this if you will add behavior to the color abstraction, as we will do.

Now, we can create an S3_rectangle by calling the rectangle_constructor(), and we can print its class, which is shown to be S3Rectangle, just as we expected. Also, if you print the S3_rectangle structure, you will see that it contains the two sides for the rectangle definition, the color class, and the attribute class names:

```
S3_rectangle <- rectangle_constructor(2, 3, "blue")
class(S3_rectangle)
#> [1] "S3Rectangle"

str(S3_rectangle)
#> List of 3
#> $ a : num 2
#> $ b : num 3
#> $ color:Class 'S3Color' chr "blue"
#> - attr(*, "class")= chr "S3Rectangle"
```

Sometimes, you will see that we have added a prefix to an object with the name of the object model we're using (S3 in this case). For example, S3Color and S3Rectangle. When you see that, it means that the particular name clashes with the corresponding object in another object model, and we need to differentiate them. If you don't do this, you may encounter quite confusing and difficult to diagnose bugs.

Public methods and polymorphism

To define a method for a class, we need to use the UseMethod() function to define a hierarchy of functions. It will tell R to look for a function whose prefix matches the current function and for a suffix in order from the vector of class names of the object being passed. The names of the methods have two parts, separated by a " . ", where the prefix is the function name and the suffix is the name of a class. As you can see, S3 generic functions work by naming conventions, not by explicitly registering methods for different classes.

We start by creating an S3area method for the S3Rectangle class, and we do so by creating a function named S3area.S3Rectangle. The UseMethod() function will make sure that the S3area.S3Rectangle function receives an object of class S4Rectangle, so inside of such a function, we can make use of the class's internals. In this case, we will take the lengths a and b and multiply them together:

```
S3area.S3Rectangle <- function(rectangle) {
    return(rectangle$a * rectangle$b)
}
```

Note that we can access such objects within the rectangle object by using the $ operator. This is not restricted to being done within a method, so really, any object can change an S3 object's internals, but just because you can doesn't mean that you should.

Now, we will call the S3area method as if it were a normal function call, to which we pass the rectangle object we created before, and we should see the area being printed to the console:

```
S3area(S3_rectangle)
#> Error in S3area(S3_rectangle): could not find function "S3area"
```

What happened? An error? Well, how can R tell that the S3area function call should actually trigger the S3area.S3Rectangle method call? For that to happen, we need to register the name with R, and we do so by calling the defining function, which actually uses the S3area name by itself. This S3area function receives an object of any type, not necessarily a S3Rectangle, and uses the UseMethod() function to tell it that it should look for the "S3area" method call for that object. In this case, we know that it will only be found for the S3Rectangle class:

```
S3area <- function(object) {
    UseMethod("S3area")
}
```

Now, we can call the S3area method as we did before, but we will get the actual area in this case. This is how you normally create methods with S3:

```
S3area(S3_rectangle)
#> [1] 6
```

Now, we will create the `S3color` method to return the color object for the rectangle. Since the color object is just a character type, there's nothing more we need to do to somehow parse that object if we just want the characters:

```
S3color.S3Rectangle <- function(rectangle) {
    return(rectangle$color)
}
S3color <- function(object) {
    UseMethod("S3color")
}
```

Now, we will print the rectangle. As you can see, the `print()` call simply shows us the internals of the object and objects contained within it:

```
print(S3_rectangle)
#> $a
#> [1] 2
#>
#> $b
#> [1] 3
#>
#> $color
#> [1] "blue"
#> attr(,"class")
#> [1] "S3Color"
#>
#> attr(,"class")
#> [1] "S3Rectangle"
```

We may want to overload this function to provide a different output. To do so, we create `print.S3Rectangle()` and simply print a string that will tell us the color of the rectangle, the fact that it's a rectangle, the length for each of its sides, and then its area. Note that both the color and the area are retrieved using the methods we defined before, `S3Color()` and `S3area()`:

```
print.S3Rectangle <- function(rectangle) {
    print(paste(
        S3color(rectangle), "rectangle:",
        rectangle$a, "x", rectangle$b, "==", S3area(rectangle)
    ))
}
```

Now, what should happen if we simply call the `print()` function, as we did before with the `S3area()` function? We should get an error, shouldn't we? Let's look at the following code:

```
print(S3_rectangle)
#> [1] "blue rectangle: 2 x 3 == 6"
```

Well, as you can see, we don't. In this case, we actually get the output we hoped we would. The reason is that the `print()` function in R is an S3 function which already registered with the `UseMethod()` function. That means that our definition `print.S3Rectangle` does not need to be registered again, and we can simply use it. That's pretty neat, isn't it? That's one of the big advantages of using parametric polymorphism. We can register functions as method calls that we may or may not end up using at some point in the future in unexpected ways, but they still provide a homogeneous interface for the user.

Encapsulation and mutability

Now, we will see how S3 handles mutability and encapsulation. To do so, we will print the a value in the rectangle, modify it, and print it again. As you can see, we are able to modify it, and from that point on we get a different result, and we do so without any method calls. That's a very risky thing to do, and you should definitely wrap this type of behavior in method calls:

```
print(S3_rectangle$a)
#> [1] 2

S3_rectangle$a <- 1

print(S3_rectangle$a)
#> [1] 1
```

 Even if you can, never modify an object's internals directly.

The proper way of modifying an object would be through some type of setter function. The `set_color.S3Rectangle()` method will be used to modify the rectangle's color, by receiving a `S3Rectangle` and a `new_color` string, and saving that new string inside of a `color` attribute in the rectangle. When you use a method like this, you're being explicit about your intentions, which is a much better way of programming. Of course, we also need to register the method call with R, as shown previously:

```
set_color.S3Rectangle <- function(rectangle, new_color) {
    rectangle$color <- new_color
    return(rectangle)
}

set_color <- function(object, new_color) {
    UseMethod("set_color")
}
```

Did you notice our error? Probably not, but it's great if you did! We did this on purpose to show you how easy it is to harm yourself when programming in R. Since R has no type checking, we inadvertently assigned a string where we should have assigned a Color. This means that the color attribute in our rectangle will no longer be recognized as a Color class after we call the set_color() method; it will be recognized as a string. If your code depends on this object being of the Color type, it will probably fail in unexpected and confusing ways and will be hard to debug. Be careful when doing assignments. Instead, we should have put rectangle$color <- color_constructor(new_color) to keep consistency.

While you can change the type of an object, you never should. As Hadley Wickham puts it, *R doesn't protect you from yourself: you can easily shoot yourself in the foot. As long as you don't aim the gun at your foot and pull the trigger, you won't have a problem.*

Now, we show how the set_color() method can be used. We will print the rectangle's color, attempt to change it to black, and print it again. As you can see, the change was not persisted in our object. That's because R passes objects by value and not by reference. This simply means that when we modify the rectangle, we are actually modifying a copy of the rectangle, not the rectangle we passed ourselves:

```
print(S3color(S3_rectangle))
#> [1] "blue"
#> attr(,"class")
#> [1] "S3Color"

set_color(S3_rectangle, "black")
#> [1] "black rectangle: 1 x 3 == 3"

print(S3color(S3_rectangle))
#> [1] "blue"
#> attr(,"class")
#> [1] "S3Color"
```

Did you notice that at the end of the `set_color.S3Rectangle()` function, we returned the `rectangle`? In other languages that may not be necessary, but in R, we do so to get back the modified object. To persist the changes in our object, we need to actually assign that resulting object into our own `S3_rectangle`, and when we do, then we can see that the color change was persisted.

This property is what gives S3 its immutability property. This is very useful when working with functional programming, but can be a bit of a hassle to work with when doing object-oriented programming. Some confusing bugs may come from this property to get you used to working this way.

Inheritance

S3 classes lack a lot of the structure normally found in other languages. Inheritance is implemented informally, and encapsulation is not enforced by the language, as we have seen before.

To implement inheritance, we will create a `square_constructor()` function that will receive the length of the sides in `a` and the name of the color. We will then use the `rectangle_construtor()` and send `a` for both lengths (making it a square), and will also send the color. Then, we will add the `S3Square` class, and finally, return the created object:

```
square_constructor <- function(a, color) {
    square <- rectangle_constructor(a, a, color)
    class(square) <- c("S3Square", class(square))
    return(square)
}
```

Now, we will create a square and print its classes. As you can see, it has the `S3Square` and `S3Rectangle` classes assigned, in order, and when we use the `print()` method on it, we actually get the print functionality from the `S3Rectangle` class, which is expected since we're signaling the inheritance:

```
S3_square <- square_constructor(4, "red")

class(S3_square)
#> [1] "S3Square" "S3Rectangle"

print(S3_square)
#> [1] "red rectangle: 4 x 4 == 16"
```

If we want to provide a specific print functionality for the square, we must overwrite the `print()` method with our own definition for `S3Square` classes, as we now do. The function is exactly the same as before, but we use the word `"square"` instead of `"rectangle"`.

```
print.S3Square <- function(square) {
    print(paste(
        S3color(square), "square:",
        square$a, "x", square$b, "==", S3area(square)
    ))
}
```

Now, when we print, we can see that the correct method is being used, because we see the word `"square"` in the output. Note that we did not have to re-register the `print()` method with the `UseMethod()` function, since we had already done so:

```
print(S3_square)
#> [1] "red square: 4 x 4 == 16"
```

Finally, remember that if the class attribute is a vector with more than one element, then the first element is interpreted as the class of the object, and the following elements are interpreted as classes that the object inherits from. That makes inheritance a property of objects, not classes, and order is important.

If we had instead written `class(square) <- c(class(square), "S3Square")` in the `square_constructor()` function, then even after creating the `print.S3Square()` function, we would still see the `print()` method calling the `print.S3Rectangle()` function. Be careful with this.

The S4 object model

Some programmers feel that S3 does not provide the safety normally associated with object-oriented programming. In S3, it is very easy to create a class, but it can also lead to very confusing and hard to debug code when not used with great care. For example, you could easily misspell a name, and R would not complain. You could easily change the class to an object, and R would not complain, either.

S4 classes were developed after S3, with the goal of adding safety. S4 provides protection, but it also introduces a lot of verbosity to provide that safety. The S4 object model implements most features of modern object-oriented programming languages—formal class definitions, inheritance, polymorphism (parametric), and encapsulation.

Classes, constructors, and composition

An S4 class is created using the `setClass()` function. At a minimum, the name of the `Class` and its attributes, formally known as **slots** in S4, must be specified. The slots are specified in with the `representation()` function, and a neat feature is that you specify the type expected for such attributes. This helps a bit with type-checking.

There are other features built-in that we are not going to look at here. For example, you could provide a function that verifies the object is consistent (has not been manipulated in some unexpected way). You can also specify default values, in a parameter called the `prototype`. If you want these features in S3, you can also implement them yourself, but they don't come as built-in features. S4 is regarded as a powerful object model, and you should definitely study it more in depth by browsing its documentation.

 All S4 related code is stored in the methods package. This package is always available when you're running R interactively, but may not be available when running R in batch mode. For this reason, it's a good idea to include an explicit `library(methods)` call whenever you're using S4.

As you can see, the conceptual difference from S3 classes is that here, we actually specify the type of object for each slot. Other changes are more syntactic than conceptual. Note that you may use the name of another S4 class for one of the slots, as we do in the case of `color` for the `S4Rectangle`. This is how you can achieve composition with S4:

```
library(methods)

setClass(
    Class = "S4Color",
    representation = representation(
        color = "character"
    )
)

setClass(
    Class = "S4Rectangle",
    representation = representation(
        a = "numeric",
        b = "numeric",
        color = "S4Color"
    )
)
```

The constructor is built automatically for you with a call to the new() function. As you can see, you simply need to pass through the name of the class you're instantiating and the values that should be assigned to the slots:

```
S4_rectangle <- new(
    "S4Rectangle",
    a = 2,
    b = 3,
    color = new("S4Color", color = "blue")
)

class(S4_rectangle)
#> [1] "S4Rectangle"
#> attr(,"package")
#> [1] ".GlobalEnv"

str(S4_rectangle)
#> Formal class 'S4Rectangle' [package ".GlobalEnv"] with 3 slots
#> ..@ a : num 2
#> ..@ b : num 3
#> ..@ color:Formal class 'S4Color' [package ".GlobalEnv"] with 1 slot
#> .. .. ..@ color: chr "blue"
```

As we did before, we retrieve the class for the object and print it. When we print it, we can see a structure that contains some @ symbols. Those are the operators used to access the slots (instead of the $ operator for S3). You can also see the nested slot for the color attribute of the Color class:

 Some slot names are forbidden due to the fact that they are reserved keywords in R. Forbidden names include class, comment, dim, dimnames, names, row.names, and tsp.

Public methods and polymorphism

Since S4 also uses parametric polymorphism (methods belong to functions, not classes) and we have already explained it a couple of times before, we are going to just point out the differences with S3 at this point. First, instead of using the UseMethod() function to register methods with R, we use the setGeneric() function, with the name of the method, and a function that calls the standardGeneric() function inside. This will provide the dispatch mechanism for S4 objects.

To actually create a method, instead of using a naming convention as we do in S3, we actually pass the name of the class and the method to the `setMethod()` function, as well as the function that should be used as a method. Second, the order there matters. If you call the `setMethod()` function before you call the `setGeneric()` method, your dispatch mechanism won't work. We did that in S3, but here, we need to reverse the order. Finally, note that we access object attributes (slots) with the @ symbol, as we mentioned before.

For completeness in the example so that the reader may compare the code for all three examples side by side, we now show how to implement the same code we showed for the S3 case:

```
setGeneric("S4area", function(self) {
    standardGeneric("S4area")
})
#> [1] "S4area"

setMethod("S4area", "S4Rectangle", function(self) {
    return(self@a * self@b)
})
#> [1] "S4area"

S4area(S4_rectangle)
#> [1] 6

setGeneric("S4color", function(self) {
    standardGeneric("S4color")
})
#> [1] "S4color"

setMethod("S4color", "S4Rectangle", function(self) {
    return(self@color@color)
})
#> [1] "S4color"
```

If you use `print()` on `S4_rectangle`, you will see that it's recognized to be of a certain type, and it will show its slots:

```
print(S4_rectangle)
#> An object of class "S4Rectangle"
#> Slot "a":
#> [1] 2
#>
#> Slot "b":
#> [1] 3
#>
#> Slot "color":
```

```
#> An object of class "S4Color"
#> Slot "color":
#> [1] "blue"
```

If we want to change this output, we override this method with our own, as we did in the case of S3. However, if we do, we will have the print() function defined to work with S4 objects, and it will stop working for objects from other object models. We encourage you to try it yourself by changing the code below to use the print method call instead of the S4print name. As you can see, we are using the same overriding mechanism as before, so we will skip its explanation:

```
setGeneric("S4print", function(self) {
    standardGeneric("S4print")
})
#> [1] "S4print"

setMethod("S4print", "S4Rectangle", function(self) {
    print(paste(
        S4color(self), "rectangle:",
        self@a, "x", self@b, "==", S4area(self)
    ))
})
#> [1] "S4print"
```

Now, we may use the S4print() method to print the desired output, as you can see in the following code:

```
S4print(S4_rectangle)
#> [1] "blue rectangle: 2 x 3 == 6"
```

Encapsulation and mutability

Now, we will take a look at the encapsulation and mutability concepts in S4. First, note that we are using the print() and not the S4print() method, because we are printing specific slots from S4_rectangle. As you can see, if we're not careful, we can still assign values directly to the internals of the object. Again, you should not do this.

Also note that if we use the method `S4color()` that we created before to encapsulate the access to the `color` attribute, we get an error telling us that the `S4color<-` function could not be found. That hints to us that we can create such a function, and we can:

```
print(S4_rectangle@a)
#> [1] 2

S4_rectangle@a <- 1

print(S4_rectangle@a)
#> [1] 1

print(S4color(S4_rectangle))
#> [1] "blue"

S4color(S4_rectangle) <- "black"
#> Error in S4color(S4_rectangle) <- "black":
#>       could not find function "S4color<-"

print(S4color(S4_rectangle))
#> [1] "blue"
```

To create a function that will encapsulate access to an object's attribute, we can use the `setReplaceMethod()` function, just as we did with the `setMethod()` function before. Note that the name of the method we are passing to the `setGeneric()` function is the one that was hinted to us in R's error, which is the name of the slot followed by the normal assignment operator in R, `<-`. Also note that there's no space between the name of the variable and symbols for the assignment operator.

Finally, note that we made sure to create an object of type `S4Color` when assigning a new value to the `color` slot. If you try to simply assign a string as we did with the S3 class, you will get an error letting you know you're trying to do something you shouldn't be doing. This is a big advantage when working with S4, as it can prevent you from committing some unexpected mistakes:

```
setGeneric("S4color<-", function(self, value) {
    standardGeneric("S4color<-")
})
#> [1] "S4color<-"

setReplaceMethod("S4color", "S4Rectangle", function(self, value) {
    self@color <- new("S4Color", color = value)
    return(self)
})
#> [1] "S4color<-"
```

Once we create such a method, we can use it to assign to the color object directly, in an encapsulated manner, which is much better than manipulating the slots directly. As you can see, the color change is persisted:

```
print(S4color(S4_rectangle))
#> [1] "blue"

S4color(S4_rectangle) <- "black"

print(S4color(S4_rectangle))
#> [1] "black"
```

Inheritance

Creating a subclass is easy; we simply need to call the `setClass()` function as we did before, and send the `contains` parameter with the name of the class it will inherit from. S4 supports multiple inheritance, but it's not something we're going to look at. The interested reader is encouraged to look into the documentation.

An interesting feature of S4 classes is that if a class extends one of R's basic types, there will be a slot called `.Data` containing the data from the basic object type. Code that works on the basic object type will work directly on the `.Data` part of the object, so it makes our programming a bit easier:

```
setClass("S4Square", contains = "S4Rectangle")
```

Note that when we instantiate the `S4Square` class, we will need to pass both attributes for the length and make sure they are the same. As we can see, the class of the object is identified correctly, and the polymorphic `S4print()` method we defined previously works fine:

```
S4_square <- new ("S4Square",
                  a = 4, b = 4,
                  color = new("S4Color", color = "red"))

class(S4_square)
#> [1] "S4Square"
#> attr(,"package")
#> [1] ".GlobalEnv"

S4print(S4_square)
#> [1] "red rectangle: 4 x 4 == 16"
```

Again, for completeness, we override the `S4print()` method with one that uses the `"square"` word instead, and we can see that it works as expected:

```
setMethod("S4print", "S4Square", function(self) {
    print(paste(
        S4color(self), "square:",
        self@a, "x", self@b, "==", S4area(self)
    ))
})
#> [1] "S4print"

S4print(S4_square)
#> [1] "red square: 4 x 4 == 16"
```

The R6 object model

S3 and S4 are really just ways to implement polymorphism for static functions. The R6 package provides a type of class which is similar to R's Reference Classes, but it is more efficient and doesn't depend on S4 classes and the methods package as RCs do.

When RCs were introduced, some users, following the names of R's existing class systems S3 and S4, called the new class system R5. Although RCs are not actually called R5 nowadays, the name of this package and its classes follows that pattern.

Despite being first released over three years ago, R6 isn't widely known. However, it is widely used. For example, it's used within Shiny (the focus of the last chapter in this book) and to manage database connections in the dplyr package.

Classes, constructors, and composition

Classes in R6 are created with the `R6Class()` function, and we pass the name of the class and lists of public and private objects. These objects can be either attributes or methods. As you can see, building a class definition in R6 produces much cleaner code, which is put together in a single definition instead of the step-by-step process used in S3 and S4. This approach is more like what you can find in other popular languages.

You may specify how the constructor should behave by using the `initialize` method. This specific method will be called when an instance of the class is created.

There are two important differences between our names in the following definition and what we used for the S3 and S4 examples. In this case, we call the print method `own_print()` and the `color` property `own_color`. The reason for the former is that R would be confused between the `color()` method and the `color` attribute. To avoid errors, we can change the name for one of them, and to keep our public interface the same, we decide to change the private attribute in this case. The reason for `own_print()` will be explained ahead:

```
library(R6)
R6Rectangle <- R6Class(
    "R6Rectangle",
    public = list(
        initialize = function(a, b, color) {
            private$a <- a
            private$b <- b
            private$own_color <- color
        },
        area = function() {
            private$a * private$b
        },
        color = function() {
            private$own_color
        },
        set_color = function(new_color) {
            private$own_color <- new_color
        },
        own_print = function() {
            print(paste(
                self$color(), "rectangle:",
                private$a, "x", private$b, " == ", self$area()
            ))
        }
    ),
    private = list(
        a = NULL,
        b = NULL,
        own_color = NULL
    )
)
```

To create an instance of a class, we call the `new()` method in the class object. We can pass some parameters, and if we do, they will be used by the `initialize` function defined for the class.

As you can see, if we use `print()` on the `R6_rectangle` object, we see a nice output letting us know what methods and attributes are public and private, as well as some extra information about them, like the fact that the default `clone()` method (used for making copies of an R6 object) is set to shallow copying instead of deep copying. We won't go into the details of what these concepts are, but the interested reader is encouraged to look into pass-by-reference versus pass-by-value mechanics.

If we had defined a `print()` method within our class, then the `print(R6_rectangle)` would have used that function by default. Note that this would be syntactically different from calling the method directly by executing a command like `R6_rectangle$print()`, but R is intelligent enough to know that if you define a `print()` method in your class, it's probably because you want to use it when using the `print()` function on the object. If that's not the case, then you should change the name of your custom print function, as we do in the case of the `own_print()` method name:

```
R6_rectangle <- R6Rectangle$new(2, 3, "blue")

class(R6_rectangle)
#> [1] "R6Rectangle" "R6"

print(R6_rectangle)
#> <R6Rectangle>
#> Public:
#>     area: function ()
#>     clone: function (deep = FALSE)
#>     color: function ()
#>     initialize: function (a, b, color)
#>     own_print: function ()
#>     set_color: function (new_color)
#> Private:
#>     a: 2
#>     b: 3
#>     own_color: blue
```

As you can see from the output, in the case of R6 classes, we have two classes instead of one. We have the class we defined ourselves, and we also have the general `R6` class added for us for the object.

Public methods and polymorphism

We have already defined the methods we want in the previous piece of code, so for completeness, we will only show how to call these methods now. As you can see, you simply use the $ operator to access a public attribute or a public method, and if it's a method, you add the parentheses at the end (surrounding any parameters you want to send as you normally would):

```
R6_rectangle$own_print()
#> [1] "blue rectangle: 2 x 3 == 6"

R6_rectangle$area()
#> [1] 6

R6_rectangle$color()
#> [1] "blue"
```

Encapsulation and mutability

Since we placed the a, b, and own_color in the private list in the class definition, they remain private, and this is how encapsulation is enforced in R6. As you can see, we were not allowed to assign directly to the a attribute as we expected, since it was placed in the private list. This makes sure that we can't have attributes or methods marked as private directly from outside the object, and prevents us from making bad decisions when coding. This is a great advantage of the R6 model.

Encapsulation in R6 is achieved through environments.

Mutability is achieved by using setters (methods used to change a class's attribute). Notice that in this case, we don't need to reassign the resulting object as we do with S3. State is actually saved within the object's environment, and it can be changed; thus, R6 has mutability:

```
R6_rectangle$a
#> NULL

R6_rectangle$own_print()
#> [1] "blue rectangle: 2 x 3 == 6"

R6_rectangle$a <- 1
#> Error in R6_rectangle$a <- 1:
```

```
        cannot add bindings to a locked environment
R6_rectangle$own_print()
#> [1] "blue rectangle: 2 x 3 == 6"

R6_rectangle$set_color("black")

R6_rectangle$own_print()
#> [1] "black rectangle: 2 x 3 == 6"
```

Inheritance

Inheritance is also more familiar when working with the R6 object model. In this case, you can simply add the `inherit` parameter to the `R6Class()` function call, and you may call the `initialize` method for the superclass by using `super$initialize()`. In this case, we use that technique to provide a more intuitive constructor interface to the user: a single value for length in the case of a square, instead of having to repeat the same value twice, which can be prone to counter-intuitive behavior if not checked. We can also override the `print()` method, just as we would normally add another method:

```
R6Square <- R6Class(
    "R6Square",
    inherit = R6Rectangle,
    public = list(
        initialize = function(a, color) {
            super$initialize(a, a, color)
        },
        print = function() {
            print(paste(
                self$color(), "square:",
                private$a, "x", private$b, " == ", self$area()
            ))
        }
    )
)
```

As you can see, in this case we get a list of classes that include the current class `R6Square`, as well as the classes this object inherits from, `R6Rectangle` and R6. Since we used an override for the `print()` method, we can use the common `print(object)` syntax instead of the ad-hoc `object$print()` syntax provided by R6:

```
R6_square <- R6Square$new(4, "red")

class(R6_square)
#> [1] "R6Square" "R6Rectangle" "R6"
```

```
print(R6_square)
#> [1] "red square: 4 x 4 == 16"
```

Active bindings

Active bindings look like fields, but each time they are accessed, they call a function. They are always publicly visible and are similar to Python's properties. If we wanted to implement the `color()` method as an active binding, we could use the following code. As you can see, you can either get or set the `color` attribute, without using an explicit method call (note the missing parentheses):

```
R6Rectangle <- R6Class(
    "R6Rectangle",
    public = list(
        ...
    ),
    private = list(
        ...
    ),
    active = list(
        color = function(new_color) {
            if (missing(new_color)) {
                return(private$own_color)
            } else {
                private$own_color <- new_color
            }
        }
    )
)

R6_rectangle <- R6Rectangle$new(2, 3, "blue")

R6_rectangle$color
#> [1] "blue"

R6_rectangle$color <- "black"

R6_rectangle$color
#> [1] "black"
```

As you can see, when an active binding is used as a *getter* (to retrieve a value), it calls the method without a value being passed. When it's accessed as a *setter* (to change an attribute), it calls the method passing the value to be assigned. It's not possible to use an active binding as a setter if the function takes no arguments.

Finalizers

Sometimes, it's useful to run a function when the object is garbage collected. If you're not familiar with garbage collection, you can think of it as a way to liberate unused memory when an object is no longer referenced by other objects in the environment.

A useful case for this feature is when you want to make sure a file or database connection gets closed before an object is garbage collected. To do this, you can define a `finalize()` method, which will be called with no arguments when the object is garbage collected. To test this functionality, you can simply add a *finalizer* as follows to some of your objects and see when you get the `"Finalizer called"` message in the console:

```
A <- R6Class("A", public = list(
    finalize = function() {
        print("Finalizer called.")
    }
))
```

 Finalizers will also be called when R exits.

The architecture behind our cryptocurrencies system

Now that the fundamentals for object-oriented programming with R have been illustrated, we will take those principles and apply them to the example we will work with for the rest of the book. We will build a system to track cryptocurrencies with object-oriented programming. If you're not familliar with cryptocurrencies, read the beginning of this chapter for a brief introduction.

The design and implemention you will see in this example evolved over various iterations and weeks. It's actually a part of the basic system I initially used in CVEST (`https://www.cvest.tech/`) to offer a single point of truth for users managing a diverse set of cryptocurrencies (although it was not implemented in R), so don't feel that you should be able to come up with a design like this right away (although many people certainly are able to, but most of the time, object-oriented systems are evolve in unpredicted ways). As Grady Booch puts it: *"A complex system that works is invariably found to have evolved from a simple system that worked. A complex system designed from scratch never works and can not be patched up to make it work. You have to start over, beginning with a working simple system."*

Let's get to it. As you may know, cryptocurrencies can be stored in exchange accounts and in wallets. Since keeping cryptocurrencies stored in exchange accounts is a very bad idea (it's risky, and a user could end up losing their assets, as has repeatedly happened), we will only focus on the cases where cryptocurrencies are stored in wallets.

Basically, what we are trying to do is to get a feed of real data about how many cryptocurrencies we posses and how much they are worth, both at a given point in time. To implement the system, the first thing we need to do is identify the primary abstractions, which are, in our case: users, assets, wallets, and exchanges. For simplicity, we will also include markets and databases in this list.

 We will use the term asset instead of cryptocurrency due to the fact that some of them are not technically currencies, but you may interchange those terms freely without confusion.

For our case, suppose we have decided from the start that even though we will read data from a single source, we may want to write data to multiple databases as we get it. Some of these databases may be local, and others may be remote. However, we don't want every piece of the system to know that there are multiple databases in use, since they really don't need this information to operate. Therefore, we will introduce another abstraction, namely storage, which will contain this information inside, and which will look like a single database to other objects that need to read or write data, and it will handle the details for them.

We include this abstraction in our list of primary abstractions, and that list is complete at this point:

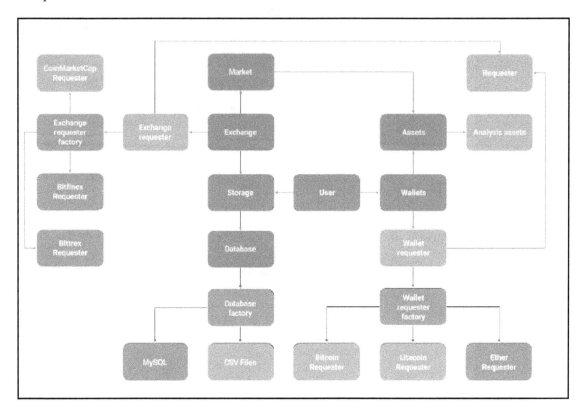

Cryptocurrency tracking architecture

Now, we need to define how this main abstraction will interact among themselves. We know that a user may have several wallets in her posession, and that in turn, these wallets have assets inside. Note that we separated the abstractions of assets and wallets because some wallets may contain more than on asset inside (for example, Ethereum wallets may contain various types of tokens). Since we anticipate this case, we will make sure we can deal with it accordingly by separating these concepts.

Users also want to be able to store their own information as well as their assets information. To do so, they will receive a storage object and they will call methods on this object, for which the public interface will be well defined.

The storage abstraction will in turn contain a single database for reading, but may contain several databases for writing, as we mentioned before. It will store these database objects inside and send them messages as necessary to accomplish the read and write operations on behalf of objects using it.

Finally, just as wallets contain assets, exchanges contain markets. The difference is that assets identify a single type of cryptocurrency, while markets use exactly two cryptocurrencies to be defined. That is why we may have a market to exchange USD for BTC (written as USD/BTC), meaning that people may use US Dollars to buy/sell Bitcoin. Other markets could be BTC/LTC or LTC/USD (where LTC stands for **Litecoin**).

The number we will be retrieving from wallets is a single number representing how much of a specific asset we posses. The number we will be retrieving from markets is a ratio representing the price, or how much of one asset is being asked for to receive one unit of the other. A BTC/USD ratio of 8,000 means that to receive one Bitcoin you're expected to give 8,000 US Dollars (which is the price as this paragraph is being written). Similarly, an LTC/BTC of 0.0086 means that you're expected to give 0.0086 Bitcoin to receive one Litecoin.

Now that these relations are more or less defined, we will need to bring more abstractions into play to write code that will make our system a reality. For example, we know that our wallet abstraction will use a similar mechanism to retrieve data from different blockchains. This can be encapsulated in a *wallet requester*. Furthermore, this wallet requester will be implemented in different ways and must be decided at runtime according to the specific wallet we're dealing with. Instead of creating a different wallet for each type of asset, and programming the mechanism to retrieve data from the blockchain inside each of them, we abstract that and create a wallet requester factory that will give our wallet abstraction the specific type of wallet requester it needs for the given asset at hand.

Similarly, our database abstraction may be implemented for various kinds of databases, so we separate the interface from the implementation and introduce a factory that will choose which specific implementation we will end up using. In our case, we will be saving the data to CSV files, but we could just as easily be using a MySQL database with what we learned in `Chapter 4`, *Simulating Sales Data and Working with Databases*.

In much the same way, our code will retrieve data from **CoinMarketCap** (`www.coinmarketcap.com`) for now, but that may change later. CoinMarketCap is not an exchange, per se; rather, it is an aggregator of price data. However, since we may want to work with price data from different exchanges in the future (like **Bittrex** or **Bitfinex),** we will provide for such abstraction, and since there's no foreseen need to treat CoinMarketCap differently from an exchange, we will just include it in that abstraction.

As a sidenote, the architecture image is not meant to be a UML diagram. **UML** stands for **Unified Modeling Language**, a tool commonly used to communicate ideas behind object-oriented systems. It's a tool you should definitely learn to use if you're planning on doing serious object-oriented programming. Also note that we will not implement the objects shown in grey color, namely Bitfinex requester, Bittrex requester, MySQL, and Ether requester. Those are left as an exercise for the user. Our system will be fully functional without them.

At this point, it seems that we have a very good idea of the abstractions we want to build and the interactions that will occur among these abstractions, so it's time to start programming. While we go through the code for the system, we will not stop to explain the concepts we have covered before; we will only explain functionality that may not be evident.

Finally, you should know that each abstraction we implement will go into its own file. This is standard practice and helps you quickly find where you need to implement or modify some code. There's a clear and intuitive hierarchy among these files. The actual code is organized in the following structure (files end with the .R extensions and directories end with the / symbol):

```
cryptocurrencies/
    assets/
        analysis-asset.R
        asset.R
        exchanges/
            exchange.R
            market.R
            requesters/
                coinmarketcap-requester.R
                exchange-requester-factory.R
                exchange-requester.R
        wallets/
            requesters/
                btc-requester.R
                ltc-requester.R
                wallet-requester-factory.R
                wallet-requester.R
            wallet.R
    batch/
        create-user-data.R
        update-assets.R
        update-markets.R
    settings.R
    storage/
        csv-files.R
```

```
        database-factory.R
        database.R
        storage.R
    users/
        admin.R
        user.R
    utilities/
        requester.R
        time-stamp.R
```

Starting simple with timestamps using S3 classes

We start by programming a class that has no external dependencies, the `TimeStamp`. We will use this class to indicate dates and times together in a single string in the format YYYY-MM-DD-HH-mm, where MM means month and mm means minutes. As you can see, with one of these strings you have the information time and date, and it will be stored with the data we retrieve from time-series for analysis in Chapter 9, *Implementing an Efficient Simple Moving Average.*

Our `TimeStamp` class will be implemented using S3. As you can see, we include the `lubridate` package to do some heavy lifting for us when transforming dates, and provide a constructor that checks whether or not the string being passed is a valid timestamp:

```
library(lubridate)
timestamp_constructor <- function(timestamp = now.TimeStamp()) {
    class(timestamp) <- "TimeStamp"
    if (valid(timestamp)) { return(timestamp) }
    stop("Invalid timestamp (format should be: 'YYYY-MM-DD-HH-mm')")
}
```

The validation is done by the `valid.TimeStamp()` function, which makes sure that only dashes (–) and digits are in the string, that the number of numbers separated by those dashes is five (year, month, day, hour, and minutes), and that the string can be parsed by the `strptime()` function, which is used to create date objects from string objects (if it's not an NA, then it could be parsed):

```
valid.TimeStamp <- function(timestamp) {
    if (gsub("-", "", gsub("[[:digit:]]", "", timestamp)) != "") {
        return(FALSE)
    }
    if (length(strsplit(timestamp, "-")[[1]]) != 5) {
```

```
            return(FALSE)
        }
        if (is.na(strptime(timestamp, "%Y-%m-%d-%H-%M"))) {
            return(FALSE)
        }
        return(TRUE)
    }

    valid <- function (object) {
        UseMethod("valid", object)
    }
```

We also provide a `now.TimeStamp()` function whose responsibility is to create a timestamp for the current time and date. It does so by invoking the `Sys.time()` function and parsing the resulting object with the format we have specified previously:

```
    now.TimeStamp <- function() {
        timestamp <- format(Sys.time(), "%Y-%m-%d-%H-%M")
        class(timestamp) <- "TimeStamp"
        return(timestamp)
    }
```

Next, we introduce a way to transform native time objects into our own `TimeStamp` objects. We simply use the `format()` function as we did before. We also introduce a mechanism to transform our own `TimeStamp` objects into native time objects:

```
    time_to_timestamp.TimeStamp <- function(time) {
        timestamp <- format(time, "%Y-%m-%d-%H-%M")
        class(timestamp) <- "TimeStamp"
        return(timestamp)
    }

    timestamp_to_time.TimeStamp <- function(timestamp) {
        return(strptime(timestamp, "%Y-%m-%d-%H-%M"))
    }
```

The `subtract.TimeStamp()` function will be important when we retrieve data, as we may want all assets that contain a date starting from a previous point in time taken from a given `TimeStamp`. The function receives two parameters: the current `TimeStamp` and the interval of how much time back we want the resulting `TimeStamp` to indicate. Depending on the chosen interval, which can be one hour, one day, one week, one month, or one year, indicated by 1h, 1d, 1w, 1m, and 1y, respectively, we will call different functions from the `lubridate` package (`hours()`, `days()`, `weeks()`, `months()`, `years()`), which receive how many units of the specified name should be used in the operation. These are easy ways to add or subtract time in R.

Note that if an unknown interval is passed, we will raise an error. Some people think that adding these `else` cases with some kind of error should be avoided, since it indicates insecure programming in the sense that you should know what options should be passed to the function, and you should never really end up in the else branch, and they would rather make sure that their code works by using unit-tests instead of checking internally with conditionals. However, we are using it to exemplify its usage and because we're not using unit-tests to prove correctness in our code. I'm also of the opinion that you can never be too careful with these types of situations, and I've found myself in situations where adding that simple else branch helped me diagnose a bug much easier:

```
subtract.TimeStamp <- function(timestamp, interval) {
    time <- timestamp_to_time.TimeStamp(timestamp)
    if (interval == "1h") {
        time <- time - hours(1)
    } else if (interval == "1d") {
        time <- time - days(1)
    } else if (interval == "1w") {
        time <- time - weeks(1)
    } else if (interval == "1m") {
        time <- time - months(1)
    } else if (interval == "1y") {
        time <- time - years(1)
    } else {
        stop("Unknown interval")
    }
    timestamp <- time_to_timestamp.TimeStamp(time)
    return(timestamp)
}

subtract <- function (object, interval) {
    UseMethod("subtract", object)
}
```

Finally, we add a convenient `one_year_ago.TimeStamp()` function, which will simply produce a current `TimeStamp` and subtract one year from it. This is one of those functions that simply evolves as the system is being developed, since I noticed I needed that functionality over and over again, so I could just make my life a little easier this way:

```
one_year_ago.TimeStamp <- function() {
    return(subtract(now.TimeStamp(), "1y"))
}
```

Now, the class is ready. Feel free to play with it to make sure it works as expected. With what you've seen so far in this chapter, you should be able to create instances and use the different methods we created. You should also try to break it to find its weak spots and possibly improve the implementation's robustness.

Implementing cryptocurrency assets using S4 classes

Now, we will implement our next abstraction with the least number of dependencies, `Asset`. We will implement it using S4, and it only depends on `TimeStamp`. We define its class using the standard methods shown before, and its attributes include `email` to identify what user an asset belongs to, a `timestamp` to identify the asset at a point in time, a `name` to know what asset we're dealing with, a `symbol` to identify the asset type within our system, a `total` to record how much of that asset a user has, and an `address` to identify what wallet the asset belongs to (a user may have several wallets for the same type of asset):

```
setClass(
    Class = "Asset",
    representation = representation(
        email = "character",
        timestamp = "character",
        name = "character",
        symbol = "character",
        total = "numeric",
        address = "character"
    )
)
```

Note that instead of using the S3 class for `TimeStamp` in the `timestamp` attribute, we decide to simply declare it as a `character` and manage the translation among types ourselves. This allows us to remain in control of this transformation process and avoid unexpected R behavior when mixing object models.

Next, we provide setter functions to change the `email` and `timestamp` attributes, since we will need them when we are retrieving asset data and saving it to disk. This is one of those design decisions that evolved as the system was developed, and we did not foresee that we would need these methods; they were added at a later point in time:

```
setGeneric("email<-", function(self, value) standardGeneric("email<-"))
setReplaceMethod("email", "Asset", function(self, value) {
    self@email <- value
```

```
        return(self)
    })

    setGeneric("timestamp<-", function(self, value)
    standardGeneric("timestamp<-"))
    setReplaceMethod("timestamp", "Asset", function(self, value) {
        self@timestamp <- value
        return(self)
    })
```

Now, we implement a dataS4 method that will allow us to retrieve the data that needs saving from our S4 objects. Note that we used the same technique as was shown before to differentiate dataS4 methods from dataS3 methods, and avoid any pitfalls with R:

```
    setGeneric("dataS4", function(self) standardGeneric("dataS4"))
    setMethod("dataS4", "Asset", function(self) {
        return(list(
            email = self@email,
            timestamp = self@timestamp,
            name = self@name,
            symbol = self@symbol,
            total = self@total,
            address = self@address
        ))
    })
```

The implementation of the AnalysisAsset will be left for the next chapter, where we introduce the types of analysis we're looking to perform with this data.

Implementing our storage layer with R6 classes

Up to this point, our code's complexity was not much more than that shown in the examples for the colors, rectangles, and squares. At this point, the code will be a bit more complex, since we are dealing with more complex abstractions and interactions among them, but we are ready to tackle the challenge with what we know so far.

Communicating available behavior with a database interface

We will start by defining the interface for databases in the `Database` class. This class is never intended to be instantiated itself. Its purpose is to simply provide an interface definition that must be respected by specific database implementations, like the `CSVFiles` implementation we will develop, and by the `Storage` implementation, to communicate with any database. The advantage of defining an interface such as this is that it provides a common language for these objects to talk to each other, and provides a reference for the programmer of what should be done and how methods should be named so that they work out of the box with the rest of the system. In Python, they would be called Abstract Base Classes. R has no formal usage for these abstract classes, but we can nevertheless implement them this way ourselves.

As you can see, our R6 `Database` interface specifies what methods should be publicly implemented and the fact that the table names used for the database should be kept private. We're adding this `table_names` list attribute instead of hardcoding the table names directly in our classes because we want to be able to easily change them in a settings file (more on this later) and we want to easily change them for the different environments we will be using this code under (mainly production and development environments).

The public methods are the getter and setter for the `table_names`, and the groups of methods used for reading and writing data, which contain a prefix stating what they are used for. It should be evident what they expect and what they return. Specifically, the `read_exchanges()` method does not receive any parameters and should return a list of `Exchange` objects (which will be defined later). The `read_users()` returns a list of `User` objects (which will also be defined later), and needs an instance of `Storage` that will be assigned to each user created so that they can read and write data. The `read_wallets()` method receives an email string and returns a list of `Wallet` objects (also to be defined later). The `read_all_wallets()` method is meant to be used only by `admins` of the system, and will return all the wallets in the system in a list, not only the wallets that belong to a specific user.

On the write side, the `write_user()` method receives a `User` object and writes it to disk, and as you can see by the `{}` symbols, it's not expected to return anything. Similarly, the other write methods receive an instance of a class and save it to disk. We need one write method for each type of class because they will need different treatments when being saved:

```
Database <- R6Class(
    "Database",
    public = list(
```

```
        set_table_names = function(table_names) {
            private$table_names <- table_names
        },
        get_table_names = function() {
            return(private$table_names)
        },
        read_exchanges = function() list(),
        read_users = function(storage) list(),
        read_wallets = function(email) list(),
        read_all_wallets = function() list(),
        read_analysis_assets = function(email) list(),
        write_user = function(user) {},
        write_wallet = function(wallet) {},
        write_assets = function(assets) {},
        write_markets = function(markets) {}
    ),
    private = list(table_names = list())
)
```

Implementing a database-like storage system with CSV files

Now that we have our `Database` interface defined, we will implement a database-like system that uses CSV files to store the information instead of an actual database.

First, we make sure we bring the `CSVFiles` class dependencies by using the `source()` function to bring files that have the definitions we need. Specifically, we bring the `Exchange` and `User` classes (which will be defined later), as well as the `Database` interface. We also define the `DIR` constant with the directory that will contain the CSV files with our system's data.

The actual `CSVFiles` class is defined using the standard R6 methods shown before. Note that it inherits from the `Database` class and provides overrides for every method in the `Database` interface, as it should. Also note that inside the constructor, that is, the `initialize` function, we are calling the `initialize_csv_files()` function and sending it the `table_names` list we receive during initialization. More on this ahead.

Since we wanted the reader to get a look at the full class definition in a single piece of code instead of piece-by-piece, we include all of it here, and explain it in the following paragraphs. It's a bit long since it contains the logic for all the methods in the Database interface, but at a high level, it's nothing more than implementation for said interface:

```
source("../assets/exchanges/exchange.R", chdir = TRUE)
source("../users/user.R", chdir = TRUE)
source("./database.R")
DIR <- "./csv-files/"

CSVFiles <- R6Class(
    "CSVFiles",
    inherit = Database,
    public = list(
        initialize = function(table_names) {
            super$set_table_names(table_names)
            initialize_csv_files(table_names)
        },
        read_exchanges = function() {
            return(list(Exchange$new("CoinMarketCap")))
        },
        read_users = function(storage) {
            data <- private$read_csv("users")
            return(lapply(data$email, user_constructor, storage))
        },
        read_wallets = function(email) {
            data <- private$read_csv("wallets")
            wallets <- NULL
            if (nrow(data) >= 1) {
                for (i in 1:nrow(data)) {
                    if (data[i, "email"] == email) {
                        wallets <- c(wallets, list(Wallet$new(
                            data[i, "email"],
                            data[i, "symbol"],
                            data[i, "address"],
                            data[i, "note"])
                        ))
                    }
                }
            } else { wallets <- list() }
            return(wallets)
        },
        read_all_wallets = function() {
            data <- private$read_csv("wallets")
            wallets <- NULL
            if (nrow(data) >= 1) {
                for (i in 1:nrow(data)) {
```

```
                wallets <- c(wallets, list(Wallet$new(
                    data[i, "email"],
                    data[i, "symbol"],
                    data[i, "address"],
                    data[i, "note"])
                ))
            }
        } else { wallets <- list() }
        return(wallets)
    },
    write_user = function(user) {
        data <- private$read_csv("users")
        new_row <- as.data.frame(dataS3(user))
        print(new_row)
        if (private$user_does_not_exist(user, data)) {
            data <- rbind(data, new_row)
        }
        private$write_csv("users", data)
    },
    write_wallets = function(wallets) {
        data <- private$read_csv("wallets")
        for (wallet in wallets) {
            new_row <- as.data.frame(wallet$data())
            print(new_row)
            if (private$wallet_does_not_exist(wallet, data)) {
                data <- rbind(data, new_row)
            }
        }
        private$write_csv("wallets", data)
    },
    write_assets = function(assets) {
        data <- private$read_csv("assets")
        for (asset in assets) {
            new_row <- as.data.frame(dataS4(asset))
            print(new_row)
            data <- rbind(data, new_row)
        }
        private$write_csv("assets", data)
    },
    write_markets = function(markets) {
        data <- private$read_csv("markets")
        for (market in markets) {
            new_row <- as.data.frame(market$data())
            print(new_row)
            data <- rbind(data, new_row)
        }
        private$write_csv("markets", data)
    }
```

```
    ),
private = list(
    read_csv = function(table_name) {
        return(read.csv (
                    private$file(table_name),
                    stringsAsFactors = FALSE))
    },
    write_csv = function(table_name, data) {
        write.csv(data,
                    file = private$file(table_name),
                    row.names = FALSE)
    },
    file = function(table_name) {
        return(paste(
            DIR, super$get_table_names()[[table_name]],
            ".csv", sep = ""))
    },
    user_does_not_exist = function(user, data) {
        if (dataS3(user)[["email"]] %in% data$email) {
            return(FALSE)
        }
        return(TRUE)
    },
    wallet_does_not_exist = function(wallet, data) {
        current_addresses <- data[
            data$email == wallet$get_email() &
            data$symbol == wallet$get_symbol(),
            "address"
        ]
        if (wallet$get_address() %in% current_addresses) {
            return(FALSE)
        }
        return(TRUE)
    }
)
)
```

Now, we will briefly explain the mechanics behind each method implementation. Let's start with `read_exchanges()`. In theory, this method should look inside the stored data and get a list of the exchanges registered in the system, create an instance for each of them, and send that back. In practice, however, it's not necessary, as just hardcoding the CoinMarketCap exchange is sufficient for our purposes. As you can see, that's all the method does: return a list with a single `Exchange` inside, which is the one for CoinMarketCap.

The read_users() method reads the data from the "user" file with the private method read_csv() defined below, and returns a list built with the lapply() function that takes every email in the data and sends it through the user_constructor(), along with a storage object received as a parameter to create User instances that are then sent back as a result of the method call. If you don't remember how the lapply() function works, take a look at Chapter 1, *Introduction to R*.

The read_wallets() method is a bit more complex. It receives an email as a parameter, reads the "wallets" file, and creates a list of Wallet instances. Since we're doing a check to see whether a specific observation in the data contains an email equal the one requested, we can simply use the lapply() function (we could, if we create a separate function that contains this, check, but we decide not to go that route). Also note that the function will only try to iterate over the row in the dataframe if the dataframe contains at least one row. This check was introduced after we found that when not having it when we had empty files, we were getting an error, since the for loop was actually being executed even if there were no rows. If the email is found to be the same as the one requested, then we append a new Wallet instance to the wallets list and return it. If there are no wallets to be created, the wallets object is coerced into an empty list. The read_all_wallets() method works in the same way but omits the email check.

The write_user() method receives a User instance, reads the data for the "users" file, creates a dataframe with the data extracted with the dataS3 method call from the User object, prints it to the console for informational purposes, and, if it's not found to already exist in the current data, it's added to it. Finally, the data is saved back into the "users" file. The actual check is performed by the private method user_does_not_exist(), which simply checks that the User email is not contained in the email column in the data, as you can see in its definition mentioned ahead.

The write_wallets() method receives a list of Wallet instances, reads the "wallets" file, and for each wallet not found to already exist in the data, adds it. It's conceptually similar to the write_user() method, and the check is performed by the private wallet_does_not_exist() method, which receives a Wallet instance and uses its contained email and symbol to get the addresses which are already associated to such combinations (recall that a single user may have multiple wallets for the same type of asset, and they would only be differentiated by their wallet addresses). If the address in the Wallet instance is found to already exist in such a subset, then it's not added.

The `write_assets()` and `write_markets()` methods are similar and should be easily understood. The difference is that they do not contain any checks for now, and that they are saving S4 and R6 objects, respectively. You can tell that by the fact that they call the `dataS4()` method and the syntax to get the `Market` data, being `market$data()`.

The private methods used to read and write the CSV files should be easy to understand. Just keep in mind that the actual filenames are coming from the `file()` private method, which uses the `table_names` contained in the superclass (`Database`) by calling the `super$get_table_names()` getter and retrieving the corresponding filename associated for a given `table_name`. The `table_name` list will later be defined in the centralized settings file, but is simply a list that contains a string for each table name (in the case of `CSVFiles`, a file name) associated to each type of object that needs to be stored.

Now, we proceed to discussing the `initialize_csv_files()` function. This function receives the `table_names` list and makes sure that the `DIR` directory exists with the `dir.create()` function. The `showWarnings = FALSE` parameter is to avoid warnings when the directory already exists in disk. Then, for each element in the `table_names` list, it will create the corresponding `filename` and see whether it exists on disk with the `file.exists()` function. If it does not, it will proceed to create an empty dataframe of the corresponding type and save it to disk:

```
initialize_csv_files <- function(table_names) {
    dir.create(DIR, showWarnings = FALSE)
    for (table in table_names) {
        filename <- paste(DIR, table, ".csv", sep = "")
        if (!file.exists(filename)) {
            data <- empty_dataframe(table)
            write.csv(data, file = filename, row.names = FALSE)
        }
    }
}
```

The different types of empty dataframes are chosen with the `empty_dataframe()` function, which receives a specific table name in the `table` parameter and returns the corresponding empty dataframe. Note that the checks assume that the words for the different objects that need to be saved are within the table names defined in the centralized settings file and that the names of two different abstractions do no appear together in a single table name:

```
empty_dataframe <- function(table) {
    if (grepl("assets", table)) {
        return(empty_assets())
    } else if (grepl("markets", table)) {
```

```
        return(empty_markets())
    } else if (grepl("users", table)) {
        return(empty_users())
    } else if (grepl("wallets", table)) {
        return(empty_wallets())
    } else {
        stop("Unknown table name")
    }
}
```

The actual empty dataframes are created by the `empty_assets()`, `empty_markets()`, `empty_users()`, and `empty_wallets()` functions. Each of these contains a specification for the data expected to be within such files. Specifically, each observation in the asset's data is expected to have an email, timestamp, name, symbol, total, and address. Each observation in the markets data is expected to have a timestamp, name, symbol, rank, price in BTC, and price in USD. The rank is a cryptocurrencies ordering based on the amount of volume transacted in the last 24 hours. The users data is only expected to contain emails. Finally, the wallets data is expected to have an email, symbol, address, and note. The note is a note that the user may specify to recognize different wallets from each other, specifically if they are being used for the same type of cryptocurrency. Maybe one Bitcoin wallet is for long-term and one for short-term; then that information could be specified in the note field. Note that you can identify the relations among these data schemes with the concepts introduced in Chapter 4, *Simulating Sales Data and Working with Databases*. Let's look at the following code:

```
empty_assets <- function() {
    return(data.frame(
        email = character(),
        timestamp = character(),
        name = character(),
        symbol = character(),
        total = numeric(),
        address = character()
    ))
}

empty_markets <- function() {
    return(data.frame(
        timestamp = character(),
        name = character(),
        symbol = character(),
        rank = numeric(),
        price_btc = numeric(),
        price_usd = numeric()
    ))
}
```

```
    }

empty_users <- function() {
    return(data.frame(
        email = character()
    ))
}

empty_wallets <- function() {
    return(data.frame(
        email = character(),
        symbol = character(),
        address = character(),
        note = character()
    ))
}
```

Easily allowing new database integration with a factory

We know at this point that we will only use the `CSVFiles Database` implementation for this example, but we can easily imagine cases where new database implementations come into play. For example, the reader will create an implementation of the MySQL database, and will want it to substitute the `CSVFiles` implementation. Isn't that right? When you expect some change in the future where you will likely need to switch one interface implementation for another, factories is a great tool to facilitate that change for yourself in the future.

Our `database_factory()` function receives a `db_setup` and `table_names` objects, both of which will come from our centralized settings file. It then takes the appropriate set of table names, depending on the environment for the database, and looks into the `db_setup` provided to find what kind of `Database` implementation it needs to instantiate. Since we only have one at this point, the only possibility will be a `CSVFiles` implementation, and if we pass any other string, then an error should be raised, as it is. The `Database` implementation actually instantiated should receive a `table_names` object and configure itself accordingly:

```
source("./csv-files.R")

database_factory <- function(db_setup, table_names) {
    table_names <- table_names[[db_setup[["environment"]]]]
    if (db_setup[["name"]] == "CSVFiles") {
```

```
            return(CSVFiles$new(table_names))
    } else {
        stop("Unknown database name")
    }
}
```

As you can see, a factory is nothing more than an `if` statement which decides what implementation should be instantiated and returned to the calling object.

Encapsulating multiple databases with a storage layer

Now that we have developed our `Database` interface and our `CSVFiles` implementation of such an interface, we are ready to develop the next layer of abstraction, our `Storage` class. It will be implemented with R6.

As you can see, the `Storage` constructor implemented in the `initialize` function receives a `settings` object which will be the full centralized settings file we have been mentioning and will use the `storage/read`, `storage/write`, and `storage/table_names` parts to create various database instances through the use of the `database_factory()` function we explained before. In the case of the `read_db` attribute, it will be a single `Database` implementation that will be used to read data. In the case of the `write_dbs` attribute, as the name implies, we will have a list of `Database` implementations where each data that is asked to be saved by other objects will be stored.

With this `Storage` abstraction, we can simply send it to objects looking for a database-like object to save and read data from, and it will take care of replicating data as necessary for us, as well as providing data to said objects. To accomplish this, you can ask that in the case of the read methods, it simply delegate the task to the `Database` implementation contained in its `read_db` attribute, and in the case of the write methods, it does the same thing for each `Database` implementation in its `write_dbs` attribute. It's as simple as that:

```
source("./database-factory.R")
Storage <- R6Class(
    "Storage",
    public = list(
        initialize = function(settings) {
            private$read_db <- database_factory(
                settings[["storage"]][["read"]],
                settings[["storage"]][["table_names"]]
            )
            private$write_dbs <- lapply(
```

```
                    settings[["storage"]][["write"]],
                    database_factory,
                    settings[["storage"]][["table_names"]]
                )
            },
            read_exchanges = function() {
                return(private$read_db$read_exchanges())
            },
            read_users = function() {
                return(private$read_db$read_users(self))
            },
            read_wallets = function(email) {
                return(private$read_db$read_wallets(email))
            },
            read_all_wallets = function() {
                return(private$read_db$read_all_wallets())
            },
            read_analysis_assets = function(email) {
                return(private$read_db$read_analysis_assets(email))
            },
            write_user = function(user) {
                for (db in private$write_dbs) { db$write_user(user) }
            },
            write_wallets = function(wallets) {
                for (db in private$write_dbs) { db$write_wallets(wallets) }
            },
            write_assets = function(assets) {
                for (db in private$write_dbs) { db$write_assets(assets) }
            },
            write_markets = function(markets) {
                for (db in private$write_dbs) { db$write_markets(markets) }
            }
        ),
        private = list(read_db = NULL, write_dbs = list())
    )
```

That's it for our storage abstractions. At this point, we have implemented a `Database` interface, a `CSVFiles` implementation of said interface, and a `Storage` layer that permits the use of multiple `Database` implementations simultaneously and decouples the read and write objects for us. We could choose to use one type of database for read operations and another one for write operations, and have some kind of external mechanism to sync them together outside of R. This could be handy for performance reasons, for example.

Retrieving live data for markets and wallets with R6 classes

This section will explain how to create a simple requester, which is an object that requests external information (from an API over the internet in this case). We will also develop our exchange and wallet infrastructure.

Creating a very simple requester to isolate API calls

Now, we will focus on how we actually retrieve live data. This functionality will also be implemented using R6 classes, as the interactions can be complex. First of all, we create a simple `Requester` class that contains the logic to retrieve data from JSON APIs found elsewhere in the internet and that will be used to get our live cryptocurrency data for wallets and markets. We don't want logic that interacts with external APIs spread all over our classes, so we centralize it here to manage it as more specialized needs come into play later.

As you can see, all this object does is offer the public `request()` method, and all it does is use the `formJSON()` function from the `jsonlite` package to call a `URL` that is being passed to it and send the data it got back to the user. Specifically, it sends it as a dataframe when the data received from the external API can be coerced into dataframe-form.

```
library(jsonlite)

Requester <- R6Class(
    "Requester",
    public = list(
        request = function(URL) {
            return(fromJSON(URL))
        }
    )
)
```

Developing our exchanges infrastructure

Our exchanges have multiple markets inside, and that's the abstraction we will define now. A `Market` has various private attributes, as we saw before when we defined what data is expected from each file, and that's the same data we see in our constructor. It also offers a `data()` method to send back a list with the data that should be saved to a database. Finally, it provides setters and getters as required. Note that the setter for the price depends on what units are requested, which can be either `usd` or `btc`, to get a market's asset price in terms of US Dollars or Bitcoin, respectively:

```r
Market <- R6Class(
    "Market",
    public = list(
        initialize = function(timestamp, name, symbol, rank,
                              price_btc, price_usd) {
            private$timestamp <- timestamp
            private$name <- name
            private$symbol <- symbol
            private$rank <- rank
            private$price_btc <- price_btc
            private$price_usd <- price_usd
        },
        data = function() {
            return(list(
                timestamp = private$timestamp,
                name = private$name,
                symbol = private$symbol,
                rank = private$rank,
                price_btc = private$price_btc,
                price_usd = private$price_usd
            ))
        },
        set_timestamp = function(timestamp) {
            private$timestamp <- timestamp
        },
        get_symbol = function() {
            return(private$symbol)
        },
        get_rank = function() {
            return(private$rank)
        },
        get_price = function(base) {
            if (base == 'btc') {
                return(private$price_btc)
            } else if (base == 'usd') {
                return(private$price_usd)
```

```
                    }
                }
            ),
            private = list(
                timestamp = NULL,
                name = "",
                symbol = "",
                rank = NA,
                price_btc = NA,
                price_usd = NA
            )
        )
```

Now that we have our `Market` definition, we proceed to create our `Exchange` definition. This class will receive an exchange name as `name` and will use the `exchange_requester_factory()` function to get an instance of the corresponding `ExchangeRequester`. It also offers an `update_markets()` method that will be used to retrieve market data with the private `markets()` method and store it to disk using the `timestamp` and `storage` objects being passed to it. Note that instead of passing the `timestamp` through the arguments for the private `markets()` method, it's saved as a class attribute and used within the private `insert_metadata()` method. This technique provides cleaner code, since the `timestamp` does not need to be passed through each function and can be retrieved when necessary.

The private `markets()` method calls the public `markets()` method in the `ExchangeRequester` instance saved in the private `requester` attribute (which was assigned to by the factory) and applies the private `insert_metadata()` method to update the `timestamp` for such objects with the one sent to the public `update_markets()` method call before sending them to be written to the database:

```
source("./requesters/exchange-requester-factory.R", chdir = TRUE)

Exchange <- R6Class(
    "Exchange",
    public = list(
        initialize = function(name) {
            private$requester <- exchange_requester_factory(name)
        },
        update_markets = function(timestamp, storage) {
            private$timestamp <- unclass(timestamp)
            storage$write_markets(private$markets())
        }
    ),
    private = list(
        requester = NULL,
```

```
            timestamp = NULL,
            markets = function() {
                return(lapply(private$requester$markets(),
    private$insert_metadata))
            },
            insert_metadata = function(market) {
                market$set_timestamp(private$timestamp)
                return(market)
            }
        )
    )
```

Now, we need to provide a definition for our ExchangeRequester implementations. As in the case of the Database, this ExchangeRequester will act as an interface definition that will be implemented by the CoinMarketCapRequester. We see that the ExchangeRequester specifies that all exchange requester instances should provide a public markets() method, and that a list is expected from such a method. From context, we know that this list should contain Market instances. Also, each ExchangeRequester implementation will contain a Requester object by default, since it's being created and assigned to the requester private attribute upon class instantiation. Finally, each implementation will also have to provide a create_market() private method and will be able to use the request() private method to communicate to the Requester method request() we defined previously:

```
    source("../../../utilities/requester.R")

    KNOWN_ASSETS = list(
        "BTC" = "Bitcoin",
        "LTC" = "Litecoin"
    )
    ExchangeRequester <- R6Class(
        "ExchangeRequester",
        public = list(
            markets = function() list()
        ),
        private = list(
            requester = Requester$new(),
            create_market = function(resp) NULL,
            request = function(URL) {
                return(private$requester$request(URL))
            }
        )
    )
```

Now we proceed to provide an implementation for `CoinMarketCapRequester`. As you can see, it inherits from `ExchangeRequester`, and it provides the required method implementations. Specifically, the `markets()` public method calls the private `request()` method from `ExchangeRequester`, which in turn calls the `request()` method from `Requester`, as we have seen, to retrieve data from the private `URL` specified.

If you request data from CoinMarketCap's API by opening a web browser and navigating to the URL shown (`https://api.coinmarketcap.com/v1/ticker`), you will get a list of market data. That is the data that will be received in our `CoinMarketCapRequester` instance in the form of a dataframe, thanks to the `Requester` object, and will be transformed into numeric data where appropriate using the private `clean()` method, so that it's later used to create `Market` instances with the `apply()` function call, which in turn calls the `create_market()` private method. Note that the `timestamp` is set to `NULL` for all markets created this way because, as you may remember from our `Exchange` class, it's set before writing it to the database. There's no need to send the `timestamp` information all the way down to the `CoinMarketCapRequester`, since we can simply write at the `Exchange` level right before we send the data to the database:

```
source("./exchange-requester.R")
source("../market.R")

CoinMarketCapRequester <- R6Class(
    "CoinMarketCapRequester",
    inherit = ExchangeRequester,
    public = list(
        markets = function() {
            data <- private$clean(private$request(private$URL))
            return(apply(data, 1, private$create_market))
        }
    ),
    private = list(
        URL = "https://api.coinmarketcap.com/v1/ticker",
        create_market = function(row) {
            timestamp <- NULL
            return(Market$new(
                timestamp,
                row[["name"]],
                row[["symbol"]],
                row[["rank"]],
                row[["price_btc"]],
                row[["price_usd"]]
            ))
        },
        clean = function(data) {
```

```
                    data$price_usd <- as.numeric(data$price_usd)
                    data$price_btc <- as.numeric(data$price_btc)
                    data$rank <- as.numeric(data$rank)
                    return(data)
            }
        )
    )
```

Finally, here's the code for our `exchange_requester_factory()`. As you can see, it's basically the same idea we have used for our other factories, and its purpose is to easily let us add more implementations for our `ExchangeRequeseter` by simply adding *else-if* statements in it:

```
source("./coinmarketcap-requester.R")

exchange_requester_factory <- function(name) {
    if (name == "CoinMarketCap") {
        return(CoinMarketCapRequester$new())
    } else {
        stop("Unknown exchange name")
    }
}
```

Developing our wallets infrastructure

Now that we are able to retrieve live price data from exchanges, we turn to our `Wallet` definition. As you can see, it specifies the type of private attributes we expect for the data that it needs to handle, as well as the public `data()` method to create the list of data that needs to be saved to a database at some point.

It also provides getters for `email`, `symbol`, and `address`, and the public `pudate_assets()` method, which will be used to get and save assets into the database, just as we did in the case of `Exchange`. As a matter of fact, the techniques followed are exactly the same, so we won't explain them again:

```
source("./requesters/wallet-requester-factory.R", chdir = TRUE)

Wallet <- R6Class(
    "Wallet",
    public = list(
        initialize = function(email, symbol, address, note) {
            private$requester <- wallet_requester_factory(symbol, address)
            private$email <- email
            private$symbol <- symbol
```

```
                private$address <- address
                private$note <- note
            },
        data = function() {
            return(list(
                email = private$email,
                symbol = private$symbol,
                address = private$address,
                note = private$note
            ))
        },
        get_email = function() {
            return(as.character(private$email))
        },
        get_symbol = function() {
            return(as.character(private$symbol))
        },
        get_address = function() {
            return(as.character(private$address))
        },
        update_assets = function(timestamp, storage) {
            private$timestamp <- timestamp
            storage$write_assets(private$assets())
        }
    ),
    private = list(
        timestamp = NULL,
        requester = NULL,
        email = NULL,
        symbol = NULL,
        address = NULL,
        note = NULL,
        assets = function() {
            return (lapply (
                    private$requester$assets(),
                    private$insert_metadata))
        },
        insert_metadata = function(asset) {
            timestamp(asset) <- unclass(private$timestamp)
            email(asset) <- private$email
            return(asset)
        }
    )
)
```

Implementing our wallet requesters

The WalletRequester will be conceptually similar to the ExchangeRequester. It will be an interface, and will be implemented in our BTCRequester and LTCRequester interfaces. As you can see, it requires a public method called assets() to be implemented and to return a list of Asset instances. It also requires a private create_asset() method to be implemented, which should return individual Asset instances, and a private url method that will build the URL required for the API call. It offers a request() private method that will be used by implementations to retrieve data from external APIs:

```r
source("../../../utilities/requester.R")

WalletRequester <- R6Class(
    "WalletRequester",
    public = list(
        assets = function() list()
    ),
    private = list(
        requester = Requester$new(),
        create_asset = function() NULL,
        url = function(address) "",
        request = function(URL) {
            return(private$requester$request(URL))
        }
    )
)
```

The BTCRequester and LTCRequester implementations are shown below for completeness, but will not be explained. If you have followed everything so far, they should be easy to understand:

```r
source("./wallet-requester.R")
source("../../asset.R")

BTCRequester <- R6Class(
    "BTCRequester",
    inherit = WalletRequester,
    public = list(
        initialize = function(address) {
            private$address <- address
        },
        assets = function() {
            total <- as.numeric(private$request(private$url()))
            if (total > 0) { return(list(private$create_asset(total))) }
            return(list())
        }
```

```
        ),
    private = list(
        address = "",
        url = function(address) {
            return(paste(
                "https://chainz.cryptoid.info/btc/api.dws",
                "?q=getbalance",
                "&a=",
                private$address,
                sep = ""
            ))
        },
        create_asset = function(total) {
            return(new(
                "Asset",
                email = "",
                timestamp = "",
                name = "Bitcoin",
                symbol = "BTC",
                total = total,
                address = private$address
            ))
        }
    )
)

source("./wallet-requester.R")
source("../../asset.R")

LTCRequester <- R6Class(
    "LTCRequester",
    inherit = WalletRequester,
    public = list(
        initialize = function(address) {
            private$address <- address
        },
        assets = function() {
            total <- as.numeric(private$request(private$url()))
            if (total > 0) { return(list(private$create_asset(total))) }
            return(list())
        }
    ),
    private = list(
        address = "",
        url = function(address) {
            return(paste(
                "https://chainz.cryptoid.info/ltc/api.dws",
                "?q=getbalance",
```

```
                        "&a=",
                        private$address,
                        sep = ""
                ))
        },
        create_asset = function(total) {
            return(new(
                "Asset",
                email = "",
                timestamp = "",
                name = "Litecoin",
                symbol = "LTC",
                total = total,
                address = private$address
            ))
        }
    )
)
```

The `wallet_requester_factory()` works just as the other factories; the only difference is that in this case, we have two possible implementations that can be returned, which can be seen in the `if` statement. If we decided to add a `WalletRequester` for another cryptocurrency, such as Ether, we could simply add the corresponding branch here, and it should work fine:

```
source("./btc-requester.R")
source("./ltc-requester.R")

wallet_requester_factory <- function(symbol, address) {
    if (symbol == "BTC") {
        return(BTCRequester$new(address))
    } else if (symbol == "LTC") {
        return(LTCRequester$new(address))
    } else {
        stop("Unknown symbol")
    }
}
```

Finally introducing users with S3 classes

Our object-oriented system is almost finalized. We're only missing the User definition. In this case, we will use S3 to define the User class. The user_constructor() function takes an email and a Storage instance in storage to create a User instance. However, before it does, it checks that the email is valid with the valid_email() function defined below. After the user has been created, the get_wallets() method is called upon it to get the wallets associated to the user before it's sent back.

The valid_email() function simply receives a string which is supposed to be an email address, and checks whether at least one @ and one . symbol are contained within it. Of course, this is not a robust mechanism to check whether or not it's an email address, and it's put here just to illustrate how a checking mechanism could be implemented:

```
source("../assets/wallets/wallet.R", chdir = TRUE)

user_constructor <- function(email, storage) {
    if (!valid_email(email)) { stop("Invalid email") }
    user <- list(storage = storage, email = email, wallets = list())
    class(user) <- "User"
    user <- get_wallets(user)
    return(user)
}

valid_email <- function(string) {
    if (grepl("@", string) && grepl(".", string)) { return(TRUE) }
    return(FALSE)
}
```

The get_wallets.User() function simply asks the storage attribute in the object to get the wallets associated to its own email address, assigns them to the wallets list attribute, and sends the User object back:

```
get_wallets.User <- function(user) {
    user$wallets <- user$storage$read_wallets(user$email)
    return(user)
}

get_wallets <- function(object) {
    UseMethod("get_wallets")
}
```

The `new_wallet.User()` function receives a `User` instance, a `symbol` string, an `address` string, and `note` string to create a new `Wallet` instance and append it to the `wallets` list attribute for the `User` instance passed to it. However, before it does, it checks in all previous registered wallets for the user. If it finds that a wallet is already registered, it simply ignores the addition and sends the same `User` instance back. This is another type of checking that you may implement in your own systems:

```
new_wallet.User <- function(user, symbol, address, note) {
    if (length(user$wallets) >= 1) {
        for (wallet in user$wallets) {
            if (wallet$get_symbol() == symbol &
                wallet$get_address() == address) {
                return(user)
            }
        }
    }
    wallet <- Wallet$new(user$email, symbol, address, note)
    user$wallets <- c(user$wallets, list(wallet))
    return(user)
}
new_wallet <- function(object, symbol, address, note) {
    UseMethod("new_wallet")
}
```

The `update_assets.User()` function simply goes through each `Wallet` instance in the `wallets` list attribute and calls its public `update_assets()` method with the current `timestamps` that was passed to it and the `Storage` instance contained within the `User` instance. As we have seen before, this results in the assets being updated and saved to the database, and the `Wallet` object takes care of that on behalf of the `User` instance:

```
update_assets.User <- function(user, timestamp) {
    for (wallet in user$wallets) {
        wallet$update_assets(timestamp, user$storage)
    }
}
update_assets <- function(object, timestamp) {
    UseMethod("update_assets")
}
```

The `save.User()` function simply uses the `storage` attribute to save the `User` instance as well as its wallets data. As we have seen, if the wallets already exist in the saved data, they will not be duplicated, and the `CSVFiles` implementation takes care of that on behalf of the `User` instance:

```
save.User <- function(user) {
    user$storage$write_user(user)
    user$storage$write_wallets(user$wallets)
}

save <- function(object) {
    UseMethod("save")
}
```

Finally, the user provides a `dataS3.User()` method to return a list with a user's email to be saved back to the database:

```
dataS3.User <- function(user) {
    return(list(email = user$email))
}
dataS3 <- function(object) {
    UseMethod("dataS3")
}
```

As we have seen in this section, after some work has been put into place, we can develop nice and intuitive abstractions that leverage the functionality implemented in other objects to provide powerful mechanisms, like saving data into a database, with very simple calls.

Helping ourselves with a centralized settings file

Finally, we show the famous centralized settings file we have been mentioning throughout the example. As you can see, it is simply a list of lists that contains parameters for how our system should behave. Centralizing these options in a single file as we do here can often be very convenient. Instead of changing code when we want different behaviors from our system, we can simply change this file, and everything will be taken care of for us:

```
SETTINGS <- list(
    "debug" = TRUE,
    "storage" = list(
        "read" = list(
            "name" = "CSVFiles",
            "environment" = "production"
```

```
        ),
        "write" = list(
            list(
                "name" = "CSVFiles",
                "environment" = "production"
            )
        ),
        "table_names" = list(
            "production" = list(
                "assets" = "production_assets",
                "markets" = "production_markets",
                "users" = "production_users",
                "wallets" = "production_wallets"
            ),
            "development" = list(
                "assets" = "development_assets",
                "markets" = "development_markets",
                "users" = "development_users",
                "wallets" = "development_wallets"
            )
        )
    ),
    "batch_data_collection" = list(
        "assets" = list(
            "minutes" = 60
        ),
        "markets" = list(
            "minutes" = 60
        )
    )
)
)
```

Specifically, note that there's a `debug` Boolean that we did not end up using, but which could be useful when debugging our system at some point. Also, note that there are two main parts to our settings file, the `storage` part and the `batch_data_collection` part. The `storage` part is the one we have used so far, and it contains the specification for which databases should be used to read and write data by providing the name of the implementation that should be used in the `name` elements, and the `environment` we're currently operating on, which can be either `production` or `development`. Both of these elements are used by the factories to set up the system appropriately before it starts operating. Also, note that the CSV files that will be created correspond to the strings found in the `table_names` element, and will be different, depending on the `environment` a database is indicated to operate under.

Saving our initial user data into the system

Before we start using our system, we need to introduce some data into it that will be used to start retrieving data for us. Specifically, we need to create some users, add some wallets to them, and save them. To do so, we create a `create-user-data.R` file that contains the script that will accomplish this for us. The script loads the S4 and R6 object models (S3 does not need to be loaded explicitly), sources the files with the definitions we directly need, which are `Storage`, `User`, and `SETTINGS`, creates two users for us, and saves them:

```
library(R6)
library(methods)

source("../storage/storage.R", chdir = TRUE)
source("../users/user.R")
source("../settings.R")

storage = Storage$new(SETTINGS)
user_1 <- user_constructor("1@somewhere.com", storage)

user_1 <- new_wallet(user_1,
                     "BTC",
                     "3D2oetdNuZUqQHPJmcMDDHYoqkyNVsFk9r", "")

user_1 <- new_wallet(user_1,
                     "LTC",
                     "LdP8Qox1VAhCzLJNqrr74YovaWYyNBUWvL", "")
save(user_1)

user_2 <- user_constructor("2@somewhere.com", storage)

user_2 <- new_wallet(user_2,
                     "BTC",
                     "16rCmCmbuWDhPjWTrpQGaU3EPdZF7MTdUk", "")

user_2 <- new_wallet(user_2,
                     "LTC",
                     "LbGi4Ujj2dhcMdiS9vaCpWxtayBujBQYZw", "")
save(user_2)
```

After the script is executed, you can look into the `csv-files/` directory and find the corresponding data inside. In this case, we used wallets with the most Bitcoin and Litecoin, which can be found online (`https://bitinfocharts.com/top-100-richest-bitcoin-addresses.html` and `https://bitinfocharts.com/top-100-richest-litecoin-addresses.html`). You may experiment using your own wallets, or any wallet whose contents you want to track. Of course, the `email` and `note` parameters don't need to be real; the only parameters that must be real are the asset symbols, which can only be `BTC` or `LTC` for the system we have implemented, and the wallets addresses for such symbols. You may leave the `note` field empty, as we do in the example.

Activating our system with two simple functions

After you have loaded some data into the system, you will be able to execute the `update-markets.R` and `update-assets.R` files, whose contents are shown below. The first one loads the required definitions, as we did previously when creating the user data, and provides the `update_markets_loop()` function, which receives a parameter that specifies the number of minutes between each time the live market data is retrieved. Every 60 minutes is a good option, and it's what we use below. The function simply creates a `Storage` instance using the `SETTINGS` specification shown before, gets the existing exchanges (which is only `CoinMarketCap` at this point), and calls the public `update_markets()` method on each of them, with the corresponding parameters:

```
library(R6)
library(methods)

source("../storage/storage.R", chdir = TRUE)
source("../utilities/time-stamp.R")
source("../settings.R")

update_markets_loop <- function(minutes_interval) {
    storage = Storage$new(SETTINGS)
    exchanges <- storage$read_exchanges()
    repeat {
        timestamp = now.TimeStamp()
        for (exchange in exchanges) {
            exchange$update_markets(timestamp, storage)
        }
        Sys.sleep(minutes_interval * 60)
    }
}
```

```
update_markets_loop(60)
```

When you execute this file, you will see some data showing the progress in your console like the one shown below. Note that we start the script with the `Rscript` command we mentioned in Chapter 1, *Introduction to R:*

$ Rscript update-markets.R

```
...
          timestamp     name symbol rank  price_btc    price_usd
1 2017-11-21-20-03 Bitcoin     BTC    1 1.00000000 8.12675e+03
          timestamp      name symbol rank  price_btc    price_usd
1 2017-11-21-20-03 Ethereum    ETH    2 0.04440240 3.61538e+02
          timestamp        name symbol rank  price_btc    price_usd
1 2017-11-21-20-03 Bitcoin Cash  BCH    3 0.14527100 1.18284e+03
          timestamp    name symbol rank  price_btc    price_usd
1 2017-11-21-20-03 Ripple     XRP    4 0.00002866 2.33352e-01
          timestamp name symbol rank  price_btc    price_usd
1 2017-11-21-20-03 Dash    DASH    5 0.06127300 4.98903e+02
          timestamp     name symbol rank  price_btc    price_usd
1 2017-11-21-20-03 Litecoin    LTC    6 0.00863902 7.03415e+01
          timestamp name symbol rank  price_btc    price_usd
1 2017-11-21-20-03 IOTA   MIOTA    7 0.00011163 9.08941e-01
          timestamp name symbol rank  price_btc    price_usd
1 2017-11-21-20-03  NEO     NEO    8 0.00427168 3.47813e+01
          timestamp   name symbol rank  price_btc    price_usd
1 2017-11-21-20-03 Monero    XMR    9 0.01752360 1.42683e+02
          timestamp name symbol rank  price_btc    price_usd
1 2017-11-21-20-03  NEM     XEM   10 0.00002513 2.04613e-01
...
```

The `update_assets_loop()` function works similarly, but it retrieves the users in each iteration, which dynamically adapts to include any user additions or deletions that may have happened while the function was waiting for its next cycle, and calls the `update_assets()` public method for each `User` instance:

```
library(R6)
library(methods)

source("../storage/storage.R", chdir = TRUE)
source("../utilities/time-stamp.R")
source("../settings.R")

update_assets_loop <- function(minutes_interval) {
    storage = Storage$new(SETTINGS)
    repeat {
        users <- storage$read_users()
```

```
        timestamp = now.TimeStamp()
        lapply(users, update_assets, timestamp)
        Sys.sleep(minutes_interval * 60)
    }
}
update_assets_loop(60)
```

An example of output for the `update-assets.R` file is shown here:

```
$ Rscript update-markets.R

...
          email          timestamp     name symbol    total
1 1@somewhere.com 2017-11-21-20-02 Bitcoin    BTC 76031.29
                         address
1 3D2oetdNuZUqQHPJmcMDDHYoqkyNVsFk9r
          email          timestamp     name symbol    total
1 1@somewhere.com 2017-11-21-20-02 Litecoin   LTC 1420001
                         address
1 LdP8Qox1VAhCzLJNqrr74YovaWYyNBUWvL
          email          timestamp     name symbol total
1 2@somewhere.com 2017-11-21-20-02 Bitcoin    BTC 14001
                         address
1 16rCmCmbuWDhPjWTrpQGaU3EPdZF7MTdUk
          email          timestamp     name symbol    total
1 2@somewhere.com 2017-11-21-20-02 Litecoin   LTC 1397089
                         address
1 LbGi4Ujj2dhcMdiS9vaCpWxtayBujBQYZw
...
```

When you execute these two files, the whole object-oriented system we developed will start working to retrieve live data periodically and save it in the corresponding CSV files. You may look directly into these files to see what data is being saved. Remember that if a wallet does not contain a positive number of an asset, it will not be shown.

When you implement your first object-oriented system, it almost feels magical. If this is the first object-oriented system you have built, I certainly hope you got that feeling, and I also hope this example was interesting and useful for you.

Some advice when working with object-oriented systems

Object-oriented programming allows for a lot of flexibility, but if it's used incorrectly, it can also cause a lot of confusion, since it's easy to develop very complex systems when much simpler solutions would suffice.

You should start a small working system before evolving it into more complex ones. Also, realize that most real-world designs are over-constrained, and you will not be able to please everyone, so you must decide on the priorities for your system.

Each part of your system should focus on a single thing, and doing that thing well. When in doubt, make shorter things. Make shorter classes and shorter methods. Doing so will force your objects to focus on a single responsibility, which will in turn improve your design and will allow you to reuse code more easily.

Make your objects as private as possible. Public classes should not have any public fields, that is, you should use encapsulation everywhere. Maximize information hiding and minimize coupling. Also, remember that names matter. Avoid cryptic abbreviations in your code, and be consistent. The same word should mean the same thing everywhere in your system.

Finally, try to keep your code as immutable as possible. This produces code that is easy to understand, is much more reusable, and is thread-safe, which can be very useful when parallelizing, as we will see in the next chapter. However, if you implement a mutable system, keep the state space as small as possible.

As general advice, your design should be easy to understand and difficult to misuse, even without documentation. Your code should be easily readable and easily maintainable, and the effort you invest in making code that is easy to change should be positively correlated with the likelihood of such change happening.

Summary

In this chapter, we have introduced the fundamentals behind object-oriented programming, and we have seen how to implement object-oriented systems within R with three different object models: S3, S4, and R6. We looked at the fundamental building blocks of object models, such as encapsulation, polymorphism, and hierarchies. We have shown you how to implement parametric polymorphism with S3 and S4, as well as regular polymorphism with R6, and we have shown how to use concepts like interfaces, even when there's no explicit support for them in R.

We have implemented a full object-oriented system to track cryptocurrencies information, and, while doing so, have looked at various patterns and techniques, as well as how the three different object models can be used together.

The type of object model to use is the subject of some controversy among R programmers, and the decision depends on how flexible, formal, or intuitive you want the code to be. In general, if you prefer more flexibility use S3, if you prefer more formality and robustness use S4, and if you prefer your code to be easily understandable and intuitive to people who come from other languages and are not familiar with S3 and S4, then use R6. However, controversy is still there.

John Chambers, the creator of the S language and one of the central developers of R, recommends S4 over S3 in his book, *Software for Data Analysis*, Springer, 2008. Google's *R Style Guide* (`https://google.github.io/styleguide/Rguide.xml`) says that you should avoid S4 whenever possible, and should use S3 instead.

Hopefully, after having read this chapter, you will have a good idea of what system you'd prefer for your next project and why. In `Chapter 9`, *Implementing an Efficient Simple Moving Average*, we will continue to expand the system we created in this chapter to make it more performant when we start dealing with large amounts of data.

9
Implementing an Efficient Simple Moving Average

During the last few decades, demand for computing power has steadily increased as the data volume has become larger and models have become more complex. It is obvious that minimizing the time needed for these calculations has become an important task and that there are obvious performance problems that need to be tackled. These performance problems arise from a mismatch between data volume and existing analytical methods. Eventually, a fundamental shift in data analysis techniques will be required, but for now, we must settle with improving the efficiency of our implementations.

R was designed as an interpreted language with a high-level expressiveness, and that's one of the reasons why it lacks much of the fine-grained control and basic constructs to support highly-performant code. As Arora nails it in the book, she edited, *Conquering Big Data with High Performance Computing, by Springer, 2016: "While R is clearly a high productivity language, it has not necessarily been a high performance language."*

It is not uncommon for the execution time of an R program to be measured in hours, or even in days. As the volume of data to be analyzed increases, the execution time can become prohibitively long, and it's often the case that data scientists and statisticians get stuck with these bottlenecks. When this happens, and if they don't know much about performance optimization, they'll probably just settle with reduced amounts of data, which can hinder their analysis. However, fear not; R programs can be slow, but well-written R programs are usually fast enough, and we will look at various techniques you can use to increase the performance of your R code.

This chapter is not meant to make you a performance optimization expert, but rather provide an overview that introduces you to the vast amount of techniques that can be used when attempting to increase your code's performance. We will look at many different techniques, each of which can have chapters and even books dedicated to them, so we will have to look at them from a very high level, but if you find yourself being constantly restricted by computing resources, they are something you will want to look further into.

Some of the important topics covered in this chapter are as follows:

- Deciding how fast an implementation must be
- The importance of using good algorithms
- Reasons why R can be slow or inefficient at times
- The big performance impact small changes can have
- Measuring your code's performance to find bottlenecks
- Comparing different implementations among themselves
- Getting the most from your computer by parallelizing
- Improving performance by interfacing with other languages

Required packages

We have already worked with some of the packages required for this chapter, such as `ggplot2` and `lubridate`. The other three packages are introduced to benchmark functions and compare their performance among themselves, and for advanced optimization techniques like **delegation** and **parallelization**, which will be explained in their respective sections.

To be able to replicate all the examples in this chapter, you also need working compilers for Fortran and C++ code. Refer to `Appendix`, *Required Packages*, for instructions on how to install them for your operating system.

Let's take a look at the following table depicting the uses of the required packages:

Packages	Reason
ggplot2	High-quality graphs
lubridate	Easily transfer dates
microbenchmark	Benchmark functions' performance

Starting by using good algorithms

To be able to communicate the ideas contained in this chapter clearly, first I need to provide some simple definitions. When I refer to an *algorithm*, I mean an abstract specification for a process. When I refer to an *implementation*, I refer to the way an algorithm is actually programmed. Finally, when I refer to a *program* or an *application*, I mean a set of such algorithm implementations working together. Having said that, it's easy to see how an algorithm can be implemented in many different ways (for example, one implementation may be using a list, while another may be using an array). Each of these implementations will have different performances, and they are related, but not equivalent, to an algorithm's time-complexity.

For those unfamiliar with the last term, each algorithm has the following two basic properties

- **Time complexity**: This property refers to the number of calculations an algorithm needs to execute, in relation to the size of input it receives. There are various mathematical tools to measure this complexity, the most common one being Big-O notation, which measures the worst-case scenario for an algorithm.
- **Space complexity**: This property refers to the amount of memory required to execute the algorithm, again in relation to the size of the input it receives, and it can be also measured with the same mathematical tools.

It's a well-known fact that an inefficient algorithm implemented very efficiently can be orders of magnitude slower than an efficient algorithm implemented inefficiently. This means that most of the time, algorithm selection is much more important than implementation optimization.

There are many other things to consider when evaluating an algorithm other than the complexities mentioned previously, such as efficiency resources usage (for example, internet bandwith), as well as other properties such as security or implementation difficulty. We won't dig into these topics in this book. However, if you want your code to perform well, you must study data structures and algorithms formally. Great resources to get started on these topics are the book by Cormen, Leiserson, Rivest, and Stein, titled *Introduction to Algorithms, by MIT Press, 2009*, and Skiena's, *The Algorithm Design Manual, by Springer, 2008*.

Just how much impact can algorithm selection have?

Calculating Fibonacci numbers is a traditional example when teaching recursiveness. Here, we will use it to compare the performance of two algorithms, one recursive and one sequential.

In case you are not familiar with them, Fibonacci numbers are defined recursively in a sequence where the next is the sum of the previous two, and the first two numbers are ones (our base cases). The actual sequence is 1, 1, 2, 3, 5, 8, 13, 21, 34, 55, 89, 144, and so on. This is called a Fibonacci sequence, and it exhibits interesting properties, such as being related to the golden ratio, which you should definitely look up if don't know what it is.

Our `fibonacci_recursive()` function receives the position of the Fibonacci number we want to calculate as n, restricted to integers greater than or equal to one. If n is a base case, that is, if it's below 1, we will simply return it (not that if we're computing the Fibonacci number at the second position, our operation n - 2 would be zero, which is not a valid position, that's why we need to use <= instead of ==). Otherwise, we will return the sum of the recursive calls to the previous two with `fibonacci_recursive(n - 1)` and `fibonacci_recursive(n - 2)`, as shown in the following code snippet:

```
fibonacci_recursive <- function(n) {
    if(n <= 1) { return(n) }
    return(fibonacci_recursive(n - 1) + fibonacci_recursive(n - 2))
}
```

As you can see in the following code snippet, our function works as expected. However, what happens when we want to retrieve the 35th or 40th Fibonacci number? As you may experience when running this code, the further the Fibonacci number is from the base cases, the more time it will take, and somewhere around the 30th position, it starts being noticeably slower. If you try to compute the 100th Fibonacci number, you'll be waiting for a long while before you get the result:

```
fibonacci_recursive(1)
#> [1] 1

fibonacci_recursive(2)
#> [1] 1

fibonacci_recursive(3)
#> [1] 2

fibonacci_recursive(4)
```

```
#> [1] 3

fibonacci_recursive(5)
 #> [1] 5

fibonacci_recursive(35)
#> [1] 9227465
```

Why is this happening? The answer is that this algorithm is doing a lot of unnecessary work, making it a bad algorithm. To understand why, let's mentally go through the execution of the algorithm for the third and fourth Fibonacci numbers and make the corresponding execution trees, as shown in the following diagram:

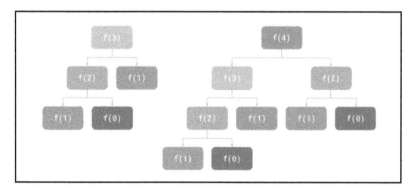

In the preceding diagram, **f(n)** is short for `fibonacci_recursive(n)`, so that we can fit all the objects inside it, and colors are used to show which function calls are repeated. As you can see, when you execute `fibonacci_recusive(3)`, the `fibonacci_recursive(1)` call is executed twice. When executing `fibonacci_recursive(4)`, that same call is executed three times. How many times will it be executed for `fibonacci_recursive(5)` and for `fibonacci_recursive(6)`? That's an exercise for you, the reader, and as you'll find, the number increases exponentially.

To be technically precise, the time complexity for the algorithm is $O(2^n)$, which is as bad as you can get. Furthermore, most of the calculations are completely unnecessary since they are repeated. The algorithm is correct, but its performance is one of the worst. As we mentioned earlier, even if you provide the most efficient implementation possible for this algorithm, it will be much slower than a very inefficient implementation of a more efficient one.

If we design a correct algorithm that avoids doing all the unnecessary calculations, we can have a much faster program, and that's exactly what the following algorithm does. Instead of making a tree of recursive calls, we will simply compute the Fibonacci numbers in order up to the one we are being asked for. We will simply add the previous two numbers and store the result in the array f, which will have n integers. We specify the two base cases and proceed with the calculation, as shown in the following code snippet:

```
fibonacci_sequential <- function(n) {
    if (n <= 2) { return(1) }
    f <- integer(n)
    f[1] <- 1
    f[2] <- 1
    for (i in 3:n) {
        f[i] <- f[i-2] + f[i-1]
    }
    return(f[n])
}
```

As you can see, each number is computed only once, which is the most efficient algorithm we can design for this problem. This avoids all the overhead from the recursive algorithm and leaves us with a linear time complexity of $O(n)$. Even if we code this algorithm without much care for performance optimization, it's execution time will be many orders of magnitude faster.

With this algorithm, we can actually compute the 1476th Fibonacci number, which is the largest one that R's internal architecture will allow for. If we try to compute the 1477th Fibonacci number, we will get infinity (Inf) as a response due to the mechanisms R uses to store integers, which is a topic we won't go into. Furthermore, the computation for the 1476th Fibonacci number is almost instantaneous, which goes to showcase the importance of choosing a good algorithm before worrying about optimizing it:

```
fibonacci_sequential(1476)
#[1] 1.306989e+308

fibonacci_sequential(1477)
#[1] Inf
```

Finally, note that we achieved an increase in speed at the expense of using more memory. The recursive algorithm discarded every Fibonacci number once it computed it, while the sequential algorithm keeps every single one in memory. For this particular problem, this seems to be a good trade-off. The trade-off among time and space is a common one in performance optimization.

Now that we have seen just how important algorithm selection can be, for the rest of the chapter we will work with a single algorithm, and we will focus on optimizing its implementation. However, the point remains that choosing an efficient algorithm is more important than implementing it efficiently.

How fast is fast enough?

Let's assume that you have chosen a good algorithm and implemented it without too much regard for optimization, as is commonly the case with first attempts. Should you invest the time to optimize it? Performance optimization can be a very costly activity. You must not try to optimize your code unless you must. Your time is valuable, and it's probably better spent doing something else.

Let's say that for some reason, you must make your implementation faster. The first thing you must decide on is how fast is fast enough. Is your algorithm required to simply finish within a couple of hours instead of a couple of days, or do you need to come down to microsecond levels? Is this an absolute requirement or should you simply do the best job you can within a specific time frame? These are important questions that you must consider before optimizing your code, and sometimes the solution is not even optimization.

It's not rare for clients to prefer spending more money on using some type of cloud resource to tackle the performance problem rather than spending valuable time optimizing an algorithm's performance, especially if they can be providing more business value doing something else.

Apart from the machine-time versus human-time trade-off mentioned earlier, there are other considerations when deciding whether to optimize an algorithm's implementation or not. Do you want your code to be easily readable? Do you want your code to be shareable? It's often the case that more performant code is also more difficult to understand. Furthermore, if you're developing code that is executed parallelly, it will impose a bunch of restrictions on the type of systems that can execute it, and you need to keep that in mind.

I suggest that you keep to the minimum number of optimizations; this will make you achieve your goal regarding how fast an implementation must run, and don't do more than that. The process will be simple: find the most important bottleneck, remove it (or at least decrease its impact), check whether or not your implementation is fast enough, and if it's not, repeat. We will go through this cycle a couple of times along this chapter, and even though it seems easy in retrospective, it can be quite difficult in reality, especially when dealing with complex algorithms.

Calculating simple moving averages inefficiently

The algorithm we will work with for the rest of the chapter is called **simple moving average (SMA)**. It's a very well-known tool for doing technical analysis of time-series, specially for financial markets and trading. The idea behind SMA is that you will compute an average at each point in time by looking back at a predefined number periods. For example, let's say you're looking at a minute-by-minute time-series, and you will compute an SMA(30). This means that at each observation in your time-series, you will take the observations that correspond to the previous 30 minutes from starting at a specific observation (30 observations back), and will save the average for those 30 observations as the SMA(30) value for that point in time.

In the later diagram, you can visualize the idea behind SMAs. The diagram shows a monotone time-series that increases by one value-unit for every time-unit, both of which start at one (that is, its value is **1** at time **1**, **2** at time **2**, and so on), along with some figures surrounding the group of observations the SMA calculation will take. As you can see, for SMA(3), we get the last three elements at every point in the time-series; similarly, for SMA(4), we get the last four elements. When you calculate the average for the subset of elements in the figure, you get the numbers in the top-left corners, which correspond to the specific SMA time-series calculated. Specifically for such a time-series, for the SMA(3) case, the result is NA, NA, **2**, **3**, **4**, **5**, **6**, **7**, and **8**, and for the SMA(4) case, the result is NA, NA, NA, **2.5**, **3.5**, **4.5**, **5.5**, **6.5**, and **7.5**.

There are a couple of following properties we should note about SMAs:

- First, note that both SMA(3) and SMA(4) are series that contain the same number of observations as the original time-series, **9** in this case.
- Second, note that they both begin with a number of NA equal to the number SMA parameter minus one. This is because in the case of SMA(3), at time **2**, we don't have three observations back, we only have two. Therefore, an NA is used to indicate that SMA(3) could not be computed at that point. The same explanation applies to all other NA values.
- Third and finally, note that every time we move one time-unit, we add one observation and remove another observation (the tail) from the current subset.

Take a look at the following figure depicting the preceding properties:

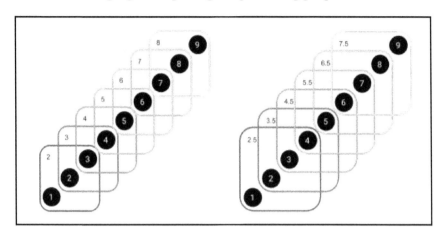

Simulating the time-series

Of course, you have been collecting data from cryptocurrency markets since you implemented your own version of the object-oriented system we developed in the last chapter, haven't you? I'm just kidding. If you have, it's probably not enough data for what we will do in this chapter, so here's a small piece of code that will simulate two time-series for Bitcoin and Litecoin price in US Dollars. The data structure is similar to the one used in the previous chapter, making the code we develop here useful for that system also.

We won't go too deep into how the function works since it should be clear for you at this point, except to point out that we're using the `time_to_timestamp.TimeStamp()` function we developed in the last chapter, and that the `simulate_prices()` function uses a quadratic model on top of an ARIMA simulation. If you don't know what an ARIMA model is, don't worry too much about it (it's not needed to understand this chapter). If you're interested in learning more about it, take a look at Shumway and Stoffer's book, *Time Series Analysis and Its Applications: With R Examples, Springer, 2011*. We are using a quadratic model because Bitcoin's price has been accelerating during the past couple of months (this is being written during November 2017). Let's take a look at the following code:

```
source("../chapter-08/cryptocurrencies/utilities/time-stamp.R")
library(lubridate)
N <- 60 * 24 * 365

simulate_market <- function(name, symbol, now, n, base, sd, x) {
    dates <- seq(now - minutes(n - 1), now, by = "min")
```

```
        ts <- unlist(lapply(lapply (
                                dates,
                                time_to_timestamp.TimeStamp),
                                unclass))
        price_usd <- simulate_prices(n, base, sd, x)
        data <- data.frame(timestamp = ts, price_usd = price_usd)
        data$name <- name
        data$symbol <- symbol
        return(data)
    }

    simulate_prices <- function(n, base, sd, x) {
        ts <- arima.sim(list(15, 15, 15), n = n, sd = sd)
        quadratic_model <- base + (x - 1) * base / (n^2) * (1:n)^2
        return(as.numeric(ts + quadratic_model))
    }

    now <- Sys.time()
    btc <- simulate_market("Bitcoin", "BTC", now, N, 8000, 8, 2)
    ltc <- simulate_market("Litecoin", "LTC", now, N, 80, 0.08, 1.5)
    data <- rbind(btc, ltc)
    data <- data[order(data$timestamp), ]
    write.csv(data, "./data.csv", row.names = FALSE)
```

Note that the parameters used to call the `simulate_market()` function try to resemble what is seen currently in Bitcoin and Litecoin prices, but keep in mind that this is a very simple model, so don't expect it to behave as the actual price time-series for these assets. Finally, we simulate 525,600 observations for each asset, which is approximately equal to the number of minutes in a year (`N <- 60 * 24 * 365`, which contains seconds per hour, hours per day, and days per year). This means we're simulating minute-by-minute data.

To visualize the Bitcoin prices we simulated, you may use the following code. It simply produces one graph that uses a sample of 1,000 elements throughout the year (more than that is unnecessary, since you won't be able to perceive more points, and it will slow down the calculations); also, another graph is produced, which shows a zoom-in effect into the first hour in the data:

```
s <- sample(1:nrow(btc), 1000)
plot(btc[s[order(s)], "price_usd"], xlab="Minutes", ylab="Price", xaxt='n')
title(main="Bitcoin price simulation for 1 year")
lines(btc[s[order(s)], "price_usd"])
plot(btc[1:60, "price_usd"], xlab="Minutes", ylab="Price", xaxt='n')
title(main="Bitcoin price simulation for 1 hour")
lines(btc[1:60, "price_usd"])
```

As can be seen, there's a strong upward trend when looking at the full year simulation, but if you zoom-in into a smaller time frame, you'll see quite a bit of price variance, which allows for useful SMA implementations. Let's take a look at the following graph:

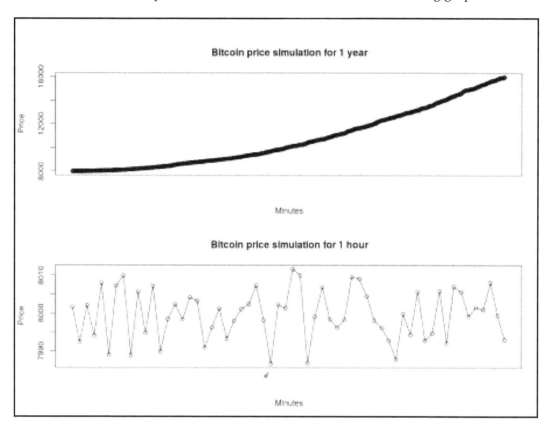

Our first (very inefficient) attempt at an SMA

As was mentioned earlier, we will work with SMA implementations for the rest of the chapter. To differentiate among them, we will change the function name for each subsequent implementation, starting with `sma_slow_1()`. All SMA implementations will receive the following parameters:

- `period`: To specify how many observations to use for the SMA.

- `symbol`: To denote the asset we want to make the calculations for
  - For this example, options will be `BTC` for `Bitcoin` or `LTC` for `Litecoin`. However, when you execute the system yourself, you'll be able to expand it with any cryptocurrency symbol you so desire.
- `data`: The actual data that contains the price time-series for every asset.

We will make two assumptions on `data`—the `timestamp` column is in increasing order and we don't have gaps in the time-series, meaning that we have price data for every minute. This allows us to skip any ordering procedures and check whether the SMA should contain NA internally when no data is available. Note that both these assumptions are fulfilled by our data simulation.

Now, we'll explain how `sma_slow_1()` works. Note that this is a very inefficient implementation, and you should definitely avoid programming this way. However, these are common errors people make, and we will be removing them one by one while we measure the impact they actually have on your code's speed. Let's see how it is done by performing the following steps:

1. First, we create an empty data frame named `result` that contains a single column called `sma`.
2. Then, we loop over all rows in the data; `end` denotes the end, or right-extreme, of the SMA interval under consideration.
3. We create a `position` integer that is the same as the `end` every time we start the loop as well as an `sma` object that will contain the actual SMA computation for the `end` position, an `n_accumulated` integer that keeps track of the number of observations we have accumulated, and a `period_prices` data frame that contains a single column to store the prices for the current SMA calculation.
4. Next, we check whether the observation at the current `end` corresponds to the `symbol` we're interested in. If it's not, we simply ignore that iteration, but if it is, we will accumulate `period_prices` starting at the `end` position (remember that `position` is equal to `end` and this point) and going backward until the number of accumulated prices is equal to the `period` we're interested in or the current `position` is lower than 1 (meaning that we're at the beginning of the time-series). To do so, we use a while-loop that checks for the condition mentioned before, increases `n_accumulated` when an observation with the same `symbol` is found and its data is appended to the `period_prices` data frame, and increases the `position` regardless of whether the observation was useful so that we don't get stuck.

5. After the while-loop is finished, we know that we have either accumulated a number of prices equal to the `period` we are interested in or we encountered the beginning of the time-series. In the first case, we compute the mean of such prices by iterating over the `period_prices` data frame, and assign that as the `sma` value for the current `end` position. In the second case, we simply record an `NA` value since we were not able to compute the full SMA. Take a look at the following code snippet:

```
sma_slow_1 <- function(period, symbol, data) {
    result <- data.frame(sma=numeric())
    for(end in 1:nrow(data)) {
        position <- end
        sma <- NA
        n_accumulated <- 0
        period_prices <- data.frame(price=numeric())
        if (data[end, "symbol"] == symbol) {
            while(n_accumulated < period & position >= 1) {
                if (data[position, "symbol"] == symbol) {
                    period_prices <- rbind(
                        period_prices,
                        data.frame(price=data[position, "price_usd"])
                    )
                    n_accumulated <- n_accumulated + 1
                }
                position <- position - 1
            }
            if (n_accumulated == period) {
                sma <- 0
                for (price in period_prices$price) {
                    sma <- sma + price
                }
                sma <- sma / period
            } else {
                sma <- NA
            }
            result <- rbind(result, data.frame(sma=sma))
        }
    }
    return(result)
}
```

If the implementation seems complicated, it's because it is. As we start improving our code, it will naturally be simplified, which will make it easier to understand.

6. Now, we want to actually see that it works. To do so, we bring the `sma-slow.R` file into memory (which contains all the slow implementations) as well as the data as shown in the following code snippet:

```
source("./sma-slow.R")
data_original <- read.csv("./data.csv")
```

Note that we take only the first 100 observations, which correspond to 50 minutes of Bitcoin price action (remember that these 100 observations only contain 50 for Bitcoin; the other 50 are for Litecoin). We can see that the SMA(5) for Bitcoin makes sense, including the first four NA (feel free to check the numbers by hand, but remember to use the data and results for your own data simulation):

```
data   <- data_original[1:100, ]
symbol <- "BTC"
period <- 5

sma_1 <- sma_slow_1(period, symbol, data)
sma_1
#>          sma
#> 1         NA
#> 2         NA
#> 3         NA
#> 4         NA
#> 5    7999.639
#> 6    7997.138
#> 7    8000.098
#> 8    8001.677
#> 9    8000.633
#> 10   8000.182
(Truncated output)
```

Before we understand how to fix this code, we need to understand why R can be slow as well as how to measure how much of an impact we're having while we are improving it.

Understanding why R can be slow

Understanding why a programming language can be slow is a fundamental skill needed to be able to increase the speed of its implementations. Any implementation in any programming language is similarly affected by an algorithm's time and memory complexities, because they are algorithms, and not implementation properties. However, the way languages handle specific implementations can vary quite a bit, and that's what we'll focus on now.

In the case of R, people often find the following four main bottlenecks:

- Object immutability
- Interpreted dynamic typings
- Memory-bound processes
- Single-threaded processes

By no means is this list complete or encountered in every implementation. It's just the most common bottlenecks I've seen people encounter, and which, after being fixed, produced the largest amount of speed improvements. They are often good starting points, but every implementation is different, so it's very difficult to suggest general rules for performance optimization, and you should keep this in mind.

Object immutability

Improving the speed of R implementations does not necessarily involve advanced optimization techniques, such as parallelization. Indeed, there are a number of simple tweaks that, while not always obvious, can make R run significantly faster. The top bottleneck people encounter with R is a lack of understanding about its object immutability property, and the overhead incurred when making copies of such objects. Simply taking care of this can produce dramatic performance improvements, and it's not too difficult once you understand how to do so. This is a good candidate to start looking for optimizations.

As an example of some of the issues that can arise, suppose you have an array of numbers named a. Now, suppose you want to update first element of a to be 10, as shown in the following code snippet:

```
a[1] <- 10
```

This assignment is much more complex than it seems. It is actually implemented via the `` `"[<-"` `` replacement function through this call and assignment:

```
a <- `"[<-"`(a, 1, value = 10)
```

At first, you may find this to be a very weird syntax, but remember that, as we saw in Chapter 1, *Introduction to R*, we can have strings that represent objects, including functions, as is the case here. The `` `"[<-"` `` parts of the line is actually a function name being called with the a, 1, and value = 10 parameters. If you execute the previous two lines, you should get the same result; that is the first element in a being equal to 10.

What actually happens is that an internal copy of a is made; the first element of such an object is changed to 10 and the resulting object is reassigned to a. Even though we are simply changing just one element of the array, in reality, the entire vector is recomputed. The larger the vector, the worse the problem is, and this can considerably slow down your implementation. It's even worse when you're using heavy data structures, such as data frames.

Languages that allow for mutabilty, such as Fortran or C++, will simply change a specific value in the array instead of producing a new copy of the full array. That's why it's often the case where code that would be just fine in other languages produces a very large, and often unnecessary, overhead when programmed similarly in R. We will see ways to mitigate this impact as we go through the chapter.

Interpreted dynamic typings

The second most important bottleneck people find is R's nature of being an interpreted and dynamically-typed language. This means that at any given line in your program, an object may be an integer, in the next line it may be a data frame, then a string, and it may be a list of data frames two lines later. This is the nature of not having fixed types for your objects, and since the interpreter can't know how to handle such objects in advance because they may be entirely different each time, it must check the object's type every time it wants to apply some kind of operation on it. This is a little exaggerated, but the point remains that since it's possible that an object's type changed, it must be continuously checked.

We will see how to avoid some of these checks to increase performance, but to deal with the interpreted and dynamically typed nature, we will have to resort to other programming languages, such as Fortran or C++, as we will show you later in the chapter. These languages fix an object's type when it's created and if you attempt to change it at some point, the program will throw an error. This may seen like an unnecessary restriction, but actually it can be very powerful when communicating some code's intent as well as to allow compilers to provide powerful optimizations for handling such objects.

Memory-bound processes

The third most important bottleneck people find is that R must have all objects in memory. This means that the computer being used for the analysis must have enough RAM to hold the entire data at once, as well as intermediate and resulting objects, and keep in mind that this RAM is shared with all the other applications running in the computer.

If R doesn't have enough RAM to hold every object in memory, the operating system will perform a **swapping** operation that, within R, will look as if you had all data in memory but data will be written and read from the hard drive in reality. Reading and writing from hard drives is orders of magnitude slower than doing equivalent operations in-memory, and R won't let you know that this is happening since it really can't (this is done by the operating system). To detect that this is happening, you should keep an eye on the tool provided by your operating system to monitor your system's resources.

Even though this is the third bottleneck in the list, when it happens, it's by far the most damaging one, as we have a disk input/output bottleneck on top of the memory bottleneck. When you encounter this problem, you'll be able to tell because R will seem to have frozen or will be unresponsive. If it's happening to you, you should definitely look for ways to eliminate it. It's the third in the list because it's not encountered as often as the previous two, not because it has less of an impact.

Single-threaded processes

The fourth most important bottleneck people encounter is the fact that R language has no explicit constructs for parallelism. An out-of-the-box R installation cannot take advantage of multiple CPUs, and it does not matter if you install R on a powerful server with 64 CPU cores, R will only use one of them.

The way to fix this is to introduce parallelism in your implementations. However, doing so is not an easy task at all. In fact, serious parallelization efforts require deep hardware and software knowledge, and often depend on the specific hardware used to execute an implementation.

Even though it's a very difficult thing to do, and maybe even because of that, R has a lot of packages whose objectives are to provide parallel solutions for specific R functions. There are some general packages you may use to create your own parallel implementations, as we will see later in the chapter, but it's definitely not the first place to start looking for performance enhancements.

Now that you understand why R can be slow, we will use this knowledge to gradually improve the SMA implementation we showed earlier, but before we do that, we must learn to measure our code's performance, and that's the focus of the next section.

Measuring by profiling and benchmarking

There's a common saying which states that you can't change what you can't measure. Even though you can technically change your code's performance in R, you definitely won't be able to know whether a change is worth it if you don't measure it. In this section, we will introduce three tools you can use to measure your code: `Rprof()`, `system.time()`, and `microbenchmark()`. The first two are included in R, and the third one requires the `microbenchmark` package to be installed. The `Rprof()` tool is used to profile code, while `system.time()` and `microbenchmark()` are used to benchmark code.

- **Profiling** means that you measure how much time a particular implementation is spending on each of its parts.
- **Benchmarking** means that you compare the total amount of time to execute different implementations to compare them among themselves, without regard for their internal parts.

Profiling fundamentals with Rprof()

Even experienced programmers have a hard time identifying bottlenecks in their code. Unless you have quite a bit of experience and a good sense of what parts of your code are slowing down its execution, you're probably better-off profiling your code before you start optimizing it. Only once you've identified the most important bottlenecks can you attempt to eliminate them. It's difficult to provide general advice on improving performance since every implementation is quite different.

The `Rprof()` function is a built-in tool for profiling the execution of R functions. At regular intervals, the profiler stops the interpreter, records the current function call stack, and saves the information to a file. We can then look at summaries of such information to find out where our implementation is spending the most time.

Keep in mind that the results from `Rprof()` are stochastic. Each time we use it, the results will be slightly different, depending on many things specific to your system, which are out of R's control. Therefore, the results we get from `Rprof()` are estimates and can vary within the sample implementation.

To use the `Rprof()` function, we simply call it without parameters before we call the code we want to measure, and then we call it again, this time sending the `NULL` parameter. The results are saved to a file in your hard drive and can be invoked with the `summaryRprof()` function call.

In this particular case, note that we sent the first 10,000 elements. If we had sent a small amount of data, the sma_slow_1() function would have finished so fast that we would not have any meaningful output (remember that Rprof() measures by time intervals). Also, the results shown here are truncated, since the actual results are much larger because they show many function calls our code used. We left the top five results for each table.

Both tables have the same information. The difference is that the $by.self table (the first one) is ordered by self, while the $by.total table (the second one) is ordered by total; self indicates how much time a function call took without regard for its child function calls, while total information includes the child function calls. This means that self data must sum to 100, while aggregated total data will commonly sum to much more than 100:

```
Rprof()
sma_1 <- sma_slow_1(period, symbol, data_original[1:10000, ])
Rprof(NULL)
summaryRprof()
#> $by.self
#>                       self.time self.pct total.time total.pct
#> "rbind"                    1.06    10.84       6.16     62.99
#> "structure"                0.82     8.38       0.94      9.61
#> "data.frame"               0.68     6.95       4.32     44.17
#> "[.data.frame"             0.54     5.52       1.76     18.00
#> "sma_slow_1"               0.48     4.91       9.78    100.00
#> (Truncated output)
#>
#> $by.total
#>                       total.time total.pct self.time self.pct
#> "sma_slow_1"                9.78    100.00      0.48     4.91
#> "rbind"                     6.16     62.99      1.06    10.84
#> "data.frame"                4.32     44.17      0.68     6.95
#> "["                         1.88     19.22      0.20     2.04
#> "as.data.frame"             1.86     19.02      0.10     1.02
#> (Truncated output)
#>
#> $sample.interval
#> [1] 0.02
#>
#> $sampling.time
#> [1] 9.78
```

As you can see in the results, the first column indicates a function call in the stack, and the numbers indicate how much time was spent in a particular function call, either in absolute (`time`) or relative terms (`pct`). Normally, you'll want to focus on the top values in the `self.pct` column of the `$by.self` table, since they show the functions that are taking the most amount of time by themselves. In this particular case, `rbind`, `structure`, and `data.frame` are the functions taking the most amount of time.

Finally, you should know that some of the names found in the functions call stack can be very cryptic, and sometimes you'll have a hard time finding references or documentation for them. This is because they are probably internal R implementations that are not meant to be used directly by R users. What I suggest is that you simply try to fix those function calls that you recognize, unless you're dealing with situations where highly-optimized code is an absolute requirement, but in that case, you would be better off reading a specialized book on the subject.

Benchmarking manually with system.time()

Now, we will look into how to benchmark your code. If you're looking for a simple measurement of execution time, `system.time()` is a good choice. You simply call a function inside of it, and it will print the following three time measures for you: .

- `user`: It is the `user` time that we should pay more attention to, since it measures the CPU time used by R to execute the code
- `system`: The `system` time is a measure of time spent by the system to be able to execute the function
- `elapsed`: The `elapsed` time is total time it took to execute the code, even if it was slowed down due to other system processes

Sometimes, `elapsed` time is longer than the sum of `user` time and `system` time because the CPU is multitasking on other processes, or it has to wait for resources such as files and network connections to be available. Other times, elapsed time is shorter than the sum of `user` time and `system` time. This can happen when multiple threads or CPUs are used to execute the expression. For example, a task that takes 10 seconds of user time can be completed in 5 seconds if there are two CPUs sharing the load.

Most of the time, however, we are interested in the total elapsed time to execute the given expression. When the expression is executed on a single thread (the default for R), the elapsed time is usually very close to the sum of the user time and system time. If that is not the case, either the expression has spent time waiting for resources to be available, or there were many other processes on the system competing for the CPU's time. In any case, if you're suspicious of your measurements, try measuring the same code various times while the computer is not spending resources in other applications.

In this particular case, we see that the execution took approximately 9 seconds to complete, which is roughly equivalent to the same time it took to execute it when measured by Rprof() in the previous section, as can be seen in the column `total.time` on the `sma_slow_1` observation of the `$by.total` table.

```
system.time(sma_slow_1(period, symbol, data_original[1:10000, ]))
#>    user  system elapsed
#>   9.251   0.015   9.277
```

If you want to measure multiple functions to compare their times, you will have to use the `system.time()` function on each of them, so it's somewhat of a manual process. A better alternative for such a thing is the `microbenchmark()` function shown in the next section.

Benchmarking automatically with microbenchmark()

If you have identified a function that is called many times in your code and needs to be accelerated, you can write several implementations for it and use the `microbenchmark()` function from the `microbenchmark` package to compare them. Its results will also normally be more reliable because, by default, it runs each function 100 times and thus is able to produce statistics on its performance.

To use the `microbenchmark()` function, you simply wrap it around a piece of code you want to measure. Some handy features are that you can make an assignment, within which it's very handy to measure and use the results in one go; also, you can pass various function calls separated by commas, and it will give you results for each of them. This way, you can automatically benchmark various functions at the same time.

Here, we will assign the results of `sma_slow_1()` to `sma_1`, as we did previously, but since it's wrapped with the `microbenchmark()` function, it will also be measured and the performance results will be stored in the `performance` data frame. This object contains the following columns: `expr` is a string that contains the function call used, `neval` is the number of times the function was executed (by default, it's `100`), and the `min`, `lq` (first quartile), `mean`, `median`, `uq` (third quartile), and `max` statistics:

```
performance <- microbenchmark(
    sma_1 <- sma_slow_1(period, symbol, data),
    unit = "us"
)

summary(performance)$median
#> [1] 81035.19
```

If you want to look at the full performance data frame, simply print it. Here, we only showed that the `median` time it took when executing the `sma_slow_1()` function call was `81,035.19` microseconds (which was the unit specified with the `unit = "us"` parameter). By default, this would have used milliseconds instead of microseconds, but we want to provide the same units for all comparisons we perform along the chapter, and microseconds is a better option for that.

We will continue to add records to the following table. Each row will contain an implementation identifier, the median microseconds it took to execute such a function, indication of the fastest implementation so far, and a percentage when being compared to the fastest one we have so far. In this particular case, since it's the only one we have done, it is obviously the fastest one and is also 100% from the best one, which is itself:

Fastest	Implementation	Microseconds median	% From Fastest
⇒	sma_slow_1	81,035.19	100%

The objective of the rest of the chapter is to extend this table to provide precise measurements of just how much performance improvements we're making as we improve our SMA implementation.

Easily achieving high benefit - cost improvements

In this section, we will show how the efficiency of R can be drastically improved without resorting to advanced techniques such as delegating to other programming languages or implementing parallelization. Those techniques will be shown in the later sections.

Using the simple data structure for the job

Many R users would agree that data frame as a data structure is a basic tool for data analysis. It provides an intuitive way to represent a typical structured dataset with rows and columns representing observations and variables, respectively, but it provides more flexibility than a matrix by allowing variables of different types (such as character and numeric variables in a single structure). Furthermore, when data frames contain only numeric variables, basic matrix operations conveniently become applicable to it without any explicit coercing required. This convenience, however, comes with a performance cost that people often don't mention.

Here, we avoid repeating the `Rprof()` results we got from profiling the `sma_slow_1()` function. However, if you look back at them, you will see that `rbind()` and `data.frame()` were among the functions that took the most time. This is precisely the performance cost mentioned earlier. If you want your implementations to be faster, avoiding using data frames can be a good start. Data frames can be a great tool for data analysis, but not when writing fast code.

As you can see in `sma_slow_2()`, the code is practically the same as `sma_slow_1()`, except that the `period_prices` object is no longer a data frame. Instead, it has become a vector, which is extended with the `c()` function in place of the `rbind()` function. Note that we are still dynamically expanding the size of an object when calling the `c()` function, which is something you shouldn't be doing for performant code, but we will take it step-by-step:

```
sma_slow_2 <- function(period, symbol, data) {
    result <- data.frame(sma=numeric())
    for(end in 1:nrow(data)) {
        position <- end
        sma <- NA
        n_accumulated <- 0
        period_prices <- NULL
        if(data[end, "symbol"] == symbol) {
            while(n_accumulated < period & position >= 1) {
                if(data[position, "symbol"] == symbol) {
```

```
                    period_prices <- c(period_prices,
                        data[position, "price_usd"])
                    n_accumulated <- n_accumulated + 1
                }
                position <- position - 1
            }
            if (n_accumulated == period) {
                sma <- 0
                for (price in period_prices) {
                    sma <- sma + price
                }
                sma <- sma / period
            } else {
                sma <- NA
            }
            result <- rbind(result, data.frame(sma=sma))
        }
    }
    return(result)
}
```

In this case, we measure its execution time just as we did earlier, but we also perform a very important verification, which is often overlooked. We verify that the values we get from sma_slow_1() are the same as those we get from sma_slow_2(). It wouldn't be a correct comparison if we measured implementations that do different things. Performing the check is also useful to increase our confidence that every change we make does not introduce unexpected behavior. As can be seen, all values are the same, so we can proceed with confidence:

```
performance <- microbenchmark(
    sma_2 <- sma_slow_2(period, symbol, data),
    unit = "us"
)

all(sma_1$sma == sma_2$sma, na.rm = TRUE)
#> TRUE

summary(performance)$median
#> [1] 33031.7785
```

We record our results in our table, and realize that removing this data frame structure allowed us to remove two-thirds of the execution time. That's pretty good for such an easy change, isn't it? Since our base case (the fastest implementation we have so far) is sma_slow_2(), we can see that sma_slow_1() would take approximately 145% more time to execute:

Fastest	Implementation	Microseconds median	% from fastest
	sma_slow_1	81,035.1900	245.32%
⇒	sma_slow_2	33,031.7785	100%

Now that we realize what an impact unnecessary data frames can have in the performance of our code, we proceed to also remove the other data frame we were using for the result object. We also replace it with a vector, and use the c() function to append to it. The same dynamic expansion problem mentioned earlier appears here, too. As you can see, everything else is kept the same.

We proceed to benchmark as we did earlier, and also check that the results we got are also the same. The cautious reader may have noted that the previous check was performed with an equality operator, while this one is performed with an inequality operator. In reality, when checking real numbers, you're better off checking that they are close enough as opposed to exactly the same. If you checked for identical numbers, you may get a FALSE result due to one of the numbers having a difference of 0.000000001, which is not significant in our case. Therefore, we establish what is a significant check for our specific use case, and test that each pair of numbers has a difference not larger than that threshold, just as we do here, with our threshold being 0.001:

```
performance <- microbenchmark(
    sma_3 <- sma_slow_3(period, symbol, data),
    unit = "us"
)

all(sma_1$sma - sma_3 <= 0.001, na.rm = TRUE)
#> TRUE

summary(performance)$median
#> [1] 19628.243
```

In this case, the median time it took to execute sma_slow_3() was of 19,628.243 microseconds. We go ahead and record that into our table, and recalculate the percentage from the best, which is sma_slow_3() at this point. Note that we are able to remove close to half the time from the already improved sma_slow_2() function, and that using the original sma_slow_1() function will take 312% more time than the latest one. It can be surprising how much performance gain you can get by simply using a simpler data structure.

Vectorizing as much as possible

Vectorization means removing a manual looping mechanism in favor of an operation optimized to do the same thing without a need for an explicit loop. It is very helpful because it helps avoid the overhead incurred on by explicit loops in R. Vectorizing is a fundamental tool in R, and you should get used to programming using it instead of using explicit loops whenever possible, without waiting until a performance stage comes into play. Once you understand how it works, it will come naturally. A good read for this topic is Ross's blog post, *Vectorization in R: Why?* (`http://www.noamross.net/blog/2014/4/16/ vectorization-in-r--why.html`).

Explicit loops may be efficient in other languages, such as Fortran and C++. However, in R, you're better off using vectorization most of the time.

There are various ways of vectorizing operations. For example, if you want to perform a matrix-vector multiplication, instead of iterating over the elements of vector and the matrix, multiplying the appropriate coefficients, and adding them together as is normally done in other programming languages, you can simply do something like A `%*%` b to perform all of those operations in a vectorized manner in R. Vectorization provides more expressive code that is easier to understand as well as more performant, and that's why you should always attempt to use it.

Another way of vectorizing is using the family of the `apply()` function R provides (for example, `lapply()`, `sapply()`, and so on). This will produce simpler code than explicit loops and will also make your implementation faster. In reality, the `apply()` function is a special case since it's not as optimized as the other functions in its family, so the performance gains won't be as much as with the other functions, but the code clarity will indeed increase.

Another way of vectorizing code is to replace loops with R built-in functions, and that's the case we will use in the next modification. In the third `if` in the code, the one after the `while` loop has finished, there's a `for` loop that adds the elements we have in the `period_prices` vector, and then it is divided by the `period` vector to produce the mean. We can simply use the `mean()` function instead of using such a loop, and that's what we do.

Now, when you read that part of the code, it reads easily as if the number accumulated prices is equal to the period, making the SMA equal to the mean of the accumulated prices. It's much easier to understand code than using the loop:

```
sma_slow_4 <- function(period, symbol, data) {
    result <- NULL
    for(end in 1:nrow(data)) {
        position <- end
        sma <- NA
        n_accumulated <- 0
        period_prices <- NULL
        if (data[end, "symbol"] == symbol) {
            while(n_accumulated < period & position >= 1) {
                if (data[position, "symbol"] == symbol) {
                    period_prices <- c(period_prices,
                        data[position, "price_usd"])
                    n_accumulated <- n_accumulated + 1
                }
                position <- position - 1
            }
            if (n_accumulated == period) {
                sma <- mean(period_prices)
            } else {
                sma <- NA
            }
            result <- c(result, sma)
        }
    }
    return(result)
}
```

Again, we benchmark and check correctness. However, in this case, we find that the median time is 20,825.879 microseconds, which is more than the current minimum from sma_slow_3(). Wasn't vectorized code supposed to be faster? The answer is that most of the time it is, but in situations like this, there's an overhead within the mean() function, due to the fact that it needs to check what type of object it's dealing with, before using it for any operations, which can cause an implementation to be slower. When we were using the explicit loop, the sums and the division incurred in a much lower overhead because they could be applied to a much smaller set of objects. Therefore, as you see in the table below, sma_slow_4() takes 6% more time than sma_slow_3(). This is not much, and since I prefer expressive code, I'll keep the change:

```
performance <- microbenchmark(
    sma_4 <- sma_slow_4(period, symbol, data),
    unit = "us"
)
```

```
all(sma_1$sma - sma_4 <= 0.001, na.rm = TRUE)
#> TRUE

summary(performance)$median
#> [1] 20825.8790
```

Take a look at the following table:

Fastest	Implementation	Microseconds median	% from fastest
	sma_slow_1	81,035.1900	412.84 %
	sma_slow_2	33,031.7785	168.28 %
⇒	sma_slow_3	19,628.2430	100 %
	sma_slow_4	20,825.8790	106.10 %

If you want to compare the overhead of the mean() function to the overhead of other ways of doing the same calculation, take a look at the following benchmark. The .Internal(mean(x)) function avoids the dispatch mechanism for methods we showed in the previous chapter and skips directly to a C implementation of the mean() function, as shown in the following code snippet:

```
x <- sample(100)
performance <- microbenchmark(
    mean(x),
    sum(x) / length(x),
    .Internal(mean(x)),
    times = 1e+05
)

performance
#> Unit: nanoseconds
#>                    expr  min   lq     mean median   uq      max neval
#>                 mean(x) 1518 1797 2238.2607   1987 2230  2335285 1e+05
#>      sum(x)/length(x)   291  345  750.2324    403  488 27016544 1e+05
#>      .Internal(mean(x)) 138  153  187.0588    160  176    34513 1e+05
```

Removing unnecessary logic

There are times when simple logic shows us that there are parts of our implementations that are unnecessary. In this particular case, the accumulation of `period_prices` can be avoided by setting `sma` to 0 initially instead of `NA`, and adding to it each price. However, when doing so, we lose track of the number of elements in the vector, so the `mean()` function doesn't make sense any more, and we proceed to simply divide the sum by `period` as we were doing earlier:

```
sma_slow_5 <- function(period, symbol, data) {
    result <- NULL
    for(end in 1:nrow(data)) {
        position <- end
        sma <- 0
        n_accumulated <- 0
        if (data[end, "symbol"] == symbol) {
            while(n_accumulated < period & position >= 1) {
                if (data[position, "symbol"] == symbol) {
                    sma <- sma + data[position, "price_usd"]
                    n_accumulated <- n_accumulated + 1
                }
                position <- position - 1
            }
            if (n_accumulated == period) {
                sma <- sma / period
            } else {
                sma <- NA
            }
            result <- c(result, sma)
        }
    }
    return(result)
}
```

Again, we benchmark and check correctness, as shown in the following code snippet:

```
performance <- microbenchmark(
    sma_5 <- sma_slow_5(period, symbol, data),
    unit = "us"
)

all(sma_1$sma - sma_5 <= 0.001, na.rm = TRUE)
#> TRUE

summary(performance)$median
#> [1] 16682.68
```

In this case, our median time was 16682.68 microseconds, making this our fastest implementation so far. Again, note how a very simple change produced a reduction of around 17% with respect to the previously fastest implementation:

Fastest	Implementation	Microseconds median	% from fastest
	sma_slow_1	81,035.1900	485.74 %
	sma_slow_2	33,031.7785	198.00 %
	sma_slow_3	19,628.2430	117.65 %
	sma_slow_4	20,825.8790	124.83 %
⇒	sma_slow_5	16,682.6800	100 %

Moving checks out of iterative processes

Suppose that we're stuck in our optimization process and don't know what we should change next. What should we do? Well, as we mentioned earlier, we should profile our code to find out our current bottlenecks, and that's what we do here. We use the Rprof() function again to profile our sma_slow_5() implementation.

The results show that the [.data.frame and [functions are our biggest bottlenecks, and although their names are a bit cryptic, we can guess that they are related to subsetting data frames (which they are). This means that our current most important bottleneck is checking whether we are at an observation that corresponds to symbol we are using, and we are performing such checks at different places in our code:

```
Rprof()
sma_5 <- sma_slow_5(period, symbol, data_original[1:10000, ])
Rprof(NULL)
summaryRprof()
#> $by.self
#>                   self.time self.pct total.time total.pct
#> "[.data.frame"        0.54    26.21       1.24     60.19
#> "["                   0.22    10.68       1.34     65.05
#> "NextMethod"          0.20     9.71       0.20      9.71
#> "sma_slow_5"          0.14     6.80       2.06    100.00
#> "Ops.factor"          0.12     5.83       0.52     25.24
#> (Truncated output)
#>
#> $by.total
#>                   total.time total.pct self.time self.pct
#> "sma_slow_5"            2.06    100.00      0.14     6.80
```

```
#> "["                  1.34    65.05    0.22    10.68
#> "[.data.frame"       1.24    60.19    0.54    26.21
#> "Ops.factor"         0.52    25.24    0.12     5.83
#> "NextMethod"         0.20     9.71    0.20     9.71
#> (Truncated output)
```

Now that we know our current largest bottleneck, we can remove it by avoiding to check whether the current observation corresponds `symbol` we receive as a parameter. To accomplish this, we simply introduce a filter at the beginning of the function that keeps only observations that contain the correct symbol.

Note that this simple filter allows us to remove the two checks we were performing earlier, since we are sure that all observations have the correct symbol. This reduces two indentation levels in our code, since these checks were nested. Doing so feels great, doesn't it? Now it seems that we have a very simple implementation which will intuitively perform much better.

To verify this, we proceed to benchmark and check for correctness, as earlier:

```
performance <- microbenchmark(
    sma_6 <- sma_slow_6(period, symbol, data),
    unit = "us"
)

all(sma_1$sma - sma_6 <= 0.001, na.rm = TRUE)
#> TRUE

summary(performance)$median
#> [1] 2991.5720
```

Also, our intuition is confirmed; our median time for sma_slow_6() is 2,991.57. That's only 17% from the previously fastest implementation we had, which was sma_slow_5(), and it takes only 3% of the time that our initial implementation took. Is this awesome or what? Take a look at the following table:

Fastest	Implementation	Microseconds median	% from fastest
	sma_slow_1	81,035.1900	2,708.78 %
	sma_slow_2	33,031.7785	1,104.16 %
	sma_slow_3	19,628.2430	656.11 %
	sma_slow_4	20,825.8790	696.15 %
	sma_slow_5	16,682.6800	557.65 %
⇒	sma_slow_6	2,991.5720	100 %

If you can, avoid iterating at all

In the previous section, we realized how large an impact can unnecessary overhead within iterations have on our implementation's performance. However, what if we could avoid iterating at all? Now that would be better, wouldn't it? Well, as we mentioned earlier, doing so is achievable with vectorization.

In this case, we will remove the while loop and replace it with a vectorized mean over the start and end positions, where end continues to be defined as it has been so far, and start is defined as the end position minus period we receive as a parameter, plus one. This ensures that we get the exact number of prices we need, and we can create an interval with start:end that will take the specific subset we need from data so that we can apply the mean() function to it:

```
sma_slow_7 <- function(period, symbol, data) {
    data <- data[data$symbol == symbol, ]
    result <- NULL
    for(end in 1:nrow(data)) {
        start <- end - period + 1
        if (start >= 1) {
            sma <- mean(data[start:end, "price_usd"])
        } else {
            sma <- NA
        }
        result <- c(result, sma)
    }
```

```
        return(result)
    }
```

Note that this change would not have been possible if we had not filtered the data at the top of the function, since we would have observations that correspond to different symbols mixed among themselves and our `start:end` interval would pick observations that contain other symbols. This goes to show that sometimes optimizations depend on each other, and one can't be applied without applying a previous one, and these relations are often found accidentally.

As always, we benchmark and check for correctness as shown in the following code snippet:

```
performance <- microbenchmark(
    sma_7 <- sma_slow_7(period, symbol, data),
    unit = "us"
)

all(sma_1$sma - sma_7 <= 0.001, na.rm = TRUE)
#> TRUE

summary(performance)$median
#> [1] 910.793
```

The median time is now `910.793` microseconds. This was expected as we know that removing explicit loops can produce big performance improvements. In this case, we were able to reduce to a little under one-third of the time from our previously fastest implementation. Note that we are now dealing with hundreds of microseconds, instead of thousands of microseconds. This means that we have achieved performance improvements in the orders of magnitude. Take a look at the following table:

Fastest	Implementation	Microseconds median	% from fastest
	sma_slow_1	81,035.1900	8,897.21 %
	sma_slow_2	33,031.7785	3,626.70 %
	sma_slow_3	19,628.2430	2,155.07 %
	sma_slow_4	20,825.8790	2,286.56 %
	sma_slow_5	16,682.68	1,831.66 %
	sma_slow_6	2,991.5720	328.45 %
⇒	sma_slow_7	910.7930	100 %

Using R's way of iterating efficiently

At this point, we're left with a single `for` loop, which we would like to remove. However, there's a bit of logic in there that gets in the way. This is where the `lapply()` function comes in handy. As you know from Chapter 1, *Introduction to R*, this function receives a list of objects that will be sent to a function provided as a second argument, and it will return the results from such function calls in a list. An added benefit of the `lapply()` function is that it takes care of the memory preallocation for us, which is a very efficient way to reduce execution time in R.

In this case, we encapsulate the logic inside our `for` loop in a separate function called `sma_from_position_1()` and use it within our `lapply()` function call. Our `sma_from_position_1()` function receives the `end`, `period`, and `data` objects we have been working with, and they keep the same meaning and perform the same vectorized mean computation we were doing earlier. However, instead of using an explicit `if...else` conditional, it uses the `ifelse()` function we introduced in Chapter 1, *Introduction to R*, which takes the condition to be checked as its first argument, the desired result in case of the condition being met as its second argument, and the desired result in case the condition is not met as its third argument. In our case, these are `start >= 1`, `mean(data[start:end], price_usd`, and `NA`, respectively.

The result we get from the function calls to `sma_from_position_1()` are unlisted into a single vector so that we get a vector result instead of a list, and that is in turn returned by `sma_efficient_1()`. Note the change in the name? At this point, this implementation can be considered an efficient one. Hurray! Take a look at the following code snippet:

```
sma_efficient_1 <- function(period, symbol, data) {
    data <- data[data$symbol == symbol, ]
    return(unlist(lapply(1:nrow(data),
                         sma_from_position_1,
                         period, data)))
}

sma_from_position_1 <- function(end, period, data) {
    start <- end - period + 1
    return(ifelse(start >= 1,
                  mean(data[start:end, "price_usd"]), NA))
}
```

Just in case you don't remember the mechanics of the `lapply()` function and you're a bit confused about the way it's being used here, let me remind you that it will take each of the elements in the list provided as the first argument, and feed them as the first argument to the function provided in the second argument. If the said function requires more parameters, those can also be passed after the function object has been provided to the `lapply()` function, which is the case of the `period` and `data` arguments you see toward the end.

Again, benchmark and check for correctness, as shown in the following code snippet:

```
performance <- microbenchmark(
    sma_8 <- sma_efficient_1(period, symbol, data),
    unit = "us"
)

all(sma_1$sma - sma_8 <= 0.001, na.rm = TRUE)
#> TRUE

summary(performance)$median
#> [1] 1137.704
```

This time, our median time is $1,137.704$ microseconds. This is more than our previously fastest implementation. What happened? If you want to know the details, you should profile the function, but in essence, the problem is that we're adding a function call that is executed many times (`sma_from_position_1()`) and function calls can be expensive, and also adding a transformation from a list to a vector we were not doing before (`unlist()`). However, we prefer to advance with version for reasons that shall become clear in a later section. Take a look at the following table:

Fastest	Implementation	Microseconds median	% from fastest
	sma_slow_1	81,035.1900	8,897.21 %
	sma_slow_2	33,031.7785	3,626.70 %
	sma_slow_3	19,628.2430	2,155.07 %
	sma_slow_4	20,825.8790	2,286.56 %
	sma_slow_5	16,682.68	1,466.63 %
	sma_slow_6	2,991.5720	328.45 %
⇒	sma_slow_7	910.7930	100 %
	sma_efficient_1	1,137.7040	124.91 %

Thera are many other vectorized functions in R that may help speed your code. Some examples are `which()`, `where()`, `any()`, `all()`, `cumsum()`, and `cumprod()`. When working with matrices, you may use `rowSums()`, `colSums()`, `lower.tri()`, `upper.tri()`, and others, and when working with combinations, you may use `combin()`. There are many more, and when dealing with something that seems like it could be vectorized, chances are that there's already a function for that.

Avoiding sending data structures with overheads

We know that operating on heavy data structures such as data frames should be avoided when possible, and here it seems that it's still possible to do just that. What if instead of passing our data frame, we extract the `price_usd` variable we're interested in and simply use that? That seems promising.

To accomplish this, at the top of the function, we not only filter for observations containing `symbol` we want, but we also extract the `price_usd` variable at that point. Now, we may send this lower-overhead data structure to our slightly modified the `sma_from_position_2()` function. It is simply modified to work with this vector instead of the full data frame:

```
sma_efficient_2 <- function(period, symbol, data) {
    data <- data[data$symbol == symbol, "price_usd"]
    return(unlist(lapply(1:length(data),
                         sma_from_position_2,
                         period, data)))
}

sma_from_position_2 <- function(end, period, data) {
    start <- end - period + 1
    return(ifelse(start >= 1, sum(data[start:end]) / period, NA))
}
```

Again, benchmark and check for correctness, as shown in the following code snippet:

```
performance <- microbenchmark(
    sma_9 <- sma_efficient_2(period, symbol, data),
    unit = "us"
)

all(sma_1$sma - sma_9 <= 0.001, na.rm = TRUE)
#> TRUE

summary(performance)$median
#> [1] 238.2425
```

This time, our mean time is `238.2425` microseconds. That's a big change. In fact, it's the largest performance improvement we have been able to produce pondered by the amount of change required, with respect to the previously fastest implementation.

Do you realize how drastic the performance improvement has been? Our first implementation takes approximately 33,900% more time to execute. Inversely, our `sma_efficient_2()` implementation takes only around 0.2% of the time that our `sma_slow_1()` implementation took. Were you expecting such a large time reduction by only writing better R code when we started this chapter? Take a look at the following table:

Fastest	Implementation	Microseconds median	% from fastest
	sma_slow_1	81,035.1900	34,013.74 %
	sma_slow_2	33,031.7785	13,865.77 %
	sma_slow_3	19,628.2430	8,238.76 %
	sma_slow_4	20,825.8790	8,741.46 %
	sma_slow_5	16,682.6800	7,002.39 %
	sma_slow_6	2,991.5720	1,255.68 %
⇒	sma_slow_7	910.7930	382.29 %
	sma_efficient_1	1,137.7040	477.54 %
	sma_efficient_2	238.2425	100%

Let's assume that we are very picky, and we want to further improve performance. What should we do? Well, let's profile our code again to find out. As you can see here, the number of function calls is reduced to just one in the `$by.self` table and only five in the `$by.total` table. Unfortunately, these results don't show us any way we can further improve performance, since all the functions shown are highly optimized already. The only thing you can attempt is to replace the `mean()` function with one of the faster alternatives shown earlier, but we won't do it in this case, since the effect of doing so was already shown previously:

```
Rprof()
sma_9 <- sma_efficient_2(period, symbol, data_original[1:10000, ])
Rprof(NULL)
summaryRprof()
#> $by.self
#>          self.time self.pct total.time total.pct
#> "ifelse"      0.02      100       0.02       100
#>
```

```
#> $by.total
#>                     total.time total.pct self.time self.pct
#> "ifelse"                 0.02       100      0.02      100
#> "FUN"                    0.02       100      0.00        0
#> "lapply"                 0.02       100      0.00        0
#> "sma_efficient_2"        0.02       100      0.00        0
#> "unlist"                 0.02       100      0.00        0
```

To further reduce the execution time of our implementation, we will have to resort to more advanced techniques such as parallelization and delegation, which are the subjects of the following sections.

Note that that's where `Rprof()` will stop being useful most of the time, since we will start using advanced tools, outside of R, to continue to improve performance, and such tools require their own profiling techniques and knowledge that we won't go into in this book.

Using parallelization to divide and conquer

So far, we have learned various ways to optimize the performance of R programs running serially, that is, in a single thread. This does not take advantage of the multiple CPU cores most computers have nowadays. Parallel computing allows us to tap into them by splitting our implementations in multiple parts that are sent to these processors independently, and it has the potential to accelerate programs when a single thread is an important bottleneck.

Parallelizing real-world applications can be a very challenging task, and it requires deep software as well as hardware knowledge. The extent of possible parallelization depends on the particular algorithm we're working with, and there are many types of parallelizations available. Furthermore, parallelization is not a yes/no decision; it involves a continuous scale. On one side of the scale, we have embarrassingly parallel tasks, where there are no dependencies between the parallel subtasks, thus making them great candidates for parallelization. On the other side, we have tasks that cannot be parallelized at all, since each step of the task depends on the results of previous steps. Most algorithms fall in between these two extremes, and most real-world parallelized applications perform some tasks serially and others in parallel.

Some tasks that are relatively easy to implement in parallel (some of them would be classified as embarrassingly parallel tasks) are converting hundreds of images from color to grayscale, adding millions of numbers, brute-force searches, and Monte Carlo simulations. The common property among these is that each subtask can be done independently of the others. For example, each image can be processed independently, or we can add various subgroups of numbers and then add the results together, and so on. The moment we introduce an order-dependency, parallelization breaks out.

How deep does the parallelization rabbit hole go?

With parallelizing and algorithm, there are a lot of decisions that must be made. First of all, we must decide what parts of the algorithm will be implemented in parallel and which parts will be implemented serially, and how to manage these parts to work correctly among themselves. Next we must decide, whether explicitly or implicitly, whether the parallelized parts will have shared or distributed memory, whether we will do data or task parallelization, whether we need to introduce some type of distributed or concurrent mechanism, and if so, what protocol will be used to coordinate them. Once we have established those high-level decisions, we must take care of the fine-grained decisions regarding the number and architecture of the processors we will use as well as the amount of memory and control permissions.

Don't worry too much about the concepts mentioned earlier; they are for more advanced usage than the intended level for this book. I will provide very general and simple explanations here to ensure that you understand the type of parallelization we will implement ourselves, but feel free to skip this section if you want.

Shared memory systems share objects stored in-memory across different processes, which can be very resource efficient, but also dangerous since one process may modify an object that is used by another process without it knowing that it happened. Another disadvantage of such systems is that they don't scale well. A more powerful, but also more complex alternative, is **distributed memory**, which makes copies of the data needed for different processes that may reside in different systems altogether. This approach can scale to thousands of CPUs, but comes at the cost of complex coordination among processes.

Data parallelism is when data is partitioned and each task is executed using a different partition. These types of parallelization help algorithm scale as more data is acquired, since we can simply create more partitions. Note that using data parallelism does not necessarily imply distributed memory, and vice versa. **Task parallelism** is when tasks are sent to different processors to be executed in parallel and they may or may not be working on top of the same data.

A disadvantage of parallel computing is that people run code on different machines, and if you are writing software that you expect to share with others, you need to be careful that your implementation is useful even when executed in different hardware configurations.

All the decisions mentioned earlier require deep technical knowledge to be properly taken, and if they seem complex, it's because they really are. Implementing parallelization can be quite complex activity, depending on the level of control you want to have over it.

Most importantly, remember that R is an interpreted language, so speed gains from utilizing compiled languages will almost always exceed speed gains from parallelizing `for` loops or other loop-hiding functions.

Practical parallelization with R

In this section, we will show you how to take advantage of multiple cores with R. We will show you how to perform a shared memory single system with multiple cores approach. This is the simplest parallel technique you can implement.

A deep look at various parallelization mechanisms available in R can be found in Theubl's doctoral thesis, *Applied High Performance Computing Using R, by Wirtschafts Universitat, 2007.*

Implementing parallel programs with R has become increasingly easier with time since it's a topic of much interest, and many people have provided, and continue to provide, better ways of doing so. Currently, there are over 70 packages in CRAN that provide some kind of parallelization functionality. Choosing the right package for the right problem, or simply knowing that a variety of options exist, remains a challenge.

In this case, we will use the `parallel` package that comes preinstalled in the recent versions of R. Other very popular packages are `doSNOW`, `doMC`, and `foreach`, but it really depends on what kind of parallelization you want to perform.

The most common parallelization technique in R is to use parallelized replacements of the `lapply()`, `sapply()`, and `apply()` functions. In the case of the `parallel` package, we have the `parLapply()`, `parSapply()`, and `parApply()` functions available, respectively. The fact that signatures among this function pairs are very similar makes the barrier to using this form of parallelization very low, and that's why I decided to showcase this technique.

Implementing the parallelization technique we will showcase is simple enough, and it involves the following three main steps once you have loaded the `parallel` package:

1. Create a cluster with the `makeCluster()` function
2. Replace a `apply()` function with one a `par*pply()` one
3. Stop the cluster you created in the first step

For our case, we will replace the `lapply()` function with `parLapply()` in our `sma_efficient_2()` implementation. However, you should avoid a common mistake done by people just starting with parallelization. Normally, they will create and later destroy a cluster within the function called to perform a task, instead of receiving a cluster from the outside and using it within. This creates performance problems, because the cluster will potentially be started many times, and starting a parallelization cluster can have quite a bit of overhead. A function that makes such a mistake is the `sma_parallel_inefficient()` function, as follows:

```
library(parallel)
sma_parallel_inefficient <- function(period, symbol, data) {
    data <- as.numeric(data[data$symbol == symbol, "price_usd"])
    cluster <- makeCluster(detectCores())
    result <- unlist(parLapply(
    cluster, 1:length(data), sma_from_position_2, period, data))
    stopCluster(cluster)
    return(result)
}
```

As you can see, `sma_parallel_inefficient()` is just `sma_efficient_2()` with the added logic for the cluster creation and deletion, and the `lapply()` replacement with `parLapply()`. You shouldn't really use this function, but it's put here to showcase how bad it can be for performance if you do. As always, we benchmark and check for correctness, as shown in the following code snippet:

```
performance <- microbenchmark(
    sma_10 <- sma_parallel_inefficient(period, symbol, data),
    unit = "us"
)

all(sma_1$sma - sma_10 <= 0.001, na.rm = TRUE)
#> TRUE

summary(performance)$median
#> [1] 1197329.3980
```

In this case, our median time is $1,197,329.398$ microseconds, which should not be too surprising after mentioning that creating and destroying a cluster multiple times can be quite inefficient. Take a look at the following table:

Fastest	Implementation	Microseconds Median	% From Fastest
	sma_slow_1	81,035.1900	34,013.74 %
	sma_slow_2	33,031.7785	13,865.77 %
	sma_slow_3	19,628.2430	8,238.76 %
	sma_slow_4	20,825.8790	8,741.46 %
	sma_slow_5	16,682.6800	7,002.39 %
	sma_slow_6	2,991.5720	1,255.68 %
	sma_slow_7	910.7930	382.29 %
	sma_efficient_1	1,137.7040	477.54 %
⟹	sma_efficient_2	238.2425	100 %
	sma_parallel_inefficient	1,197,329.3980	50,2567.50 %

Now, we proceed to remove the logic that creates and destroys the cluster out of the function, and instead receive the `cluster` as a parameter to `sma_parallel()`. In that case, our implementation looks just like the one we had before, except for the use of `parLapply()`. It's nice to be able to achieve something as complex as parallelization with simply this change, but it's really a product of having simplified our code up to what we have now. If we attempted to parallelize our initial `sma_slow_1()` implementation, we would have a hard time doing so. Take a look at the following code snippet:

```
sma_parallel <- function(period, symbol, data, cluster) {
    data <- as.numeric(data[data$symbol == symbol, "price_usd"])
    return(unlist(parLapply(
        cluster, 1:length(data), sma_from_position_2, period, data)))
}
```

Again, we benchmark and check for correctness, as shown in the following code snippet:

```
cluster <- makeCluster(detectCores())
performance <- microbenchmark(
    sma_11 <- sma_parallel(period, symbol, data, cluster),
    unit = "us"
)

all(sma_1$sma - sma_11 <= 0.001, na.rm = TRUE)
#> TRUE

summary(performance)$median
#> [1] 44825.9355
```

In this case, our median time is `44,825.9355` microseconds, which is roughly worse than we were able to achieve with `sma_slow_2()`. Wasn't parallelization supposed to be much faster? The answer is yes, when working with larger inputs. When we use data that has millions of observations (not the 100 observations we have been using for these tests), it will be faster, because its execution time won't increase as much as the one for other implementations. Right now, `sma_paralle()` is paying a big fixed cost that is not a good investment when working with small datasets, but as we start working with larger datasets, the fixed cost starts being small as compared to the performance gains. Take a look at the following table:

Fastest	Implementation	Microseconds Median	% From Fastest
	sma_slow_1	81,035.1900	34,013.74 %
	sma_slow_2	33,031.7785	13,865.77 %
	sma_slow_3	19,628.2430	8,238.76 %
	sma_slow_4	20,825.8790	8,741.46 %
	sma_slow_5	16,682.6800	7,002.39 %
	sma_slow_6	2,991.5720	1,255.68 %
	sma_slow_7	910.7930	382.29 %
	sma_efficient_1	1,137.7040	477.54 %
⟹	sma_efficient_2	238.2425	100 %
	sma_parallel_inefficient	1,197,329.3980	50,2567.50 %
	sma_parallel	44,825.9355	18,815.25 %

To finalize the section, remember to call `stopCluster(cluster)` when you want to stop using the cluster. In this case, we will leave it running as we will continue to perform more benchmarks through the rest of the chapter.

Using C++ and Fortran to accelerate calculations

Sometimes, R code just isn't fast enough. Sometimes, you've used profiling to figure out where your bottlenecks are, and you've done everything you can think of within R, but your code still isn't fast enough. In those cases, a useful alternative can be to delegate some parts of the implementation to more efficient languages such as Fortran and C++. This is an advanced technique that can often prove to be quite useful if know how to program in such languages.

Delegating code to other languages can address bottlenecks such as the following:

- Loops that can't be easily vectorized due to iteration dependencies
- Processes that involve calling functions millions of times
- Inefficient but necessary data structures that are slow in R

Delegating code to other languages can provide great performance benefits, but it also incurs the cost of being more explicit and careful with the types of objects that are being moved around. In R, you can get away with simple things such as being imprecise about a number being an integer or a real. In these other languages, you can't; every object must have a precise type, and it remains fixed for the entire execution.

Using an old-school approach with Fortran

We will start with an old-school approach using Fortran first. If you are not familiar with it, Fortran is the oldest programming language still under use today. It was designed to perform lots of calculations very efficiently and with very few resources. There are a lot of numerical libraries developed with it, and many high-performance systems nowadays still use it, either directly or indirectly.

Here's our implementation, named `sma_fortran()`. The syntax may throw you off if you're not used to working with Fortran code, but it's simple enough to understand. First, note that to define a function technically known as a `subroutine` in Fortran, we use the `subroutine` keyword before the name of the function. As our previous implementations do, it receives the `period` and `data` (we use the `dataa` name with an extra `a` at the end because Fortran has a reserved keyword `data`, which we shouldn't use in this case), and we will assume that the data is already filtered for the correct symbol at this point.

Next, note that we are sending new arguments that we did not send before, namely `smas` and `n`. Fortran is a peculiar language in the sense that it does not return values, it uses side effects instead. This means that instead of expecting something back from a call to a Fortran subroutine, we should expect that subroutine to change one of the objects that was passed to it, and we should treat that as our `return` value. In this case, `smas` fulfills that role; initially, it will be sent as an array of undefined real values, and the objective is to modify its contents with the appropriate SMA values. Finally, the n represents the number of elements in the data we send. Classic Fortran doesn't have a way to determine the size of an array being passed to it, and it needs us to specify the size manually; that's why we need to send n. In reality, there are ways to work around this, but since this is not a book about Fortran, we will keep the code as simple as possible.

Next, note that we need to declare the type of objects we're dealing with as well as their size in case they are arrays. We proceed to declare `pos` (which takes the place of position in our previous implementation, because Fortran imposes a limit on the length of each line, which we don't want to violate), n, `endd` (again, `end` is a keyword in Fortran, so we use the name `endd` instead), and `period` as integers. We also declare `dataa(n)`, `smas(n)`, and `sma` as reals because they will contain decimal parts. Note that we specify the size of the array with the `(n)` part in the first two objects.

Once we have declared everything we will use, we proceed with our logic. We first create a `for` loop, which is done with the `do` keyword in Fortran, followed by a unique identifier (which are normally named with multiples of tens or hundreds), the variable name that will be used to iterate, and the values that it will take, `endd` and 1 to n in this case, respectively.

Within the `for` loop, we assign `pos` to be equal to `endd` and `sma` to be equal to 0, just as we did in some of our previous implementations. Next, we create a `while` loop with the `do...while` keyword combination, and we provide the condition that should be checked to decide when to break out of it. Note that Fortran uses a very different syntax for the comparison operators. Specifically, the `.lt.` operator stand for less-than, while the `.ge.` operator stands for greater-than-or-equal-to. If any of the two conditions specified is not met, then we will exit the `while` loop.

Having said that, the rest of the code should be self-explanatory. The only other uncommon syntax property is that the code is indented to the sixth position. This indentation has meaning within Fortran, and it should be kept as it is. Also, the number IDs provided in the first columns in the code should match the corresponding looping mechanisms, and they should be kept toward the left of the logic-code.

For a good introduction to Fortran, you may take a look at *Stanford's Fortran 77 Tutorial* (`https://web.stanford.edu/class/me200c/tutorial_77/`). You should know that there are various Fortran versions, and the 77 version is one of the oldest ones. However, it's also one of the better supported ones:

```fortran
      subroutine sma_fortran(period, dataa, smas, n)
      integer pos, n, endd, period
      real dataa(n), smas(n), sma
      do 10 endd = 1, n
          pos = endd
          sma = 0.0
          do 20 while ((endd - pos .lt. period) .and. (pos .ge. 1))
              sma = sma + dataa(pos)
              pos = pos - 1
 20       end do
          if (endd - pos .eq. period) then
```

```
          sma = sma / period
      else
          sma = 0
      end if
      smas(endd) = sma
10  continue
    end
```

Once your code is finished, you need to compile it before it can be executed within R. Compilation is the process of translating code into machine-level instructions. You have two options when compiling Fortran code: you can either do it manually outside of R or you can do it within R. The second one is recommended since you can take advantage of R's tools for doing so. However, we show both of them. The first one can be achieved with the following code:

```
$ gfortran -c sma-delegated-fortran.f -o sma-delegated-fortran.so
```

This code should be executed in a Bash terminal (which can be found in Linux or Mac operating systems). We must ensure that we have the `gfortran` compiler installed, which was probably installed when R was. Then, we call it, telling it to compile (using the `-c` option) the `sma-delegated-fortran.f` file (which contains the Fortran code we showed before) and provide an output file (with the `-o` option) named `sma-delegated-fortran.so`. Our objective is to get this `.so` file, which is what we need within R to execute the Fortran code.

The way to compile within R, which is the recommended way, is to use the following line:

```
system("R CMD SHLIB sma-delegated-fortran.f")
```

It basically tells R to execute the command that produces a shared library derived from the `sma-delegated-fortran.f` file. Note that the `system()` function simply sends the string it receives to a terminal in the operating system, which means that you could have used that same command in the Bash terminal used to compile the code manually.

To load the shared library into R's memory, we use the `dyn.load()` function, providing the location of the `.so` file we want to use, and to actually call the shared library that contains the Fortran implementation, we use the `.Fortran()` function. This function requires type checking and coercion to be explicitly performed by the user before calling it.

To provide a similar signature as the one provided by the previous functions, we will create a function named `sma_delegated_fortran()`, which receives the `period`, `symbol`, and `data` parameters as we did before, also filters the data as we did earlier, calculates the length of the data and puts it in `n`, and uses the `.Fortran()` function to call the `sma_fortran()` subroutine, providing the appropriate parameters. Note that we're wrapping the parameters around functions that coerce the types of these objects as required by our Fortran code. The `results` list created by the `.Fortran()` function contains the `period`, `dataa`, `smas`, and `n` objects, corresponding to the parameters sent to the subroutine, with the contents left in them after the subroutine was executed. As we mentioned earlier, we are interested in the contents of the `sma` object since they contain the values we're looking for. That's why we send only that part back after converting it to a `numeric` type within R.

The transformations you see before sending objects to Fortran and after getting them back is something that you need to be very careful with. For example, if instead of using `single(n)` and `as.single(data)`, we use `double(n)` and `as.double(data)`, our Fortran implementation will not work. This is something that can be ignored within R, but it can't be ignored in the case of Fortran:

```
system("R CMD SHLIB sma-delegated-fortran.f")
dyn.load("sma-delegated-fortran.so")

sma_delegated_fortran <- function(period, symbol, data) {
    data <- data[which(data$symbol == symbol), "price_usd"]
    n <- length(data)
    results <- .Fortran(
        "sma_fortran",
        period = as.integer(period),
        dataa = as.single(data),
        smas = single(n),
        n = as.integer(n)
    )
    return(as.numeric(results$smas))
}
```

Just as we did earlier, we benchmark and test for correctness:

```
performance <- microbenchmark(
    sma_12 <- sma_delegated_fortran(period, symboo, data),
    unit = "us"
)

all(sma_1$sma - sma_12 <= 0.001, na.rm = TRUE)
#> TRUE

summary(performance)$median
#> [1] 148.0335
```

In this case, our median time is of 148.0335 microseconds, making this the fastest implementation up to this point. Note that it's barely over half of the time from the most efficient implementation we were able to come up with using only R. Take a look at the following table:

Fastest	Implementation	Microseconds Median	% From Fastest
	sma_slow_1	81,035.1900	54,741.11 %
	sma_slow_2	33,031.7785	22,313.71 %
	sma_slow_3	19,628.2430	13,259.32 %
	sma_slow_4	20,825.8790	14,068.35 %
	sma_slow_5	16,682.6800	11,269.79 %
	sma_slow_6	2,991.5720	2,020.87 %
	sma_slow_7	910.7930	615.26 %
	sma_efficient_1	1,137.7040	768.54 %
	sma_efficient_2	238.2425	160.93 %
	sma_parallel_inefficient	1,197,329.3980	808,823.26 %
	sma_parallel	44,825.9355	30,280.94 %
⟹	sma_delegated_fortran	148.0335	100 %

Using a modern approach with C++

Now, we will show you how to use a more modern approach using C++. The aim of this section is to provide just enough information for you to start experimenting using C++ within R on your own. We will only look at a tiny piece of what can be done by interfacing R with C++ through the Rcpp package (which is installed by default in R), but it should be enough to get you started.

If you have never heard of C++, it's a language used mostly when resource restrictions play an important role and performance optimization is of paramount importance. Some good resources to learn more about C++ are Meyer's books on the topic, a popular one being *Effective C++* (Addison-Wesley, 2005), and specifically for the Rcpp package, Eddelbuettel's *Seamless R and C++ integration with Rcpp by Springer, 2013*, is great.

Before we continue, you need to ensure that you have a C++ compiler in your system. On Linux, you should be able to use gcc. On Mac, you should install Xcode from the application store. O n Windows, you should install Rtools. Once you test your compiler and know that it's working, you should be able to follow this section. We'll cover more on how to do this in Appendix, *Required Packages*.

C++ is more readable than Fortran code because it follows more syntax conventions we're used to nowadays. However, just because the example we will use is readable, don't think that C++ in general is an easy language to use; it's not. It's a very low-level language and using it correctly requires a good amount of knowledge. Having said that, let's begin.

The #include line is used to bring variable and function definitions from R into this file when it's compiled. Literally, the contents of the Rcpp.h file are pasted right where the include statement is. Files ending with the .h extensions are called header files, and they are used to provide some common definitions between a code's user and its developers. They play a similar role to what we called an interface in the previous chapter.

The using namespace Rcpp line allows you to use shorter names for your function. Instead of having to specify Rcpp::NumericVector, we can simply use NumericVector to define the type of the data object. Doing so in this example may not be too beneficial, but when you start developing for complex C++ code, it will really come in handy.

Next, you will notice the // [[Rcpp::export(sma_delegated_cpp)]] code. This is a tag that marks the function right below it so that R know that it should import it and make it available within R code. The argument sent to export() is the name of the function that will be accessible within R, and it does not necessarily have to match the name of the function in C++. In this case, sma_delegated_cpp() will be the function we call within R, and it will call the smaDelegated() function within C++:

```
#include
using namespace Rcpp;

// [[Rcpp::export(sma_delegated_cpp)]]
NumericVector smaDelegated(int period, NumericVector data) {
    int position, n = data.size();
    NumericVector result(n);
    double sma;
```

```
for (int end = 0; end < n; end++) {
    position = end;
    sma = 0;
    while(end - position < period && position >= 0) {
        sma = sma + data[position];
        position = position - 1;
    }
    if (end - position == period) {
        sma = sma / period;
    } else {
        sma = NA_REAL;
    }
    result[end] = sma;
}
return result;
}
```

Next, we will explain the actual `smaDelegated()` function. Since you have a good idea of what it's doing at this point, we won't explain its logic, only the syntax that is not so obvious. The first thing to note is that the function name has a keyword before it, which is the type of the `return` value for the function. In this case, it's `NumericVector`, which is provided in the `Rcpp.h` file. This is an object designed to interface vectors between R and C++. Other types of vector provided by `Rcpp` are `IntegerVector`, `LogicalVector`, and `CharacterVector`. You also have `IntegerMatrix`, `NumericMatrix`, `LogicalMatrix`, and `CharacterMatrix` available.

Next, you should note that the parameters received by the function also have types associated with them. Specifically, `period` is an integer (`int`), and `data` is `NumericVector`, just like the output of the function. In this case, we did not have to pass the `output` or `length` objects as we did with Fortran. Since functions in C++ do have output values, it also has an easy enough way of computing the length of objects.

The first line in the function declare a variables `position` and n, and assigns the length of the data to the latter one. You may use commas, as we do, to declare various objects of the same type one after another instead of splitting the declarations and assignments into its own lines. We also declare the vector `result` with length n; note that this notation is similar to Fortran's. Finally, instead of using the `real` keyword as we do in Fortran, we use the `float` or `double` keyword here to denote such numbers. Technically, there's a difference regarding the precision allowed by such keywords, and they are not interchangeable, but we won't worry about that here.

The rest of the function should be clear, except for maybe the `sma = NA_REAL` assignment. This `NA_REAL` object is also provided by `Rcpp` as a way to denote what should be sent to R as an `NA`. Everything else should result familiar.

Now that our function is ready, we save it in a file called `sma-delegated-cpp.cpp` and use R's `sourceCpp()` function to bring compile it for us and bring it into R. The `.cpp` extension denotes contents written in the C++ language. Keep in mind that functions brought into R from C++ files cannot be saved in a `.Rdata` file for a later session. The nature of C++ is to be very dependent on the hardware under which it's compiled, and doing so will probably produce various errors for you. Every time you want to use a C++ function, you should compile it and load it with the `sourceCpp()` function at the moment of usage.

```
library(Rcpp)

sourceCpp("./sma-delegated-cpp.cpp")

sma_delegated_cpp <- function(period, symbol, data) {
    data <- as.numeric(data[which(data$symbol == symbol), "price_usd"])
    return(sma_cpp(period, data))
}
```

If everything worked fine, our function should be usable within R, so we benchmark and test for correctness. I promise this is the last one:

```
performance <- microbenchmark(
    sma_13 <- sma_delegated_cpp(period, symboo, data),
    unit = "us"
)
all(sma_1$sma - sma_13 <= 0.001, na.rm = TRUE)
#> TRUE
summary(performance)$median
#> [1] 80.6415
```

This time, our median time was `80.6415` microseconds, which is three orders of magnitude faster than our first implementation. Think about it this way: if you provide an input for `sma_delegated_cpp()` so that it took around one hour for it to execute, `sma_slow_1()` would take around 1,000 hours, which is roughly 41 days. Isn't that a surprising difference? When you are in situations that take that much execution time, it's definitely worth it to try and make your implementations as optimized as possible.

You may use the `cppFunction()` function to write your C++ code directly inside an `.R` file, but you should not do so. Keep that just for testing small pieces of code. Separating your C++ implementation into its own files allows you to use the power of your editor of choice (or IDE) to guide you through the development as well as perform deeper syntax checks for you.

Looking back at what we have achieved

As you know, up to now, we have benchmarked our code using a subset of the data that contains only the first 100 observations. However, as we saw at the beginning of the chapter, performance can vary for different implementations, depending on the size of the input. To bring together all our efforts in the chapter, we will create a couple of functions that will help us measure how the execution times for our implementations change as we use more observations from our data.

First, we bring our requirements into R, mainly, the `microbenchmark` and `ggplot2` packages and the files that contain our implementations.

Next, we create the `sma_performance()` function that takes a `symbol`, a `period`, the `original_data`, a list named `sizes` whose elements are the number of observations that will be taken from `original_data` to test our implementations, a `cluster` to avoid the overhead of initializing it within our `sma_parallel()` function as we saw in the corresponding section, and the number of times we want to measure each implementation.

As you can see, for each size in sizes, we take the corresponding number of observations in the `data` object, and we send it along with the other necessary arguments for the `sma_microbenchmark()` function. Then, we add the `size` value into the `result` data frame, which is provided by the `summary()` function applied on top of the resulting object from the `microbenchmark()` function from `sma_microbenchmark()`. We need to add this ourselves because the `microbenchmark()` function doesn't have any knowledge about the size of the data it's dealing with. Finally, we flatten the list of data frames in the `results` list with the `do.call("rbind", results)` function call, which sends a single data frame as output.

The `sma_microbenchmark()` function is very simple. It only receives some parameters and passes them forward to each of the implementations that will be measured by the `microbenchmark()` function. Note that we are leaving inside the `sma_paralel_inefficient()` function, but it's commented out to avoid any scale issues in the graph we will end up producing (since it is very slow, it will skew our graph).

The resulting object from the `sma_performance()` function returns a data frame with the results for all the tests, which is used as input for the `graph_sma_performance()` function in the form of `results` objects. It also receives the `sizes`, which will be used to define the values in the x axis. As you can see, we call `remove_arguments()`, which we mention as we move ahead. It creates a graph using the `ggplot()`, `geom_point()`, and `geom_line()` functions as we saw earlier, and we use logarithmic scales for both axes.

The `remove_arguments()` function does exactly what it says—it removes the parenthesis and the arguments from the function calls so that we keep only the function name. This is done to reduce the space in the graph's legend. To accomplish this, we use the `gsub()` function we saw in `Chapter 1`, *Introduction to R*.

To use the code we just presented, we simply create the `sizes` list we are missing and use all the other objects we had defined previously in this chapter. In this particular case, we want to measure the first 10, 100, 1,000, and 10,000 observations. If you want, you can increase this list with larger amounts. Remember that the total amount of observations in the simulated data is a little over 1,000,000.

The resulting graph shows the number of observations in the *x* axis and the microseconds median in the *y* axis. Both axes use logarithmic scale, so keep in mind when interpreting the relations. As you can see, when the size of the input is smaller (toward the left of the graph) the execution time difference is smaller, and as we increase the input size, differences start being larger and larger, specially considering the logarithmic scales.

Some interesting things to note are as listed as follows:

- `sma_efficient_1()`: The function was shown to be slower than the `sma_slow_7()` for 100 observations, is actually faster when using 10,000 observations. This shows that the tradeoff made sense, specially as inputs increase.
- `sma_efficient_2()`: This implementation is faster, for 10 observations, than the Fortran implementation. That's pretty surprising and shows that the overhead incurred in calling Fortran code is not worth it for that input size. However, `sma_efficient_2()` quickly becomes slower as input size increases.

- `sma_parallel()`: This implementation is slow due to all the overhead it incurs as we saw in the corresponding section, but it's also the implementation where percentage time increase is the least as input size increases. This should makes us wonder what happens when we're dealing with the full data? Will it be faster, at that point, that the Fortran or C++ implementations which seem to be increasing faster? That's left as an exercise for the reader.

Finally, for the curious reader, what do you think will happen if you use the `sma_delegated_cpp()` implementation along with the parallelization approach we showed? If you want to know the answer, you should definitely try it yourself.

Other topics of interest to enhance performance

We saw an overview of the most important and common techniques used to optimize R implementations. However, there is still a lot we have not covered. In the following sections, we will briefly mention some of them.

Preallocating memory to avoid duplication

Memory preallocation is an important technique we covered implicitly when we used the `lapply()` function, since it does preallocation for us. However, a more explicit explanation can be useful. As we have already seen, dynamically growing objects in R is not great for performance. Instead, you should define an object with the full size you will need and then perform updates on its elements instead of recreating them. To accomplish this, you may use something like `double(10)` to define an vector of doubles that will contain 10 elements at most. Whenever you define an object's size before you start using it, will help you avoid recreating new objects each time its size is increased and will save you a lot of time.

However, accurate preallocation is not always feasible because it requires that we know the total number prior to the iteration. Sometimes, we can only ask for a result to store repeatedly without knowing the exact total number. In this case, maybe it is still a good idea to preallocate a list or vector with a reasonable length. When the iteration is over, if the number of iterations does not reach the preallocated length, we can take a subset of the list or vector. In this way, we can avoid intensive reallocation of data structures.

When it comes to preallocating memory, R is no different from the other programming languages. However, being an interpreted language, it imposes less restrictions; thus, it is easy for users to overlook this types of issues. R will not throw any compilation error if a vector's memory is not preallocated. You should keep this in mind when writing fast code.

Making R code a bit faster with byte code compilation

Even though R is an interpreted language, it can go through a small phase before code execution called **byte code compilation**, which is a less strict compilation procedure. Under some scenarios, it can save between 5% to 10% of time if already optimized functions are not being used heavily. All base R functions are byte code compiled by default.

To byte code compile your functions, you use the `cmpfunc()` function wrapped around the function you want to compile, after loading the `compiler` package. You may also send an `options` arguments such as `options = list(optimize = 3))`, where the optimize element should be an integer between 0 and 3. The higher the number, the more effort R will put into optimizing the compilation. The following lines show how to create a function called `sma_efficient_2_compiled()`, which is a compiled version of the `sma_efficient_2()` function:

```
library(compiler)
sma_efficient_2_compiled <-
    cmpfun(sma_efficient_2, options = list(optimize = e))
```

Just-in-time (JIT) compilation of R code

R also supports **Just-in-time** (**JIT**) compilation. When JIT compilation is enabled, R will automatically byte code compile any code that is executed without explicitly having called one of the compile functions. To activate JIT compilation, use the `enableJIT()` function.

The level argument tells R how much code to compile before execution; 0 disables `JIT`, 1 compiles functions before their first use, 2 also compiles functions before they are duplicated, and 3 also compiles loops before they are executed:

```
library(compiler)
enableJIT(level = 3)
```

JIT compilation can also be enabled by setting the `R_ENABLE_JIT` environment in the operating system before starting R. The value of `R_ENABLE_JIT` should be set to the value of the level argument.

Using memoization or cache layers

If you have deterministic algorithms, every time you provide equal inputs, you should receive equal outputs, and if that's the case and the process to go from inputs to outputs is very time-consuming, you may use memoization or cache layers. The basic idea is that you store some copies of the inputs and outputs, and whenever an input is sent to a function, before computing the output, you check whether or not that specific input's output has been computed before. If it has, send that instead of doing all the work again. This means you should only be computing the output for each input once.

You should try to implement such a layer in the `fibonacci_recursive()` function we created at the beginning of this chapter to see how big of an impact these kind of techniques can have, even when using slow algorithms.

Sometimes, these types of techniques are also used even when the output for a given input changes through time. All you have to do in such cases is to provide a mechanism that will invalidate or delete the stored input/output relation after a specific amount of time so that it's actually recalculated next time the input is used.

Improving our data and memory management

R, as any programming language, is constrained by CPU, RAM, and I/O, and in this chapter, we focused on increasing the speed for the CPU part. However, considerable performance gains can be achieved by also making our RAM and I/O usage more efficient.

Measuring RAM (memory) usage is best done outside of R using the tools provided by your operating system for exactly this purpose. The information that these tools report varies depending on the operating system, but here are the key metrics you should keep an eye on: CPU usage, free memory, physical memory, swap size, and bytes read/written per second.

If you encounter high CPU utilization, the CPU is likely the main bottleneck for R's performance. Use the profiling techniques in this chapter to identify which parts of the code are taking most of the CPU's time is the way to go.

If you encounter enough free system memory with high disk I/O, your code is likely performing lots of read/write operations to disk. Remove any unnecessary I/O operations and store intermediate data in the memory if there is sufficient memory.

If you encounter low CPU utilization and low free system memory with a large swap size, the system is likely running out of physical memory and is thus swapping memory onto the disk. In this case, see whether you have enough resources to handle the loads you're sending to R, and if you do, try to use the `rm()` function to remove unused objects that are waiting memory from R's session.

If you encounter a scenario similar to the last one, but you know that you don't have enough memory to handle the full data you're working with, even if you did so efficiently, you may try to partition your data. Can you work with a subset of the data by parts and then bring the results together? If so, you should try that. For example, if your full data doesn't fit in memory and you're trying to find the maximum value, you may want to split your data into four parts, load each them one by one, calculate the maximum for each of them, and remove them from memory after you do, while keeping the maximum and then getting the maximum of the four maximums you computed separately.

Another possibility for a scenario like the previous one is to simply migrate your data handling to a database. Databases are specialized tools for dealing with data, and can avoid data being a bottleneck in R since only the preprocessed subset of the data you need is brought into R. Most of databases nowadays also perform very efficient simple operations, like finding the maximum. You can leverage the techniques we showed in `Chapter 4`, *Simulating Sales Data and Working with Databases*, to accomplish this.

Using specialized packages for performance

Another good way to increase the performance of your implementations is to look for specialized functions published in CRAN packages or elsewhere. Before you go about changing your own code, take a look and see if you can find a very efficient implementation somewhere else. There's tremendous variation in CRAN packages' quality and speed, but leveraging them can definitely save you a lot of time.

Two very powerful packages to help you develop efficient implementations are the `data.table` and `dplyr` packages. They can provide efficient ways of dealing with data frames, and in the case of `dplyr` other objects as well. The **Basic Linear Algebra Subprogram (BLAS)** library can also be very helpful when performing linear algebra operations. It's written using Fortran and is highly optimized.

Flexibility and power with cloud computing

Sometimes, you don't even need more computing power or efficient resources usage. Sometimes, you just need to run R on some other computer without tying up your own for hours or days. In those cases, using cloud computing resources can be very useful.

Cloud computing resources are not only useful when you want to use an extra machine, they are a very efficient way to get hold of supercomputers to do some work for you. It's very easy to build a machine with 64 CPU cores and 512 GB of RAM memory. Using a system like that may be cheaper than you think, and it can be leveraged for very costly computations that would take way too much time in commodity hardware.

Specialized R distributions

Finally, if none of the previous options have worked for you, you may also use specialized R distributions. These distributions are maintained independently of the common R distribution and are focused on optimizing specific aspects within R. Some of them are built to provide fine-grained controlled for parallelization, and some do it for you automatically. Learning to use those distributions can be require a significant time investment, which may or may not be beneficial for your particular case.

Summary

In this chapter, we saw the most important reasons behind slow R code: programming without understanding object immutability, the nature of interpreted dynamic typings, memory-bound processes, and single-threaded processes. We learned that the first one can be reduced by properly using R, the second one can be reduced by delegating to statistically typed languages such as Fortran or C++, the third one can be reduced using more powerful computers (specifically with more RAM), and, finally, the fourth one can be reduced using parallelization.

We also mentioned some variables that we may want to take into account when deciding whether or not to optimize our implementations, how small a difference in implementation may result in big performance enhancements, and how the performance gains from these enhancements can become larger as the size of the inputs increases. Finally, we also learned how to profile and benchmark to improve our implementations.

In the next and final chapter, we will learn to use the `Shiny` package to create interactive dashboards that will make use of the SMA implementation we developed throughout this chapter.

10
Adding Interactivity with Dashboards

Shiny enables you to write powerful interactive web applications entirely in R. Using R, you can create a user interface and server, and Shiny will compiler your R code into the HTML, CSS, and JavaScript code needed to display your application on the web. What makes a Shiny application particularly powerful is that it can execute R code on the backend, so your application can perform any R calculation you can run on your desktop. You may want your application to process some data based on user inputs and provide some interactivity to make data analysis more intuitive. In this chapter, we will show you how to accomplish this.

Shiny implements the *functional reactive programming* paradigm that powers many of today's most modern web applications. We will explain what it is and how it works within Shiny. We will show how to work with streams of events coming from application users and how to react to them accordingly. To do so, we will work through an example that receives inputs from users and provides data and graphs in return. By the end of the chapter, you'll realize how easy it can be to create powerful web applications that take your R skills to the next level.

Some of the important topics covered in this chapter are as follows:

- The Shiny web applications architecture
- The functional reactive programming paradigm
- How reactivity is implemented within Shiny
- Receiving inputs from users interactions
- Sending outputs in responses to the web browser
- Adding interactions to Shiny applications

Required packages

We have already worked with the first two packages, namely ggplot2 and lubridate. The shiny package is used to build web applications directly from R, while the shinythemes and ggthemr packages are used to apply themes to style our web application. For more information, take a look at Appendix, *Required Packages*. Required packages for this chapter are shown in the following table:

Package	Reason
ggplot2	High-quality graphs
lubridate	Easily transform dates
shiny	Create modern web applications
ggthemr	Apply themes to ggplot2 plots
shinythemes	Apply themes to Shiny applications

Introducing the Shiny application architecture and reactivity

In its simplest form, a Shiny application requires a server and a **user interface** (UI). These components form the basic architecture behind all Shiny applications. The ui object controls the layout and appearance of your application, and the server function contains the logic needed by the application. If you know how web applications work, you can think of them as the *frontend* and the *backend*, respectively. The shinyApp() function creates and launches a Shiny application from an explicit UI/server pair. It will compile R code into web-friendly languages HTML, JavaScript, and CSS.

Below we have the simplest possible Shiny application, which has an empty server and a UI with a basic message. If you are in an interactive R session, your web browser should launch and show the application. If it doesn't, you can navigate to the URL yourself, which is in the form http://127.0.0.1:6924/, where 127.0.0.1 is the IP of your own computer and 6924 is the port Shiny is using to listen for connections. As you can see in your web browser, it is nothing amazing, but it's a functioning web application created only using R:

```
library(shiny)
server <- function(input, output) { }
ui <- fluidPage("This is a Shiny application.")
```

```
shinyApp(ui, server)
```

> Having a fixed port, instead of a randomly assigned port, which changes on every `shinyApp()` call, makes development easier. To use a fixed port, change the function call to `shinyApp(ui, server, options = list(port = 6924))` with a port of your preference.

Note that your R session will be busy while the application is active, so you will not be able to run any R commands. R is monitoring the application and executing the application's reactions. To get your R session back, press *Ctrl* + *C*, or if you are using RStudio, click on the stop sign icon.

For simplicity, we're creating our Shiny applications in a single file. However, with bigger applications, you will likely split the components into `ui.R` and `server.R` files (which are the standard files used for Shiny applications).

As we will see throughout the chapter, Shiny provides a great paradigm for developing web applications which is used in many cutting-edge systems nowadays. It's known as *functional reactive programming*. It's not a simple concept to grasp, but it's very powerful, and we will learn to use its fundamentals in this chapter. However, before we do, I will try to provide a simple explanation of what it is and how it works within Shiny.

What is functional reactive programming and why is it useful?

Let's start with the reactive programming part. **Reactive programming** is programming with *asynchronous data streams*. We start by defining these terms at a general level.

A *stream* is a sequence of ongoing events ordered in time. In reality, almost anything can be thought of as a stream, but simple examples are balls bouncing, where an *event* is considered every time a ball hits the floor. It can happen repeatedly many times, without specific patterns, stop for a while, then continue, and then stop again. Users clicking in a website is also a *stream*, where each click is an *event*. As you can imagine, there are *streams* everywhere around us.

The other term that needs to be defined is *asynchronous,* which literally means *without syncronization.* Normally, *synchronous* functions wait at the line of a function call until the function being called is finished executing, possibly returning a value. This is the way we have been programming so far. However, *asynchronous* functions don't necessarily wait for the functions they call to be finished. This means that our functions need to *react* to it whenever it arrives.

If we join these two terms, we can understand that programming with *asynchronous data streams* works by writing code that is able to react to *events* as they happen, continuously and randomly. In the case of this chapter, these *events* will be user interactions (clicks or keystrokes) with our application, which means that our R code will be responding directly to these clicks and keystrokes as they happen.

If it is still hard to get a grasp on the idea, think about it as a spreadsheet with formulas. When you change a value that other cells depend on or are listening to (analogous to receiving some input from a user in our application), then other cells react accordingly and present the newly computed value (which will be output change we show to the user). It's really that simple. The *listening* to the stream is called **subscribing.** The functions we are defining are *observers,* and the stream is the *observable* being *observed.* This is precisely the *Observer Design Pattern.* Take a look at Gamma, Helm, Johnson, and Vlissides's book *Design Patterns: Elements of Reusable Object-Oriented Software, by Addison-Wesley, 1994.*

On top of that, you are given a great set of tools that allows you to create, filter, and combine any of these *streams.* That's where the *functional programming* magic kicks in. Functional programing allows for composition, and that's exactly what we will use it for, to *compose streams.* A *stream* can be used as an input to another one. Even multiple *streams* can be used as inputs to many others. Furthermore, you may use any of these raw or transformed streams anywhere in your code. That's really what makes Shiny such a great tool.

Functional Reactive programming raises the level of abstraction of your code, so you can focus on the interdependence of events that define your application's logic, rather than having to constantly fiddle with a large amount of implementation details. *Functional-reactive* code is also likely to be more concise.

The benefit is more evident in modern applications that are highly interactive. Applications nowadays have an abundance of real-time events that enable a highly interactive experiences, and *functional reactive programming* is a great tool for that.

How is functional reactivity handled within Shiny?

Reactivity is what makes your Shiny applications responsive. It seems like the application instantly updates itself whenever the user makes a change. However, in reality, Shiny is rerunning your R expressions in a carefully scheduled way every couple of microseconds, which creates the illusion of responsiveness. You don't need to know how reactivity occurs to use it, but understanding reactivity will make you a better Shiny programmer.

Remember that when we executed our very simple Shiny application in a previous section, the R console stopped being interactive? Well, that was happening because executing the `shinyApp()` function makes R busy by constantly monitoring and updating expressions as necessary, which is what creates the responsive experience for users.

Now, imagine you have a complex application with lots of interactivity, then running every expression every couple of microseconds would completely saturate your processor, and your users would have a terrible user experience. That's why Shiny needs to be smart enough to only update those expressions that require it. Whenever a user submits an action (*event*), expressions that handle such events become *invalidated*, effectively marking themselves as being in need of an *update*, and this behavior is propagated among all expressions that depend on them. When a few microseconds have passed, R will check which expressions are marked for being updated, and only update those.

The mechanism just described can reduce the number of expressions that are recomputed from thousands to none, in case there has not been any user action, and to a few at most, since it's very hard for a user to accomplish a lot in a few microseconds which in turn would result in a few required updates, instead of a full application update each time. This mechanism allows R to handle complex Shiny applications, and it's the key to reactivity. It allows the application to be updated as fast as possible, making input/output coordination almost instantly.

The building blocks for reactivity in Shiny

The building blocks of reactivity in Shiny are built around three types of functions: input, output, and rendering functions. Input functions most of the time end with the `Input` string (not always) and I will refer to them as `Input()` functions. Output functions always end with the `Output` string and I will refer to them as `Output()` functions. Finally, rendering functions begin with the `render` string and similarly I will refer to them as `render*()` functions.

`Input*()` functions are used within the `ui` object and they generate *reactive values*, which are values received from an interaction through a web browser, and are passed through the `input` parameter in the `server` function. The `render*()` functions are used within the `server` function and make use of *reactive values* to produce *observables* that go back into the `ui` object, through the `server` function's `output` parameter. Finally, `*Output()` functions are used in the `ui` object to show the content of these observables in the web browser.

Reactive values are received in the `server()` function through the `input` parameter, which is a list whose elements contain elements that are *linked* with the `ui` object through strings that act as unique identifiers. The `output` parameter in the `server` function is also a list, but it's used to receive observables that will be sent to the web browser.

Functions that know how to deal with *reactive values* are known as *reactive functions*. Not every R function is a reactive function, and they need special construction mechanisms provided by Shiny, and if you try to use a *reactive value* in a *non-reactive function*, you will get an error (this is an easy mistake when starting to use Shiny). The `render*()` functions are used to create reactive functions. Another way of doing so is with the `reactive()` function we will explain later in the chapter.

Reactive functions are commonly used to generate observables that may be used by other reactive functions or by `render*()` functions. However, reactive functions can also produce side effects (for example, writing to a database). If reactive functions have `return` values, they are *cached* so that the function is not required to be re-executed if its corresponding *reactive values* have not changed.

The input, output, and rendering functions

Each `*Input()` function requires several arguments. The first one is a string with the name for the widget, which will only be used by you. The second one is a label which will be shown to the user in your application. The remaining arguments for each `*Input()` function vary depending on its functionality. They include things like initial values, ranges, and increments. You can find the exact arguments needed by a widget on the widget function's help page, (for example, `? selectInput`). The following table shows all available `*Input()` functions with an indication of what they are used for:

The `Input*()` function	Use
`actionButton()`	Action button
`checkboxGroupInput()`	Group of checkboxes

`checkboxInput()`	Single checkbox
`dateInput()`	Date selection
`dateRangeInput()`	Date range selection
`fileInput()`	File upload
`helpText()`	Help text for input forms
`numericInput()`	Numeric input field
`radioButtons()`	Set of options in radio buttons
`selectInput()`	Set of options in drop-down
`sliderInput()`	Numeric input slide bar
`submitButton()`	Submit button
`textInput()`	Text input field

Each of the `*Output()` functions requires a single argument, which is a character string that Shiny will use to identify the corresponding *observer* from the `output` parameter in the `server` function. Users will not see this name, it will only be used by you. The following table shows the list of all the available `*Output()` functions with an indication of what they are used for. You may find more information about them using their corresponding help pages (for example, `? tableOutput`):

The `*Output()` **function**	Use
`dataTableOutput()`	Data table
`htmlOutput()`	Raw HTML
`imageOutput()`	Images
`plotOutput()`	Graphs
`tableOutput()`	Tables
`textOutput()`	Text
`uiOutput()`	Raw HTML
`verbatimTextOutput()`	Verbatim text

Finally, each render*() function takes a single argument, an R expression surrounded by braces ({ }). These expressions can contain one simple line of text or they can involve many lines of code and function calls. The following table shows the list of all render*() functions with an indication of what they are used for. You guessed it, you may find more information about them using their corresponding help pages (for example, ? renderText):

The render*() function	Use
renderDataTable()	Data table
renderImage()	Image
renderPlot()	Graph
renderPrint()	Any printed output
renderTable()	Data frame, matrix, or other table-like structure
renderText()	String
renderUI()	Shiny tag object or HTML

Shiny applications combine the *Input(), *Output(), and render*() functions to produce powerful web applications. The simplest applications will be composed of only reactive values and observers, without too much logic between them. However, it's also possible to place as many expressions as we want between them, which allows for more complex applications.

There are many more ways to work with reactivity in Shiny. A very friendly introduction video can be found at RStudio's *Learn Shiny* video tutorials (https://shiny.rstudio.com/tutorial/).

Designing our high-level application structure

That's enough theory, let's get to action building our own application. The application we will build will make use of the previous chapter, so if you haven't read that one, please do. The dashboard we will build will make more sense if you do. This dashboard will show graphs with the price data points from the previous chapter's data simulation, as well as the SMA calculations we developed. Furthermore, it will allow us to explore the price data using a dynamic table.. By *dynamic*, we mean that responds to user input.

Setting up a two-column distribution

The layout you choose to use for your application depends on its objectives. In this case, a two-column layout will suffice. To accomplish this, we use the `fluidPage()` function and assign it to the `ui` object. This function adjusts content according to the web browser's dimensions:

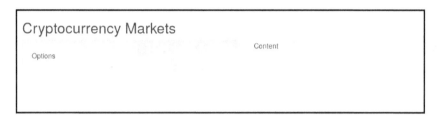

Inside the `fluidPage()`, we use the `titlePanel()` function to provide a title for our application and the `sidebarLayout()` function to create a two-column layout. This last function requires two other functions to be called inside it to create the corresponding content for each column. These two functions are called `sidebarPanel()` and `mainPanel()`, and they receive the content we want to create inside of them as parameters. The column on the left will be used to display available options for users and the one on the right to show actual content as a result of the user inputs, so we use some strings as placeholders that describe exactly that:

```
ui <- fluidPage(
    titlePanel("Cryptocurrency Markets"),
    sidebarLayout(
        sidebarPanel("Options"),
        mainPanel("Content")
    )
)
```

 The `fluidPage` simply generates HTML, which is sent to the web browser. You may print the `ui` object in the R console as we progress along the chapter to see the HTML it created.

This code will create a very basic structure as the one shown in the next image. As we move along, we will make the application more and more complex, but we need to start somewhere.

As you can see, nesting function calls will be a common pattern in the `ui` object to structure the application. This can be tricky, and if for some reason, you miss a comma (",") somewhere, you may find a cryptic message as the one shown . If that's the case, making sure your commas are correctly placed is a good start for fixing this error:

```
Error in tag("div", list(...)) : argument is missing, with no default
Calls: fluidPage ... tabsetPanel -> tabPanel -> div ->   -> tag
```

Introducing sections with panels

To show a section for graphs and a separate one for data tables, we will use the `tabsPanel()` function in conjunction with the `tabPanel()` function. The `tabsPanel()` function receives and arranges one or more `tablePanel()` function calls, where each of them receives the name for a tab and its actual content:

```
ui <- fluidPage(
    titlePanel("Cryptocurrency Markets"),
    sidebarLayout(
        sidebarPanel("Options"),
        mainPanel(
            tabsetPanel(
                tabPanel("Simple Moving Averages", "Content 1"),
                tabPanel("Data Overview", "Content 2")
            )
        )
    )
)
```

Since we created two tabs with the titles, *Simple Moving Averages* and *Data Overview*, respectively, that's what we see as the tab names. If you are running the application yourself at this point, you may click on them and you will see the `Content 1` or `Content 2` strings, depending on which one you click on:

Note that the `tabsetPanel()` function took the place of the `"Content"` string we previously had in its place. This will be a common pattern. As we start introducing more and more elements to the application, they will replace previous placeholders. Once you get used to Shiny, you may completely avoid the creation of placeholders.

Inserting a dynamic data table

Now we will add a dynamic table with the data we simulated in the previous chapter, so first of all, we need to bring that data into the application, and we do so with the line shown below. You should place this data-loading line above the `ui` object in your app. This way, it will only be run once, when starting up the Shiny application, as any code that would normally be run when executing an R script:

```
ORIGINAL_DATA <-
read.csv("../chapter-09/data.csv", stringsAsFactors = FALSE)
```

At this point, we need to introduce the `DT` package. It provides an easy way to create dynamic tables for Shiny applications. Since we will reference it through its package name, we don't need to load it with `library(DT)`. Referencing it by its package name helps us separate the native Shiny functions from those that come from external packages.

To implement this, we need to modify the `server` function we had not touched up to this point. We need to introduce some logic into it that will allow us to move data from R into the web interface. To accomplish this, we assign it to the `table` element in its `output` parameter, which will function as an observer. The element name we assign to it can be any valid list element we wish, but it's a good idea to just use names that describe the contents of the observer. Keep in mind that these names must be unique as Shiny will use them to identify what objects to pass back and forth between the `ui` object and the `server` function. The observer is created with the `renderDataTable()` function from the `DT` package. This function works as any other `render*()` function, it receives a single parameter, which is an expression that returns a value which will be the content of the observer.

In this case, the data table created with the `datatable()` function, again from the DT package. To create this data table, we are simply passing the `ORIGINAL_DATA` object we loaded previously. Now that the server-side adjustment is finished, we add a `fluidRow()` instead of "Content 2" in the `ui` object to introduce a row that will adjust its length according to the web browser's dimensions, and inside of it, we call the `dataTableOutput()` function from the DT package. Note that the string sent as the only parameter to this function is the name of the element we assigned to the `output` parameter in the `server` function. This is the mechanism that Shiny uses to move data from the `server` to the `ui`:

```
ui <- fluidPage(
    titlePanel("Cryptocurrency Markets"),
    sidebarLayout(
        sidebarPanel("Options"),
        mainPanel(
            tabsetPanel(
                tabPanel("Simple Moving Averages",
                        "Content 1"),
                tabPanel("Data Overview",
                        fluidRow(DT::dataTableOutput("table"))
                )
            )
        )
    )
)

server <- function(input, output) {
    output$table <-
    DT::renderDataTable(DT::datatable({return(ORIGINAL_DATA)}))
}
```

Now that our code is ready, we should see a table appear in the **Data Overview** tab. This table is dynamic in the sense that you may order its columns by clicking on the column titles, as well as change the number of observations shown, and search through its contents. Also note that a pagination mechanism was automatically added for us along with an observation counter. These tables are very easy to create, yet very useful, and we will see later in this chapter how to expand their functionality even more.

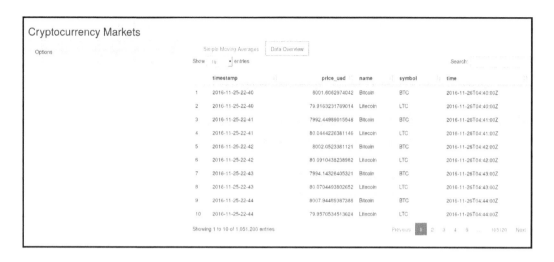

Introducing interactivity with user input

The interactivity we saw previously with the dynamic data table works within the web browser itself using JavaScript, and it does not need to go through the `server` function to provide the interactivity, only to pass the table itself. However, many interesting interactivity features need to go through the `server` so that we can provide custom responses for them. In this section, we show how to add various types of inputs to our application.

Setting up static user inputs

First, we will show how to filter the timestamps in the data to only show observations that fall within a range defined by the user. To do this, we need to first define four timestamps: the minimum, the initial left limit, the initial right limit, and the maximum. These four values will be used by our date range widget to define the allowed range for the user (the minimum and maximum values are used for this), as well as the initial date range (the initial left and right limits are used for this), which may be different from the limits of the allowed range.

Therefore, we need to extract such values, and we do so by making use of the `TimeStamp` class we created in `Chapter 8`, *Object-Oriented System to Track Cryptocurrencies*. Note that we use the `days()` function from the `lubridate` package (you should add the `library(lubridate)` line at the top of your file), just as we did in the mentioned chapter.

Since we only need to create these objects once, they should go just below the code that is used to load the `ORIGINAL_DATA`, before the `ui` object definition:

```
DATE_MIN <-
timestamp_to_date_string.TimeStamp(min(ORIGINAL_DATA$timestamp))

DATE_MAX <-
timestamp_to_date_string.TimeStamp(max(ORIGINAL_DATA$timestamp))

DATE_END <-
timestamp_to_date_string.TimeStamp(time_to_timestamp.TimeStamp(
    timestamp_to_time.TimeStamp(min(ORIGINAL_DATA$timestamp)) + days(2)))
```

The `timestamp_to_date_string()` function in the `TimeStamp` class had not been created and we added it for this chapter. It is very simple and is shown in the following code. Its objective is to simply get the first 10 characters of a `TimeStamp`, which correspond to the format YYYY-MM-DD:

```
timestamp_to_date_string.TimeStamp <- function(timestamp) {
    return(substr(timestamp, 1, 10))
}
```

Now that we have created these objects, we may use the following code to expand the `ui` object. What we did was replace the `"Options"` string with a function call to `dateRangeInput()`, which is the function used to create a date range, as the name implies. It receives as parameters the unique identifier that will be used to retrieve its *reactive values* within the `server` through the `input` parameter, the `label` shown to the user, the `start`, `end`, `min`, and `max` values mentioned earlier, the `separator` we want to use among the web browser input boxes, the date `format` we want to use, and what day of the week it is considered to start on (`0` for Sunday, `1` for Monday, and so on):

```
ui <- fluidPage(
    titlePanel("Cryptocurrency Markets"),
    sidebarLayout(
        sidebarPanel(
            dateRangeInput(
                "date_range",
                label = paste("Date range:"),
                start = DATE_MIN,
                end = DATE_END,
                min = DATE_MIN,
                max = DATE_MAX,
                separator = " to ",
                format = "yyyy-mm-dd",
                weekstart = 1
```

```
                )
            ),
        mainPanel(
            tabsetPanel(
                tabPanel("Simple Moving Averages",
                         "Content 1"),
                tabPanel("Data Overview",
                         fluidRow(DT::dataTableOutput("table"))
                )
            )
        )
    )
)
```

On the server side, we will add more logic within the *reactive experssion* passed as a parameter to the `datatable()` function. Instead of simply sending the raw `ORIGINAL_DATA` dataframe, we will filter it before we send it. To do so, we first assign a copy of it to the `data` object and extract the two date values from the widget we created in the `ui` object, using their references within the `input` parameter. Then, we check whether any of these is different from their initial values. In case they are, we update the `data` object with only those observations that are within the range specified, which we accomplish with a standard dataframe selection. Finally, we sent this filtered `data` to the `datatable()` function, and proceed as we did earlier.

The result of these changes to the `ui` and `server` is that we can now filter the dates allowed in the dynamic table shown in the **Data Overview** tab, which is something we could not do before. The date range widget in action is shown in the following screenshot. Try to change its dates and see how the dynamic table updates:

Setting up dynamic options in a drop-down

Now we will see how to add a drop-down input whose entries adapt to the tab the user is currently viewing. Specifically, we will add the possibility for the user to select which asset they want to use to filter the data. If you looked carefully, you may have noticed that the dynamic data table contains observations for both Bitcoin and Litecoin, which may be fine when we're just looking at the table, but it will be a problem when we attempt to show a price time-series because we will have data for more than one asset. We want to provide a mechanism to select only one of them, but we want to keep the option of looking at all of them together in the dynamic data table, just as we are doing now.

We start by creating the object that contains the unique asset names we currently have in the data. This is much better than hardcoding their names directly into code, since they will be automatically updated when our data changes, which would not be the case if we hardcoded them. This line should go just below the previous *global* objects, which only needs to be created once:

```
DATA_ASSETS <- unique(ORIGINAL_DATA$name)
```

Since the input widget in this case has dynamic logic, we can't just create inside the `ui` object, we need to create it in the `server` function and pass it along to the `ui` object. The way to do it is by introducing a new observer into the `output` parameter, named `select_asset` in this case, which is created with the `renderUI()` function since it will contain a Shiny `*Input()` function. As we did with the `data` in the previous section, we will assign the *default* asset names, and only in the case that the user is the second tab which is the **Data Overview** tab (more on where this comes from below), will it also add the `All` option to the drop-down. Otherwise, it will just keep the asset names without the `All` option, which is what we want for the SMA graphs we will create later:

```
server <- function(input, output) {
    output$table <- DT::renderDataTable(DT::datatable({
        data  <- ORIGINAL_DATA
        start <- input$date_range[1]
        end   <- input$date_range[2]
        if (time_to_date_string.TimeStamp(start) != DATE_MIN |
            time_to_date_string.TimeStamp(end) != DATE_END) {
            data <- data[
                data$timestamp >= time_to_timestamp.TimeStamp(start) &
                data$timestamp <= time_to_timestamp.TimeStamp(end), ]
        }
        return(data)
    }))

    output$select_asset <- renderUI({
```

```
        assets <- DATA_ASSETS
        if (input$tab_selected == 2) {
            assets <- c("All", assets)
        }
        return(selectInput("asset", "Asset:", assets))
    })
}
```

To actually provide a mechanism for the `server` to understand what tab the user is currently viewing, the `ui` object needs to be adjusted so that the `tabsetPanel()` function receives an `id` parameter with the name of the object that contains the current tab number, `tab_selected` in this case (which is the name used to check in the `server` function). Also, each tab within must have a value assigned with the `value` parameter, as is shown. This way we make sure that the **Data Overview** tab is identified with the 2 value.

Also note that we added the `htmlOutput()` function call within the just introduced `wellPanel()` function call in the `sidePanel()` function. The `wellPanel()` visually groups panels to provide more intuitive interfaces for users, and the `htmlOutput()` function uses the name of an observer to know what to show in the web browser, the `select_asset` element of the `output` object in this case:

```
ui <- fluidPage(
    titlePanel("Cryptocurrency Markets"),
    sidebarLayout(
        sidebarPanel(
            wellPanel(
                dateRangeInput(
                    "date_range",
                    label = paste("Date range:"),
                    start = DATE_MIN,
                    end = DATE_END,
                    min = DATE_MIN,
                    max = DATE_MAX,
                    separator = " to ",
                    format = "yyyy-mm-dd",
                    weekstart = 1,
                    startview = "year"
                ),
                htmlOutput("select_asset")
            )
        ),
        mainPanel(
            tabsetPanel(
                id = "tab_selected",
                tabPanel(
                    "Simple Moving Averages",
```

```
                    value = 1,
                    "Content 1"
                ),
                tabPanel(
                    "Data Overview",
                    value = 2,
                    fluidRow(DT::dataTableOutput("table"))
                )
            )
        )
    )
)
```

Having performed these changes, now we can see that our application shows an asset name drop-down with options `Bitcoin` and `Litecoin` when the user is in the **Simple Moving Averages** tab, and which also includes the `All` option when they are in the **Data Overview** tab, just as we wanted and as can be seen in the following screenshot:

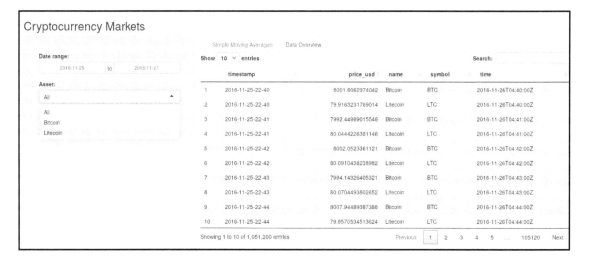

Setting up dynamic input panels

The final two inputs we will introduce will be used for the SMA graphs later on. The first one is used to select which SMA implementation the user wants to use. The options are the `sma_efficient_1()`, `sma_efficient_2()`, `sma_delegated_fortran()`, and `sma_delegated_cpp()` functions we created in the previous chapter. The second one is used to define the period used for the SMA calculation, and which is used as input in one of the previous functions.

Since code can start being too repetitive and taking too much space, and since you have most likely understood the nesting patterns used in the creation of the `ui`, I will avoid repeating the full `ui` object declaration, and simply point where changes need to be made.

In this case, we want to add the following code after the `wellPanel()` function has ended and before the `sidebarPanel()` function ends. The following code will be the second parameter to `sidebarPanel()`, so don't forget to add a comma (",") after the `wellPanel()` function finishes, otherwise you will get an error.

The `conditionalPanel()` function checks for a JavaScript condition, specified using a string, to decide whether or not a panel should be showed to the user. Since the `input` object is sent to the web browser through a JavaScript object conveniently named `input`, we can use that to get the value we're looking for, which is whether or not the user is looking at the first tab, "`Simple Moving Averages`". If she is, then we will show the panel:

 JavaScript uses the dot (".") notation to access elements instead of the `money` ($) notation used in R.

The panel shown is `wellPanel()` with two input objects inside: `radioButtons()` and `sliderInput()`. The first one receives the available options for the user in a list sent through the `choices` parameter (each element's name is what is shown to the user, while each element's value is used internally in R which are the SMA implementation names in this case), as well as the `selected` one by default. The second one receives the `min`, `max`, and default `value` for the numeric slider. Both receive the unique identifier and label as the first two arguments, as every other `*Input()` function does:

```
conditionalPanel(
    condition = "input.tab_selected == 1",
    wellPanel(
        radioButtons(
            "sma_implementation",
            "Implementation:",
            choices = list(
                "C++" = "sma_delegated_cpp",
                "Fortran" = "sma_delegated_fortran",
                "Efficient 1" = "sma_efficient_1",
                "Efficient 2" = "sma_efficient_2"
            ),
            selected = "sma_delegated_cpp"
        ),
        sliderInput(
            "sma_period",
```

```
            "Period:",
            min = 5,
            max = 200,
            value = 30
        )
    )
)
```

We will leave the actual graphs creations for later, so we don't need to change anything on the `server` side. At this point, the *reactive values* coming out of `input$sma_implementation` and `input$sma_period` will not be used. A screenshot showing how these inputs is shown as following. If you navigate to the **Simple Moving Averages** tab, they should be shown, but if you navigate to the **Data Overview** tab, they should be hidden:

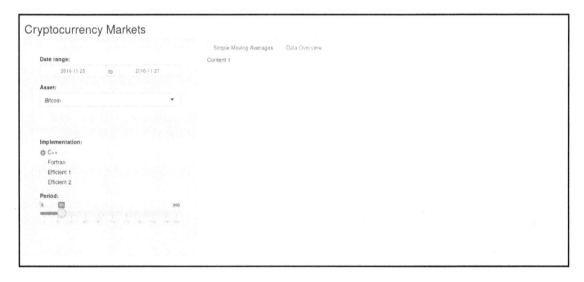

As you can see, allowing users to interact with the application is not too hard, and is accomplished by using the `*Input()` functions in the `ui` object, whose *reactive values* in turn may be used in the `server` function.

Adding a summary table with shared data

Now we will add a summary table on top of our dynamic data table. This summary table should be updated according to the assets selected (note the plural since we allow for the `All` case in this tab). Take a moment to try to think how you would implement this yourself? If you tried to replicate the pattern shown previously for the `data` object we showed before, you would have a correct but inefficient solution. The reason is that the logic to filter the data would be duplicated, which is unnecessary.

To avoid this pitfall we show next how to share streams among different *reactive functions* using the `reactive()` function, which is a function that used to prepare *reactive values* for other *reactive functions*. In this case, we move all the logic we had created before into the expression sent as a parameter to this function and assign it to the `data` object, which is now a *reactive function* itself. Note that we also added a bit of code to check whether the current asset selection is different from `All` and if it is, then use that value to filter the data, similarly to how we filter it using dates.

Once we have done that, we can replace the logic we had inside the `datatable()` function with a simple call to the `data()` reactive function, which will provide the expected dataframe. And now that we have extracted this logic, we can reuse the `data()` call in an other place, as we do in the `output$summary_table` observer created with the `renderTable()` function. As you can see, it's being passed a dataframe created with statistics for the minimum, median, mean, and maximum of the dataframe returned by the `data()` function. In this case, we can guarantee that the data used in the `output$table()` and `output$summary_table()` functions is the same:

```
server <- function(input, output) {

    data <- reactive({
        data  <- ORIGINAL_DATA
        start <- input$date_range[1]
        end   <- input$date_range[2]
        if (input$asset != "All") {
            data <- data[data$name == input$asset, ]
        }
        if (time_to_date_string.TimeStamp(start) != DATE_MIN |
            time_to_date_string.TimeStamp(end) != DATE_MAX) {
            data <- data[
                data$timestamp >= time_to_timestamp.TimeStamp(start) &
                data$timestamp <= time_to_timestamp.TimeStamp(end), ]
        }
        return(data)
    })
```

```
output$table <- DT::renderDataTable(DT::datatable({return(data())}))

output$select_asset <- renderUI({
    assets <- DATA_ASSETS
    if (input$tab_selected == 2) {
        assets <- c("All", assets)
    }
    return(selectInput("asset", "Asset:", assets))
})

output$summary_table <- renderTable(data.frame(
    Minimum = min(data()$price_usd),
    Median = mean(data()$price_usd),
    Mean = mean(data()$price_usd),
    Max = max(data()$price_usd)
))
}
```

Be careful if you're using stochastic data (for example, random numbers) if you're duplicating data logic instead of using a `reactive()` function, since you will probably not end up with the same data in both places.

We also need to introduce the corresponding function call in the `ui` object, which we place in the corresponding `tabPanel()`. To place in this the dataframe we just created, we use the `tableOutput()` function with the corresponding `summary_table` string as parameter. The code is as follows (note that I omit the `ui` code around this snippet):

```
tabPanel(
    "Data Overview",
    value = 2,
    fluidRow(tableOutput("summary_table")),
    fluidRow(DT::dataTableOutput("table"))
)
```

After implementing these changes, you should see a summary table with the mentioned statistics on top of the dynamic data table, and they should update as different values are sent as inputs for dates and asset selection.

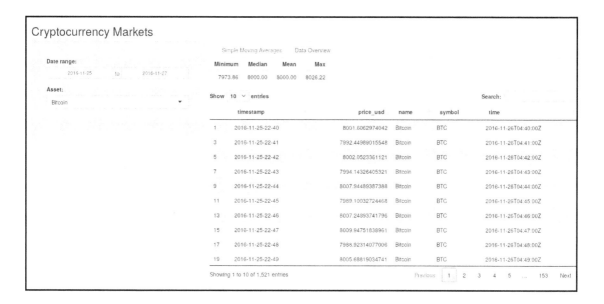

Adding a simple moving average graph

Now we will create our first **simple moving average** (**SMA**) graph. This graph will be created with the   package, and will show two lines. The black line will be the actual price data, and the blue line will be SMA.

Before we begin, and since `ggplot2` graphs which make use of dates are better created with actual dates instead of timestamp strings, we add the `time` column to the `ORIGINAL_DATA` dataframe with the corresponding dates. This should be placed immediately after having loaded the data:

```
ORIGINAL_DATA$time <- timestamp_to_time.TimeStamp(ORIGINAL_DATA$timestamp)
```

Next we show how our `sma_graph()` function is implemented. As can be seen, it will receive two parameters, the `data` dataframe and the `sma` vector coming out of one of the SMA implementations mentioned before. The function is very simple, it creates a graph with `time` on the *x* axis and `price_usd` on the *y* axis, adds points and lines for such data, and then adds a second blue line with the values from the `sma` vector. The `group = 1` parameter is used to avoid any errors by telling the `ggplot()` function that there's a single group in that data, and the `size = 1` parameter is just to make the line stand out a little bit more.

Note that we return the graph object. Finally, you should keep in mind that using the geom_line() function introduces interpolation into the example, which may misrepresent the discrete data we have for prices, but it can also be helpful to understand the price dynamics, and that's why we use it:

```
sma_graph <- function(data, sma) {
    g <- ggplot(data, aes(time, price_usd))
    g <- g + geom_point()
    g <- g + geom_line(group = 1)
    g <- g + geom_line(aes_string(y = sma),
                       group = 1, color = "blue", size = 1)
    return(g)
}
```

Now, to follow good practices, we place the SMA calculation in a reactive() function of its own (just below the data *reactive function* we created before). Note that it's a *reactive function* that depends on another *reactive function*, data() to be precise.

The following code (which omits the rest of the server function), shows that this sma definition makes use of the do.call() function to execute the implementation name we receive as a *reactive value* from the input$sma_implementation widget. The do.call() also receives a list as the second parameter, and this list contains the parameters that will be sent to the actual function we want to call. In this case, it's the input$sma_period, the symbol (which in this case will be a single one because we restricted data for this tab to have a single asset), and the actual data through the call to the data() *reactive function*:

```
sma <- reactive({
    return(do.call(
        input$sma_implementation,
        list(input$sma_period, data()[1, "symbol"], data())
    ))
})
```

Having implemented this sma() reactive function, we can implement the observer output$graph_top() as follows (again, we omitted some code around):

```
output$graph_top <- renderPlot({
    return(sma_graph(data(), sma()))
})
```

Finally, we need to update our `ui` object to replace the `"Content 1"` placeholder with a `fluidRow()` and a `ploutOutput()` inside. We send the `"graph_top"` unique identifier to the observer we are interested in:

```
fluidRow(plotOutput("graph_top"))
```

This was simple enough, wasn't it? Now we can run our application, and it should show us a graph for the first two days in the data, with a blue **SMA(30)** on top as the one shown in the following screenshot:

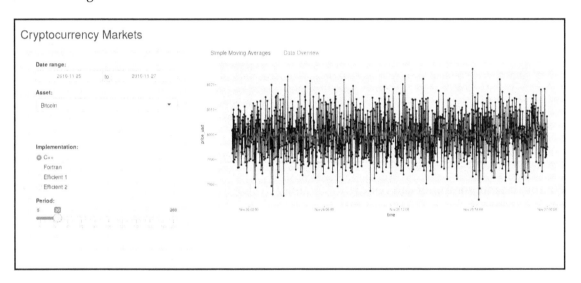

Note that you can change the options and the graph will update accordingly. For example, if we chose only the first day in the data and decide to graph only an **SMA(5)** on top of it.

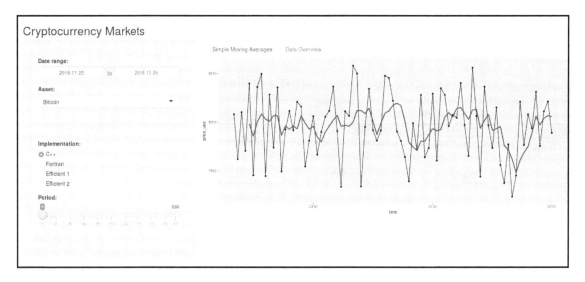

Finally, if your computer can handle it, you may decide to show the full data (which is quite a bit of observations, so do be careful). In that case, the SMA would not be visible, but it will still be plotted for us. The result is shown in the following image:

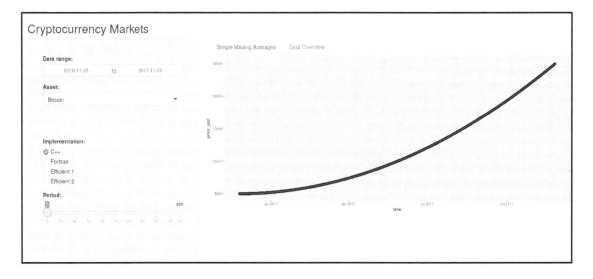

Adding interactivity with a secondary zoom-in graph

Finally, we are going to add some interactivity to our graph by implementing another similar graph, which will exhibit a *zoom-in* effect on the one we created before. The idea is that we can select an area of the graph we just created and the one we will place below it will update to only show the specific area we have selected. Seems interesting, doesn't it?

To accomplish this, we need to modify the `plotOutput()` we inserted at the end of the previous section to include a `brush` parameter with a call to the `brushOpts()` function, which in turn receives the name of the unique identifier for the brush input we are creating. This parameter is used to create a special type of input, which retrieves a selected area from the graph shown in the web browser. We also add another `fluidRow()` with another `plotOutput()` just below it to contain the graph that will provide the *zoom-in* effect. The code is as follows:

```
tabPanel(
    "Simple Moving Averages",
    value = 1,
    fluidRow(plotOutput("graph_top", brush = brushOpts("graph_brush"))),
    fluidRow(plotOutput("graph_bottom"))
)
```

Now the `input$graph_brush` reactive value will contain a list with four elements inside `xmin`, `xmax`, `ymin`, and `ymax`, which are the coordinates that conform the area selected in the top graph. Our `ranges()` reactive function will use them to send the appropriate values as limits to the bottom graph. The way it works is that it will check whether `input$graph_brush` is `NULL`, and if it's not, meaning that an area is selected, then it will return a list with two elements, x and y, where each of these elements contains the appropriate coordinates. If `input$graph_brush` is `NULL`, then the x and y elements of the returned list will be `NULL`, which signals the `coord_cartesian()` function, which we will use on top of the `sma_graph()`, to avoid placing any constraints in the axes for the graph. The actual function is shown in the following code, and as other functions created with `reactive()`, it should be placed inside the `server` function.

Also note that we need to make a small transformation to the values for the *x* axis because they are returned as integers, and not dates which is the type of object being used by ggplot() for that axis. We simply use the as.POSIXct() function to transform such integers into valid dates, using the oring = "1970-01-01", which is what ggplot() uses by default. If we don't make the transformation, we will get an error:

```
ranges <- reactive({
    if (!is.null(input$graph_brush)) {
        return(list(
            x = c(as.POSIXct(input$graph_brush$xmin,
                             origin = "1970-01-01"),
                  as.POSIXct(input$graph_brush$xmax,
                             origin = "1970-01-01")),

            y = c(input$graph_brush$ymin,
                  input$graph_brush$ymax)
        ))
    }
    return(list(x = NULL, y = NULL))
})
```

Now we are able to create the output$bottom_graph observer just as we created the previous graph, but in this case we will add the coord_cartesian() function on top of the graph object returned by sma_graph() to limit the axes values. Note that we use the expand = FALSE to enforce the limits coming from the ranges() reactive function, we just created in the preceding code:

```
output$graph_bottom <- renderPlot({
    return(sma_graph(data(), sma()) +
           coord_cartesian(xlim = ranges()$x,
                           ylim = ranges()$y, expand = FALSE))
})
```

Having implemented these changes, we should have the desired effect. To test it, we can open the application and see the two identical plots one on top of the other, like the following screenshot shows:

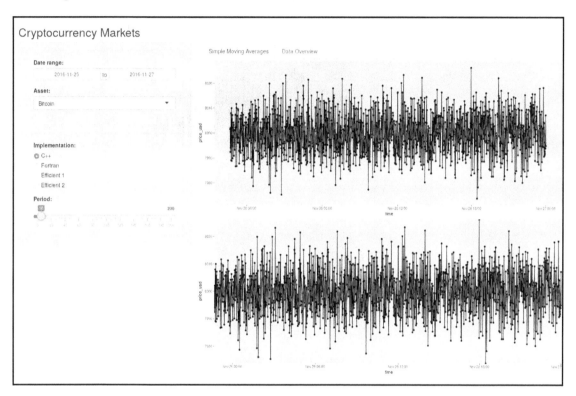

However, if we select an area on the top graph, then the graph on the bottom should update showing only that specific part of the graph. Pretty cool, isn't it?

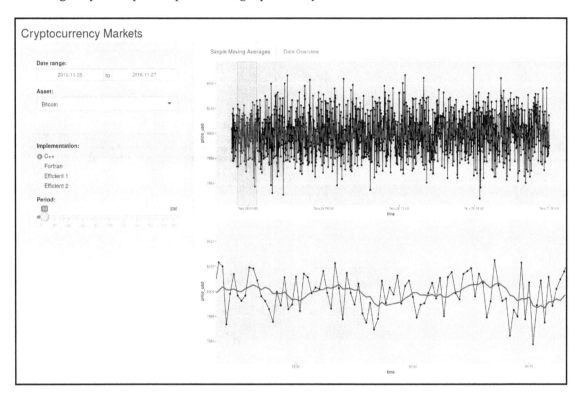

Finally, you should know that another way to introduce interactive graphics is to use well known JavaScript like `Plot.ly` (which we used in `Chapter 5`, *Communicating Sales With Visualizations*). Shiny creates websites that use JavaScript in the background so this technique is a natural fit. However, this is an advanced technique and its use is more involved than what we have shown here, so we won't show it but you should know it's possible in case you want to pursue it yourself.

Styling our application with themes

Up to this point, we have been using the theme provided by default by Shiny, but now that our application is finished, we want to stylize it with some tech-looking colors. In that case, we can use the `shinythemes` and `ggthemr` packages, which provide us with an easy way to apply themes to Shiny applications and `ggplot2` graphs, respectively.

All we need to do to apply the themes is to tell the `ggplot2` framework to apply the *flat dark* theme provided by the `ggthemr` package, and to make sure that the *outer* side of the graph is also stylized we use the `type = outer` parameter, as is shown here. The code should be placed wherever we placed our `ggplot2` code for cohesiveness, which is in the `functions.R` file for this chapter:

```
library(ggthemr)
ggthemr('flat dark', type = 'outer')
```

To stylize the Shiny application itself, we send the `theme` parameter, using the `shinytheme()` function, to the `fluidPage()` function just before our `titlePanel()` function call, as is shown here:

```
ui <- fluidPage(
    theme = shinytheme("superhero"),
    titlePanel("Cryptocurrency Markets"),
    ...
)
```

We also change the SMA line in the graphs to white, which you already know how to do, and with these changes, now our application looks pretty high tech. The following shows the **Simple Moving Average** tab:

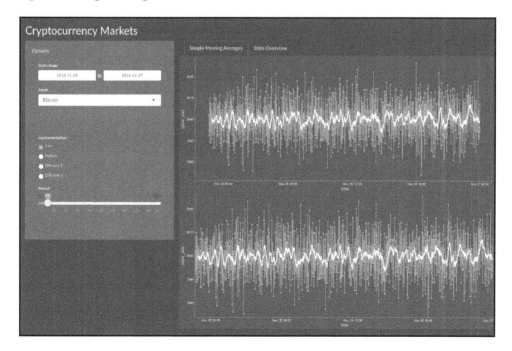

And here you can see a screenshot of the **Data Overview** tab:

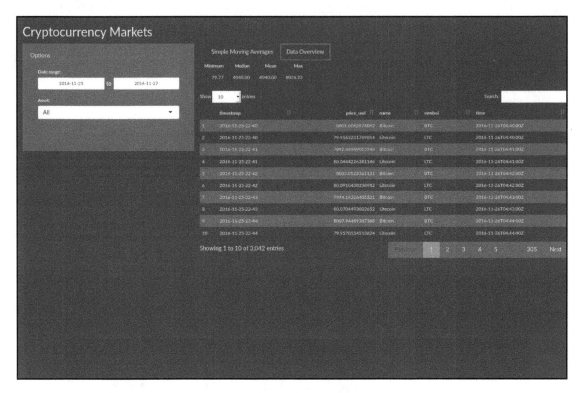

To find other themes you can look at the `shinythemes` repository (http://rstudio.github.io/shinythemes/) and the `ggthemr` repository (https://github.com/cttobin/ggthemr). To make sure the readers realize what the full code looks like at once, I place here the full code for the application as well as the function used for graphs:

```
library(shiny)
library(ggplot2)
library(lubridate)
library(shinythemes)

source("../chapter-08/cryptocurrencies/utilities/time-stamp.R")
source("../chapter-09/sma-delegated.R", chdir = TRUE)
source("../chapter-09/sma-efficient.R")
source("./functions.R")

ORIGINAL_DATA <-
read.csv("../chapter-09/data.csv", stringsAsFactors = FALSE)
```

```
ORIGINAL_DATA$time <-
timestamp_to_time.TimeStamp(ORIGINAL_DATA$timestamp)

DATA_ASSETS <- unique(ORIGINAL_DATA$name)

DATE_MIN <-
timestamp_to_date_string.TimeStamp(min(ORIGINAL_DATA$timestamp))

DATE_MAX <-
timestamp_to_date_string.TimeStamp(max(ORIGINAL_DATA$timestamp))

DATE_END <-
timestamp_to_date_string.TimeStamp(time_to_timestamp.TimeStamp(
    timestamp_to_time.TimeStamp(min(ORIGINAL_DATA$timestamp)) + days(2)))

ui <- fluidPage(
    theme = shinytheme("superhero"),
    titlePanel("Cryptocurrency Markets"),
    sidebarLayout(
        sidebarPanel(
            "Options",
            wellPanel(
                dateRangeInput(
                    "date_range",
                    label = paste("Date range:"),
                    start = DATE_MIN,
                    end = DATE_END,
                    min = DATE_MIN,
                    max = DATE_MAX,
                    separator = " to ",
                    format = "yyyy-mm-dd",
                    weekstart = 1,
                    startview = "year"
                ),
                htmlOutput("select_asset")
            ),
            conditionalPanel(
                condition = "input.tab_selected == 1",
                wellPanel(
                    radioButtons(
                        "sma_implementation",
                        "Implementation:",
                        choices = list(
                            "C++" = "sma_delegated_cpp",
                            "Fortran" = "sma_delegated_fortran",
                            "Efficient 1" = "sma_efficient_1",
                            "Efficient 2" = "sma_efficient_2"
                        ),
```

```
                        selected = "sma_delegated_cpp"
                    ),
                    sliderInput(
                        "sma_period",
                        "Period:",
                        min = 5,
                        max = 200,
                        value = 30
                    )
                )
            )
        ),
        mainPanel(
            tabsetPanel(
                id = "tab_selected",
                tabPanel(
                    "Simple Moving Averages",
                    value = 1,
                    fluidRow(plotOutput("graph_top",
                                        brush = brushOpts(
                                        "graph_brush"))),
                    fluidRow(plotOutput("graph_bottom"))
                ),
                tabPanel(
                    "Data Overview",
                    value = 2,
                    fluidRow(tableOutput("summary_table")),
                    fluidRow(DT::dataTableOutput("table"))
                )
            )
        )
    )
)

server <- function(input, output) {

    data <- reactive({
        data <- ORIGINAL_DATA
        start <- input$date_range[1]
        end <- input$date_range[2]
        if (input$asset != "All") {
            data <- data[data$name == input$asset, ]
        }
        if (time_to_date_string.TimeStamp(start) != DATE_MIN |
            time_to_date_string.TimeStamp(end) != DATE_MAX) {
            data <- data[
                data$timestamp >= time_to_timestamp.TimeStamp(start) &
                data$timestamp <= time_to_timestamp.TimeStamp(end), ]
```

```
    }
    return(data)
})

sma <- reactive({
    return(do.call(
        input$sma_implementation,
        list(input$sma_period, data()[1, "symbol"], data())
    ))
})

ranges <- reactive({
    if (!is.null(input$graph_brush)) {
        return(list(
            x = c(as.POSIXct(input$graph_brush$xmin,
                             origin = "1970-01-01"),
                  as.POSIXct(input$graph_brush$xmax,
                             origin = "1970-01-01")),
            y = c(input$graph_brush$ymin,
                  input$graph_brush$ymax)
        ))
    }
    return(list(x = NULL, y = NULL))
})

output$table <- DT::renderDataTable(DT::datatable({
    return(data())
}), style = "bootstrap")

output$select_asset <- renderUI({
    assets <- DATA_ASSETS
    if (input$tab_selected == 2) {
        assets <- c("All", assets)
    }
    return(selectInput("asset", "Asset:", assets))
})

output$summary_table <- renderTable(data.frame(
    Minimum = min(data()$price_usd),
    Median = mean(data()$price_usd),
    Mean = mean(data()$price_usd),
    Max = max(data()$price_usd)
))

output$graph_top <- renderPlot({
    return(sma_graph(data(), sma()))
})
```

```
    output$graph_bottom <- renderPlot({
        return(sma_graph(data(), sma()) +
            coord_cartesian(xlim = ranges()$x,
                            ylim = ranges()$y, expand = FALSE))
    })
}

shinyApp(ui, server, options = list(port = 6924))
```

Other topics of interest

When working with Shiny there are common tasks that can be used to customize your web applications. Some of these tasks are adding static images, HTML, and CSS. In the following sections we will briefly look into how these can be accomplished with Shiny. Finally, we will also mention some options you have to share your application with others, without having to setup your own web server, so that they can use it in their web browser, through an internet connection.

Adding static images

Images can enhance the appearance of your application and help your users understand the content. Shiny looks for the img() function to place image files in your application. To insert an image, simply call with the src specifying the images location. You can also include other HTML friendly parameters such as height and width (they will be passed as *pixel values*):

```
img(src = "image.png", height = 250, width = 250)
```

The image.png file must be in a folder named www in the same directory as the app.R script. Shiny will share any file placed here with your user's web browser, which makes www a great place to put images, style sheets, and other things the browser will need to build the wap components of your Shiny application.

Adding HTML to your web application

It's easy to add HTML elements to your Shiny application using HTML tags. There are many elements you can add to your page using syntax like `tags$h1()` or `tags$p()` for a first-level heading and a paragraph, respectively. In the following piece of code, you can see how these would be used to create a page with one first-level heading, followed by a paragraph, a second-level heading, and then another paragraph.

The full list of HTML tags can be found in the Shiny HTML Tags Glossary (`https://shiny. rstudio.com/articles/tag-glossary.html`):

```
ui <- fluidPage(
    tag$h1("This is a first level heading"),
    tag$p("This is a paragraph."),
    tag$h2("This is a second level heading"),
    tag$p("This is a another paragraph.)
)
```

Sometimes, however, you may need more control on the HTML you want to use. In that case you can actually specify HTML directly into your application by using the `HTML()` function. In this case, Shiny will not perform any escaping on your behalf, and you will have full HTML powers, you simply need to pass it raw HTML as is shown here. Note that this raw HTML may be included in other tags, as is the case here, where it's wrapped by a `div` HTML tag:

```
tags$div(
    HTML("Raw HTML")
)
```

Adding custom CSS styling

Shiny uses the Bootstrap framework for structure and styling. If you're new to CSS **Cascading Style Sheets** (**CSS**) or are not familiar with Bootstrap, it would be a good idea to read the *Getting Started* guide (`https://getbootstrap.com/docs/3.3/getting-started/`) before attempting to apply your own styling.

To include your own CSS, you have a couple of options, but we will only show how to use the `includeCSS()` function and how to apply styles directly into HTML tags. The `includeCSS()` function is provided by Shiny and can be used to include a CSS file directly from the `www` directory mentioned in the previous section. Its usage is fairly simply.

Even though it's usually not a great idea because it's hard to find your styles and it's even harder to be consistent, sometimes it's useful to apply a style directly into a HTML tag. If you want to do so, you can send a `style` parameter to a specific tag.

Let's assume that you have a file called `style.css` in the `www` directory that provides all the styles you want, except the green color you want to apply to the *first-level* heading. Then, you may use the following code which includes both techniques:

```
ui <- fluidPage(
    includeCSS("style.css"),
    h1(style = "color: blue;", "A blue heading"),
)
server <- function(input, output) { }
shinyApp(ui, server)
```

Sharing your newly created application

Although Shiny applications end up as HTML files you can't simply copy them to your server. They require a Shiny server, just like the one we have been working with through this chapter. There are two ways to run Shiny applications (as any other application), locally or remotely. Locally means that you fire up an R installation with Shiny and the required dependencies, and run it just as we have been doing during this chapter. Remotely means that you can access it through a website, which can be very cool and convenient at times.

To run locally you need to have the files for the application in the computer that will execute them. There are many ways to do so, but the most common one is to upload them to a Git repository, download them from there, and follow the steps you already know. Furthermore, if your files are in a Git repository hosted in GitHub (https://www.github.com), you may use the `runGitHub()` function with the name of the repository and the username of the account that holds the repository. In that case, the downloading, unpacking, and execution will be done for you. For example, to run the application we developed through this chapter, you may use the following line:

```
runGitHub("", "")
```

If you want to provide remote access to your application, you have many options, but the main ones are three: ShinyApps, RStudio Connect, and Shiny Server. **ShinyApps** (`https://www.shinyapps.io`) offers this service for free for small applications with limited visits and can scale up in paid versions. **RStudio Connect** (`https://www.rstudio.com/products/connect/`) is a publishing platform for Shiny applications and R Markdown reports. With it, you can publish directly from RStudio. Finally, **Shiny Server** (`https://www.rstudio.com/products/shiny/shiny-server/`) is an open source version of the Shiny server you've been using in this chapter, with the added benefit that you can run it in the Linux servers you control (of course, this includes servers from cloud providers). RStudio also sells a yearly subscription to Shiny Server Pro, which provides security, administration, and other enhancements when compared to the open source version.

Summary

As we saw throughout the chapter, using the *functional reactive programming* paradigm to create powerful web applications using Shiny is not necessarily difficult. It only requires good concept understanding and a bit of exploration.

We showed how to provide inputs for users to be able to send *reactive values* to the backend, that is, the `server`, and have it respond adequately to such streams of events. We also showed how to add more sophisticated interactions such as the the two graphs with the zoom-in effect.

This is the final chapter for the book, and you saw how to use many of the tools provided by Shiny to create interactive applications. However, we have just scratched the surface of what is possible with Shiny and R in general. I hope you take what you have learned in this book and create amazing applications. Thank you for making it this far! I wish you the best of luck.

Required Packages

In this appendix, I will show you how to install the software you need to replicate the examples shown in this book. I will show you how to do so for Linux and macOS, specifically, Ubuntu 17.10 and High Sierra. If you're using Windows, the same principles apply but the specifics may be a bit different. However, I'm sure it will not be too difficult in any case.

There are two types of requirements for executing all the code in this book: external and internal. Software outside of R, is what I call external requirements. Software inside of R, meaning R packages, are what I refer to as internal requirements. I will walk you through the installation of both of these.

External requirements – software outside of R

Some of the R packages required to reproduce the code in this book have external dependencies, which can either be installation or execution dependencies. We will go through the installation of each external dependency in the following sections. Installing external dependencies is not difficult, but it may be an unfamiliar process that requires us to do some work outside of R. Once we install these external dependencies successfully, installing R packages should be easy.

Before we proceed, I just want to say that you won't always know in advance what external dependencies you need before attempting to install an R package. Normally, you will simply try to install the package and see what happens. If no problems arise, then you are all set. If problems do arise, the output from the console will hint you into what you need to do next. Most of the time, a quick online search for the error or a look into the package's documentation will be enough to understand how to proceed. As you get more experience, you'll be able to quickly diagnose and solve any problems.

The following table shows the external software that we need to install, as well as which chapters it's used in, why it is used, and the URL where you can get it. The URLs for the Fortran and C++ compilers I have provided in the following table are for macOS. In the case of Linux, I haven't provided any because we will install them using the Terminal through the package manager, and you don't need to navigate to an external website to download their installers. Finally, all of this software is free and you should install the latest version. The external software required for R packages to work are given in the following table:

Software	Chapters	Reason	Download URL
MySQL Community Server	4	Provide MySQL database	`https://dev.mysql.com/downloads/mysql/`
GDAL system	5	3D graphs in Linux	`http://www.gdal.org/index.html`
XQuartz system	5	3D graphs in macOS	`https://www.xquartz.org/`
Fortran compiler	9	Compile Fortran	`https://gcc.gnu.org/wiki/GFortranBinaries`
C++ compiler	9	Compile C++	`https://developer.apple.com/xcode/`

Depending on your setup, some of the Terminal commands you execute (both in Linux and macOS) may need to be prepended with the `sudo` string to allow them to actually modify your system. You can find more information in Wikipedia's article on the `sudo` command (`https://en.wikipedia.org/wiki/Sudo`), and in your operating system's documentation.

Dependencies for the RMySQL R package

`Chapter 4`, *Simulating Sales Data and Working with Databases*, has an execution dependency on MySQL databases. This means that the `RMySQL` R package can be installed just fine without having a MySQL database in the system, but when R uses it to interface to a MySQL database, you must have one available and running with an appropriate configuration, otherwise you will run into errors.

Now I will show you how to install the MySQL Community Database, in both Ubuntu 17.10 and macOS High Sierra. During the installation, you may be asked for an optional username and password, and if that is the case, you should take the opportunity and actually specify these instead of leaving it blank since we will need actual values from within R. If you do, you can skip the following sections about setting up username/password combination.

Ubuntu 17.10

Installing MySQL in Ubuntu is straightforward. You simply need to update your package manager and install the `mysql-server` package, as shown here:

```
$ apt-get update
$ apt-get install mysql-server
```

The database should be automatically executed for you, which you can verify by following the next section titled *Both*. If it's not, you can use the following command to start the database:

```
$ sudo service mysql start
```

Check out Rackspace's post *Installing MySQL Server on Ubuntu* (`https://support.rackspace.com/how-to/installing-mysql-server-on-ubuntu/`) for more detailed instructions.

macOS High Sierra

The first thing you need to do is to install **Xcode** (`https://developer.apple.com/xcode/`). To do so, you need to open the App store in your computer, search for `Xcode`, and install it. If you have any development work with your macOS, it's probable that you already have it installed as it's a basic dependency for most development under macOS.

Next, I recommend that you use the excellent **Homebrew** package manager (`https://brew.sh/`). It's the closest you can get to a tool like `apt-get` in Ubuntu. To install it, you need to execute the following line in your Terminal. Note that the actual URL in the command may change, and you should make sure it matches the one shown in Homebrew's website.

 The following command is split using the "\" symbol. If you want to use it as a single line, you can delete such symbol and join the two lines into one.

Let's have a look at the following command:

```
$ /usr/bin/ruby -e "$(curl -fsSL \
  https://raw.githubusercontent.com/Homebrew/install/master/install)"
```

Once you have both Xcode and Homebrew installed, then you can install MySQL by simply executing the following line in your Terminal, and you should be all set:

```
$ brew install mysql
```

In case you had any trouble installing MySQL this way. You can try the more manual route by going to the MySQL Community download page (`https://dev.mysql.com/downloads/mysql/`), downloading the appropriate DMG file, and installing it as any other macOS application.

Setting up user/password in both Linux and macOS

Once you have the MySQL database installed on your computer, you need to make sure that you can access it with an explicit user/password combination. If you have already set them up, you should be able to access the database as shown ahead.

The `<YOUR_PASSWORD>` value is shown in the second line and without Command Prompt (**$**) because it should not be included in the first line, and you should wait for MySQL to request it, which is usually after you execute the first line, and this is done with an invisible prompt, meaning that you won't see what you are typing (for security reasons):

```
$ mysql -u <YOU_USER> -p
<YOUR_PASSWORD>
```

If you see information similar to what is shown ahead and you get Command Prompt like `mysql>`, then you're all set, and you should use that user/password combination when connecting to the database from within R:

```
$ mysql

Welcome to the MySQL monitor. Commands end with ; or \g.
Your MySQL connection id is 15
Server version: 5.7.20-0ubuntu0.17.10.1 (Ubuntu)

Copyright (c) 2000, 2017, Oracle and/or its affiliates. All rights
reserved.

Oracle is a registered trademark of Oracle Corporation and/or its
affiliates. Other names may be trademarks of their respective
owners.

Type 'help;' or '\h' for help. Type '\c' to clear the current input
statement.

mysql>
```

If you were not able to connect, or you don't have an explicit user/password combination, then we need to create it. To do so, you need to figure out how to log in to your MySQL server, which will depend on the configuration used to install your database (which can vary even for similar operating systems). It's probable that you are able to access it by simply executing the following command in the Terminal:

```
$ mysql
```

Once you are in MySQL Command Prompt, you should execute the following line to create the user/password combination for your local installation. After doing so, you should be all set, and you should be able to login explicitly using this user/password combination as was shown previously:

```
mysql> CREATE USER ''@'localhost' IDENTIFIED BY '';
mysql> GRANT ALL ON *.* TO ''@'localhost';
```

Finally, just to be clear, when you see the following code in the corresponding chapter, you need to use the same user/password you created here in the place of the `<YOUR_USER>` and `<YOUR_PASSWORD>` placeholders:

```
db <- dbConnect(
    MySQL(),
    user = <YOU_USER>,
    password = <YOUR_PASSWORD>,
```

```
    host = "localhost"
)
```

Dependencies for the rgl and rgdal R packages

Chapter 5, *Communicating Sales with Visualizations*, makes use of the `rgl` and `rgdal` packages to create 3D and geographical data graphs. These two packages have the trickiest external dependencies from the ones we will see in this book, so we will provide different ways of installing them in case one of them is not useful for you.

We need to install **GDAL** (**Geospatial Data Abstraction Library**) system libraries (http://www.gdal.org/) with geospatial, and **X11** (https://www.x.org/wiki/) in Ubuntu or Xquartz (https://www.xquartz.org/) in macOS to create windows with dynamic content.

> In the case of Windows, you don't need something external like X11 or Xquartz, since Windows handles the necessary windows natively.

Ubuntu 17.10

To install GDAL and X11, we need various system libraries in Ubuntu. The easiest way to accomplish this is to use the following lines. If you had no problems, you should be all set:

```
$ apt-get update
$ apt-get install r-cran-rgl
```

If using the previous lines gave you an error, or otherwise did not work, you can try to install GDAL in a more explicit way using the following lines. The last two lines can be combined into a single one if you prefer, they were split due to space restrictions:

```
# apt-get update
$ apt-get install mesa-common-dev libglu1-mesa-dev libgdal1-dev
$ apt-get install libx11-dev libudunits2-dev libproj-dev
```

If you still get some kind of error with the previous commands, you can try to add the `ubuntugis` repository information, update your package manager, and then retry the previous code:

```
$ add-apt-repository ppa:ubuntugis/ubuntugis-unstable
$ apt-get update
```

macOS High Sierra

To install GDAL in macOS, you may use the Homebrew package install we mentioned earlier. Of course, Xcode can also be installed in your computer at this point:

```
$ brew install proj geos udunits
$ brew install gdal2 --with-armadillo --with-complete --with-libkml --with-unsupported
```

Finally, we need to install the Xquartz System (similar to X11 for Ubuntu). To do so, go to the Xquartz website (https://www.xquartz.org/), download the appropriate DMG file, and install it as you would with any other application for macOS.

Dependencies for the Rcpp package and the .Fortran() function

Chapter 9, *Implementing an Efficient Simple Moving Average*, shows how to delegate code to Fortran and C++ to increase speed. These languages have compilers of their own that must be used to compile the respective code so that it can be used by R. How to compile such code is shown in the chapter. What we will do here is show how to install the compilers.

The compiler for C++ code is called gcc and the one for Fortran is called gfortran. It's probable that you have both already available in your computer, since they are dependencies for R, but in case you don't, it's easy enough to install them.

Ubuntu 17.10

To install both compilers in Ubuntu, simply execute the following lines in your Terminal:

```
$ apt-get update
$ apt-get install gcc ggfortran
```

macOS High Sierra

To install the C++ compiler in macOS, simply install **Xcode** (https://developer.apple.com/xcode/). As we mentioned earlier, it can be installed through the App Store application you should have in your computer.

To install the Fortran compiler, you can use the Homebrew package manager as shown ahead. However, if for some reason it doesn't work, you can also try using the binaries found at GNU's website (`https://gcc.gnu.org/wiki/GFortranBinaries`):

```
$ brew install gfortran
```

Internal requirements – R packages

An R *package* is a related set of functions, help files, and data files that have been bundled together. At the time of writing this, **Comprehensive R Archive Network (CRAN)** (`https://cran.r-project.org/`) has over 12,000 packages available for R. This is a huge advantage when using R, since you don't have to reinvent the wheel to make use of very high quality packages that probably implement the functionality you're looking for, and if there aren't any such packages, you can contribute your own!

Even if CRAN doesn't have a package with the functionality you need, it may exist in personal Git repositories in GitLab, GitHub, Bitbucket, and other Git hosting websites. As a matter of fact, two of the packages we will install come from GitHub, not CRAN, specifically `ggbiplot` and `ggthemr`. Finally, you may install specific versions of packages, as we will do with the `caret` package.

All the packages used in this book are shown in the following table, with an indication of the chapter they are used in, the version that you should install, and the reason why we use them in the book. In the examples in the book, we use R packages which are not shown in the following table, but since they are built-in, we don't have to install them ourselves, and thus are not shown. For example, that's the case with the `methods` and `parallel` packages, which are used to work with the S4 object system and perform parallel computations, respectively. The R packages that we need to install are mentioned in the following table:

Package	Chapters	Version	Reason
ggplot2	2, 3, 5, 9, and 10	Latest	High-quality graphs
ggbiplot	2	Latest	Principal component plots
viridis	2 and 5	Latest	Color palette for graphs
corrplot	2 and 3	Latest	Correlation plots
progress	2 and 3	Latest	Show progress for iterations
RMySQL	4	Latest	Interface to MySQL database

ggExtra	5	Latest	Graphs with marginal distributions
threejs	5	Latest	Interactive globe graph
leaflet	5	Latest	Interactive high-quality maps
plotly	5	Latest	Interactive high-quality graphs
rgl	5	Latest	Interactive 3D graphs
rgdal	5	Latest	Manipulating geographical data
plyr	5	Latest	Appending to data frames
lsa	6	Latest	Cosine similarity computation
rilba	6	Latest	Efficient SVD decomposition
caret	6 and 7	Latest	Machine learning framework
twitteR	6	Latest	Interface to Twitter's API
quanteda	6	Latest	Text data processing
sentimentr	6	Latest	Text data sentiment analysis
randomForest	6	Latest	Random forest models
ggrepel	7	Latest	Avoid overlapping labels in graphs
rmarkdown	7	Latest	Markdown documents with executable code
R6	8	Latest	R6 object model
jsonlite	8	Latest	Retrieve data from JSON APIs
lubridate	8, 9, 10	Latest	Easily transform dates
microbenchmark	9	Latest	Benchmark functions' performance
shiny	10	Latest	Create modern web applications
shinythemes	10	Latest	Apply themes to Shiny applications
ggthemr	10	Latest	Apply themes to ggplot2 graphs

To install these packages, you can use the `install.packages(ggplot2)` command and change the package to be installed for each of the ones shown in the previous table. However, a more efficient way to install all of them is to send a vector with all the package names we want to install to the `install.packages()` function, as is shown in the following code. Finally, note that you may send the `dependencies = TRUE` argument to tell R to try to install any missing dependencies for you:

```
install.packages(c(
    "ggplot2",
    "viridis",
    "corrplot",
    "progress",
    "RMySQL",
    "ggExtra",
    "threejs",
    "leaflet",
    "plotly",
    "rgl",
    "rgdal",
    "plyr",
    "lsa",
    "rilba",
    "twitteR",
    "quanteda",
    "sentimentr",
    "randomForest",
    "ggrepel",
    "rmarkdown",
    "R6",
    "jsonlite",
    "lubridate",
    "microbenchmark",
    "shiny",
    "shinythemes",
    dependencies = TRUE
))
```

Note that the previous vector omits three packages: `ggbiplot`, `ggthemr`, and `caret`. They are omitted because the first two can only be installed directly from GitHub (not CRAN), and the third one needs a specific version because the latest one contains a bug that affects some of our code at the time of this writing. To install the `ggbiplot` package, we need the user of the owner of the package in GitHub. If you go to the packages URL (`https://github.com/vqv/ggbiplot`), you can see that it's `vqv`. Now, to perform the actual installation, we use the `install_github()` function from the `devtools` package, and we provide it with a string that contains the name of the user (`vqv`) and the name of the repository (`ggbiplot`), separated by a diagonal (`/`).

 If you prefer, you may load the `devtools` package into memory, and then call the `install_github()` function directly.

Let's look at the following command:

```
devtools::install_github("vqv/ggbiplot")
```

Similarly, to install the `ggthemr` package (`https://github.com/cttobin/ggthemr`), we use the following line:

```
devtools::install_github("cttobin/ggthemr")
```

Finally, to install the `caret` package, we can use CRAN, but we must specify the version we want, which is `6.0.76` in this case. To accomplish this, we use the `install_version` function from the same `devtools` package. In this case, we send it the name of the package and the version we want:

```
devtools::install_version("caret", version = "6.0.76")
```

By now, you should have everything you need to fully replicate the code in the book. If you run into any problems, I'm confident that online and Stack Overflow (`https://stackoverflow.com/`) searches will be very helpful.

Loading R packages

At this point, you should be able to load the R packages you need for this book, and you can do so using the `library()` or `require()` functions, both of which take the name of the package you want to load as an argument.

You may be wondering why you need to load packages into R to use them. If every package were loaded into R by default, you may think you were using one function but really be using another. Even worse, it's possible for there to be internal conflicts: two different packages may use the exact same functions names, resulting in strange and unexpected results. By only loading packages that you need, you can minimize the chance of these conflicts.

Index